Fleeing the Iron Cage

Fleeing the Iron Cage

*Culture, Politics, and Modernity
in the Thought of Max Weber*

Lawrence A. Scaff

UNIVERSITY OF CALIFORNIA PRESS
Berkeley   Los Angeles   London

University of California Press
Berkeley and Los Angeles, California

University of California Press, Ltd.
London, England

Printed in the United States of America
1   2   3   4   5   6   7   8   9

Library of Congress Cataloging-in-Publication Data

Scaff, Lawrence A.
    Fleeing the iron cage: culture, politics, and modernity in the
thought of Max Weber / Lawrence A. Scaff.
        p. cm.
    Bibliography: p.
    Includes index.
    ISBN 0-520-06435-6 (alk. paper)
    1. Weber, Max, 1864–1920—Views on culture.   2. Culture.
3. Civilization, Modern.   4. Social ethics.   5. Social sciences—
Philosophy.   I. Title.
HM101.S2817 1989
306'.092'4—dc19   88-26113
                                                                CIP

To my parents

Contents

Preface

Studying Max Weber was virtually a requirement for my generation of theoretically inclined students in the social sciences at Berkeley. The "myth of Heidelberg" was encountered at nearly every turn in the fields that interested me most—political and social theory, sociology, political science, history, philosophy—and usually in such a way as to convince initiates that his contributions, somehow, stood at the center of every worthwhile controversy. Indeed, coming to terms "critically" and "analytically" (as we liked to say) with an imperious Weber became de rigueur in a bewildering variety of settings, from the intramural dispute in science over "value judgment" to general reflection on the nature of rationality. Positions had to be identified, taken, and defended, and typically they were in relation to Weber.

Looking back on these discussions, I am now struck by the extent to which critic and defender alike assumed that Weber's importance stemmed entirely from his contributions as a "founder" of the social sciences as we have come to know them in America—Weber along with Emile Durkheim and perhaps Georg Simmel in the first rank, with others like George Herbert Mead, Vilfredo Pareto, and Ferdinand Tönnies trailing along behind. As I read further into Weber's work, picking up the political essays and turning especially from translations to the original German texts, this assumption seemed to become increasingly questionable. I began to doubt that the "social science" of our own age, either in form or in content, had much to do with Weber's version of

Wissenschaft or with the problems *he* had in mind. It appeared that even our best authorities had put together a peculiarly domesticated rendition of his ideas. (The outstanding case in point is surely Talcott Parsons, a "theorist" who violated Weber's most cherished views about "theory," while nevertheless claiming the Weberian patrimony as his own.) But I also began to glimpse a rather different Weber, an outsider who simply was not constrained by institutional or disciplinary boundaries, a scholar who, unlike Durkheim, had no design on establishing a new discipline or school, a thinker whose interests extended to all of culture—ancient and modern, Occidental and Oriental—a figure who spent most of his mature years in the diaspora beyond the protection and ease of the university, who alternated between flights into the intellect and escapes in travel. I came to realize that Weber was simply not one of us, with our fastidious "research programs" and concern for "professionalism." For him "seriousness" and "integrity" were the first principles of life, and especially the life of the mind. It often seems that we hardly know what this means any more.

My own first encounter with Weber actually occurred in more innocent circumstances, when in response to a careless query about new and important work in social theory, my father with a "Read this!" placed a copy of Reinhard Bendix's *Max Weber, An Intellectual Portrait* in front of me. If I was impressed by anything while poring through this work, an exposition that could hardly have been expected to sustain the casual interest of a high school student, then it was by the universal and comparative sweep of Weber's reflections on world civilizations, written, I thought, in the tradition of the great classics of cultural anthropology and world history. In retrospect I must say that Bendix's summary contained little of the actual spirit of Weber; it was "a curious kind of 'reader,'" as C. Wright Mills once noted, "a Weber Reader without any Weber, a collection of paraphrases." Nevertheless, the episode aroused a curiosity about the meaning of Weber's thought that I have sustained and to which I have returned more than once, a curiosity the present study tries to satisfy.

My interest, then, is in that "other" Weber, the man we have not known, the thinker we have missed in the rush to establish the conceptual boundaries and methodological foundations of the social sciences. I have tried to read him afresh, unburdened by the old controversies or interpretations, and with a mind open to the possibilities of his thought. To do this, I have approached Weber in his own times, through his own fin-de-siècle culture, his own language, problems, and intellectual experience. The result is, I hope, a different understanding that will make Weber's ideas available to the questions and interests of the next generation of readers.

This journey in search of Weber has accumulated several intellectual debts that it is a pleasure to acknowledge. A number of years ago, at a time when it would have been easy to do otherwise, Sheldon Wolin provided encouragement and support, for which I remain deeply grateful. Wolfgang J. Mommsen opened the doors of the Max-Weber-Edition at the University of Düsseldorf for me; I appreciate his assistance and that of his staff, who aided my search for sources and instructed me in my struggles to read Weber's unbelievably bad handwriting. I owe a word of thanks to my colleague and fellow *Weber-Kenner*, Gangolf Hübinger, who has sustained a conversation about our shared interests over several years and two universities. I have benefited especially from the generous counsel, encouragement, and friendship of Wilhelm Hennis, whose writings and acute suggestions have proved to be especially helpful for moving this study toward completion. A year spent in his "Seminar für wissenschaftliche Politik" at the University of Freiburg marked an important stage in the development of my thinking. At various times several colleagues in addition to those already mentioned have read and commented on parts of this work, among whom I should like to thank Guenther Roth, Donald N. Levine, Robert Eden, and, in particular, Robert Antonio. Birgitta Nedelmann encouraged me to take a closer look at the Weber-Simmel partnership, a suggestion that proved to be extremely valuable. A word of acknowledgment is also due three archives: the Bundesarchiv Koblenz, the Fondazione Luigi Einaudi for access to the Weber-Michels correspondence, and the helpful and efficient staff of the Zentrales Staatsarchiv in Merseburg, where the most important papers are housed. My investigations would not have been possible without support from the Deutscher Akademischer Austauschdienst, the University of Arizona Foundation, and the Fulbright Commission—especially the award of a Fulbright Fellowship for 1984–85 at the University of Freiburg in Freiburg im Breisgau, where some of the text was written. The entire manuscript has profited from the patient scrutiny of Lieselotte Hofmann, copyeditor for the University of California Press.

Finally, I want to acknowledge the support of my parents, who have followed the course of this work with great interest, as well as the contribution long ago of the Drieschner family, from whom I received my first real understanding of German language and culture. I have saved until last a special word of appreciation for my two daughters, who have shared some of the journey with me, and for my wife, Susan, whose love of life and literature has made it all worthwhile.

Parts of my text, mainly in Chapters 2 through 4, have been published previously in journal articles in the *American Political Science Review*, the *British Journal of Sociology*, the *Kölner Zeitschrift für Soziologie und Sozialpsychologie*, and the *Sociological Review*, and have benefited from comments by these journals' reviewers. I have revised and expanded all of this material for the present study.

Abbreviations

JB	*Jugendbriefe*. Edited by Marianne Weber. Tübingen: J. C. B. Mohr (Paul Siebeck), 1936.
Lebensbild	Marianne Weber, *Max Weber: Ein Lebensbild*. Tübingen: J. C. B. Mohr (Paul Siebeck), 1926.
MWG	*Max Weber Gesamtausgabe*. Tübingen: J. C. B. Mohr (Paul Siebeck), 1984–.
PE	*The Protestant Ethic and the Spirit of Capitalism*. Translated by Talcott Parsons. New York: Scribner's, 1958.
S&F	*The Methodology of the Social Sciences*. Edited and translated by E. A. Shils and H. A. Finch. New York: Free Press, 1949.
Selections	*Max Weber, Selections in Translation*. Edited by W. G. Runciman. Cambridge: Cambridge University Press, 1978.
SVSP	*Schriften des Vereins für Sozialpolitik*.
WuG	*Wirtschaft und Gesellschaft*. Edited by J. Winckelmann. 2 vols. Cologne: Kiepenheuer & Witsch, 1964.

ARCHIVES

AMW	Archivo Max Weber, Fondazione Luigi Einaudi, Turin
MWE	Archive of the Max-Weber-Edition, University of Düsseldorf
NJ	Nachlass Georg Jellinek, Bundesarchiv Koblenz
NWS	Nachlass Werner Sombart, Zentrales Staatsarchiv Merseburg, Repository 92
NW	Nachlass Max Weber, Zentrales Staatsarchiv Merseburg, Repository 92

Introduction

The encounter with Max Weber is a disquieting affair, like the encounter with our century. For Weber is very much a thinker of the modern age of war, revolution, science, and the state. The spirit of our contemporary life is captured in the concepts and questions he left behind: bureaucracy, domination, rationality, charisma, the "ethic" of work, disenchantment. He saw the predicament of our "fate" in an age of bureaucratic domination; the problem of the "irrationality" of a purely instrumentally, or means-ends, oriented culture; the questionable deep attraction of "charismatic" enchantment in the face of misplaced meaning. Yet in his work he pursued these themes with such ruthless determination and on so vast a scale as to rule out success or perfection, just as he proceeded to invoke standards of "integrity" and "responsibility" so exacting that they seemed to elude the modern world.

Several particular considerations help account for the intense and troubled atmosphere surrounding Weber, some having to do with the person he was, others with his scholarship. Consider, for example, a few of the most obvious external aspects of his life: Notwithstanding his reputation for learning and teaching, Weber's longest sojourn in a university was remarkably only five semesters at Freiburg at the very start of his career. As a man who early in life expressed a deep longing for a political career, he never served in elected public office, although his wife, Marianne, and several friends and colleagues did. As for the professional assignments he accepted—coediting the *Archiv für Sozial-*

wissenschaft und Sozialpolitik, editing and overseeing the *Grundriss der Sozialökonomik* (*Outline of Social Economics*) project, or helping organize the German Sociological Society—Weber was never entirely comfortable with them, his complaints or attempts to withdraw commencing almost as soon as he accepted the responsibilities. He never really recovered from the illness that struck at age thirty-four, as a reading of the unique and candid correspondence with Robert Michels stunningly reveals. For that reason alone, if not for political considerations, it seems wildly improbable that he might have played a central role in politics after 1918, as friends from the Heidelberg Circle wanted to believe. As Weber himself recognized, he was excitable, unreliable, and lacked the "calm nerves" necessary for public office. His reputation as a lone wolf, a troublemaker, and alarmist was not undeserved, and if the humorless and stark criticism of his political essays is any indication of intentions, Weber certainly wanted it that way. Yet as a scholar, he never really completed any of his major projects, never writing a book after the "habilitation" in 1891, employing instead the journal article and handbook essay as his major vehicles of expression. This circumstance holds especially for his alleged magnum opus, *Economy and Society*, a work others compiled in his name, whose title should have read *Die Wirtschaft und die gesellschaftlichen Ordnungen und Mächte* (literally, *The Economy and the Social Orders and Powers*), and whose contents were governed in part, as Johannes Winckelmann has now shown, by its position in the *Outline of Social Economics* and the failure of colleagues to meet their authorial commitments.[1]

Everything considered, Weber's life and work present a troubling panorama, a disunified collage of frustrated ambition, renunciation, disappointment, and prodigious mental exertion. Those closest to Weber characterized his nature in similar ways: a "truly daemonic temperament" (Michels), a "titan bound" (Marianne Weber), a "spirit possessed" (Paul Honigsheim), or "the modern man who permitted himself no deceptions" (Karl Jaspers). Ranking first among Weber's few fears was the thought that others "could think of him as a commonplace professor, for whom specialized knowledge is the only thing of importance." Indeed, as Honigsheim elaborated retrospectively, "Many con-

---

1. Johannes Winckelmann, *Max Webers hintergelassenes Hauptwerk* (Tübingen: J. C. B. Mohr [Paul Siebeck], 1986); to avoid confusion, I shall continue to refer to Weber's title as *Economy and Society*.

ceived of Max Weber as only a man of learning [*Gelehrte*], but that means they did not understand him at all."[2]

So how did Weber understand himself? In the world of his contemporaries he was the enfant terrible of the younger generation, and with the exception of a single unguarded observation about Michels, he identified with no one. Weber's stance with respect to colleagues was uniformly a claim of critical distance, reserve, originality, or as he once said without mincing words "the utmost objective relentlessness of a kind that can produce *discord* now and then, even if I choose the most polite form of criticism conceivable" and that "in *any* case brands me as a (scientific) *partisan*, which I also *want* to be."[3] But in the timeless fictional world of his imagination, Weber was free to read into himself symbolic figures like John Gabriel Borkman, Ibsen's haunted, driven, and doomed man of achievement; Don Quixote, the tragicomic worldly pilgrim; Tristan, the hero suffering and struggling for self-knowledge; and above all others—Faust.

If there is an element of truth in these many characterizations, then how *should* Weber be understood? What could be the meaning of his reputed identifications? In answering large questions like these, which stand at the center of this entire inquiry, one is led almost invariably to retrace the contours of certain well-worn categories: Weber as "founder" of sociology (Parsons, Bendix), leader of the "revolt against positivism" (Hughes), theoretician of *Machtpolitik* (Mommsen, Aron), defender of "bourgeois reason" (Marcuse, Lukács), or proponent of "decisionism" and "value nihilism" (Habermas, Strauss).[4] But as one turns from the comfort of the old and familiar to the life and thought

2. Hermann Glockner, *Heidelberger Bilderbuch: Erinnerungen* (Bonn: Bouvier, 1969), 102; Paul Honigsheim, "Der Max-Weber-Kreis in Heidelberg," *Kölner Vierteljahrshefte für Soziologie* 5 (1926): 271.

3. Letter to Heinrich Herkner, 11 May 1909, NW 18: 19–20.

4. Talcott Parsons, *The Structure of Social Action* (Glencoe, Ill.: Free Press, 1949); Reinhard Bendix, *Max Weber: An Intellectual Portrait*, 2d ed. (Berkeley: University of California Press, 1977); H. Stuart Hughes, *Consciousness and Society: The Reorientation of European Social Thought, 1890–1930* (New York: Random House [Vintage Books], 1958), chap. 8; Wolfgang J. Mommsen, *Max Weber and German Politics, 1890–1920*, trans. M. Steinberg (Chicago: University of Chicago Press, 1984); Raymond Aron, "Max Weber and Power-Politics," and Herbert Marcuse, "Industrialization and Capitalism," in *Max Weber and Sociology Today*, ed. O. Stammer (New York: Harper & Row, 1972), 83–100, 133–51; Georg Lukács, *Die Zerstörung der Vernunft* (Berlin: Aufbau-Verlag, 1955); Jürgen Habermas, *Toward a Rational Society*, trans. J. Shapiro (London: Heinemann, 1971), chap. 5; Leo Strauss, *Natural Right and History* (Chicago: University of Chicago Press, 1953).

as a whole that is said to be in question, one cannot fail to sense a dissonance between interpretive generalizations long since taken for granted and the record of actual work and accomplishment. For what Weber thought, wrote, questioned, and achieved had to do with far more than founding a new science, defending national or class interests, or rebelling against a rationalist heritage. He was more than merely a scientist, and he was never fully a politician. Even to conceive his essential questions arrayed along a single axis between "science" and "politics" is already to risk missing what is most important.

Some observers of the age were alert to other possibilities. Jaspers spoke of Weber embodying the most fundamental philosophical impulse—knowledge of self and the "fate" of the times: "Through him we arrived at the clearest consciousness of the present and the immediate moment." Honigsheim remarked that "it was really something quite special within his kingdom of contradiction and nonconformity that gave it the power of creating a community." Ludwig Curtius saw in Weber "the dictator of a spiritual [geistig] kingdom that encompassed all the problems of modern life."[5] Perhaps one should say that if Gladstone was for Weber the "dictator of the battlefield of elections," then Weber became for his audience the colossus astride the terrain of "culture" where the struggle to form modern consciousness was occurring. Occasionally, later thinkers, writing from within entirely different traditions, have glimpsed similar dimensions: Weber is said to have shown "under what conditions a historical dialectic is possible" and to have offered a "historical understanding of the Vielseitigkeit of the creative choice, and a philosophy which questioned history" and its rumored determinisms.[6] Or in Löwith's idiom, Weber was, like Marx, motivated by "the question of the fate of man in the contemporary human world," but then understood the scientific expression of his ideas to represent "the specific historical character of the whole of our modern existence and of its problems." This "science" was fragmentary, the life unsatisfactory, yet they "nevertheless," or precisely for that reason, "encompass the totality of our time."[7]

5. Karl Jaspers, Max Weber: Eine Gedenkrede (Tübingen: J. C. B. Mohr [Paul Siebeck], 1926), 10; Honigsheim, "Der Max-Weber-Kreis in Heidelberg," 271; Ludwig Curtius, Deutsche und Antike Welt: Lebenserinnerungen (Stuttgart: Deutsche Verlags-Anstalt, 1950), 362.

6. Maurice Merleau-Ponty, "The Crisis of the Understanding," in The Primacy of Perception and Other Essays, ed. J. M. Edie (Evanston: Northwestern University Press, 1964), 210.

7. Karl Löwith, Max Weber and Karl Marx (1932), trans. H. Fantel (London: Allen & Unwin, 1982), 20–21, 30.

Weber's own writings contain the same monumental theme, the general problematic directed toward understanding what he in the 1890s called "the fate imposed upon us" and at the end of his life "the fate of our times." Instead of dismissing such phrases as rare, recondite, or exaggerated rhetoric, I propose to take them as a point of entry into the deepest level of Weber's thinking about historical development, his own activity, and what he came to regard in his most telling figure of speech as the "iron cage" of a specialized, "vocational humanity" compelled to renounce the "Faustian universality of humankind" and live within a rationalized and disenchanted world. In my judgment, if we follow Weber's lead in this direction—that is, toward the culture and politics of the modern age—we should be rewarded with the recovery of a much more challenging and unusual body of thought than has generally been encountered before. Furthermore, we shall also discover a set of problems whose horizons extend far beyond commonplace learning and connect the entire sphere of Weber's thinking with the most serious questions of modern thought.

Thus, the central theme of these essays is found in the problem of culture, and especially modern culture and the "science of culture" Weber proposed for coming to terms with our world. I have moved Weber closer to the "modern" than is usually the case in discussions of his thought,[8] for I think it *is* at the center of his concerns as a writer whose self-defined vocation was to see whether any meaning at all could be wrested from a postcritical, disenchanted world, an "age of subjectivist culture" in his own phrase. Even in those places where Weber's interests become historical or obviously conceptual, one eye is always trained on what has become of our "conduct of life" and our "fate." Far from being a source of weakness or ambiguity, as some have suggested,[9] it is this essentially cultural element in Weber's work that provokes and fascinates.

A closely related theme that is woven into the fabric of my discussion

8. The recent exception is Scott Lash and Sam Whimster, eds., *Max Weber: Rationality and Modernity* (London: Allen & Unwin, 1987). However, most of this collection's seventeen contributions belong within the narrow and well-worn confines of the problem of "rationalization." Only with the innovative chapter by Wilhelm Hennis (a partial translation of *Max Webers Fragestellung: Studien zur Biographie des Werks* [Tübingen: J. C. B. Mohr (Paul Siebeck), 1987], chap. 2, a suggestion by Jeffrey Alexander, pp. 199–205, and the essays of the editors, pp. 259–90 and 355–77, does an understanding of Weber's relation to the "modern" in its broadest cultural sense begin to emerge.

9. See Wolfgang Schluchter, "Value-Neutrality and the Ethic of Responsibility," in Guenther Roth and Wolfgang Schluchter, *Max Weber's Vision of History: Ethics and Methods* (Berkeley: University of California Press, 1979), 110–12.

has to do with Weber's connection to the achievements of his two most important predecessors: Marx and Nietzsche. Weber himself was alert to the possibilities of pursuing such a line of inquiry, as evidenced in the remarks attributed to him at the end of his life:

> One can judge the honesty of a contemporary scholar and above all a contemporary philosopher according to how he takes a stand in relation to Nietzsche and Marx. Whoever denies that he could not have accomplished the most important parts of his own work without the work done by both of them deceives himself and others. The world in which we live as intellectual beings is largely a world bearing the imprint of Marx and Nietzsche.[10]

The "philosopher of history" against whom this comment was directed, Oswald Spengler, had evidently failed the test by claiming to "refute" Nietzsche's philosophy and Marx's historical predictions through a stylish and misguided "academic prophecy" of his own. Weber could not restrain his scorn: confronted by such alternatives, he retorted, our allegiance should be commanded not by someone like Spengler, but by his opponents. As for Marx, "Should he arise from his grave today and look around, despite several important deviations working against his prophecies, he would have every reason to say, truly this is flesh of my flesh and bone of my bones."[11] The same could have been said for Nietzsche.

This story from 1920 may well be apocryphal, but it is in any case certainly allegorical: as a reflection on modernity, a claim that we moderns live in a post-Marxian and post-Nietzschean world, it can become a statement of Weber's own intellectual genesis. The brief confrontation with the philosophy of history succeeds in illuminating an essential part of the substructure of Weber's thought, without which his contributions would not have been possible at all. Omissions are important in these self-reflections: Kant and Hegel remain in the shadows. There appears to be a special connection to Marx and Nietzsche, distinctive traces of their thinking, for it is only with them that we move to the center of Weber's world, a world presupposed at the very beginning of his intellectual development. It is important to ask what Weber could have owed to an encounter with both of these antagonistic spirits, to the master of dialectic *and* the dialectician of mastery.

These themes, primary and secondary, appear at the foundations of Weber's thought. They suggest the problem in his own terminology, in

---

10. Cited in Eduard Baumgarten, *Max Weber: Werk und Person* (Tübingen: J. C. B. Mohr [Paul Siebeck], 1964), 554–55.

tandem with Nietzsche's critique of the Kantian philosophy, of proposing a level of discourse that can come to terms with the "presuppositions" of knowledge and science. My aim is to search for the ground of his inspiration, the ideas that led to his inquiries, and thereby to restore the excitement, originality, and danger to Weber's intellectual journey, the unsettled and questionable aspects that make it worth investigating.

The first two chapters of this study are devoted primarily to what might be called the "early Weber"—that is, the closing decades of the nineteenth century and the considerable body of thought Weber produced in the 1890s when he was in his twenties and thirties, a good deal of which is still worth considering in connection with the *problems* of his life and work. With few exceptions this early period has been completely ignored,[12] and studies of Weber have instead selected 1903–4 as the point of departure, the years when he turned forty and published the first installments of his "Roscher and Knies" study, *The Protestant Ethic and the Spirit of Capitalism*, and the major editorial statement for the *Archiv für Sozialwissenschaft und Sozialpolitik*, "The 'Objectivity' of Social Scientific and Sociopolitical Knowledge." The hiatus and apparent new beginning are explained by Weber's illness, commencing in 1898, and his return to writing and productive scholarship about five years later—a recovery that was in fact never more than partial. But to accept this division is to overlook the implications suggested by Marianne Weber's reminder that to those who knew him, her husband-to-be's "intellectual and moral personality was established early in life," and by age twenty-four he "was a man whose basic structure was complete and self-contained, a man whom insights and experiences could enrich but no longer remold."[13] With this in mind, it seems appropriate to attempt to restore the early writings to the position they actually occupied in the formation of Weber's thinking about the origins of capitalism and the development of the modern world.

Using this starting point in Weber's work before Weberian sociology, the three middle chapters then take up a wide range of issues having to do with Weber's evolving mature conceptions of culture, sociology, and

11. Ibid., 554, alluding, of course, to *Genesis* 2:23.
12. The judgment of Jeffrey C. Alexander, *The Classical Attempt at Theoretical Synthesis: Max Weber* (Berkeley: University of California Press, 1983), is representative: "There is no 'early Weber' in the sense that there is an early Marx or early Durkheim. In Weber's early writings, we do not find a theoretical position that is crucial to the unfolding of the mature theory" (7).
13. *Lebensbild*, 90; Eng. trans., 85.

politics—that is, those aspects of his work and texts that have normally attracted the most attention, from *The Protestant Ethic* to "Politics as a Vocation" and the studies published posthumously as *Economy and Society*. In these chapters I have been guided by the aim of identifying the predicament of what Weber calls modern "subjectivist culture," and then of showing how and why he isolates and comes to terms with the competing "life-orders" and "value-spheres" of the historically given human world. Since this body of writing is the most familiar part of Weber's contribution, I have also tried as much as possible to avoid treading across familiar terrain in order to explore instead some of the landscape that is still relatively unknown. In charting this course, I have found, somewhat to my surprise, that a great deal could be gained by paying close attention to Weber's complex relationship with his lifelong friend and colleague, the philosopher and sociologist Georg Simmel. Such a claim may startle those who have sought guidance elsewhere, as in the work of a logician like Heinrich Rickert,[14] but I have become convinced that Simmel, among all of Weber's contemporaries, is the key figure. In any case, where Weber's problems are concerned, it can never be a matter of finding traces of convergence or influence with respect to one or another contemporary. Weber, like Simmel, craved originality, and the significance of what he can plausibly be said to have borrowed, derived, or synthesized from elsewhere is minuscule when contrasted with the inventiveness of his own contributions.

In the final two chapters I expand the discussion more fully into the circle of important thinkers who surrounded Weber in the prewar years and who, together with Weber, were responsible in a major way for initiating the terms of discourse over "modernity" in the twentieth century. It is clearly valuable to situate Weber in the intellectual environment of these contemporaries in order to establish the nomenclature of the problematic dialogue of which he was a part, the range of its positions, and the meaning of Weber's own responses. Only through this kind of comparison does Weber's position become fully understandable and available for critical use.

As for the themes of this study, I have conceived my contribution primarily as a work of interpretation and synthesis that develops its point of view by interweaving exposition with analysis and commen-

14. The main contribution in this respect is Thomas Burger's *Max Weber's Theory of Concept Formation: History, Laws, and Ideal Types*, 2d ed. (Durham: Duke University Press, 1987), in which he begins by speaking of a "convergence" between Weber and Rickert, a notion that in my judgment vastly overstates Weber's agreement on matters of importance with his junior colleague and childhood friend.

tary. For the most part I have not reserved criticisms for particular sections. In the last chapter, however, I intentionally depart from this design somewhat by offering a few observations concerning modernity and its politics that extend beyond Weber's discussion, but that are, I believe, consistent with the questions that characterize it. If we are to learn anything at all important from the classics of the past century, then it must be to pursue their problems and questioning with aspirations that they would themselves have recognized and appreciated.

Lastly, a few words should be added about my approach in writing this study. My main purpose has been to develop, sustain, and support a line of thinking about Weber, a "reading" of his work in our all-too-fashionable idiom, and to do so through an understanding of what *he* wrote and said in the context of his times, culture, and contemporaries. It may seem obvious to say this, but it needs to be emphasized because of the countless studies of Weber that proceed in exactly the opposite way, pursuing themes or defining problems external to Weber's concerns while nevertheless claiming to be "about" Weber. Such approaches may yield interesting results on their own, but they do not offer an opportunity to listen to Weber and to learn from him. In my discussion I have attempted as much as possible to have Weber speak directly to us, in his voluminous written work and through his correspondence, most of which is still unpublished. For interpretive and comparative purposes, I have often used the ideas of his contemporaries, especially some of those immediate colleagues and friends whose work he knew best. As for other critical and interpretive writing, I have relied in a limited way mainly on major and relatively recent interpretations of Weber that are significant for illuminating the problems of his thought and for clarifying my own point of view. However, no attempt has been made to survey or incorporate the vast secondary literature on Weber into my themes, for to do so is in my judgment only an invitation to trivialize and misdirect our understanding.

A word of caution is in order with respect to Weber's work itself. The condition of his writings, especially in translation, is deplorable, to say the least—worse than for any other major thinker of the last century—and has led one astute observer to conclude that our knowledge of Weber has become fundamentally flawed.[15] A great deal of Weber's

15. Friedrich H. Tenbruck, "Wie gut kennen wir Max Weber? Über Maßstäbe der Weber-Forschung im Spiegel der Maßstäbe der Weber-Ausgaben," *Zeitschrift für die gesamte Staatswissenschaft* 131 (1975): 719–41; and "The Problem of Thematic Unity in the Work of Max Weber," *British Journal of Sociology* 31 (1980): 316–51.

work, especially that published before 1900, is not readily available and is therefore generally unread. Much of what is available in German is poorly edited, contextually obscure, even mistitled, a circumstance the current *Max Weber Gesamtausgabe* should remedy. In English the situation is much worse, with piecemeal translations, edited texts, partial and unsystematic readers. In addition, some of Weber's most famous and important writings suffer from inaccurate and misleading translation, and even the best English versions often prove insufficiently precise for intelligent interpretation. Such problems are, of course, magnified when one considers the thousands of letters and archival entries that still await publication in any form. Until this material becomes available and the textual deficiences are rectified—a prospective condition still years away—it will not be possible even to attempt a definitive study of Weber and his work.

Given this state of affairs, I have found it useful to consult those archival sources available to me and have considered it absolutely indispensable to return to Weber's original German texts. In citing from an archival document, I have always followed that archive's own numbering system; all translations from these materials are my own. With respect to Weber's published work, my procedure has been to cite the German text, if possible in one of the volumes of collected essays, and then to cite the equivalent English text, when one exists. In the interest of accuracy, I have often included Weber's original terminology. Whenever possible, I have tried to use the wording in the available translation. But in the majority of cases I have had to substitute my own translations for quoted passages, even though this may further complicate access to Weber's work. My intention, of course, is precisely the reverse. Unfortunately, considering the condition of the translations, there is no other, easier solution to the problem of grasping the meaning of his thought. What is needed, above all, is to encounter Weber once again from the beginning and with a sense of judgment alert to the potentials of what he actually wrote and said.

CHAPTER I

Epigones of a Great Age

If I have understood anything at all of my times sympathetically, it is its type of heroism, the modern-heroic life form and
attitude of the overburdened, over-disciplined *moralist of accomplishment* "working at the edge of exhaustion."

—*Thomas Mann*

Max Weber's late-nineteenth-century intellectual and political environment was dominated by four trends and the critical issues connected
with them: the demise of "liberal" politics and culture, particularly the
partisan "National Liberalism" of the preceding generation; the con-
comitant steady growth of socialism as an ideology, science, organization, and cultural movement; a shift in the socio-cultural sciences,
broadly conceived, toward economic categories, concepts, and explanations —thus from jurisprudence and philosophical disciplines to political economy and social history; and the appearance of an uneasy
concern over the prospects of "cultural decline," a kind of *Kultur-
pessimismus* resulting from the increasing "rationalization" of modern
life. It was, above all, these themes and the interpretation of their historical and sociocultural meaning that set the stage for Weber's thinking
from its beginnings in the 1880s to its final phases in the immediate
aftermath of World War I. They provided the substantive context within
which even his contributions to the sciences developed.

Of these issues none was more far-reaching and troublesome for
turn-of-the-century politics than the complexities associated with liberalism and its travails. While any politically aware member of Weber's
generation would have been alert to these struggles, Weber personally
experienced the demise of liberalism and its competition with alternatives in an acute form and at especially close range. Growing up as the
oldest son in a political household in Berlin, his father being a prominent member of the National Liberal Party, young Weber had every

opportunity to observe, debate, and judge the tumultuous public life of the Bismarckian and Wilhelmian era. Furthermore, he did so while fully absorbed into the aspiring national culture of urban, upper-middle-class life. Indeed, it would be difficult to find anyone among Weber's contemporaries more ideally situated to observe and experience the very spirit of liberalism in action. As contemporaries noted, "The best traditions of the liberal middle class encompassed Weber's youth," and, politically considered, he was "in a sense born into the liberal party circle."[1]

Most specifically, Weber lived through the phenomenon he later in life called "the evolution of the mentality of bourgeois virtue,"[2] an evolution of which he was himself a part and one that serves as the initial focus of our inquiries. Our questions must be: what were those "best traditions" that appeared to play so strong a formative role? What was the evolution that Weber observed, and how did he respond to it?

THE DECLINE OF BOURGEOIS LIBERALISM

To retrace Weber's engagements with the German middle class and "burgherly nature" to their source in the *juste milieu* of the nineteenth century is to uncover the conflict-ridden story of "the calm, unself-conscious life of an older generation and the nervous, self-observing haste of its descendants," adopting Rilke's characterization of the emergent pattern.[3] Deliberately siding with the newer generation, Weber did not escape the hegemony of this cultural archetype, which he sketched elsewhere in passages recalling his own self-conscious encounters as "a restless and systematic struggle with life" conducted "in deep spiritual isolation."[4] Among all the trends, the crisis in bourgeois liberalism most directly affected Weber's thought and action, for the conspicuous and ironic identification formed with his hereditary social class was fundamental to his entire orientation. "I am a member of the middle classes [*bürgerliche Klassen*], feel myself as such, and am educated in their views and ideals," was the striking version of this affirmation in the

1. Albert Salomon, review of *Max Weber: Eine Gedenkrede*, by Karl Jaspers, and *Max Weber: Ein Lebensbild*, by Marianne Weber, *Die Gesellschaft* 3 (1926): 188; Käthe Leichter, "Max Weber als Lehrer und Politiker," in *Max Weber zum Gedächtnis*, ed. R. König and J. Winckelmann (Cologne: Westdeutscher Verlag, 1964), 132.

2. A phrase used in a lengthy letter to Robert Michels, containing reflections on Weber's youthful encounter with the liberalism of his father's generation, 11 August 1908 (AMW 60).

3. From Rilke's 1902 comments, "Thomas Mann's *Buddenbrooks*," in *Thomas Mann*, ed. H. Hatfield (Englewood Cliffs, N.J.: Prentice-Hall, 1964), 8.

4. "Die protestantische Ethik und der Geist des Kapitalismus," *GARS* 1:97–98; *PE*, 107–8.

Freiburg Inaugural Address.[5] It was an affirmation repeated a number of times over the next decades.

The theme of liberalism's demise has several dimensions to it, both specific and general, political and cultural. Many are peculiar to the German sociopolitical situation in the 1870s and 1880s, especially the "revolution from above" effected by Bismarck in social policy. Weber was acutely aware that policy shifts during these decades marked a practical end to possibilities for the growth of parliamentary authority and prefigured an unavoidable, severe constitutional and social crisis. But on the few occasions when he commented directly on the nineteenth-century liberal, middle-class, and nationalist generation, he usually did so with the aim of assembling reminders of its long-forgotten hopes, sacrifices, successes, and shattering disappointments, once even remarking that persecution of the socialists under Bismarck was "trifling compared to what our bourgeois fathers and grandfathers faced in the struggle against absolutism."[6] So it was also with his comments on that generation's leading figures, such as Rudolf von Bennigsen, whose parliamentary talents were re-created in Weber's later memory as a model to emulate.[7]

Weber had an exceptionally thorough knowledge of these predeces-

---

5. "Der Nationalstaat und die Volkswirtschaftspolitik, Akademische Antrittsrede" (1895), *GPS*, 20; translated as "The National State and Economic Policy (Freiburg Address)," *Economy and Society* 9 (1980): 444. Among the similar later statements, a few appear in exchanges with Michels, the bourgeois renegade, to whom Weber slyly defended his 1907 critique of bureaucratization in the Social Democratic Party (SPD) as "a speech of a class-conscious bourgeois" addressed to "the cowards in his own class" (letter of 6 November 1907, AMW 50). Or when Marianne inherited stock in the family's Oerlinghausen textile firm, Weber issued a sardonic report that the rentier existence "had stripped away our déclassé status in favor of the most miserable bourgeois qualities" (12 August 1907, AMW 47).

6. Letter to Michels, 4 August 1908, AMW 59; Weber added, "In this respect Fritz Reuter is typical." As a member of the Jena Burschenschaft (student fraternity), Reuter (1810–74) was arrested in 1833 after the Hambach Festival, put on trial, and sentenced to death in 1836, but was subsequently pardoned and released after seven years' imprisonment. Reuter made his reputation as a popular writer of epics and satire, using the Mecklenburg dialect with great effect; Weber read from his works at Sunday gatherings (Marianne Weber, *Lebensbild*, 147; Eng. trans., 139), and he is obliquely referred to in *MGA*, I/3 (1892), 96. Reuter was related to Gottfried Keller (1819–90), noted Swiss novelist of the bourgeoisie, also cited by Weber in *MWG*, I/15:95, and *GARS* 1:98; *PE*, 107.

7. Weber's father had been a member of Bennigsen's National-Liberal *Reichstag* faction. Addressing the historical questions decades later, Weber noted that these figures had "left almost no documentation behind, not even a man like Bennigsen" (letter of 11 August 1908, AMW 60). At this time Weber's colleague Hermann Oncken, having completed a study of Lassalle, was compiling the definitive biography of Bennigsen: *Rudolf von Bennigsen: Ein deutscher liberaler Politiker nach seinen Briefen und hintergelassenen Papieren*, 2 vols. (Stuttgart: Deutsche Verlags-Anstalt, 1910); like Weber, Oncken complained in his foreword about the poverty of evidence and Bennigsen's own disinclination to write the history of the liberal movement.

sors and their views, the politicians and professorial representatives of the *Bildungs-* and *Besitzbürgertum:* in addition to Bennigsen, the historians Theodor Mommsen and Heinrich von Treitschke, his uncles Hermann Baumgarten and Julius Jolly, and his own father, Max Weber, Sr., to name only a few—all models of "bourgeois" conviction for the apostate son. "I knew the older generation precisely," Weber once noted, "and, subjectively considered, I had my most difficult inner struggles with them"—a truly important self-disclosure.[8] Immersion in this particular world produced in Weber a spiritual as well as political predicament, an expression of internal doubts and fears in addition to a questioning of the direction taken by public life. Even Weber's most striking metaphor of the time revealed deep apprehension: "One has the impression of sitting on a speeding train, while doubting whether the next switch will be correctly set."[9] The comment was aimed at uncertainties at the end of the eighties, but in fact it expressed a pervasive disquiet tugging at the ordered exterior of Weber's life and work.

Reservations of this kind, first appearing in the 1880s, were certainly provoked for Weber in part by an increasingly embittered critique of *Reich* institutions from the pen of the Strassburg historian Hermann Baumgarten.[10] As *the* prominent opponent of Treitschke's "national history," this respected relative and friend was important for young Weber as a skillful critic of the growing complacency and confusion within liberalism's ranks in the eighties and as a remarkably foresighted (and isolated) analyst of the crippling effects of Bismarck's Caesarist demagogy. An "old liberal" from the days of the Frankfurt Parliament, imbued with atavistic liberal-democratic hopes, Baumgarten understood that the new *Reich* had transformed the political environment: not the earlier concern with ideal legal forms and postulated rights, but observation of the power position and political experience of classes, status

8. Letter of 11 August 1908, AMW 60; In the *Lebensbild,* Marianne Weber records the attendance at the Weber's Charlottenburg home, where young Max was permitted after dinner to pass out cigars among the male dignitaries and National Liberal deputies (41–42; Eng. trans., 39–40).

9. Letter to Baumgarten, 21 December 1889, *JB,* 324, repeated on p. 330, and preceded with a comment on the campaign leading up to the 1890 elections: "Apparently liberalism has unfortunately not yet reached its lowest point" (323).

10. Baumgarten's significance is especially emphasized by Wolfgang J. Mommsen, *Max Weber and German Politics, 1890–1920,* trans. M. Steinberg (Chicago: University of Chicago Press, 1984), chap. 1, who notes quite correctly that "the only meaningful and lasting influence on Weber during his student years" (11) came from this respected family member, whose lectures Weber had attended during his military service. Mommsen's critical study of Weber the "politician," written from a neoliberal point of view, was first published in 1959, with a revised edition in 1974.

groups, and their organized representatives had become the focus for an emerging national politics. Performing a critique on his own earlier self-criticism,[11] Baumgarten came within this context to advocate a new constitutional system incorporating the actual substance rather than the mere appearance of parliamentary rule. However, after the reversal of national policy in 1878, his position grew sharply negative. The images of impending doom in Weber's early writings, the sarcastic jibes at his own generation's historical illiteracy, and the polemics directed against the "unpolitical" *Bürgertum* and Bismarck's questionable and destructive "legacy" followed quite precisely the thinking set down in Baumgarten's stinging critique.

Thus, reporting to his uncle from Berlin in the mid-eighties, Weber noted that the atmosphere of the time was marked by "the incredible ignorance of the history of this century among my contemporaries." Bismarck's founding deeds were eulogized, Treitschke's nationalist polemics greeted with "frenetic jubilation," while a "mystical national fanaticism" and philistine realpolitik carried the day; otherwise, except for native Berliners, Weber observed, "tabula rasa rules here."[12] The record of middle-class liberalism and its twelve years of legislative achievements, beginning with the North German Confederation in 1866, was simply obliterated in the prevailing political climate, determined as it was by the "fatal gift of Bismarck's Caesarism," which Weber labeled "the basic mistake."[13] In the judgment of the precocious nephew, as for the uncle, it appeared incontestable that liberalism's future as a political program and cultural force was in peril, and both agreed that the decisive events in the fortunes of liberalism had come not with the *Reichsgründung*, but with fateful choices made in 1877–78.

A great deal is revealed in Weber's unconventional insistence on this "turning point" (as he called it), a claim that is reemphasized in his later political writings and correspondence. Unlike many contemporaries, who viewed the political scene as an unbroken pattern of national progress or interpreted 1848 (the failure of liberal revolution), 1866–70 (Bismarck's military successes against Austria-Hungary and France), or

11. *Der deutsche Liberalismus: Eine Selbstkritik* (Frankfurt: Ullstein, 1974), originally published in 1866. Expressing views he later questioned, Baumgarten had written that "the middle class is little fitted for political action" (42) and had appealed for strong leadership and praised a bureaucracy "which included the real political strength of the *Bürgertum*" (47). Framed through categories adopted by Weber, his ambivalence speaks volumes about liberalism's weaknesses.
12. Letters of 14 July 1885, 25 April 1887, 30 April 1888: *JB*, 174, 232, 298.
13. Letter of 8 November 1884, *JB*, 143.

even 1890 (Bismarck's resignation) as the great divide for modern Germany, Weber maintained that all the conditions for political paralysis, bureaucratic domination in the *Obrigkeitsstaat* (authoritarian state), and "feudalization" of the social order were present only in the aftermath of deliberate choices made in 1877–78. All would come to this view, he added, "who had *experienced* the events, as I did" [14]—that is, from within liberal political circles in Berlin.

Weber's critical and gloomy assessment rested on three observations: First, in these months all prospects for increasing parliamentary responsibility and power had come to an abrupt end, following the collapse of negotiations between Bennigsen and Bismarck. Second, the new post-election strategy, appealing to a right-of-center majority, called for state intervention combined with repression of the Left: protectionism (including tariffs on grain and iron), civil service "reform" (actually a purge of liberal elements in the bureaucracy), state-sponsored social security programs, and the antisocialist law. Third and most important, the economic basis for the policy shift was secured by an "unholy" alliance between industrial capitalism and the large agrarian interests, particularly the favored Junker estates in the East. This powerful bloc dominated foreign and domestic politics through World War I, and it aroused Weber's ire on countless occasions before and after 1900.

But the deeper questions Weber puzzled through had to do with the causes and consequences of this momentous turnabout. Criticizing liberalism from within, he thought stubborn complacency rather than ideological incoherence had finally overtaken its promise. As the century approached its end, the "founding" generation from the 1860s seemed able only to "endure social legislation with an almost passive mistrust" because it "simply did not *recognize* certain problems"— namely, those arising around the "social question" and the attendant changes in social structure affecting labor-relations and the material conditions of life for industrial and agrarian workers. [15] The liberal sphere of action would remain "limited," Weber predicted, "as long as economic and social questions continue so exclusively in the foreground," a situation expected to persist indefinitely. [16] The more profound reason for this outcome lay elsewhere, however: not only in Bismarck's policies and legacy, but in the shared responsibility for them.

14. Letter of 4 August 1908, AMW 59.

15. Letters to Baumgarten, 30 April 1888, *JB*, 299; and Michels, 11 August 1908, AMW 60.

16. Letter to Baumgarten, 3 January 1891, *JB*, 329.

"The terrible annihilation of independent conviction that Bismarck brought about is naturally the main cause or one of the main causes of everything harmful in our present circumstances. But in this respect aren't we at least as guilty as Bismarck himself?"[17] The "you are to blame for yourselves" thrust of this message, to speak with Nietzsche, was one that Weber never surrendered in his personal efforts to come to terms with bourgeois liberalism's legacy.

As for consequences, one could minimally expect a decreasing importance of parties as such (excluding the special case of Social Democracy, which opposed the entire system in any case) and an attempt to rule through patronage, interest-group support, and extraconstitutional maneuvering; a decline in the quality of political leadership and emasculation of the process by which selection of leaders occurred; and the paradoxical political hegemony of the model "unpolitical" citizen—taken together a basic formula for perpetuating the authoritarian state buttressed by sham constitutionalism. Four decades after the great "turning point," Weber thought these results had been fully realized: "Since 1878 the nation has been unaccustomed to sharing, through its elected representatives, in the determination of its political affairs. Such participation, after all, is the precondition for developing political judgment."[18] And without political judgment, according to this view of the world, all is lost. One had to begin again, searching for a new way of thinking, even a new science that would measure up to the needs of the times. For Weber this search was already under way in his early writings.

THE CRISIS IN LIBERAL CULTURE

The significance Weber attached to policy shifts in 1877–78 should not be overestimated or considered in isolation. Underlying the political crisis was a growing challenge to nineteenth-century liberal culture itself, a mood of questioning that became an irrepressible force in the 1890s, especially among the intelligentsia in the urban centers of Eu-

17. Letter to Baumgarten, 18 April 1892, *JB*, 346.
18. "Parlament und Regierung im neugeordneten Deutschland: Zur politischen Kritik des Beamtentums und Parteiwesens" [Parliament and Government in a Reconstructed Germany: Toward a Political Critique of Officialdom and Party Politics] (1918), in *MWG* I/15:449; Eng. trans. in *EaS*, 1391–92. Weber also argued that these "later developments have *completely vindicated* the basic political premises of the National Liberals" (1388), referring to their warnings, which he shared, concerning the baneful consequences of the shift in 1877–78.

rope: Paris, London, Vienna, Berlin. Weber emerged from the very center of Berlin's upper-middle-class intellectual life, growing up and studying there precisely during those decades in which the city was transformed from a provincial administrative capital into a cosmopolitan, industrialized, modern metropolis, becoming the world's fifth largest city by 1910. If he belonged to a specific generational grouping, a special formation of the zeitgeist or, in Hughes' phrase, a "cluster of genius,"[19] then it was the generation of the nineties, set apart because of its shared consciousness of a dynamic and wrenching destabilization of transmitted cultural traditions, a deeply felt discontinuity in the formative life experiences characterizing the turn of the century and determining its identity and collective fate.

Entering the maelstrom of fin de siècle culture is a daunting adventure, but its dangers can be reduced somewhat by categories already defined and explored recently by cultural historians. One attractive route to the kind of understanding we seek is set forth in Schorske's study of Freud's Vienna and Viennese modernism, an investigation concerned throughout with the cultural movement of "ubiquitous fragmentation" and "infinite innovation," or with what Arnold Schoenberg called "a death-dance of principles" and rival value-spheres.[20] Two suggestive themes emerge from an appraisal of the Viennese milieu, and they appear to be repeated throughout industrializing urban civilization: a break with the progressive historical outlook of the nineteenth century, and a replacement of liberal rationalism with a new protagonist on the stage of history—the "psychological" human type. These themes combine to form a full-scale crisis in what can be called liberal culture.[21]

The cultural movement invariably takes the form of a collective generational revolt by "*die Jungen*," the representatives of youth and renewal who begin to appear across the cultural spectrum—in art, poetry,

19. H. Stuart Hughes, *Consciousness and Society: The Reorientation of European Social Thought, 1890–1930* (New York: Random House [Vintage Books], 1958), 17; Mary Gluck, *Georg Lukács and His Generation, 1900–1918* (Cambridge: Harvard University Press, 1985), has addressed the problem of characterizing a "generation" among the intellectuals in this period (see esp. 43–44).

20. Carl E. Schorske, *Fin-de-Siècle Vienna: Politics and Culture* (New York: Random House [Vintage Books], 1981), xix.

21. In this context by "culture" I generally mean that intellectual, spiritual, and aesthetic condition that characterizes a way of life, or life-style, a usage consistent with Raymond Williams' in *Keywords: A Vocabulary of Culture and Society* (London: Croom Helm, 1976), 76–82. Culture's "liberal" characteristics have to do minimally with (a) faith in necessary "progress" in history; (b) belief in human improvability through the application of "reason," often in the form of scientific knowledge; and (c) an ethos of achievement through specialized work.

music, drama, architecture, literature, philosophy, the sociocultural
sciences—and interestingly also in Weber's own self-descriptions of the
nineties.[22] The revolt is often accompanied by the alienation of the intellectuals from politically dominant groups, then in some cases from
"society" as a whole—recall in this connection Weber's use of the "salon des refusés" figure of speech to describe both his Heidelberg circle
and the German Sociological Society—and for many by a flight from
political engagement either into the hothouse of "aesthetic culture" or
into the cold and clear air of "intellect."

For our purposes, however, the most powerful part of the analysis of
cultural crisis is the juxtaposition of *two* rival cultures at the turn of the
century: as a starting point a public and moralistic culture, confident in
the humane powers of science and derived from the even older eigh-
teenth- and nineteenth-century liberal historicist outlook discernible in
thinkers as disparate as Kant, Hegel, and Ranke. In the latter half of
the century it was typified by the civic-minded generation of the "great
age" of national unification, but now in the years of Bismarck's tena-
cious control its members are growing increasingly disillusioned, like
Baumgarten, or sliding into complacency, like Max Weber senior. Opposed to this configuration of values was an emerging "aesthetic culture," representative of the new, amoral *Gefühlskultur*, or culture of
"feeling" and "experience," out of which grew a special sensitivity to
art, psychic nuance, emotional states, expressiveness, and interiority. It
was a marginal, particularizing culture closely linked with the oppositional identity of outsiders or with the sloganeering of "art for art's
sake." Here one finds the culture of Baudelaire's dandy (the model for
the early George Circle), of Mallarmé's symbolism, the youth movement, urban modernism, *Jugendstil* (art nouveau) in art and architecture, Oscar Wilde's dramas and Richard Strauss' operas, experimentation with new forms of therapeutic living in the counterculture of
Schwabing and Monte Verità near Ascona, Simmel's "sociological impressionism," Lukács' flirtation with antimodern aestheticism, and

22. In his maiden speech before the Verein für Sozialpolitik, (Association for Social
Policy), Weber contrasted the situations of the "older generation" and "we youth" (*wir
Jüngeren*): "Die ländliche Arbeitsverfassung," *Verhandlungen des Vereins für Sozialpolitik*, in *SVSP* 58 (1893): 84. Similarly, in the Freiburg Inaugural Address, Weber referred
to "we youthful members of the German historical school" and to the "right of youth to
be true to itself and its ideals" (*GPS*, 16, 24; "The National State," 440, 448). The many
post-1897 literary contributions of Georg Simmel, among Weber's friends, to the Munich
Journal *Jugend—the* new voice of youth and the inspiration for *Jugendstil*, or "art nouveau"—constitute the most spectacular instance of this trend.

later, in Weber's Munich, the aesthetically styled apocalyptic counter-
politics of the *Räterepublik*. It is precisely this culture and its carriers
that Weber confronts at a number of critical junctures, beginning in the
nineties.[23]

These fundamental contrasts in culture—historical versus psychological outlooks, moralistic and scientific opposed to aesthetic orientations, a kind of humorless and upright *Buddenbrooks* liberalism against
the stirrings of an experimental but deeply serious attitude toward
life—all appear to be valid everywhere in urban Europe and not simply
in Freud's imperial city. They set the outer boundaries of Weber's path
through life, an enormously convoluted route that moves on the one
hand toward distance and self-restraint rather than into the new cultural space defined by subjectivity and interiority, yet on the other hand
traverses an intellectual terrain containing a fascination for modern cultural innovation, including lifelong engagement with figures like Wagner and Ibsen, Richard Strauss and Stefan George, Maeterlinck and
Dostoevski. Or to put the matter on a different plane, in the age after
Marx and Nietzsche, Weber chose to follow the adventures of the subjective consciousness, but from a distance within the horizon of a commanding historical imagination. That is not all, however, for in Weber's
northern imperium important variations and modifications complicated
the cultural landscape even further.

The cultural polarity is fundamental for Weber's fin-de-siècle world.
Nevertheless, the remarkable cohesion of the Viennese urban élite and
the *traditional* aestheticism and sensuality of Catholic Austrian culture
were not shared elsewhere in German-speaking Europe. As Schorske
points out, "Traditional Austrian culture was not, like that of the German north, moral, philosophical, and scientific."[24] In the vast and powerful northern neighbor, compared with the microcosm of Vienna, one
could encounter, not surprisingly, a more differentiated cultural environment, manifested partly in the stern requirements of a dogmatic (and
pietist) Protestantism and partly in the long-standing and in a sense
tradition-minded attraction for *Wissenschaft* and for "philosophical
culture," as Weber's Berlin compatriot, Georg Simmel, with good reason entitled his major collection of essays. These cultural strata were

23. As one small example, in 1894 Weber purchased and displayed many of Max
Klinger's *Jugendstil* etchings, which he kept for twelve years (*Lebensbild*, 213–15, 362;
Eng. trans., 201–4, 359). Klinger was widely considered the representative of Nietz-
schean ideas in art; his work was celebrated by the Vienna Secession in 1902 (Schorske,
Fin-de-siècle Vienna, 254–55), an appropriate indication of his stature among the rebels.
24. *Fin-de-siècle Vienna*, 7.

then overlaid in the 1890s with a neoliberal appeal for "ethical culture" that Weber enjoyed ridiculing, probably to the discomfort of those colleagues and friends, such as Ferdinand Tönnies, Werner Sombart, Gerhart von Schulze-Gävernitz, and Robert Michels, who at one time or another helped articulate its message.[25] And to these levels of culture one should still add the specifically "political culture" that was so significant for the formation of Weber's thinking about the *vita activa*, a quite mixed heritage of Bismarckian achievement and its lessons for "the primacy of foreign policy" with all their troubling, ambivalent, and robust implications.

We should not miss the extent to which these rival cultural strata overlaid each other and the liberal culture of the *Bürgertum*. But to sort through the various layers is to see, additionally, that Weber's individualistic conscience was forged not simply in the present-day public world of fathers and sons but also in the milieu of a preliberal, ascetic Protestantism, the site of a universalizing ethos, or what Thomas Mann, borrowing from Nietzsche, appropriately called an "ethical atmosphere" that took seriously its tragic sense of history, the rightness and necessity of social reform, and a kind of stubborn opposition to all eudaemonic conceptions of life. The ascetic approach to life invented a new "modern-heroic life form," represented by the overburdened, overdisciplined *moralist of accomplishment* 'working at the edge of exhaustion.'"[26] A more apt characterization of Weber's "heroic" facet, depicting *one* side of his cultural identification, is scarcely imaginable. Often wanting to feel crushed under the burden of work, he wrote openly to Marianne of his "inner treadmill," of "desperately clinging to scientific work as to a talisman, without being able to say what it should ward off."[27] There was hardly an aspect of the morally grounded ideals flourishing in this atmosphere that Weber did not absorb: Simply consider the appeals scattered through his work from the earliest stages for "matter-of-factness" (*Sachlichkeit*) or "objectivity," clarity about the world as it "is," a sense of "proportion" and "distance," personal "integrity," disciplined striving for the impossible, the inevitability of "struggle," and "responsibility" before history (which was even raised to the level of a distinctive ethos, an "ethic of responsibility"). More-

25. Tönnies was a charter member, and he and Sombart delivered lectures inaugurating the formation of the international chapter in Zürich in 1896; Schulze-Gävernitz lent his support as Weber's colleague in Freiburg.

26. *Reflections of a Nonpolitical Man* (1918), trans. W. Morris (New York: Ungar, 1983), 54, 103.

27. Letter of 4 August 1898, from a sanatorium in Konstanz, NW 30/1:66; *Lebensbild*, 249; Eng. trans., 236.

over, neither politics nor culture itself escaped Weber's Calvinist eye: the former was rendered "diabolic" and "tragic," while the latter came in his vision to be burdened with "guilt."

For the generation of the nineties, however, the most overt public expression of the "ethical" standpoint was championed elsewhere, in the Society for Ethical Culture introduced into Germany in 1892. Largely an Anglo-American invention, this association sought to bolster the older liberal, moral-scientific outlook under new social conditions shaped by rapid industrialization and urbanization.[28] "Ethical culture" wanted to be a social movement, but it remained essentially an idea and an organization, putting forward the best face of naive, reformist liberal idealism. Its Berlin program of 1892, vigorously defended by Tönnies, called for "introducing a philosophical way of thinking" into national life in order to promote general "moral idealism," a "healing of the soul" for the working class, and a "simpler and more natural way of life for the well-to-do."[29] The meaning of such "ethical" content was perfectly captured in Michels' invariably passionate rhetoric: "If an ethic truly wants to earn the name 'ethic,' then it must enlist the sympathies of the entire world, resound in everyone's ears, set everyone's hearts pounding, and not least of all relentlessly tear away the cloak of injustice"—not to mention hypocrisy![30]

Regarded as a strength by its defenders across the social and political spectrum, such emotive and exhortatory appeals became an annoyance for Weber at an early stage and provoked some ironic commentary. Already in 1895 he remarked to his brother Alfred that his appeal in the "Inaugural Address" to "reason of state" and the inevitability of the "struggle for existence" had given "ethical culture" a "firm kick."[31]

28. See Horace L. Friess, *Felix Adler and Ethical Culture: Memories and Studies* (New York: Columbia University Press, 1981).

29. Ferdinand Tönnies, *Ethische Kultur und ihr Geleite* (Kiel: Feincke, 1893), 11–13.

30. Robert Michels, "'Endziel', Intransigenz, Ethik," *Ethische Kultur* 11 (1903): 393; one of a series of eight articles Michels published in the movement's journal from 1903 to 1905, while he was still numbered among the radicals in the German and Italian Socialist parties.

31. Letter of 17 May 1895, NW 30/4:15–16. Later during the war the society's leading spokesman and editorial overseer, Friedrich Wilhelm Förster, was to become enmeshed in Weber's reflections on the "ethical problem" in the politically charged atmosphere of Munich's *Räterepublik*. In "Politics as a Vocation" Förster served as one of Weber's models for the "cosmic-ethical 'rationalist'" propagating the morally uncompromising but from Weber's point of view politically irresponsible thesis "from good comes only good; but from evil only evil follows" (*GPS*, 541–43; G&M, 122–24), which was indeed a leading maxim in Förster's popular treatise on ethics and political education: *Politische Ethik und politische Pädagogik; Mit besonderer Berücksichtigung der kommenden deutschen Aufgaben*, 3d ed. (Munich: Reinhardt, 1918), especially "the errors of Machiavellism," 192–210.

Similarly, in his work on the stock exchange, Weber warned against proposals for "unilateral economic disarmament" by those wanting to compel economic institutions to be moral: a strong stock exchange "cannot be a club for 'ethical culture,'" but must instead function justifiably as an instrumental "means for power in the economic struggle."[32] Never one to show great attraction for "formalism," whether in morality, the law, or science, Weber put as much distance as possible between his positions and this politics of moral rearmament based on an absolutist ethics of pure intentions. Perhaps had it been able to camouflage more effectively the whiff of noblesse oblige if not moral superiority in its message, "ethical culture" might have proved more attractive. But as idea and mode of conduct it nevertheless presented an emotionally alluring message for those thirsting for the older and plainer verities, a message that among other things interpreted the cultural crisis as fundamentally moral in nature, an instance of decadence in "values," and sought solutions for it simply in "right living," the harmonies of "nature," the power of moral example, and ethical perfectionism. Such views represented, at their best, the latest wave of well-intentioned reformism. Their inability to trigger anything but scorn in Weber's judgments shows how far he had traveled away from the comfortable assumptions of a venerable burgherly cultural heritage.

As a "moralist of accomplishment" Weber took his dialectical point of departure not in ethical systems, but in the "cultural tasks" (*Kulturaufgaben*) facing the nation's two generations. At the end of his 1893 speech to the Verein für Sozialpolitik (Association for Social Policy), the single episode responsible more than any other for establishing his reputation, Weber turned to the particular situation of the age: Addressing an audience drawn, as he said, "overwhelmingly from older and more experienced men," he suggested that the "countless illusions" demanded at first in order even to create a nation had been quickly followed by unresolved social conflicts and a search for new directions in social policy necessary to address them. "We cannot once again revive the naive and enthusiastic vigor that animated the generation before us," he argued, "because we confront tasks of a different kind from those of our fathers"—tasks that led well beyond liberalism. In the face of the future, Weber acknowledged feeling a certain "resignation" and, speaking for his own generation, fear of "the cruel curse of epigonism,"

---

32. "Die Börse" (1896), *GASS*, 321–22.

of imitative and undistinguished emulation ensured by a quirk of history.[33]

These unique figures of speech are suggestive for understanding Weber's particular response to the travails of *Bürgerlichkeit*. The "epigones" appeared before and after the great Verein für Sozialpolitik encounter with patriarchal power, once to defend the one companion of the age with whom he "had a strong emotional friendship," Paul Göhre,[34] and once to defend himself, and in both instances to establish an imagery for transforming the predicament of generational succession and for coming to terms with the course of cultural development. "We are epigones of a great age," Weber suggested, and "the stormy impulse of idealism" has become impossible "through our clearer knowledge of the prosaic laws of social life."[35] For the older generation, "German history appeared to have come to an end," and with it the best hopes of a *national* liberalism and the "bourgeoisie's capacity for political judgment [*Urteilsfähigkeit*]," whereas for the newer generation, historical responsibility was just beginning: It demanded lifting "the veil of illusions" through "a prodigious work of *political* education."[36]

Weber's sense for the meaning of his enigmatic language was determined by a single question: how to avoid the "hard fate of the political *epigone*," in the words of the Freiburg Address; or, in Nietzsche's phrasing, how to "forget the superstition that you are epigones."[37] The meaning of this question could indeed already be found in Nietzsche's "untimely" early writings, where the "late survivals, mere epigoni" who are self-satisfied and comfortable ("*die Behaglichen*"), are cast against those who "study history as a means to *life*": in the past the classical Greeks, and in the present those prepared to make themselves into "a

33. "Die ländliche Arbeitsverfassung," *SVSP* 58 (1893): 84–85.

34. According to Ernst Troeltsch, "Max Weber" (1920), in *Max Weber zum Gedächtnis*, 44.

35. "Zur Rechtfertigung Göhres," *Die Christliche Welt* 6 (24 November 1892): 1109.

36. *GPS*, 21, 24; "The National State," 444, 447. I have explored this theme in an early paper, "Max Weber's Politics and Political Education," *American Political Science Review* 67 (1973): 128–41, an essay that now seems to me importantly a product of its own times and my education, though the issues are perennial: they have to do with practical knowledge and practical judgment. I would decline to deprecate or stigmatize Weber's notion of political education, as do Stephen P. Turner and Regis A. Factor, *Max Weber and the Dispute over Reason and Value: A Study in Philosophy, Ethics, and Politics* (London: Routledge & Kegan Paul, 1984), 87–89, in this case and in others.

37. *GPS*, 21; "The National State," 444; Friedrich Nietzsche, "On the Uses and Disadvantages of History for Life," *Untimely Meditations*, (1873–76), trans. R. J. Hollingdale (Cambridge: Cambridge University Press, 1983), 94 (pt. II, sec. 6; this reference and similar ones will henceforth be cited as "II, 6").

mirror where the future may see itself," or all those whose biographies appear under the inscription "'a fighter against his age.'"[38] Weber heard the voices of the sirens, but his vocation took shape precisely around such struggles, in opposition to the times, against the spirit of "technical progress," or, as he once said, "'against the stream' of the material constellations of interests."[39] An answer to his own question had to be sought in alternatives to the comfortable assumptions of a political and cultural liberalism in decline. The search for an intellectually adequate, critical, and constructive response led Weber initially toward a new form of inquiry: the comparatively youthful science of political economy.

WEBER'S TURN TO POLITICAL ECONOMY

During his lifetime Weber explored a variety of vocational fields and came to symbolize many things to many different people. As Robert Michels, one of the very few colleagues for whom he ever expressed an "affinity," once commented, "Max Weber was a very complex person: a man of strict and exact science, a scholar from head to toe who loved science as passionately as a young bride, a political economist, specialist in public law, sociologist, historian of religion, but also a practical politician, organizer, and not least possessed of a truly daemonic nature."[40] These valedictory phrases recall Weber's contrasting characterization of Michels as a "moralist" whose personal ethos seemed outwardly so dissimilar to his own.[41] Yet Weber probably also saw in himself a repudia-

---

38. Friedrich Nietzsche, *Werke in drei Bänden*, ed. K. Schlechta (Frankfurt: Ullstein, 1983), 1: 145, 218, 237, 251, 284. The problem of the "epigones" is especially evident in "On the Uses and Disadvantages of History for Life," secs. 1, 5, 6, 8, and 10. After discussing the Germans as a "nation of heirs" and praising the "unhistorical culture" of Greek antiquity, Nietzsche writes, "What I mean by this—and it is all I mean—is that the thought of being epigones, which can often be a painful thought, is also capable of evoking great effects and grand hopes for the future in both an individual and in a nation, provided we regard ourselves as the heirs and successors of the astonishing powers of antiquity and see in this our honour and our spur" (Hollingdale trans., 103). Weber's evocation of the *Epigonentum* should be read from this angle.

39. "Zur Lage der bürgerlichen Demokratie in Russland," *Archiv* 22 (1906): 348; also *GPS*, 61; *Selections*, 282.

40. Robert Michels, *Bedeutende Männer: Charakterologische Studien* (Leipzig: Quelle & Meyer, 1927), 109; originally published in the *Basler Nachrichten* in 1920, a month after Weber's death.

41. In a letter to Gisela Michels-Lindner, 25 December 1909, AMW 67; Weber continued, "Even though I often differ from him on particulars and also on matters important in themselves, I too repeatedly find so many affinities in our fundamental *mode* of seeing and comprehending things. And that happens to me so rarely."

tion of the world's stupidity in favor of the stubborn radicalism of the "outsider" guided by a unique spirit. But setting aside for the moment the riddle of the "daemonic," the most consistently applied identification Weber chose for himself from among those listed by Michels was not so much "sociologist" as *Nationalökonom*, or political economist. "We political economists have a pedantic custom . . ." was the characteristically sobering pronouncement in the opening sentence of "Science as a Vocation." [42]

As a young student concerned with the subject matter of the human sciences generally, Weber had pursued wide-ranging interests in philosophy, theology, political economy, political science (*Staatswissenschaft*), and, especially, jurisprudence and history, attending lectures by some of the great men in these disciplines at Heidelberg, Strassburg, Göttingen, and Berlin. Among these subjects he chose as his starting point not the "new" science of political economy but the thoroughly respectable subjects of history and law, completing his dissertation and "habilitation" in the philosophical faculty at Berlin's Humboldt University on narrowly defined legal-historical topics dealing with the history of medieval trading companies and the agrarian history of Rome. [43] These were studies intended for the cognoscenti and, strictly speaking, were the only books Weber ever wrote. Read today, they must strike one as palatable mainly for the "fact-greedy gullet" of the "subject matter specialists," whose proclivities Weber himself identified. [44] Yet they also revealed an interest, as Käsler has suggested, in "that theme which guided all of his work: the origins and consequences of 'modern' capitalism." [45]

Marianne Weber has recorded the familiar story of her husband's early professional orientation and struggles: qualifying as a *Referendar* (junior barrister) in 1886 at twenty-two, acquiring a law degree and

42. The speech delivered to the Freistudentische Bund in Munich on 7 November 1917, not later than that date, as has often been supposed: *GAW*, 582; G&M, 129. Weber's famous companion speech, "Politics as a Vocation," was given to the same student association on 28 January 1919, and, like the earlier talk, then revised for publication early in 1919; on this dating, see Wolfgang Schluchter's excursus in his study coauthored with Guenther Roth, *Max Weber's Vision of History: Ethics and Methods* (Berkeley: University of California Press, 1979), 113–16.

43. Completed in 1889 and 1891, under the direction of Professors Levin Goldschmidt and August Meitzen, respectively: see the documentation in *Max Weber zum Gedächtnis*, 10–12; and the discussion in Guenther Roth, "Introduction" to *EaS*, xxxiv–xliv.

44. "Die 'Objektivität' sozialwissenschaftlicher und sozialpolitischer Erkenntnis," *GAW*, 214; S&F, 112.

45. Dirk Käsler, *Einführung in das Studium Max Webers* (Munich: Beck, 1979), 30–31.

admission to the bar three years later, dull courtroom work as an un-salaried law clerk, preparation for a career as an attorney, thoughts of applying for the position of legal counsellor in Bremen, and in general "an extraordinary longing for practical activity" with political pros-pects.[46] This longing was to go unfulfilled, however, as academic oppor-tunities multiplied: In 1892 Weber replaced the ailing Levin Gold-schmidt as a lecturer on commercial law and law of exchange at Berlin; he considered an offer there the following year of an associate profes-sorship in law; and finally he accepted the offer of a chair in political economy at Freiburg. Given the dramatic turn in his interests toward political economy, the last opportunity challenged Weber's imagination, even though it really meant a change of disciplines and extensive new preparations. He moved to Freiburg as an *Ordinarius* (full professor) at age thirty in the fall of 1894.

The general significance of Weber's turn to political economy and choice for Freiburg, especially in relation to his interests in cultural tasks and problems, was strikingly revealed in Marianne's retrospective observations about her husband's thinking: "As a science political economy is still elastic and 'young' in comparison with jurisprudence; in addition, it lies on the boundary of the most varied academic fields; it leads directly to the history of culture and ideas, as well as to philo-sophical problems; and finally it is more fruitful for a political and sociopolitical orientation than the more formal problematic of legal thought."[47] The slow march toward political economy actually began as early as 1883, when in his second Heidelberg semester Weber at-tended Karl Knies' lectures on "political economy" and "finance"— lectures "which I certainly must hear," Weber commented in a letter, "even if uninteresting due to the subject matter, but nevertheless very thoroughgoing." But he resumed his attendance the following semester with a far more positive impression, noting Knies' "quite brilliant re-marks."[48] Study of "Adam Smith and others" to master some of politi-cal economy's "basic concepts" contributed to a clearer understanding of the subject. Shortly thereafter Weber turned to Gustav von Schmoll-er's "political economy essays" in the *Preussische Jahrbücher*, finding them more congenial than expected.[49]

46. Letter to Baumgarten, 3 January 1891, *JB*, 326; *Lebensbild*, chaps. 4–5 passim; also concisely set forth in Wilhelm Hennis, *Max Webers Fragestellung: Studien zur Bio-graphie des Werks* (Tübingen: Mohr, 1987), 120–22.
47. *Lebensbild*, 212; Eng. trans., 200.
48. Letters to his father, 23 February and 5 May 1883, *JB*, 71, 74.
49. Letter to his father, 3 September 1883, *JB*, 75.

Weber's youthful letters, covering the crucial years of intellectual development when he was in his twenties, continue to record a maturing
attraction for political economy in the face of dissatisfaction with the
older sciences. Thus, explaining the progress of his studies, the Berlin
doctoral candidate noted arriving reluctantly at the conclusion that certain "practical" problems of the times "were not to be understood
with the means of our science [that is, jurisprudence], so that for me
the impulse toward scientific work for its own sake significantly de-
creased"; he found an engaging alternative in the "company of young
political economists, naturally most of them primarily opponents of
Manchesterism, something good for me, I think, for as a political
economist I'm still poorly informed." [50]

As political economy gained in stature, at least in the broad sense
propagated by Schmoller among the *Kathedersozialisten* (the "socialists
of the chair" in the universities) and those in the Verein für Sozialpolitik, so Weber moved steadily in its direction. His shift toward the new
perspective, with its radical and postliberal concern for the "social
question," led him to pursue contacts with what he called a new
"school" composed of "political economists and *Sozialpolitiker*," or
politicians committed to an activist social policy. Nearly eight years
after his initial exposure to Knies and Schmoller, Weber found he had
"become approximately one-third political economist," presumably
with the remaining fractions of his mind still reserved for law and history.[51] This intellectual journey continued with the Freiburg appointment, the longest continuous academic position ever held by Weber
(two and a half years); the collaboration there with another political
economist, Gerhart von Schulze-Gävernitz; the invitation to succeed his
former teacher Knies at Heidelberg; and his extensive public service and
activities during the decade.

Weber was highly self-conscious of the change brought about in his
thinking, a movement in thought, as it were, not so much from history
to sociology, as Antoni would have it,[52] as from the older liberal histo-
riography of a Mommsen or Ranke to the new political economy of the
Kathedersozialisten and others who took the "social question" seriously. He was also fully aware of the growing attraction at the time for
economic categories and explanations: "We find the economic mode of

50. Letter to Baumgarten, 30 September 1887, *JB*, 271–73.
51. Letters to Baumgarten, 30 April 1888 and 3 January 1891, *JB*, 299, 327.
52. Carlo Antoni, *From History to Sociology: The Transition in German Historical
Thinking*, trans. H. White (London: Merlin, 1962), chap. 4.

analysis advancing in all spheres: social policy [*Sozialpolitik*] in place of politics, economic power-relations in place of legal relations, cultural and economic history in place of political history." In short, the "economic point of view" has "come into fashion."[53] Against those who thought the recently won popularity meant a victory for the autonomy and hegemony of the economic, or a clear triumph for the "pure Platonic interest of the technologist,"[54] Weber warned that the new "fashionableness" risked losing sight of the source of values, the nature of value-conflict, and the realities of *political* relations and power. For him the essential meaning of the shift in perspective emerged in the claim that, as a science, political economy had to be practical, political, national, and, above all, *modern*. Each attribute was important for defining Weber's earliest Weltanschauung.

In the first place, Weber touted the new approach as a means for achieving a modus vivendi between theoretical work and practical activity, at least to the extent that an operative compromise could ever be achieved. His writings and public activities of the nineties issued in numerous ventures into eminently practical-political topics or into public education, from courses on political economy for Friedrich Naumann's Protestant reformers, to service on the Ministry of the Interior's commission to study the stock exchange, to lectures before workers' and women's clubs.[55] The lecture courses were especially significant for revealing Weber's purposes, since they were expressly intended to recruit

53. *GPS*, 15; "The National State," 439.
54. *GPS*, 16; "The National State," 440. Weber's phrasing is awkward, to say the least. What he had in mind as "pure Platonism" is clarified by Simmel's reminder, couched in a Nietzschean language: "One should not be misled by the tremendous amount of intelligence that created the theoretical foundations of modern technology and which, indeed, seems to put Plato's dream of making science reign supreme over life into practice" (*The Philosophy of Money* [1900], trans. T. Bottomore and D. Frisby [London: Routledge & Kegan Paul, 1978], 483). In this case it was "economic science" wanting to dominate and determine "life," and indeed *seeming* to do so. But this flattering world-picture concealed a dangerous modern substitution and reversal: the actual domination of human ends and choices not by *episteme* (or reflection), but by *techne* (or technical means), a pattern concluding in alienation. Weber returned to this theme and Plato's relation to it in "Science as a Vocation."
55. With respect to the last two items, see, for example, Weber's account in "Die Ergebnisse der deutschen Börsenenquete," *Zeitschrift für das gesammte Handelsrecht* 43–45 (1895–96): 83–219, 457–514; 29–74; 69–157; also the reports of his speeches on "Agrarpolitik" in Frankfurt (*Frankfurter Zeitung*, 17 February, 8 and 15 March, 1896); and on "Die bürgerliche Entwickelung Deutschlands" in Saarbrücken (*St. Johanner Zeitung*, 13 January 1897), after which he was proposed as a *Reichstag* candidate from that Saar district (*Lebensbild*, 236), an offer he declined. *Die Christliche Welt* 8 (10 May 1894): 459, reported Weber speaking to a Berlin women's association on a favorite topic, "Grundzüge der modernen sozialen Entwicklung" (fundamentals of modern social development).

a liberal audience for this practical science: The "old aesthetic-philo-sophical education of civil society [*bürgerliche Gesellschaft*]" is com-pletely outmoded, Naumann confided to his followers; and the void will now be filled by a political economy, Weber explained, whose overrid-ing purpose is to make sure "that the full range of problems is properly recognized and the practical questions are *correctly asked.*"[56] In satis-fying this aim Weber always chose for himself the most controversial subjects: labor relations, the power of the Junkers, and the goals of state policy. He made a point in the political-educational setting of attacking the inclinations of his liberal contemporaries who believed in the "natu-ral laws" of progress, warning them of the realities of power and the naiveté and paradoxes of action based solely on "good" intentions. Just as Marx's earliest polemics were aimed against utopian socialism, so we might say Weber's targeted the excesses of a "utopian liberalism."

Political economy possessed another "practical" component in the unusual sense Weber gave to it as a so-called science of humanity: "The question that leads us through thought beyond the grave of our own generation is not how human beings of the future will *feel*, but how they will *be*, a question that in truth underlies all economic-political work."[57] That is why, of course, for Weber political economy offered *the* unrivaled solution to the riddle of epigonism. It was a science of the world of "being," a science investigating, above all, the "economic and social conditions of existence [*Daseinsbedingungen*]" that shape "the *quality of human beings.*" Even "as an explanatory and analytic sci-ence, political economy . . . when it makes *value-judgments* is bound to that distinctive mark of humanity which we find in our own essence [*Wesen*]."[58] The nature of that "distinctive mark" as a desire for perfec-tion of the soul, along with the meaning of this startling language of *Dasein* and "essence," moves us far beyond these limited passages into the heart of Weber's deepest reflections, including what he later called the transcendental presuppositions for his version of "science" in the

56. Friedrich Naumann, "Der evangelisch-soziale Kursus in Berlin," *Die Christliche Welt* 7 (2 November 1893): 1083; Max Weber, "Die Evangelisch-sozialen Kurse in Berlin im Herbst dieses Jahres," *Die Christliche Welt* 7 (3 August 1893): 767. As one of seven speakers, Weber was responsible for eight hours devoted to "Landwirtschaft und Agrar-politik." The sessions in Berlin ran for a week before an audience of about 500, including (for the first time) twenty-three women.

57. *GPS*, 12; "The National State, 437. The most insightful discussion of this theme is Hennis, *Max Webers Fragestellung*, chap. 3, "Eine 'Wissenschaft vom Menschen': Max Weber und die deutsche Nationalökonomie der Historischen Schule," which breaks new ground by demonstrating Weber's indebtedness to political economy and especially to Karl Knies, in contrast to the neo-Kantianism of his day.

58. *GPS*, 13; "The National State," 437.

sense of *Wissenschaft*, of knowing and the pursuit of knowledge. For the moment, however, let us only say that in this way of thinking Weber believed he had found a means to penetrate through the veil of general sociocultural forms to the particulars of their inner consequences for individual human existence.

In addition to these notions, political economy (*Nationalökonomie* or *Volkswirtschaft*) had a strong national component for Weber, much as it did earlier for Friedrich List. In contrast to the classical theory of value and exchange, List's theory of the "national system" stressed development of national "productive forces" and acceptance in principle of state management and economic intervention.[59] Similarly, Weber's analysis of *actual* foreign and domestic affairs stressed conflict and the clash of opposed material and ideal interests, a cycle of never-ending encounters in which the state itself was centrally involved. Weber was simply not a follower of the theorists of community, whether exemplified in Tönnies' and the socialists' commitment to *Gemeinschaft* (communal association) or in Otto von Gierke's and the "Germanists'" defense of *Genossenschaft* (cooperative fellowship). Moreover, to state the case for political economy in this manner is also to suggest that Weber's "nationalism" was the logical political correlate of his economic thought. More precisely, Weber placed political economy in the service of what he called "the permanent economic and political *power* interests of the nation," insisting that the popular "economic point of view" contained in itself no unquestioned standard of practical judgment, but only a normally unacknowledged "chaos of value-standards." A standard for judgment had to be sought elsewhere, and at this level Weber found it in the problematic sphere of politics—that is, in arguments from "reason of state" and "permanent national interest." Such a standpoint was needed to make the controversial claim, as he did, that "the science of political economy is a *political* science."[60]

Last of all, political economy as a form of inquiry and way of or-

59. For the historical developments, consult Harald Winkel's excellent survey, *Die deutsche Nationalökonomie im 19. Jahrhundert* (Darmstadt: Wissenschaftliche Buchgesellschaft, 1977). Although Weber himself published nothing of substance on the schools of economic thought, even though he planned to do so, the colleague with whom he taught a joint seminar, Schulze-Gävernitz, commented directly at this time on List and the new political economy: "Die gegenwärtigen Mittel zur Hebung der Arbeiterklasse in Deutschland," *Ethische Kultur* 3 (1895): 137–39, 149–52. Moreover, in their seminar Weber and Schulze-Gävernitz evidently devoted considerable attention to the problem of the "ideals," associated with a "tendency," that were used for both "explanation" and "evaluation" of economic events (Weber's letter to Lujo Brentano, 1 January 1897, NW 30/4:10).

60. See principally *GPS*, 14–18; "The National State," 438–42.

dering the world built its content on characteristics of the modern. Weber spelled out this surprising connection in detail in the *Kategorienlehre*, or "conceptual introduction," to his Heidelberg lectures, a document that provides a revealing first glimpse at the "sociological categories of economic action" worked out more comprehensively some twenty years later in the first part of *Economy and Society*, also entitled a *Kategorienlehre*. While the content of "economy" and "economic action," historically considered, is always highly variable, Weber insisted that from his perspective "*abstract* theory starts from the modern occidental type of human being and his economic action." It does so in order to bear in mind as "models" the most highly concentrated, extensive, and "advanced" instances and characteristics of economic life. *Volkswirtschaft* is a species of exchange economy—"the regulation of commodity supply through exchange"—that is "peculiarly modern," because it assumes economic activity based on (a) formally "free" labor; (b) freedom of exchange; (c) private property; and (d) presumably "automatic," or market, regulation of production, distribution, budgeting, and commodity use through the exchange of goods. The requisite definitions then followed a consistent, if somewhat complicated form:

> Under "economic action" we understand a specific kind of *external and purposive aspiration*—i.e., conscious, well-planned behavior with respect to nature and humans—that is *compelled* by those needs, which require *external means* for their satisfaction, regardless of whether they are "material" or "ideal" in kind, and which serve the purpose of *providing for the future*.[61]

Subsequently Weber translated this cumbersome language into the idea of a purposive-rational (*zweckrational*) or instrumental orientation to utility satisfaction,[62] which became in the course of his thinking a leading and distinctive characteristic not only of the economic order, but of the modern world generally and modern self-consciousness, in contrast to other possible action-orientations, such as the "traditional," the "evaluative," or the "affective." What the science of political economy provided was essential access to an understanding of *that* world—Weber's world and ours as well.

Weber fully intended to rewrite and publish this raw material from what he called his *Grundrisse*, the "basic outline" for the lectures on

---

61. "Die begrifflichen Grundlagen der Volkswirtschaftslehre; Erstes Buch" (Heidelberg, 1898), 1, 14–16, a privately printed handout for the summer semester; copy on file at the Max-Weber-Arbeitsstelle, Munich. There is a similar formulation in Weber's political economy lecture notes from this period, in NW 31/1 : 132.

62. See *WuG*, 43; *EaS*, 63.

political economy he had prepared in Freiburg and Heidelberg. As late as the summer of 1899, a full two years after the family dispute that led him to have a breakdown, he still expressed the desire to complete his manuscript and have it published as a book.[63] But the efforts only intensified Weber's illness and had to be terminated for years, until all of his extensive reading began to reemerge in his later work, especially in the preparation and writing for parts of *Economy and Society*, commencing around 1909. By then Weber's views on political economy and the sociocultural sciences generally, including sociology, had matured in a number of ways, a development that forms a later chapter in this story. However, the initial insight into a type of modern "rationality" characterized by objectification of efficient, means-ends calculation, conscious or planned manipulation of external objects, and cunning, if compulsive "needs" gratification, connected the early and later studies and remained basically unchanged in its substance. Many have seen this as Weber's only significant insight about modernity, one expressed in a putative predominance of the formal over the substantive, or the universal over the particular.[64] In fact, it served as the starting point for a highly complex and varied tracing of the origins and fate of Occidental rationalism.

Having set the stage with a discussion of the political and cultural crises that shaped Weber's late-nineteenth-century mentality and acted on his judgments about the sociocultural sciences, we are now in a position to set his thinking in motion. How did he respond to the demise of liberalism and the promise of political economy? What substantive results were achieved in his version of political economy as he worked through the configuration of problems confronting the new political and intellectual communities?

63. A letter to Marianne, 24 August 1898 (NW 30/1:76), written from the Konstanz sanatorium, asks her to bring the "notebook of lectures on practical political economy" so that he can "change the beginning." On 23 July 1899 (NW 30/4:78–79), Weber writes his mother that he wants to have the "Grundriss" in manuscript form next year and available as a book the year afterward. But this was a wishful promise, for in the same letter he also reports continuing nervousness and inability to talk or to read his lectures.

64. In *The Critique of Pure Modernity: Hegel, Heidegger, and After* (Chicago: University of Chicago Press, 1986), 9–17, David Kolb employs precisely this characterization of Weber's alleged position as a strategy for showing the more illuminating and comprehensive views of modernity in Hegel and Heidegger. But such characterizations are really a caricature: they succeed only by failing to explore the full range of Weber's thinking.

CHAPTER II

In Search of the Modern: From Patriarchalism to Capitalism

The bourgeoisie, wherever it has achieved domination, has destroyed all feudal, patriarchal, idyllic relations. . . . [It] compels them to introduce so-called civilization . . . it creates a world after its own image.

—Karl Marx

From its earliest reception, Weber's work has been closely associated with the idea of an interpretive, or *verstehende*, sociology that defines its subject matter as "social action" and its methodology as the postulate of the "subjective interpretation of action." But a recent study has sought to undermine this received view, arguing for a fundamental incompatibility between Weber's "substantive studies" and "methodological principles," revealed by the way in which those studies "adhere far more closely to a Marxist structuralism than they do to *verstehen* principles."[1] The intention behind inventing such a "structuralist" Weber is to show that "meaningful social action" is always subjected to "structural," or "objective," constraints, that Weber's sociology shares with Marxism a "deterministic perspective" having an internal logic independent of individual consciousness, and that *this* sociology is epistemologically "autonomous." Such Weberian revisionism may be new, contentious, or both. It is portentous in any case as part of the struggle for the mastery of Weber, a struggle that is important since Weber is thought to occupy a central terrain in the contemporary social sciences. Whoever controls the interpretation of Weber can entertain hopes of also governing scientific activity.[2]

1. Bryan S. Turner, *For Weber: Essays on the Sociology of Fate* (London: Routledge & Kegan Paul, 1981), 9.
2. The *hopes* should be emphasized, so as to avoid the impression, which I do not intend, that a Weberian legacy of a kind *Weber* would willingly embrace has seized control in significant segments of the social sciences. I do not think this is the case, as a treatment like Jeffrey C. Alexander, *The Classical Attempt at Theoretical Synthesis: Max*

It must be said, however, that this argument puts us on precisely the wrong ground. We are compelled to choose between two allegedly divergent strains in Weber's thought, strains that Weber himself somehow failed to conceptualize in terms adequate to our present understanding. The basis of the choice is uncertain: Is it textual, theoretical, polemical, or political? In addition, the choice is not attuned to the dynamics of Weber's entire thought, but to a partial instrumentation of its modes, splitting Weber's voice into two dissonant lines, pitting Weber against Weber. To choose *for* Weber is also to choose *against* him; to accept a "structuralist" Weber is to reject the sociology that typically bears his name. The paradox will merely mislead instead of yielding a more fruitful orientation. The question to ask is not, which side must we be on, but rather, what assumptions must be present for this kind of choice to be possible at all?

Two appear indispensable: What Weber really means can be separated from and substituted for what he only says, and genuine meaning can then be extracted by squeezing Weber's thought into preformed categories of the interpreter's making. Thus, Weber can be imagined to play "the Jeremiah of modern capitalism"—in conjunction, one supposes, with Marx's Isaiah.[3] Unfortunately, neither assumption can be accepted. Yet a serious problem lies concealed in this line of argument, and it can be restated in the following way. From its inception there are two analytically distinguishable tendencies in Weber's substantive work: one in which status groups, social classes, patterns of domination, and material interests define the analytic core; and a second in which religious ethics, normative orders, patterns of legitimation, and ideal interests define a rather different set of core notions. This distinction is present *within* the substantive work itself, not between the work and any set of "methodological principles." It has to do with the very content of Weber's thought, not with oppositions between substance and form, rhetoric and meaning, structuralism and subjectivism, materialism and idealism. The problem is not to find a point of leverage from which Weber can be catapulted either closer to "Marxist structuralism" or farther away from it, but rather to discover what the relationship is

Weber (Berkeley: University of California Press, 1983), convincingly and unintentionally demonstrates. On this point I agree with Friedrich H. Tenbruck, "Das Werk Max Webers: Methodologie und Sozialwissenschaften," *Kölner Zeitschrift für Soziologie und Sozialpsychologie* 38 (1986): esp. 13.

3. Turner, *For Weber*, 352, 354, where he claims that "Weber did not adhere to his own interpretative principles."

between these two tendencies in his thought, why that relationship is important, and what consequences it can have.

Far from establishing the autonomy of sociology as a field, Weber's approach was intentionally and self-consciously embedded within a set of general ideas about the nature of history, society, and human understanding. It is these essential conceptions, rather than alleged incompatibilities between content and method, that demand reflection. Together with the two analytic tendencies, they were already present in Weber's earliest intellectual accomplishments, and thus it is to his work before 1900 that we should first direct our attention.

Adopting this perspective, we can say that the most general question for Weber in his early writings, one that unified his studies of antiquity, medieval Europe, and nineteenth-century Germany, was, What is the relationship between changes in economic structure (especially capital formation, the process of production, and the organization of labor), changes in social structure, and changes in political authority and rule? And what consequences did such "structural" changes have for the conduct of life in different social strata? The questions should be stated this way to emphasize Weber's early interest in developmental transformations and their cultural significance. Of course, today "development" and "structure" have acquired all sorts of connotations having little to do with Weber's questions. I am interested not in untangling these meanings, but in seeing what can be learned from *Weber's* use of "developmental" and "structural" language in those writings in the new "political economy" that constitute his *first* analysis of capitalist development.[4]

AGRARIAN ORIGINS

It is a little-noted fact that Weber's lifework began with a concern for agrarian systems and their historical role in the rise of capitalism. The important proximate starting points for Weber's early work on capitalism can be found mainly in two places: the studies of G. F. Knapp, the doyen of agrarian political economists and the authority on East Elbia (the seven German provinces east of the Elbe River) prior to Weber's studies; and the evolutionary schema of theorists like Carl Rodbertus

4. The first analysis is quite like the "last" one presented in Weber's 1920 university lectures, *General Economic History*, trans. F. Knight (New York: Collier, 1961), and discussed in Randall Collins, *Weberian Sociological Theory* (Cambridge: Cambridge University Press, 1986), chap. 2, as modified from an earlier article.

and Karl Bücher, who had aimed for sweeping reconceptualizations of history in terms of material production.

Knapp was important because he had asked Marx's old question about the essential characteristics of capitalism, but then, instead of investigating the industrial revolution or the formal properties of economic "laws," had sought an understanding of the nature of capitalist development in historical relations. According to this view, the answer to the question What *is* capitalism? could best be grasped when one asked, When and where did capitalism *begin*? Everyone thinks first of English industry circa 1750, Knapp pointed out; however, the actual origins are to be found in sixteenth-century agriculture, he argued, and not in peasant agriculture but in the English leasehold system or, in the German case, specifically the large-scale *Gutswirtschaft* of the eastern provinces, erected on the foundation of the patriarchal *Grundherrschaft*, where one could observe formation of large enterprises, accumulation of profits by an entrepreneurial class, and commercial production for a market—for Knapp the sufficient conditions for capitalist development, whether agrarian or industrial. Intentionally leaving open the question of the status of labor, Knapp then suggested that capitalist enterprise can be consistent with either "free" or various forms of "unfree" labor (e.g., compulsory service, villeinage). In England free agrarian labor was present already in the sixteenth century, whereas in Prussia free wage-labor was a later step along the path of economic rationalization, appearing after the legal emancipation of the peasantry in 1807.[5] Interest in this "agrarian thesis" has been popularized once again by Immanuel Wallerstein and his followers, only without acknowledging Knapp's contributions. Weber certainly accepted its problematic, calling Knapp's work "of exceptional significance" and praising the "brilliant investigations" of the Strassburg political economist and his school.[6]

5. See Georg F. Knapp, *Die Bauern-Befreiung und der Ursprung der Landarbeiter* (Leipzig: Duncker & Humblot, 1887); and "Die Erbuntertänigkeit und die kapitalistische Wirtschaft" (1891), in *Die Landarbeiter in Knechtschaft und Freiheit: Gesammelte Vorträge*, 2d ed. (Leipzig: Duncker & Humblot, 1909), 45–64; cf. Weber's comparison of England and the *Grundherrschaft* and *Gutswirtschaft* in Prussia in "Entwicklungstendenzen in der Lage der ostelbischen Landarbeiter," *Archiv* 7 (1894): 14. The interesting essay by Martin Riesebrodt, "From Patriarchalism to Capitalism: The Theoretical Context of Max Weber's Agrarian Studies," *Economy and Society* 15 (1986): 476–502, is essentially correct about the theoretical sources for Weber's early writings, except for the emphasis placed on *Genossenschaft* ideas and the work of Schmoller, neither of which appear to me crucially significant in themselves.

6. *Die Lage der Landarbeiter im ostelbischen Deutschland* (1892), *MWG* I/3:67 n. 2; "Capitalism and Rural Society in Germany" (1904), in G&M, 374. Another impor-

On the other hand, Rodbertus and later Bücher had attempted to address the problem of evolutionary stages and sequences, a problem that had also taken shape in Marx's writings and one that was emphasized in Weber's own time by Engels. Despite its one-sided and sometimes misleading formulations, Rodbertus' reconstruction of the *oikos* and the ancient economy was praised by Weber as "uncommonly fruitful and stimulating" for his own work on antiquity and on the "developmental" problem generally.[7] That work proceeded in some measure as a critical reception of Rodbertus' attempt to treat antiquity in its own terms, in opposition to Eduard Meyer's view of the ancient world as a "completely modern culture" with a money economy, production for a market, an industrial sector, commercial classes, an urban proletariat, and incipient capitalism.[8] Weber instead stressed the uniquely *un*modern characteristics of a world that could not be understood with a market-centered analysis, at most using the concept "oikos economy" as an analogue to the "isolated household economy" of Germany's patriarchal estates.[9] With respect to his investigations of the ancient and

---

tant source for the "agrarian thesis" is R. H. Tawney's later work on English conditions: *The Agrarian Problem in the Sixteenth Century* (New York: Franklin, 1912). Of course, Marx himself had not completely missed agrarian change, although he thought it was triggered by industrialization: "In the sphere of agriculture, modern industry has a more revolutionary effect than elsewhere, for this reason, that it annihilates the peasant, that bulwark of the old society, and replaces him by the wage-labourer. Thus the desire for social changes, and the class antagonisms are brought to the same level in the country as in the towns. The irrational, old-fashioned methods of agriculture are replaced by scientific ones" (*Capital* [1897] [New York: International Publishers, 1967], 1:505).

7. Letter to Brentano, 20 February 1893, *JB*, 363–65, a reply to Brentano's essay, "Die Volkswirthschaft und ihre konkreten Grundbedingungen," *Zeitschrift für Sozial- und Wirthschaftsgeschichte* 1 (1893): 77–148. Judging from this letter and what is known of Weber's early reading, we can be sure he was familiar with Engels' 1884 preface to *The Poverty of Philosophy*, a polemic against Rodbertus' socialist credentials in a "priority" dispute with Marx, as well as with his study that same year, *The Origin of the Family, Private Property, and the State*. Other positive remarks on Rodbertus are in "Agrarverhältnisse im Altertum," *Handwörterbuch der Staatswissenschaften*, ed. J. Conrad (Jena: Fischer, 1897), 18, and the 2d, rev. ed. of 1898, 1:85.

8. See the arguments in "Die wirtschaftliche Entwicklung des Altertums" (1895), *Kleine Schriften* 2d ed., 3 vols. (Halle: Niemeyer, 1924), vol. 1; summing up his views, Meyer writes that "the seventh and sixth centuries [B.C.] in Greek history correspond in the development of modern times to the fourteenth and fifteenth centuries, the fifth to the sixteenth" (118–19)!

9. "The organization of the large [East Elbian] estates ... carried within itself the shell of the isolated household economy, or more precisely that which Rodbertus calls oikos economy" ("Entwicklungstendenzen," *Archiv*, 4). Among recent scholars, M. I. Finley has sided with Weber against Meyer: see *The Ancient Economy* (Berkeley: University of California Press, 1973), esp. chap. 5; and *Ancient Slavery and Modern Ideology* (New York: Viking, 1980), 42–48; also Alfred Heuss, "Max Webers Bedeutung für die Geschichte des griechisch-römischen Altertums," *Historische Zeitschrift* 201 (1965), esp. 539–42.

modern worlds, Weber's reception of Bücher's ideas, partly an extension of Rodbertus' work, followed very much the same course. Especially the threefold typology—household economy, city economy, and national economy (*Volkswirtschaft*)—with its evolutionary application was a terminology he also regarded as a fruitful starting point, borrowing it for analytic and expository purposes, even though it was eventually criticized, altered, and used without the assumptions of progressive stages.[10]

What Weber retained from these beginnings is a complex matter. In his early work on the East Elbian territories, for instance, he largely accepted Knapp's views about the sixteenth-century transformation and the basic characteristics of capitalist production, but he also sought to reconceptualize the problem of capitalism's development in terms that would make sense out of the economic *and* political demise of the traditional patriarchal system of domination in the East. To accomplish this project, Weber had to look more closely than did Knapp and others at the systematic relationships connecting economic production, social stratification, and political power. Also, Weber came to reject any ordering of these relations in a mechanistic or dialectical theory of "stages," whether espoused by Rodbertus, Bücher, Marx, or Engels. The questions raised in these controversies were partly historical, partly theoretical. Thus, Weber reworked Rodbertus' thesis of the unqualified "autarchy of the oikos" on historical grounds and with historical evidence, as Meyer pointed out,[11] but he also revised the entire idea of a necessary progression through steplike stages, an evolutionary theory, while retaining the developmental perspective in historical studies through elaboration of "type" concepts. The shift from "real" historical stages (i.e., stages thought to be real), as found in Bücher and Engels, for example, to hypothetical and heuristic types was Weber's solution *in nuce* to the theoretical dilemma presented by a naive superimposition of historical and conceptual forms.

It is in light of these starting points that we should understand

10. See "Agrarverhältnisse im Altertum" (1897), 4, 18; also the categories in "Grundriss zu den Vorlesungen über Allgemeine ('theoretische') Nationalökonomie" (Heidelberg, 1898), 7–8, 11, 12, where Bücher's work is cited under "Die typischen Entwicklungsstufen des Gewerbes," "Die typischen Vorstufen der Volkswirtschaft," "Die Stadtwirtschaft und der Ursprung der modernen Unternehmungsformen," "Die Entstehung der Volkswirtschaft." Rodbertus's writings are also extensively cited on pp. 9, 16, 18, 19, 23.
11. "Die wirtschaftliche Entwicklung des Altertums," *Kleine Schriften*, 1 : 83 n. 1. On Weber, Meyer, Bücher, and their generation's scholarship on antiquity generally, see M. I. Finley, *Economy and Society in Ancient Greece* (London: Chatto & Windus, 1981), 3–23.

Weber's self-proclaimed reputation as the younger generation's "enfant terrible." [12] The epithet is thought usually to derive from his sharp and unconventional practical-political views, but there is in fact a significant theoretical-scientific source for it as well. Knapp himself recognized the extent of Weber's innovations at an early stage: Commenting on Weber's lengthy study for the Verein für Sozialpolitik, Knapp declared that "this work above all has led to the perception that our expertise has been surpassed, that we must start to learn all over again." [13] The factual details amassed by Weber in his systematic analysis of the Verein's questionnaires would not have surprised Knapp, for such facts were well known to those who had studied the problem, but the interpretive perspective according to which Weber ordered his observations would have provoked surprise and controversy. Indeed, it continued to provoke controversy; as Weber said of the polemical aspects of the "Inaugural Address" in Freiburg three years later, "not agreement, but opposition" encouraged the resolve to publish his views. [14] The oppositional element was also remarkably evident in most of his scientific work during these years and stimulated the controversial response to its publication.

Knapp's unusually generous praise can be attributed to several novel aspects of Weber's theoretical contributions: his creation of a new analytical language by calling on the conceptual resources of the German historical school and the different classical traditions of political economy, including those associated with Marx; his conception of the conditions of agrarian life in terms of the "organization of labor," or *Arbeitsverfassung*; and his attempt to work out a satisfactory explanation of certain "developmental" patterns in society. With respect to these elements, perhaps it hardly need be said that Weber's novel approach came to comprise the distinctive mode of thought we now call "Weberian." As for the latter, it should be noted that Weber's "developmentalism" took modern Europe as its point of departure, but in the end came even to include all of antiquity and a great deal of world civilization within its perspective. Each innovation is crucial to understanding the formation of Weber's thinking, and thus each invites close consideration.

12. In his report on the East Elbian study, "Die ländliche Arbeitsverfassung," *Verhandlungen des Vereins für Sozialpolitik*, in *SVSP* 58 (1893), 62.
13. From Knapp's introductory remarks preceding Weber's speech, "Die ländliche Arbeiterfrage," in *SVSP* 58 (1893), 7; also *Die Landarbeiter in Knechtschaft und Freiheit*, 90–91.
14. "Der Nationalstaat und die Volkswirtschaftspolitik, Akademische Antrittsrede," *GPS*, 1.

WEBERIAN STRUCTURALISM

The analytic language Weber employs in his early studies contains some intriguing and problematic features. Turning to the 1892 text to which Knapp referred, one finds Weber introducing the study with a statement about the problem of a general "process of transformation," of "economic stages of development," changes in stratification, "social class formation" and conflict, and competing "material" and "subjective" (ideal) interests.[15] The first substantive chapter then takes up a class analysis of the agrarian social structure of the Eastern Territories, one that exposes the morphology of relations (*Verhältnisse*), especially relations of domination, and oppositions (*Gegensätze*) among the economically and politically relevant strata. The emphasis is on relationships, conflicts, and dynamic processes. At this analytic level the concepts Weber uses can be designated relational, for they may connect one social unit with another, or refer to patterned social interactions, or have characteristic properties identifiable with reference to properties of other concepts—as can be seen, for example, in referring to "labor" as "rent of capital."[16]

This relational language is then continued and augmented through subsequent texts: we hear more of labor-power and capital, production and exchange, material and ideal interests, division of labor, class struggle and contradictions, relations of domination, and "proletarianization." The structural terminology of superstructure (*Überbau*) and base (*Unterbau, Basis*) also makes an occasional appearance as a way of distinguishing configurations of relations, although always in a critical context. Relational concepts can be said to form the core of Weber's analysis in the sense that they do not vary a great deal from study to study, regardless of time, place, circumstance, and analytic problem.

15. "Vorbemerkung," *Die Lage der Landarbeiter im ostelbischen Deutschland* (1892), *MWG* I/3:61–67. It is worth emphasizing that Weber's famous statement from his "mature" work in the *Sociology of Religion*—"Not ideas, but material and ideal interests, directly govern men's conduct. Yet very frequently the 'world images' that have been created by 'ideas' have, like switchmen, determined the tracks along which action has been pushed by the dynamic of interest" (*GARS* 1:252; G&M, 280)—contains a conceptual language and point of view already present in his earliest writings. Dirk Käsler's concise survey of the early work, *Einführung in das Studium Max Webers* (Munich: Beck, 1979), 30–77, has the singular advantage of showing the connections between it and Weber's later writings.

16. "Entwicklungstendenzen in der Lage der ostelbischen Landarbeiter" (1894), *GASW*, 477, translated by Keith Tribe as "Developmental Tendencies in the Situation of East Elbian Rural Labourers," *Economy and Society* 8 (1979): 182. This is the second, revised version of the *Archiv* essay bearing the same title cited above in note 5.

Thus, "class" can be usefully applied to antiquity as well as to nineteenth-century Europe, as can concepts of material and ideal interests,
forms of domination, various kinds of "unfree" and "free" labor, and
the like. Specific historical expressions of these relational concepts do
change, of course, but never at random, for they are always situated
within a process of "development."

Weber's developmental language is the most intriguing aspect of the
early writings. From the 1889 dissertation to the essays of 1896–98 on
antiquity, there appear concepts like "developmental stage [or level],"
"phase," or "tendency" (*Entwicklungsstufe, Entwicklungsstadium,
Entwicklungstendenz*), "stage [or level] of culture" and civilization
(*Kulturstufe*), "transitional stage" and "technical progress."[17] For Weber these developmental concepts should be understood not as historical laws, "necessary" and "real" entities, or aspects of an attempt to
stake out an epistemological position, but rather as part of a terminology considered adequate for ordering significant explanatory questions. They illustrate what might be called the "Weberian heuristic"—
that is, the restrained nominalism of his view regarding the status of
concepts in gaining knowledge of historical processes of change.

Reflecting later on his own usage, Weber was to make this view quite
explicit, arguing that concepts like "level of culture" or "stage of development" were at most conceptual means of representation, comparison,
or analogical thinking, useful for bringing forth "the historical *peculiarity* of each individual development in its causal dependency." They
were only concepts, never "real essences" or something like an "Hegelian 'Idea,'" just as they were exclusively a means to knowledge, never
the "ends of cultural history."[18] Thus, neither the historicist nor the

17. In his translation of *Roscher and Knies: The Logical Problems of Historical Economics* (New York: Free Press, 1975), Guy Oakes has chosen *evolution* rather than *development* for this terminology. I use *development* because it has somewhat broader connotations in English, suggesting the appropriate relationships between Weber's analysis,
the "developmental" theories of the nineteenth century, and the most recent debates over
"development" and "modernization." The term *evolution* often has Darwinian or socio-
biological connotations that Weber wanted to avoid, *except* in those instances where he
criticized the importation of biological metaphors into social analysis. In addition, Weber's German did permit the use of *evolution* when that was the intended meaning; for
example, "Was heisst Christlich-Sozial?" *Die Christliche Welt* 8 (17 May 1894): 477,
where he speculates about the "evolution of technology [*Technik*]" coming to an end in
the West.
18. "Der Streit um den Charakter der altgermanischen Sozialverfassung in der
deutschen Literatur des letzten Jahrzehnts" (1904), in *GASW*, 517, a review Weber un-
dertook for his presentation at the St. Louis Universal Exposition in 1904, "Capitalism
and Rural Society in Germany," both of which took up Knapp's research and were concerned generally with clarifying issues Weber had addressed in the nineties. Like "Agrarverhältnisse im Altertum," these texts form a bridge to Weber's later work. An explicit

Marxist concept of "developmental *law*" with its universalist and realist connotations, ever appears in Weber's arsenal, nor does any precise classification of step-by-step progressions from "inferior" to "superior" stages according to a definitive criterion, such as "freedom," "class conflict," or "adaptation." The latter procedure, found in the Hegelians, the Social Darwinists, Auguste Comte, and Herbert Spencer, and in historicists like Wilhelm Roscher, Bruno Hildebrand, and Carl Lamprecht, was rejected out of hand by Weber for its capacity to conceal political illusions or personal preferences and thus distort the understanding of historical relationships.

Of course, it is both the "relational" and "developmental" terminologies that have led some writers to see the not-so-invisible hand of Marx in Weber's earliest studies.[19] Thus, Löwith has cautiously suggested that some evidence points toward Weber's predilection for "a free application of the method of historical materialism," taking "the contradiction between relations of production and forces of production as a guide for explanation."[20] Or abandoning Löwith's caution, Fleischmann has even gone so far as to say that Weber grasped for Marx's guidance early in his work, "'verifying' the correctness of the Marxist theory," only to turn away from it later, presumably under Nietzsche's aegis.[21] The truth of the matter is that on the one hand "Weber took Marx seriously, and learned from Marx," but on the other hand he was emphatically not like his colleague Sombart, notable as the "Proteus of German social scientists,"[22] who as a young socialist and scholar received Engels' grudging praise as a "somewhat eclectic Marxist."[23] In

critique of the concept "developmental law" is presented in *Roscher and Knies*, in *GAW*, 22–30, Eng. trans., 73–80.

19. Concepts like *Verhältnis* and *Entwicklungsstufe* are important for Marx in some of his best-known works, such as the *Manifesto*, a fact that is often obscured in translation. There can no longer be any doubt that Weber had direct knowledge of Marx before 1900: for example, his handwritten notes for the unfinished political economy *Grundriss* project (on file at the Max-Weber-Arbeitsstelle, Munich) contain excerpts from the controversial section on the "rate of profit" in *Das Kapital: Kritik der politischen Ökonomie*, vol. 3, ed. F. Engels (Hamburg: Meisner, 1894), 132–51, as part of what was evidently intended as a comprehensive critique of Marx's value theory in the context of socialist thought. Thanks are due Dr. Karl-Ludwig Ay for providing access to these notes.

20. Karl Löwith, "Die Entzauberung der Welt durch Wissenschaft," *Merkur* 18 (1964): 504.

21. Eugène Fleischmann, "De Weber à Nietzsche," *Archives européennes de sociologie* 5 (1964): 194.

22. Phrases from Vernon K. Dibble, "Social Science and Political Commitments in the Young Max Weber," *Archives européennes de sociologie* 9 (1968): 98; Paul Honigsheim, *On Max Weber*, trans. J. Rytina (New York: Free Press, 1968), 9.

23. Engels' letter to Lafargue, 26 February 1895, in Karl Marx and Friedrich Engels, *Werke* (Berlin: Dietz, 1973–), 39:414, responding to Sombart's "good article" on vol. 3

comparison with some of his contemporaries, Weber was not weaned on the Marxist dialectic, and it would be misleading to treat him as if he were.

We can begin to see Weber's innovations and the distance between his views and the Marxism of his day most clearly by raising two questions: First, is there a central concept, nodal point, or idea—such as "equality" in Tocqueville, "alienation" in Marx, "anomie" in Durkheim, the "unconscious" in Freud—around which Weber's thought develops? Is there anything in his early writing that would qualify as a kind of conceptual breakthrough? Second, what is Weber's understanding of social and historical explanation? Can it be said that he accepts the basic form of "Marxist structuralism" and works within the limits of its assumptions?

The first question appears more difficult to answer for Weber than for other major nineteenth-century social theorists. Concepts like domination, rationalization, and bureaucratization come to mind. However, none of these is satisfactory as a starting point, even though all become prominent after 1905. Instead, another concept seems an attractive candidate: *Arbeitsverfassung*, the key theoretical term in Weber's major writings from 1892 to 1894. This term, which resists precise translation, was common among political economists, Weber included, as a shorthand way of characterizing the historically given "constitution," "condition," or "organization" of labor, or labor-relations.[24] It was not a purely formal category like those used in classical economics, and for this reason it found favor in the "historical school" of political economy. In its most general usage the concept was unusual because of a double origin and meaning. Combining both juridical and socio-cultural connotations, legalistic and Aristotelian perspectives, it could refer both to "environmental" conditions (including legal norms) acting on the individual conceived as a "unit of labor" and to the "material" and "mental" state of labor in the abstract. Thus, one could speak of "labor" as both concrete activity and abstract potential, and of the

---

of *Das Kapital* (Capital III), "Zur Kritik des ökonomischen Systems von Karl Marx," *Archiv* 7 (1894): 555–94, published when the *Archiv*'s editor was the socialist and former schoolmate of Freud's, Heinrich Braun. Engels also wrote directly to Sombart (11 March 1895, 427–30), praising the review and suggesting only that Marx's thought be considered "not a doctrine, but a method." Engels died before he could publish his own reply to the *Capital III* debate over the concept of "value," a contribution now in *Werke*, 25:895–917.

24. For the problems of translation, see Keith Tribe's note to his translation of "Developmental Tendencies," 203.

"constitution of labor" as a summation of a *particular* configuration of material conditions, social structure, legal principles, and even psychological or ethical motivations—in short, as the embodiment of a way of life.

Weber did employ the concept in this general cultural sense, but he also modified the standard connotation in two important ways. First, he sought to give *Arbeitsverfassung* a particular meaning that would render it useful for causal explanations. This required postulating a distinction among different kinds of explanatory factors: for example, in the East Elbia studies labor's situation was said to be "determined" variously by economic forces, such as the "mode of enterprise" (*Betriebsweise*); by political-psychological considerations, such as the workers' "desire for freedom," a so-called ideal interest that was quite "irrational" from a "materialist" standpoint, as Weber remarked; and by the existing system of social stratification. Weber's most novel suggestion was then to identify the *Arbeitsverfassung* specifically with "relations" of social stratification within the larger socioeconomic system, as appears repeatedly in passages in which he weighs the significance of multiple causal factors:

> Thus, for the factors discussed so far—size of the enterprise [*Betriebsgrösse*] and intensity of cultivation [*Wirtschaftsintensität*]—we found that in their significance for the workers' situation they were less influential than the inherited *Arbeitsverfassung* (which at the same time includes the social stratification of all the inhabitants of the large estates, or rather is identical to it) and less influential than the traditional living standard of the workers, which is based upon this *Arbeitsverfassung*.[25]

Or in the language of the revised version of the "Developmental Tendencies" essay:

> As we see again and again, it is the *kind of Arbeitsverfassung*, therefore the kind of social stratification and grouping of the rural workers, that is decisive for the workers' material situation. And if it further appears that with current power-relations [*Machtverhältnisse*] in rural areas the monetary reorganization of the *Arbeitsverfassung* seriously endangers the workers' material situation, then a change in the mode of enterprise [*Betriebsweise*] (which has the tendency to bring about this monetary reorganization) carries the same dangers within itself. Indeed this is the case with the intensive mode of enterprise.[26]

25. "Entwicklungstendenzen," *Archiv*, 28, published, incidentally, in the same issue as Sombart's review of *Capital III*.
26. "Entwicklungstendenzen," *GASW*, 498; I have translated the passage rather literally (cf. "Developmental Tendencies," 196) in order to stay as close as possible to Weber's own terminology and causal imputations.

These are somewhat difficult passages, part of an argument in which Weber attempts convincingly to demonstrate the relative explanatory autonomy of the *Arbeitsverfassung*, now sociologically defined, in relation to economic factors (e.g., *Betriebsgrösse, Betriebsweise*) and political factors (e.g., *Machtverhältnisse*) in determining the contemporary "material situation" of agrarian labor. Briefly, his argument seeks to show that none of the economic variables can in themselves account for workers' material situation; the *Arbeitsverfassung* (i.e., system of social stratification) and its "developmental tendencies" must always be included as what would nowadays be called an independent variable, a viewpoint lost on even some of Weber's most knowledgeable colleagues.[27]

The second innovative modification appears at this point as well, for clearly Weber proposed that any specific *Arbeitsverfassung* be viewed as a "type"—that is, a logically coherent statement of the characteristic properties of a particular system of social and economic relations. The nature and consequences of any developmental pattern could only be clarified, Weber seemed to suggest, on the basis of a specification and comparison of heuristic types. (Parenthetically, Weber's later so-called methodological commentary on "ideal types" is a reflection on this early practice, not a legislative prescription for work in progress.) Putting the claim abstractly, we might say that from Weber's perspective there are no useful teleological categories for explaining a necessary constitution and reconstitution of labor in the course of its struggles, but rather logical "types" accounting for probable and historically emergent configurations of stratification and production.

In contrast to Marx's early position, there are no ontological claims concerning labor that ground this analysis in presuppositions about "essential being." But this is not to say that Weber avoids the paradox hovering over Marx's discussions—that is, whether to side with "nature" or with human history and culture. Although he does not defend a standpoint from which to *condemn* the "separation" between a given sociocultural form and something called "authentic human nature," Weber does call for a clarification of those critical "value standards" whereby political economy *judges* social arrangements and postulates corrective ideals. The need to criticize the heteronomy of standards and

---

27. See especially Weber's corrections to Kaerger's misinterpretation of these points only in the first, *Archiv* version of "Entwicklungstendenzen," 33–36 n. 1.

purposes in any form of knowledge perhaps explains the desire he once expressed to spend more time among the "fleshpots of philosophy."[28]

These ideas, an elaboration of the meaning and use of *Arbeitsverfassung*, qualify as a Weberian structuralism. The much-abused name *structuralism* is deserved because Weber conceives of action as partially under the sway of material (that is, economic) forces external to the individual, even of "developmental tendencies against which the individual is powerless,"[29] and it is Weberian because it refuses to concede a monopoly in human affairs to economic rationality, just as it declines to grant hegemony in human science to what one might call a foundational ontology. We may nevertheless still wonder whether it is possible to be more specific about Weber's causal claims. Does he work within the boundaries of a world conceived as forces of production, relations of production, and superstructure? Or does he propose modifications in the familiar "materialist" terminology?

The language Weber employs suggests a fundamental modification. For one thing, he avoids the requisite terminology of forces and relations of production (*Produktivkräfte, Produktionsverhältnisse*); his early analysis of capitalism is centered much more on labor, interest, and social structure or stratification (*soziale Struktur, soziale Schichtung*). Moreover, when he speaks directly to the issue, he advocates what can be designated reciprocal causality. For example, in one representative passage summarizing results from the second inquiry into East Elbia, Weber proposed that it was neither the "iron law of wages"— that is, Lassalle's revision of Ricardo's wage theory—nor the "intensity of cultivation," but rather the "historically evolving social stratification of the agricultural population" that was the "decisive factor" for explaining workers' "fate" and conditions of life in the East:

> The causal relationship is at least partially reversed here. With our modern scientific method we have become used to viewing technical-economic conditions [*Bedingungen*] and interests basically as primary, from which a people's social structure and political formation [*Gestaltung*] are derived . . . but here we see quite clearly that it is a matter of reciprocal effects in which the purely economic factor does not by any means play the leading role. Population distribution, division of trades, division of land, the legal forms of the organization of labor [*Arbeitsverfassung*] within individual districts have a much more decisive significance for the material and social-ethical

28. Letter to Marie Baum, 4 February 1908, NW 30/7:57–58.
29. Letter to Friedrich Naumann, probably 1897, archive of the MWE.

condition of the agricultural worker, for his total standard of living, than do possible differences between favorable or unfavorable economic conditions for agricultural enterprise in certain areas, or than the relationship of profits from one form of production to profits from another form. It is these relations of social stratification [*soziale Schichtungsverhältnisse*] that almost entirely determine the workers' standard of living, and as a result of this standard of living—not the reverse—almost entirely determine their wages, their total economic condition.[30]

Once again the relations of social stratification, the *Arbeitsverfassung* in its particular sense, receive primary emphasis and reveal Weber's reliance on categories with specific historical and social applicability. In addition, by speaking of "reversal" and "reciprocity," Weber signals a revision of the influential Marxist causal model. What can we make of his alternative, which is still far from self-evident?

The surface clarity of Weber's undogmatic understanding of cause and effect in the above passage masks a complex line of reasoning, beginning with an apparently commonplace distinction between "technical-economic conditions and interests" on the one side and "social structure and political organization" on the other, the former viewed as primary by Marxist science, the latter as epiphenomenal. Such a separation of causal factors implies that for Weber, as for a number of recent interpreters, Marx was a determinist in the strong sense: that is, "productive forces" (both technological and economic) were taken to be "the determining factor in historical development."[31] But for his own purposes Weber deliberately separates "social stratification" as relations (the *Schichtungsverhältnisse*) from the productive "base" of society and ascribes independent causal significance to such *social* relations. Thus, in this revised model there are three kinds of relations—economic, social, and political—and Weber is free to use each as an independent causal agent. It must be stressed that "relations of production" in Marx are redefined as "relations of social stratification" by Weber; in other words, economic content as "production" is excluded from the conceptualization of the social sphere.

In addition, we must see that Weber abandons the idea of a level-

---

30. From Weber's report, following Paul Göhre's, on the sequel to the Verein für Sozialpolitik investigation of agrarian labor, carried out for Naumann's Protestant Social Congress: "Die deutschen Landarbeiter," in *Bericht über die Verhandlungen des 5. Evangelisch-sozialen Kongresses* (Berlin: Rehtwisch & Langewort, 1894), 66.

31. Quoting William Shaw, *Marx's Theory of History* (Stanford: Stanford University Press, 1978), 53; see also G. A. Cohen's "primacy thesis" in *Karl Marx's Theory of History: A Defence* (Princeton: Princeton University Press, 1978), esp. 134.

structure causal model, ordered from the foundation upward, in favor of what should be understood as a network model of causality. Put another way, the hierarchical metaphor dominating Marx's writing is replaced by a cyclical one. The network, or cycle, imagery conveys the idea that the relative influence of any kind of factor, economic or otherwise, must be considered a *possibility* to be checked against experience. Thus, in contrast to the line of reasoning concerning East Elbia quoted at length above, Weber does insist in his Roman studies on the primacy of *economic* changes—disappearance of commerce, development of a rural natural economy—as the most basic causal factors explaining the *political* decline of the Empire.[32] Such a view of causality also contains the symbolization that permits Weber later on to speak of "causal chains" or to deride the "theorists of the superstructure" for their belief in an ability to postulate "ultimate" or "essential" causes in which a theory of history can be grounded.[33]

Thus, it will not prove adequate (and not only because of Hegelian innuendos) to suppose that Weber wanted either to join with Marx in standing right side up or to change the intellectual environment by having Marx's followers learn anything like the mysteries of Althusserian consciousness-raising. Weber attempted rather to alter the terms of discourse, not simply by reconstructing what he called "Marx's theoretically shattered system"[34] from its original pieces, but by substituting new conceptual blocks of his own.

THE TYPOLOGY OF AGRARIAN ECONOMIES

Weber's investigation of the territories east of the Elbe was not only part of a series of inquiries into agrarian relations throughout history, it

---

32. "Die sozialen Gründe des Untergangs der antiken Kultur" (1896), *GASW*, 308; a remarkably imprecise translation of this important Freiburg lecture, "The Social Causes of the Decline of Ancient Civilization," is appended to *The Agrarian Sociology of Ancient Civilizations*, trans. R. I. Frank (London: NLB, 1976), 389–411, the final 1909 version of "Agrarverhältnisse im Altertum" under a somewhat misleading title. (An older and more accurate translation is to be found in the *Journal of General Education* 5 [1950]:75–88.) The independent "factors" Weber admits into his early studies can be economic, social, political, legal, technological, psychological, cultural, ideological, and even biological (e.g., nutrition, diet) and geographical.

33. See his 1910 statement at the first meeting of the German Sociological Society, in *Verhandlungen des Ersten Deutschen Soziologentages* (Tübingen: J. C. B. Mohr [Paul Siebeck], 1911, 101; *GASS*, 456.

34. Report in *Die Hilfe* 2 (6 December 1896): 5; also "Zur Gründung einer national-sozialen Partei" (1896), *GPS*, 26.

was also one illustrative case for a larger theoretical scheme—a typology of agrarian economies—that he used to order his thinking about
apparently discontinuous agrarian socioeconomic forms. Since this
scheme focused attention on the historical transformation of agrarian
economies, it was directly linked to the problem of modern capitalism's
origins, distinguishing characteristics, unique productive dynamics, systematic development, and ultimately paradoxical and problematic "rationality." Elaboration of the typology suggested an understanding of
historical change that conceived "development" as a complex interaction of economic, social, psychological, and political-legal factors, or
most particularly as the result of penetration and transformation of an
existing "traditional" form of human organization by a more "rationalized" mode of production, administration, or social action.

Two innovative claims characterized Weber's point of departure. In
the first place, he contended that contrary to popular belief, the ubiquitous *Arbeiterfrage* (literally, the worker question) was not merely a
problem of industrial wage-labor in the cities and hence of incipient
urban "class conflict" between expropriated labor-power and expropri-
ating capital. It was instead a larger "social" question that not only
included but also arose from the conditions of agricultural labor, partly
for quantitative reasons—agricultural workers in Germany in 1890
numbered over six million, or about one seventh of the national population—but more importantly for qualitative reasons: As Weber noted,
through most of Western history agrarian labor represented the "broad
foundation of the state and nation" as the source of productive capacity,
labor-power for cities, recruits into armies, and especially as the trans-
mitter of sociocultural norms.[35] The debate over agrarian classes and
production, found in every country in the industrializing West and in
Weber's Germany pitting landowners' rosy view of labor against socialists' charges of a "modern serfdom," was just as critical as disputes
over the condition of the urban "proletariat" and the meaning of
industrialization.[36]

35. "Die Erhebung des Vereins für Sozialpolitik über die Lage der Landarbeiter," *Das Land* 1 (1893): 8.

36. Weber actually uses the phrase "*modernes Leibeigenschaftsverhältnis*" in quotation marks, literally "modern relations of serfdom" or "bondage" (ibid., 8). As he would
have known, the phrase is a reference to Engels' remarks about a "second serfdom" (often
incorrectly attributed to Marx) in a letter to Marx, 15 December 1882, citing Engels' own
essay on the history of agrarian relations in the German "mark": see Marx and Engels,
Werke, 35:128. Engels' work provided one convenient target for Weber's writings on
agrarian society.

Weber suggested, second, that the key to understanding labor problems in the agrarian sector lay not in application of a general formula,
such as the separation of the worker from the means of production, but
rather in the recognition that labor-intensive agricultural production
must confront the "natural" fact of inevitable seasonal fluctuations in
labor requirements affecting both amounts and kinds of labor-power
and influencing a vertical and horizontal differentiation within the division of labor. Any particular agrarian *Arbeitsverfassung* could be seen
simply as an attempt to answer the question posed by such contingencies: How does a society solve the problem of variable requirements for
labor in the agrarian economy? Weber insisted that the way in which
this "most difficult problem" of variations in requirements for labor-
power was settled would then have far-reaching consequences not only
for agricultural production and the socioeconomic system of which it
was a part, but for the development of culture and civilization itself.[37]

In his more theoretical discussions in the 1890s, Weber answered his
own question in two ways, or rather with repect to conditions prevailing in the "two essentially different economic spheres" of Germany:
"One looks to the west, the other to the east; one is long since an 'industrial state,' the other has remained until now an 'agrarian state.' The
fundamental problem of our entire national economic policy lies in the
unbalanced relationship of these halves . . . that belong together politically, but diverge economically."[38] Thus, in the western and southern
agricultural regions studied by his Verein für Sozialpolitik collabora-
tors, Weber observed a "type" of *Arbeitsverfassung* characterized by an
"individualism carried to an extreme" and by the self-interest and relative "freedom" of the smallholder.[39] The system of smallholdings prevailing there had developed in stark contrast to the large eastern estates
run with dependent labor, a comparison whose significance had previously struck Tocqueville's attention:

> It was chiefly along the Rhine that at the close of the eighteenth century
> German farmers owned the land they worked and enjoyed almost as much

37. *Die Lage der Landarbeiter*, 68; "Die Erhebung des Vereins," 24.
38. From a discussion in response to a lecture by Karl Oldenberg, *Verhandlungen des
8. Evangelisch-sozialen Kongresses* (Göttingen: Vandenhoeck, 1897), 111.
39. Weber stated these ideas at the beginning of his 1893 Verein report in *SVSP* 58:
64–66; also "Capitalism and Rural Society in Germany," in G&M, 367–68. Dibble,
"Social Science and Political Commitments in the Young Max Weber," has shown that
among the six authors of the Verein's agrarian studies Weber alone stated conclusions at
this level of comparative generalization; on the studies and Weber's participation see especially Martin Riesebrodt, "Einleitung" and "Editorischer Bericht," in *MWG* I/3: 1–33.

freedom as the French small proprietor; and it was there, too, that the revolutionary zeal of the French found its earliest adepts and took most permanent effect. On the other hand, the parts of Germany which held out longest against the current of new ideas were those where the peasants did not as yet enjoy such privileges—and this is, to my mind, a highly suggestive fact.[40]

Tocqueville's "highly suggestive fact" surfaced at the center of Weber's own inquiries forty years later, when he observed that, in contrast to the East, nothing like a "labor question" could be uncovered in agricultural districts along the Rhine. The reasons for its absence had to do with an individualistic rationalization of the old *Feldgemeinschaft* of the village settlement, repeated fragmentation of land ownership through legal division among all heirs (hence, lack of primogeniture, entail, or other quasi-feudal practices), relative social equality between smallholders and large landowners, and absence of a local aristocracy with legal-administrative powers. Certain developmental consequences followed from such an organization of labor. Economically, the fragmented pattern of landholding tended to perpetuate production inefficiencies, which could, however, be overcome by increasing the intensity and raising the quality of labor, as was often the case. Socially, the smallholder achieved a kind of equality by owning the means of production and viewing his labor not as an imposed "duty" but as a freely chosen activity based on material interest, thereby eliminating "alienation" and "exploitation" as important issues. Politically, this system was associated with autonomous local administration and weak organization; thus it proved to be a quixotic base of support for the centralized national state.

In any case, by the 1890s the important problems of agrarian labor resided elsewhere—in the provinces of East Elbia—and Weber responded to the dilemmas confronted there by sketching four main types of agrarian economies in Western civilization that had organized labor, and therefore the entire social system, in radically different ways.[41] The "slave state" sought to perpetuate a continuous labor supply through military conquest and strict control of laborers' social institutions, such as marriage, family, and private property. At the other extreme, along a

40. Alexis de Tocqueville, *The Old Régime and the French Revolution* (1856), trans. S. Gilbert (Garden City, N.Y.: Doubleday [Anchor Books], 1955), 25. Weber never cited this classic, yet the passage is entirely consistent with his views, which undoubtedly included knowledge of French and British developments. At one public lecture he reportedly "described democratic agrarian relations in France and feudal relations in Great Britain" (*Frankfurter Zeitung*, 8 March 1896).

41. See especially the summation in "Die Erhebung des Vereins," 24–26.

continuum of state control of labor, some "colonial" systems have relied on the peculiar conditions of surplus or "nomadic" labor, piece-wages, and surplus land to accomplish similar tasks of agrarian production. Somewhere between these two stands the "patriarchal" system, characteristic of quasi-feudal orders and the "second serfdom" in Europe; it successfully bound labor to the land by enforcing various complex forms of economic, social, and legal dependency. Finally, the solution most characteristic of the "modernizing state" has been based on formally "free" labor, wage payments, intensive cultivation, technological innovation, and highly rationalized capital accumulation—an emerging "capitalist" type.

This suggestive fourfold typology can be reinterpreted and summarized, if somewhat more concisely than Weber's original account, by making explicit the categories that are in fact used for comparing and distinguishing types: productive factors, the relevant social unit of production, the characteristic social structure, authority relations pertinent to each type, the kind of political movement, the "cultural level" of laboring groups, the degree of technological innovation, and the "developmental tendency" associated with each configuration. Each type tends toward a rationalization of its categories, so that all are systematically interrelated: for example, the factors of production operative in slave systems (unfree labor, large estates, irregular capital formation) are logically connected to a particular social unit of production, a particular social structure, and the like. An abbreviated tabulation of the types can help clarify these relationships (see Table 1).

Weber's comparative studies of the *oikos* economy of antiquity, the colonial economy of contemporary Argentina,[42] and the economic and social structure of Western Europe convinced him that the "slave," "colonial" and "patriarchal" types were all incapable of sustained "technological" innovation and economic "rationalization." All depended on the persistence of certain specific historical conditions—for example, continual military conquest, uninterrupted access to surplus land, permanent isolation from market forces—that were difficult to sustain in the modern world and were at any rate not conducive to development of a "rational" system of production and exchange. In other words, there could be no doubt that the fourth, "capitalist" type contained the

---

42. The brief remarks on Argentina are found mainly in "Die Erhebung des Vereins," 25; "Argentinische Kolonistenwirthschaften," *Deutsches Wochenblatt* 7 (1894): 20–22, 57–59; and a review of B. Lehmann, *Die Rechtsverhältnisse der Fremden in Argentinien,* in *Zeitschrift für das gesammte Handelsrecht* 42 (1894): 326–27.

TABLE I.

THE TYPOLOGY OF AGRARIAN ECONOMIES

Types

Characteristics	Slave	Colonial	Patriarchal	Capitalist
Factors of Production:				
Labor	unfree	free, nomadic; piece-wages	bonded, settled; share-rights, payment in kind	free, mobile; contractual relations, money wages
Land	oikoi, large estates	freeholding, surplus land	estates	commercial enterprise
Capital formation	irregular	irregular	virtually none	systematic, continuous
Social unit of production	community of slaves	nomadic band	monogamous extended family	monogamous nuclear family
Social structure	master/slave	colonist/indigene	lord/serf, patron/client	entrepreneur/wage-laborer
Authority relations	bureaucratization, military rule	laissez-faire	bureaucratization, personal relations of domination	rationalized state, centralized administrative rule
Political movement	slave rebellion	amorphous, disorganized	apathetic labor, latent antagonism among orders	mobilized labor, manifest class conflict
Cultural level of labor	low	low	medium	high
Technological innovation	low	medium	medium	high
Developmental tendency	stagnation	wastefulness, exhaustion	autarchy, isolation	rational production for a market, rising real wages, expansion
Weber's main histori-	Roman Empire	Argentina (19th	Germany (16th–	Germany (19th

most powerful forces of economic rationalization. Yet, paradoxically, the full theoretical delineation of "developmental tendencies" *within* this type would point up socioeconomic and political conflicts, the opposition among classes and interests, from which possible consequences or "objective possibilities" for its own transformation could be inferred.

The usual caveats are in order when interpreting this typology. It intentionally exaggerates the distinguishing characteristics of each type, emphasizing that which is logically most typical for purposes of consistency, internal coherence, and precise comparison with actual historical cases. What matters most, as Weber repeatedly insisted in his later methodology essays, such as "'Objectivity' in Social Science and Social Policy," is not type construction for its own sake, but rather clarification of the "typical" with an eye toward historical analysis. At their best, types serve an orienting function and suggest questions, hypotheses, and relationships for investigation; they are never to be confused with the data of "history."[43] Weber uses them himself this way in his early writings, where there is in reality very little discussion of the types as such, but a great deal of writing about their internal dynamics and historical transformations, especially in relation to the historical cases that interested him most: Germany from the sixteenth century to the present, Roman antiquity, and colonial Argentina.

At this point in Weber's early writings we have encountered the concrete application of "ideal type" analysis and the initial conception of rationalization. The definitive demonstration of this generalization comes in the key "transitional" text, "Agrarverhältnisse im Altertum," one of two instances in Weber's published writings that span the early and later phases of his thought.[44] It must be remembered that this essay on "agrarian relations" dates from 1897–98 (the first and second versions), not 1909 (the final form), and is in origin a companion piece for

43. Note Weber's remark that all "*theoretical* constructions" are "pure mental images [*gedankliche Bildungen*], whose relationship to the empirical reality of the immediately given is problematic in every individual case" ("Die 'Objektivität' sozialwissenschaftlicher und sozialpolitischer Erkenntnis," *GAW*, 205; S&F, 103), or the important criticism of "naturalism" from Plato through Hegel and Marx: "Nothing, however, is more dangerous than the *confusion* of theory and history stemming from naturalistic presuppositions, whether in the form of a belief that one has recorded the 'actual' content, the 'essence' of historical reality in such conceptual images [*Begriffsbilder*]; or that one uses them as a procrustean bed into which history must be forced; or even that one hypostatizes the 'ideas' as a 'true' reality, as real 'forces' standing behind the play of appearances and working themselves out in history" (*GAW*, 195; S&F, 94).

44. All three versions of this text were published in the *Handwörterbuch der Staatswissenschaften*, ed. J. Conrad, with the last, nearly eight times longer than the original, reprinted in *GASW*, 1–288.

"The Social Causes of the Decline of Ancient Civilization" written in 1896. A comparison of these versions shows the emergence in the last text of clearly identified "ideal types" of the "organizational stages" characteristic of agricultural societies in antiquity. Weber now defends the use of such types not only as means for classification and comparison, but as rational reconstructions of particular "developmental stages." In fact, the terminology of "stages" and "types" is so closely associated in Weber's mind that the actual words are used interchangeably.[45] Furthermore, the 1909 text uses the terms "rationalization" and "rationalization process" ("*Rationalisierungs'-Prozess*"), often in quotation marks, to generalize about and explain structural relationships and changes both *internally* to a single type and *externally* among different types.[46] Rationalization is now discussed by Weber in terms of functional specialization in the division of labor, structural differentiation of social and economic life, and (in one brief aside) secularization of culture. This is precisely the terminology and theoretical perspective of the earlier 1897–98 texts, only with time the "ideal types" have become more explicit, the methodological underpinnings more self-conscious, and the problem of "rationalization," subsequently clarified in Weber's later writings, more precise.

Weber proposed the use of types not only as a way of settling the *Methodenstreit* (dispute over methods) between "historical" and "theoretical" economics, or between Schmoller's descriptive monographic methods and Menger's abstract "marginal utility" models, but also as a strategy for fighting clear of the Hegelian legacy, so deeply influential for Marx, of an objectivist philosophy of history with its "emanatist" understanding of concepts and its assumption of a necessary and law-like progression through universal stages. Weber seemed to have this in mind when he once remarked, "Two paths stand open: Hegel's or—*our* way of approaching things. . . . I will only be interested in the quality of the 'authentic' Hegel, for each of us has his own version."[47] Weber's version appears to have settled under the heading "emanatism," defined as an attempt "to surmount the '*hiatus irrationalis*' between concept and reality by the use of 'general' concepts—concepts which, as meta-

45. As an illustration, the English translation even renders "*Stadien*" (literally "stages") as "types" in one key passage: compare *GASW*, 44, with *Agrarian Sociology*, 78.
46. *GASW*, 38–39; Weber's statements demonstrate that the "developmental" language is supplemented and superseded by the language of "rationalization."
47. Letter to Franz Eulenburg, 11 May 1909, NW 30/7: 125–26.

physical realities, comprehend and imply individual things and events as their instances of *realization*."[48] But to use such concepts was to prejudge history, to superimpose schemata on events, outcomes, and meanings. The "type" concept, Weber thought, would instead facilitate theoretical judgment, not guarantee validity, in an open texture of interpretive possibility.

As is well known, Weber also thought clarity could be brought to the interpretation of *Marx's* historical generalizations—"far and away the most important case," according to Weber—if the concepts and "developmental laws" created by "the great thinker" were treated as "ideal types" capable of suggesting contingent "hypotheses" about social and historical relations that could be checked through investigation. Reflecting on his own experience in the nineties, Weber acclaimed "the eminent, indeed unique *heuristic* significance of these ideal types, if one uses them for *comparison* with reality; similarly," he noted on the other hand, "their perniciousness, as soon as they are considered empirically valid or even as *real* (i.e., in truth: metaphysical) 'effective forces,' 'tendencies,' etc., is known to everyone who has worked with Marxian concepts."[49] But, by contrast, for his own practice when employing the indispensable conceptual apparatus of political economy—"city economy," "state," "development," and so on—Weber insisted on speaking the more ambiguous and complex, but more intellectually defensible nominalist language of "types," "tendencies," and "probabilities of action."

It is possible to read Weber's discussion as an alternative to the rough scheme of stages of development in the division of labor and modes of production suggested by Marx in *The German Ideology* and manuscripts like the "Grundrisse" (which Weber could not have known): from tribal and communal to slave systems, feudalism, capitalism, a deviant "asiatic" mode of production, and so forth. The comparison may suggest the omission of other types from Weber's contribution— say, "agrarian communism" as the earliest form of agricultural production, or some similar variant as the final "fully rational" transcendence of private property and the capitalist division of labor. Certainly Weber was well aware of such possibilities through his reading of Rodbertus

48. *GAW*, 15; *Roscher and Knies*, 66.
49. "Die 'Objektivität,' " *GAW*, 204–5; *S&F*, 103. Many examples illustrating this discussion of "types," the most sustained anywhere in Weber's work, are drawn from his early writings: "city economy," "household economy," "value," "exchange," "development," "individualism," "liberalism," and of course "feudalism" and "capitalist culture."

and Bücher, classical anthropologists like Lewis Henry Morgan and Johann Jakob Bachofen, not to mention Marx and Engels themselves.[50] But doubting their historicity, in the published early work he did not directly address these problems, suggesting only that in Germany all further specific distinctions would fall within the range of alternatives already sketched in various types of *Arbeitsverfassung*. Interestingly, the question does emerge later in the *General Economic History*, Weber's posthumously published lecture notes from 1920, where he again reveals a deep skepticism about the elaboration of further pre- or postcapitalist types of agrarian organization. On balance, two reasons seem to predominate: There is in such discussions an absence of concrete historical evidence, combined with the strong convictions of an ideological dispute between socialism and Manchester liberalism; the issues are really ideological, not historical. Moreover, Weber was convinced that contemporary forms of "agrarian communism" conceived as the corrective to capitalist exploitation did not mark a further step along the path of economic rationalization, but instead represented a displacement of economic rationality by political goals (e.g., social justice, solidarity) and would most likely lead back toward forms of dependency imposed by the new "patriarch," the state. In this view, "collectivization" would signify little more that a revival of "patriarchalism," perhaps made more palatable by a few concessions to "capitalist" commercial norms.

It should also be said that, as a concept, "agrarian communism" seems to make sense only *prior* to the agrarian *economic* types Weber wants to describe, at an entirely different level of analysis. This is so because it lacks any basis in mechanisms of exchange, as can be seen even in Weber's most fundamental conceptions of his subject matter. As we have already noted, for him political economy as the study of *Volkswirtschaft* is a modern science based on assumptions about economic action derived from modern economic experience. *Volkswirtschaft* itself, Weber maintains, is a species of exchange economy or, more specifically, an economy and its science based on "the regulation of commodity supply through exchange." Therefore, considered logically and historically, what Weber designates as its "conceptual opposite" has to be "commodity supply in the primitive household without exchange"

---

50. See the bibliographies in Weber's 1898 "Grundriss," especially under sec. 8 ("Die ältesten Existenzbedingungen der menschlichen Wirtschaft" [the oldest conditions of existence in human economy]), no. 2 ("Die primitiven menschlichen Gemeinschaftsformen" [primitive human forms of community]).

or "all completely communistic social organizations."[51] These notions of autarchic communities "which only produce and operate with *consumable* goods" are rationally conceivable only outside the scope of modern political economy and prior even to Rodbertus' concept of the "oikos economy."

One can conclude that Weber's typology was open to amendment and revision, especially at the level of sub-types, in the course of historical investigations and in light of unfolding social experience. It was not exhaustive, but neither was it incomplete in view of the temporality of all historical knowledge.

THE PROBLEM OF DEVELOPMENT

From the preceding discussion, it is clear that the elemental clash between patriarchal and capitalist orders lies at the very heart of Weber's concern in his early work. Although the issues are complex, a monumental theme can be reconstructed from the mass of details: it is not merely the "bread and butter question" (Engels)[52] or quantitative changes in the relationships between wage levels, grain prices, and ground rents, but rather the qualitative transformation of the "unmodern patriarchal organization of labor [*Arbeitsverfassung*]"[53] at the hands of the modernized, "rational," impersonal, large-scale capitalist enterprise. For Weber the transformation represents an irreversible "developmental tendency," and therefore the question to ask is not whether it can be stopped or reversed, but rather, what its social, political, and cultural consequences are.[54]

It was really this question that fired Weber's imagination, for he saw far more clearly than others of his generation that the traditional social structure of the East, characterized by "lazy rentiers and an apathetic,

51. "Die begrifflichen Grundlagen der Volkswirtschaftslehre, Erstes Buch" (Heidelberg, 1898), 14.

52. "Die Messer- und Gabelfrage," from Engels' reference to Chartism: *MWG* I/3: 920; also " 'Privatenquêten' über die Lage der Landarbeiter," *Mitteilungen des Evangelischsozialen Kongresses*, no. 5 (1892): 4; "Die deutschen Landarbeiter," 81–82.

53. *MWG* I/3:895.

54. Reinhard Bendix, *Max Weber: An Intellectual Portrait*, 2d ed. (Berkeley: University of California Press, 1977), chap. 2; and Wolfgang Schluchter, "Der autoritär verfasste Kapitalismus: Max Webers Kritik am Kaiserreich," in *Rationalismus der Weltbeherrschung: Studien zu Max Weber* (Frankfurt: Suhrkamp, 1980), 134–69, tend to emphasize social consequences, whereas Keith Tribe, "Prussian Agriculture—German Politics: Max Weber 1892–97," *Economy and Society* 12 (1983): 181–226, has emphasized political aspects of Weber's East Elbian studies.

traditionalistic mass" and resting on semifeudal survivals, a "community of interest" between labor and land, unquestioned hierarchies of traditional authority, and the legal-administrative prerogatives of the estates, was a system doomed to oblivion. At best it could be appreciated only in "historical-aesthetic" memory.[55] Arising from its ashes were "fungible" entrepreneurs guided solely by considerations of "economic efficiency" and laborers "torn out of the collective unity of the family" to become "*only* labor-power for the owner and in their own eyes as well."[56] The future of agrarian society offered what Weber saw as a "latent" class struggle between these two strata.[57] On the one side was typically an absentee entrepreneurial class driven by fear of declining status in relation to the pacesetting urban bourgeoisie, a stratum better positioned than landed wealth to gain access to a "modern way of life [*Lebensführung*] demanding steadily increasing *cash* expenditures."[58] On the other side stood an increasingly mobilized agrarian labor force, whose changed position in the eastern provinces meant not only proletarianization or a reservoir of recruits for the "industrial reserve army," but also "Polenization" as the estates lost their German populations to the promise of "freedom" in the cities, "this driving force of the modern world."[59] The status of the formally "free" laborers, emancipated from dependencies, contains a deep paradox: "More intensive cultivation was successful for them in *one* way, and to be sure culturally successful, but not materially: they became acquainted with *freedom*, and in order to obtain it they were prepared to sacrifice even their own material well-being." Under prevailing relations of domination, Weber concluded, "homelessness and freedom are one and the same."[60] The headlong flight from the benign tyranny of patriarchalism in the countryside terminated in the sinister iron cage of industrial labor in the cities.

The resulting conflict-ridden system of socioeconomic relations effectively undermined the bases of the "authoritarian state" at either end of

55. *Verhandlungen des 8. Evangelisch-sozialen Kongresses*, 109; debate over "Die ländliche Arbeitsverfassung," *SVSP* 58:129.

56. "Entwicklungstendenzen," *Archiv*, 23.

57. "Zum Pressstreit über den Evangelisch-sozialen Kongress," *Die Christliche Welt* 8 (12 July 1894): 672.

58. "Entwicklungstendenzen," *Archiv*, 4.

59. *MWG* I/3:920.

60. "Entwicklungstendenzen," *Archiv*, 41; "'Privatenquêten,'" no. 6 (1892): 4; and "Die deutschen Landarbeiter," 68, where Weber speaks of the *modern* "psychological illusions" of freedom that condition the agrarian workers' existence and whose power in economic life cannot be understood from a "materialist-economic standpoint."

the social order: both reliable peasants and self-assured Junkers were dying breeds. For those remaining survivors on the estates, caught in the web of traditionalism, the influx of migrant seasonal labor led just as surely, according to Weber's "thesis of displacement,"[61] to a general decline in living standards and even more importantly to the cultural "decadence" or "fatality" of an older way of life that *because of* its national political successes had "dug the grave of its own social organization."[62] In terms of the typology, "modern nomadism" threatened a shift from patriarchalism to a "colonial" type. As for the emerging new order, Weber repeatedly insisted that neither the bourgeoisie nor the urban working class was in a position to fill the spreading void at the political center. A seemingly regional or even local crisis in the agrarian *Arbeitsverfassung* threatened to undo the whole fabric of national life. What had begun as a rather limited empirical inquiry thus turned in Weber's hands into a thoroughgoing critique of modern development and prospects for the future.

One aim of this argumentation was to suggest that the simple question—Is the *Gutswirtschaft* of the East Elbian territories "capitalist" or "feudal?"—was itself misleading and likely to generate a set of false issues. According to Weber's highly differentiated picture of social, economic, and political conditions in the East, what one observed through the nineteenth century was the *emergence* of capitalist productive forms, whose characteristics, rates of development, and location were dependent on numerous factors. No doubt the patriarchal system was a drag on economic rationalization, yet capitalist and patriarchal forms of the labor relation continued to exist side by side even beyond 1900. From the viewpoint of national development and power, any state would be better off without patriarchalism; when it nevertheless persisted, then it was for political reasons, usually the "reactionary" defense of entrenched and traditionalistic material interests that were "irrational" from the standpoint of economic rationality. With the coming triumph of the "capitalist" developmental form in the countryside, one could foresee there the kind of class formation and "exploitation" of labor associated with urban industrialism.[63]

61. "*Verdrängungsthese*" is given a sociocultural meaning, in contrast to Freud's identical language for repression in the psyche.
62. "Entwicklungstendenzen," *Archiv*, 3 and 5, where Weber uses the Nietzschean terminology of *Decadence* and *Verhängnis* (fate, fatality); *MWG* I/3:927.
63. When comparing Russian and Prussian agrarian relations, Theda Skocpol, *States and Social Revolutions* (New York: Cambridge University Press, 1979), 109, 144–47, exaggerates the rate and extent of the transition from feudal to capitalist forms in East

Weber's critique of agrarian labor's "exploitation" (*Ausbeutung*), a term appearing only occasionally,[64] or its "material situation," as he tended to say more often, can remind us of Marx's early discussions of "alienated labor" or Tocqueville's disturbing passages on the degradation of workers under conditions of an increasingly rationalized division of labor. But for Weber the struggle is repetitive and familiar: "Now we stand once again before the old problem," namely "the emancipation of the lowest stratum of the old society" or the "emancipation of labor from property," first acted out in antiquity, most fatefully in Rome, and repeating itself in new circumstances.[65] From this perspective, antiquity entered Weber's field of vision because, like East Elbia in the nineteenth century, it also raised questions about the transformation of agrarian economies under conditions of mixed socioeconomic and political forms, sharing features of dependent-feudal relations and capitalist appropriation. Yet outcomes were radically different in the two historical cases. To ask why this was so was to push the analysis beyond a *histoire événémentielle* to the higher plane of theoretical conceptualization.

Now Weber was careful to deny any direct lessons from the study of history, either for comforting theories of progress or for strategies of political action. In his words, a study of antiquity could be expected to have only "historical interest," for "a modern proletarian and a Roman slave would be as unable to understand one another as a European and

---

Elbia. It is surely false to suggest that following the Stein-Hardenberg reforms after 1807 a "vast majority" of the Eastern peasantry were forced to become wage-laborers. If Weber's work demonstrated anything, it was that the transformation of the peasantry into "wage laborers" was quite gradual and went through numerous "mixed" and intermediate forms, subject to local and regional variations. Weber chose to view the change as a "developmental tendency," and in fact it was "completed" only after World War I. Skocpol tends to have the argument both ways: that is, *if* formally "free" wage-labor on the estates of the East had been a truly significant force by 1848–49, then one would have expected some expression of agrarian revolt during those two revolutionary years. Instead there was deathly silence, in contrast to at least a few outbursts in western Germany. Why? The question is answered (147) by pointing out that the Stein-Hardenberg reforms had left the Eastern peasantry as weak economically and politically as in the eighteenth century. That is precisely the point! By 1848–49 the old "patriarchal" system was still intact and regionally dominant, although under pressure from new wage forms. By 1892 it was in full retreat economically, but still shored up through political and legal means. Of course, this was the central "contradiction" guiding Weber's analysis, one perceived also by the Social Democrats in their first serious debate on the "agrarian question" in the nineties. For evidence, see Max Rolfes, "Landwirtschaft, 1850–1914," in *Handbuch der deutschen Wirtschafts- und Sozialgeschichte*, vol. 2, ed. H. Aubin and W. Zorn (Stuttgart: Klett, 1976), esp. 508 for wage-labor.

64. For example, in "Entwicklungstendenzen," *Archiv*, 18; and *MWG* I/3: 923, 925, at the conclusion of this major study.

65. *MWG* I/3: 923; "Agrarverhältnisse im Altertum" (1897), 1.

a Chinese. Our problems are of a completely different character."[66] It can hardly be accidental that in this same introductory passage from "The Social Causes of the Decline of Ancient Civilization" Weber reproduces Marx's epigram from the first German Preface to *Capital I*— "This story is about you (*de te narratur fabula*)"—in an identical context, but with a precisely opposed meaning.[67] For Weber, history issues a harder lesson: It is never simply a story about ourselves, but rather a record of differences, contingencies, unanticipated consequences, and paradoxical meanings. The rhetoric of difference can function to create a necessary distance between past and present, antiquity and modernity, text and audience, Marx and Weber himself—distance that is necessary as a precondition for judging the meaning of the great transformation.

Yet the exercise of judgment raises the possibility of exploring certain suggestive historical analogies. As Weber notes, to study ancient civilization is to observe a process of "internal self-dissolution" (*innere Selbstauflösung*), and to study the patriarchal system in nineteenth-century Germany is to observe a repetition of that process. In Greek and Roman antiquity, for example, the struggle for emancipation of labor took the form of a clash between slave and market economies, unfree and free labor. Ancient civilization experienced a nascent "agrarian capitalism," a budding "exchange economy" like that of the medieval city, even what Weber calls an "upper-middle-class politics" (*grossbürgerliche Politik*) based on a combination of commercial and landed interests. But in antiquity, market production and free labor lost ground, the ancient *polis* remained essentially a center of consumption and not production, and the "superstructure of the exchange economy" was eventually subordinated to the "base of a [natural] economy without exchange." In the case of Rome, Weber contends, the *polis* even finally transformed itself into "an enormous *oikos*." This transformation marked a victory of economic over political forces, a victory that would spell the end of the civilization of antiquity and the gradual emergence of conditions that Weber foresaw as "a new basis for agrarian society."[68]

66. "Die sozialen Gründe des Untergangs der antiken Kultur," *GASW*, 291; *Agrarian Sociology*, 397.

67. From Horace's *Satires*, 1.1.69–70.

68. These ideas and quotations are from *MGA* I/3 : 923; *GASW*, 291–94; "Agrarverhältnisse im Altertum" (1897), 7–10, 16. The most famous analogies between antiquity and modernity appear in the final paragraph of the 1909 revision of "Agrarverhältnisse," where Weber comments on a "bureaucratization of society" that "will gain mastery over capitalism *sooner or later*, just as in antiquity" (*GASW*, 278; *Agrarian Sociology*, 365).

What I am suggesting, therefore, is that in this part of his work on the German East and on agrarian society in antiquity Weber's theme is defined by the double interplay between *polis* and *oikos* in antiquity, polity and economy in the modern age. In both Greek and Roman antiquity the theme is emphasized by an argument that is designed to document the way in which the *oikos* came to obscure and replace the *polis* in Western culture, and with ambivalent consequences for the course of ancient civilization: on the one hand a decline into feudalism, on the other the restoration of the family as a viable social and productive unit.[69] At the end of this historical process stands the patriarchal "organization of labor" with its forms of socioeconomic dependency and political domination, confronted once again by the corrosive, revolutionizing, and now victorious forces of capitalist production and exchange. In the contemporary age of Western culture the question then became, Could it be possible to say along which developmental path the clash of dynamic forces would move modern society?

Approaching the theme philosophically, one might add that this last way of posing the problem of historical meaning finds a parallel in Nietzsche's masterful essay, which Weber would have encountered early, on the "Uses and Disadvantages of History for Life" in the *Unzeitgemässe Betrachtungen*, at the end of which a rationale emerges for any inquiry or speculations about antiquity. Like Weber, Nietzsche understands the Greeks' cultural achievements as presupposing a reinterpretation of "history." The Greeks too, he writes, whose culture was also a "chaos" of warring elements, were in "danger of being overwhelmed by what was past and foreign, of perishing through 'history.'" But they "gradually learned *to organize the chaos* by following the Delphic teaching ['know yourself'] and thinking back to themselves, to their real needs . . . they again took possession of themselves; they did not long remain the overburdened heirs and epigones of the entire Orient." In Nietzsche's symbolic language, what they overcame was the stance of those who embrace an ethics of happiness, who revere culture as "a *decoration of life*."[70] Recalling Weber's critique of "eudaemonian ethics" and "ethical culture," we see here the beginnings of his scathing

---

Along these lines he also suggests that "in terms of its function the migrant laborers' barracks is the money economy's analogy to the slave barracks of antiquity" ("Entwicklungstendenzen," *GASW*, 492).

69. See *Die römische Agrargeschichte* (Stuttgart: Enke, 1891), 275.

70. *Untimely Meditations*, trans. R. J. Hollingdale (Cambridge: Cambridge University Press, 1983), 122–23 (II, 10).

repudiation of those "last men who invented happiness" and "modern intellectuals" who "play at decorating a sort of domestic chapel" confronted in the pages of "Science as a Vocation."[71] For one problem in Weber's thought, as in Nietzsche's, was the "chaos" of value and existential conflict, the probability that the meaning of culture would not be clarified through the course of historical evolution, indeed the questioning of the faith that could assume happiness to result from a necessarily "progressive" world of limitless possibilities. Such questioning defines one purpose behind Weber's reading of the significance of this most modern transformation.

WEBER'S PESSIMISTIC STANDPOINT

The skeptical distance Weber places between himself and what appears in the *Protestant Ethic* as the "rosy blush" of the spirit of religious asceticism's "laughing heir, the Enlightenment" suggests one point at which Nietzsche's presence can be felt in his work.[72] But the sense of a parallel with Nietzsche is itself qualified by at least some of Weber's explicit political argumentation. While it is significantly true that Weber was "neither a 'critic by principle' nor an 'apologist' of the capitalist system" and could not be "clearly assigned to any given scientific school of thought or political party,"[73] it is nevertheless also correct to emphasize that Weber did not doubt the long-term strength of either capitalist development or pressures for increasing social and cultural "democratization." As the most politically attuned of scholars, he was therefore deeply worried not about an alleged "problem of democracy," but about the effects of the "developmental tendencies" he observed on class structure and leadership in the new industrial state.

In some respects his orientation was shared by a select number of like-minded social scientists. For instance, a young colleague, Schulze-Gävernitz, had asked, as did Weber, how the position of labor could be strengthened in politics. Previous radical thought provided little guidance for an answer: "Marx's great mistake," Schulze-Gävernitz had written, was to assume the emergence of "class domination by the bour-

---

71. "Wissenschaft als Beruf," *GAW*, 598, 611; G&M, 143, 154; in the former passages Weber is in fact quoting from Nietzsche, *Thus Spoke Zarathustra*, part I (Introduction), sec. 5.

72. *GARS*, 1:204; *PE*, 181–82; *"rosige Stimmung"* (rosy blush) connotes more precisely a pleasant "mood" or "high spirits" Weber associates with the eudaemonic moral outlook of Enlightenment thought.

73. Riesebrodt, "From Patriarchalism to Capitalism," 498 (translation revised).

geoisie" in Germany equivalent to that in England; but the German state instead produced "a Junker-feudal superstructure much more than a bourgeois-liberal one."[74] Given such a retrograde class structure, in comparison with England's, the most adequate *Sozialpolitik* revolved around promotion of industrialization, an alliance between working and middle classes, and certain legal reforms (e.g., freedom of association) and legislative enactments (e.g., use of state lands for resettlement in the East, a program of "land for the masses"). We find Weber's position here, too, but it is accompanied by a more radical skepticism about the probable future of labor-relations and the prospects for finding that "catilinarian energy of the deed" or for recruiting effective leadership from *any* class in the new state.[75]

Furthermore, in Weber's early thought this irreducible skepticism assumes a theoretical form and argument. It can be summarized in the following way as a series of statements about the contradiction between "economic" and "political" domination:

First: In contemporary Germany, political power, consolidated through the Junkers and their control of the state bureaucracy, is used to maintain the economic supremacy of the same aristocratic class. Or as Weber wrote, "Instead of being able to base itself on a secure material foundation, political power must now be placed conversely in the service of economic interests."[76] Thus, there is a kind of "political determinism."

Second: But in the face of contemporary developmental tendencies, the real decline in the economic strength of the eastern estates will undermine and eventually destroy their assumed political jurisdictions, national power, and leadership position in the state. Thus, a case can be made for an "economic determinism."

Third: Nevertheless, it is in the "ideal interest" of all strata in society

---

74. "Die gegenwärtige Mittel zur Hebung der Arbeiterklasse in Deutschland," *Ethische Kultur* 3 (1895): 151.

75. *GPS*, 22; "The National State," 446. Weber was not alone in this judgment; consider Marx's early comment in his "Kritik der Hegelschen Rechtsphilosophie" (1844): "But in Germany every class lacks the logic, insight, courage and clarity, which would make it a negative representative of society. Moreover, there is also lacking in every class . . . that genius which pushes material force to political power, that revolutionary daring which throws at its adversary the defiant phrase, *I am nothing and I should be everything*" (*The Marx-Engels Reader*, 2d ed., ed. R. Tucker [New York: Norton, 1978], 63).

76. "Entwicklungstendenzen," *Archiv*, 4.

for national political power and leadership to be restructured in accordance with long-term transformations in economic strength or the "material situation" of different classes. In this sense there is a "codeterminism" of political and economic factors.

Fourth: How is such restructuring to be accomplished? Short of revolution, it must come about through political initiative and education, as Weber argued quite directly in the Freiburg Address. This is, of course, an explicitly value-laden *political* argument, but it can also be seen as a philosophical claim of the kind Weber develops in subsequent writing for the relative "autonomy" of politics.

Weber's arguments reveal a remarkable pattern of reasoning that is scattered in its different parts throughout his early work. But nowhere is the force of the arguments more obvious than in the 1897 debate with Karl Oldenberg, a representative of the opposing view, the incurable romantic proponent of the distinctive moral achievements, solidarity, and productivity of agrarian society. Oldenberg foresaw a choice between a policy of "cosmopolitan" and adventurous export and a policy of autarchic agrarian development and national independence, between "industrialization and extreme individualism" and "agrarian civilization, the age-old master." Embracing the agrarian alternative, he expounded an early version of "dependency theory," but ironically in defense of agrarian conservatism or the "feudal-Junker superstructure."[77] In Weber's eyes this analysis was noteworthy as a "Philippic" against industrialization and capitalism, a mythical picture presupposing the actuality of an "idyllic politics" of precapitalist, patriarchal solidarity, whose message to modern youth should read, "I want peace and quiet, so go find another homeland."[78]

What Weber called his "Jeremiad" contained all of the necessary and contrary elements: capitalist development, like political struggle, was "inescapable for us" and a matter of "our fate"; "only the path within which it moves can be economically influenced." In the German case attempts at resistance resulted in oddly distorted manifestations: "bu-

77. Karl Oldenberg, *Deutschland als Industriestaat* (Göttingen: Vandenhoeck, 1897), esp. 41, a speech of 10 June 1897 to the annual meeting of the *Evangelisch-sozialer Kongress*, followed immediately in the proceedings by a reply from Weber.
78. From Weber's remarks on Oldenberg's lecture, *Verhandlungen des 8. Evangelisch-sozialen Kongresses*, 105, 108. It was the attack on capitalism that writers on the Left like the young Robert Michels and Georg Lukács shared with Oldenberg: see Michels' use of Oldenberg in *Probleme der Sozialphilosophie* (Leipzig: Teubner, 1914), 81.

reaucratic religiosity" in the middle class, "feudalization of bourgeois capital," a philistine politics and political environment.[79] In one of his most revealing perorations, Weber added,

> There are optimists and pessimists in the consideration of the future of German development. Now, I don't belong to the optimists. I also recognize the enormous risk which the inevitable outward economic expansion of Germany places upon us. But I consider this risk inevitable, and therefore I say, "So must you be, you will not escape from yourself."[80]

This is passionate and perhaps exaggerated rhetoric, to be sure, but its meaning is hardly self-evident. Given Weber's well-known, vigorous commitment to a national *Machtpolitik* of new tasks and grand horizons, a politics in the mode of Gaullist grandeur, so to speak, one may well wonder at the collision of identifications with "fate," "inevitability," "pessimism," and "development" against the philistine literati and epigoni. What, precisely, did Weber have in mind?

Few passages in Weber's early writings are more significant or complex, for they are passages reverberating with the echo of ideas from Nietzsche and Burckhardt back to Goethe. Weber was prepared to travel part way with Nietzsche, to side with "pessimism" against the naive evolutionists, those "historical men" who imagined this as either the best of all possible worlds or a world soon to be crowned with happiness. But what was the substance of this particular "pessimism"? In the symbolic and surprisingly differentiated language Weber chose for conveying his meaning, to affirm the "risk" accompanying "historical inevitability" was to find a way of repudiating the "romantic pessimism" of Oldenberg, just as Nietzsche had cast off Schopenhauerian denial of life in favor of a "pessimism of strength." In fact, Nietzsche identified romantic pessimism—"the last *great* event in the fate of our culture"—with both Schopenhauer's philosophy and Wagner's music, and opposed it to a classical, "*Dionysian* pessimism," a will to the tragic, to what Plato (and Weber following him) called *mania*.[81] For

79. Weber's discussion of Oldenberg's lecture, *Verhandlungen des 8. Evangelischsozialen Kongresses*, 109–11. It is worth remembering in this connection that because of Nietzsche's apotheosis of the "will to power," Weber also included him in the charge of "philistinism," as noted in marginalia in Weber's copy of Simmel, *Nietzsche und Schopenhauer*, now catalogued in the Max-Weber-Arbeitsstelle library, Munich: see Wolfgang J. Mommsen, *Max Weber: Gesellschaft, Politik und Geschichte* (Frankfurt: Suhrkamp, 1974), 261 n. 125.
80. Weber's discussion of Oldenberg's lecture, 123.
81. For examples of this language, see especially Nietzsche's 1886 preface to *The Birth of Tragedy; or, Hellenism and Pessimism*, trans. W. Kaufmann (New York: Random

Weber the turn away from the intelligentsia's gray and retrospective romanticism was also, as happened so often, a turn toward the classical brilliance of Goethe's Olympian spirit. The key to understanding Weber's stance is found in the last sentence—"So must you be, you will not escape from yourself"—a line borrowed appropriately from the stanza on the "Dämon" in Goethe's cycle, "Urworte, Orphisch," a quotation from a famous poem that would have been immediately recognizable to Weber's audience, and a line, furthermore, that introduces one of the great and problematic leitmotifs in his thought.[82]

For Goethe, as for Weber, the "daemon"—*das Dämonische*—was present as "fate," as the characteristic and preformed essence of individual identity, the unchanging and self-directive "law" of destiny. As in Greek tragedy, individuals were seen to be propelled forward according to their own internal developmental "forms," "stamped" on them for eternity, thus paradoxically present as both limitation and infinitude, actuality and possibility. By invoking Goethe's prophetic imagi-

---

House [Vintage Books], 1967), 17–27; idem, *The Gay Science*, trans. W. Kaufmann (New York: Random House [Vintage Books], 1974), 327–31 (sec. 370); idem, *Werke in drei Bänden*, ed. K. Schlechta (Frankfurt: Ullstein, 1983), 1:9–10; 2:244–46; Max Weber, "Wissenschaft als Beruf," *GAW*, 591; *G&M*, 136; cf. Mommsen, *Max Weber: Gesellschaft, Politik und Geschichte*, 134.

82. The poem was evidently a favorite of Weber's, as he used this line a second time in his memorial speech for his good friend and Heidelberg colleague, Georg Jellinek, who had just died, at the wedding of the Jellineks' daughter, Dora, on 21 March 1911 (in *Max Weber zum Gedächtnis*, 13). The full stanza reads:

Dämon

Wie an dem Tag, der dich der Welt verliehen,
Die Sonne stand zum Grusse der Planeten,
Bist alsobald und fort und fort gediehen
Nach dem Gesetz, wonach du angetreten.
So musst du sein, dir kannst du nicht entfliehen,
So sagten schon Sibyllen, so Propheten;
Und keine Zeit und keine Macht zerstückelt
Geprägte Form, die lebend sich entwickelt.

Daemon

As stood the sun to the salute of planets
Upon the day that gave you to the earth,
You grew forthwith, and prospered, in your growing
Heeded the law presiding at your birth.
Sibyls and prophets told it: You must be
None but yourself, from self you cannot flee.
No time there is, no power, can decompose
The minted form that lives and living grows.

On the first occasion Weber applied Goethe's line to the "fateful" development of the nation, the second time to the person and the formation of personality.

nation and disclosing it within the unanticipated context of historical national "development," Weber chose to emphasize the conjunctive formation of these paradoxes in their timeless and contemporary bearing: risk was accompanied by certainty, the agonistic by the necessary. In the terms of this discussion, "fate" became symbolic for the sense of which historical development could be said to be constrained by "structure," yet open to "living" as opposed to mechanical, stagelike "evolution." Put somewhat differently, if there could ever be any meaning to declaring with Marx that humans "make their own history," for Weber it would be because "the possible is often reached only by striving to attain the impossible that lies beyond it."[83] However, in this view "fate" and not simply "will" was responsible for the painfully indifferent results of history.

By invoking Goethe's belief in the "daemonic" in human affairs, did Weber cast his lot with the forces of irrationalism and hopelessness in history? Was his a counsel of despair? With these questions we are led beyond a merely stylish conception of pessimism to Weber's deepest commitments, to the presuppositions even of his version of political economy. For Weber the "fateful" source of pessimism lay not in rumored cultural decadence, nor even in the paradox of "unanticipated consequences" in history, but rather in the experience of "historical inevitability" and the displacement of human action and meaning between infinite possibility and finite impossibility. Weber may have adapted the thought from Goethe, but among contemporaries he shared it most closely with the revisionist Greek "classicism" of Burckhardt and Nietzsche, for like Burckhardt's, Weber's pessimism was classical and Hellenic, and like Nietzsche's, it was cast in the image of the hard lessons of Thucydidean politics. "It seems to me," Weber once wrote in comments on Burckhardt's *Griechische Kulturgeschichte,*

> that the struggle of all against all in the sphere of *foreign* policy was the unalterable primary factor for the Hellenic states. (Burckhardt understands it as the outwardly directed agon.) And I think the atmosphere that produced this condition of permanent threat to all of existence ("in the midst of life we are overtaken by death") sounds its strongest note in the specific Hellenic pessimism that Burckhardt depicts so well.[84]

83. "Der Sinn der 'Wertfreiheit' der soziologischen und ökonomischen Wissenschaften" (1917), *GAW*, 514; S&F, 24.
84. A letter written in Rome to Carl Neumann, 11 November 1900, NW 30/4:82–83. In another letter to Neumann (14 March 1898, NW 30/4:72), Weber mentions he is most attracted to Burckhardt's "universal history," especially in relation to cultural development and decline. Burckhardt's work was noted for its discussion of the "daemonic"

What Weber saw in Burckhardt's interpretation of the culture of antiquity—including "the highly visible and unqualified 'public character' [Öffentlichkeit] of all of existence" in the *polis*, in contrast to the modern city—depended on his own vision and agonistic drive, not only with respect to the meaning of antiquity, but also in relation to his definition of the pessimistic standpoint.

Weber's objectification of the "daemonic" self had to be presented as a critique of pleasant expectations or, even more strikingly, of the "endless longing for human happiness" rampant among his liberal contemporaries: "*We alone do not engage in Sozialpolitik in order to create human happiness,*" Weber proclaimed again and again; furthermore, he reasoned, "precisely from our pessimistic standpoint we arrive at a point of view, and especially I do personally, that appears to me much more idealistic"—more so, that is, than the "greatest happiness" principle:

> I believe we must renounce the aim of creating a positive feeling of happiness through any kind of social legislation. We want something else and can only want something else. We want to protect and sustain that which appears *valuable* in people: self-responsibility, the deep impulse toward achievement, toward the spiritual [*geistig*] and moral excellence of humanity, even where it confronts us in its most primitive form. Insofar as it is in our power, we want to configure external relations not so that human beings feel satisfied, but so that in view of the necessity of the unavoidable struggle for existence the best in them will be brought out, the physical and spiritual [*seelisch*] characteristics that we want the nation to preserve.[85]

In these lines, then, are to be found the meaning of *Weber's* pessimism of strength, the positive statement of the presuppositions for both his science of political economy and his practical engagements on the side of social reform. Weber called this agonistic idealism of a new *arete* "irrational" in the sense that it rested on *practical* judgment and was put forward in tension with the world as it "is" and without regard to the internal, machinelike logic of "material" and "technical progress"— hence, all the more reason to affirm it with unrestrained vigor.

---

and "pessimism" in Greek culture: *Griechische Kulturgeschichte*, 2 vols. (Berlin: Spemann, 1898), 2:70–76, 373–93. Weber also generalized this reading of the culture of antiquity to ascetic Protestantism, where he found a "sober pessimistic evaluation of humanity and everything human" that was closely tied to the profound "inner isolation of the individual," an interpretation uniquely his own ("'Kirchen' und 'Sekten' in Nordamerika," *Die Christliche Welt* 20 [1906]: 581).

85. "Die deutschen Landarbeiter," 80–81; cf. *GPS*, 13.

Viewed after nearly a century of history, the contours of Weber's "pessimistic" argumentation and the substance of his first investigations of the great transformation in Western culture might provoke any number of reactions—to the foreboding warnings, conceptual innovations, bittersweet assessment of a world lost forever, or passionate engagement on the side of the "excellence of humanity" and national greatness. Whatever our standpoint, the "permanent threat to all of existence" and the "daemon who holds the fibers" of our very lives are phrases with a peculiarly sobering effect in the nuclear age. They return in Weber's concluding reflections on the modern age, there cast against the murmurs of "disenchantment." The old analogies with antiquity survive intact: "We live as did the ancients," Weber remarks, "only we live in a different sense"; "Many old gods, disenchanted and hence in the form of impersonal forces, ascend from their graves, strive to gain power over our lives, and resume the eternal struggle with each other." [86] The struggle among these "gods," the way in which we may live within the life-order of this "eternal return," draws us to the next phase in Weber's pursuit of the unfolding life-history of Western culture.

86. "Wissenschaft als Beruf," *GAW*, 604–5; G&M, 148–49.

CHAPTER III

Culture and Its Discontents

Only give me life, then I will create a culture for you out of it!
—*Friedrich Nietzsche*

The years between 1898 and 1903 were the darkest of Weber's life. They were years of illness, disappointment, wanderings to the south, and struggle toward a partial, self-willed recovery. In the *Lebensbild* Marianne Weber provides the only published, firsthand version we have of her husband's breakdown—a "fall" or "crash" in her words— triggered, figuratively speaking, by a patricidal quarrel, long in preparation, that took place at their home in Heidelberg on 14 June 1897. Hers is a guarded account, hedged in by discretion and pride, that only hints at the reasons for Weber's altered situation.

But the momentous episode can in fact be recovered from Weber's own hand. Having on 10 June just obliterated Karl Oldenberg and the defenders of patriarchal solidarity with a passionate "Jeremiad," rebellious youth asserted itself a second time against the founding generation, but now in the most dangerous setting and personal manner imaginable. For alone among the family's four brothers, Max interposed himself between mother and father, defending Helene Weber's rights to freedom while castigating Max Weber senior's "grotesque impertinences" and "patriarchal" demands. Accusing the father of "deceitfulness," "lies," "jealousy," "intolerance," and "egoism" (as he wrote within hours of the event), Max junior showed him the door for the last time. With a defensive declaration that he now felt "better" and "freer," the son announced his intention never to see the old patriarch again, "either now, or in future years." "I am absolutely fed up with this man," he wrote to his brother Alfred; "Henceforth, Papa doesn't exist for us

[Marianne and myself]."[1] To defend *his* honor, Max senior spent another week with his wife near Heidelberg, before departing alone on the day of their thirty-fourth wedding anniversary. In Berlin, having heard the father's side of the affair as a mediator, Alfred reported to Max that their father felt "deeply offended," a response Max dismissed as a "typical maneuver."[2] But when the father suddenly died four weeks following this exchange, on 10 August, a dismissal could no longer suffice. Death wish had become irrevocable fact.

It was Friedrich Meinecke, Weber's former Freiburg colleague, who in reviewing Marianne Weber's biography first commented on the "tragic" possibilities latent in the Weber family circle. These remarkable events and relationships suggested to him the classical, mythic dimensions of a Tantalus-like family genealogy, with the oldest son fated to be hounded by the furies of bad conscience.[3] Perhaps emboldened by successful combat elsewhere, one son took up Oedipus' staff, and the raw, unrestrained, and unapologetic ferocity of his self-insertion into the long-standing parental quarrel, combined with its shocking end, secured a catastrophic outcome.

Within a year of the Heidelberg confrontation, exhaustion and recurrent depression had driven Weber from his normal regime of work, promising not simply renewed appreciation of "the purely human side of life,"[4] as he at first naively hoped, but rather a long descent into the abyss. Was collapse inevitable? Was Weber's symbolic act necessary for his later accomplishments? Could his reflections on the "orders of life" and modern "fate" have been gained without such sacrifice? Does his fall and return follow the line of Nietzsche's thought that only "blood

1. All quoted words and phrases are from five letters Max Weber wrote to Alfred (15, 19, 23, [?] June, 13 July, NW 30/4:60−67, in Marianne's partial transcripts) concerning what he refers to on 15 June as the events of yesterday evening. In writing the biography of her husband, Marianne, who witnessed the explosion herself, chose not to quote this revealing documentation, with the exception of one unattributed and mild paraphrase (*Lebensbild*, 243; Eng. trans., 231). But her transcriptions in the Nachlass Weber allow one to correct her own published comments, as well as the inaccurate sequence of events conjured by Arthur Mitzman, *The Iron Cage: An Historical Interpretation of Max Weber* (New York: Knopf, 1970), chap. 4.

2. Letter to Alfred, 13 July 1897, NW 30/4:66−67.

3. Friedrich Meinecke, "Max Weber" (1927), in *Max Weber zum Gedächtnis*, ed. R. König and J. Winckelmann (Cologne: Westdeutscher Verlag, 1964), 143−47. These possibilities were then catalogued under battlefield headlines like "assault on the Junker hegemony" and "retreat from ascetic rationalism" in Mitzman's heavy-handed exposé, *The Iron Cage*. Guenther Roth's assessment, "Max Weber's Generational Rebellion and Maturation," in his collection with Reinhard Bendix, *Scholarship and Partisanship: Essays on Max Weber* (Berkeley: University of California Press, 1971), 6−33, aims for balance.

4. Letter to Marianne, 4 August 1898, NW 30/1:65−66; *Lebensbild*, 249; Eng. trans., 236.

and cruelty lie at the bottom of all 'good things,'"[5] or Freud's extrapolation of the patricide that lies beneath all "culture"? Who can say with any certainty? We may never know precisely what this "descent into hell" (Marianne's term) meant to Weber, or how he managed some measure of recovery. But in any case it seems likely that Meinecke's surmise is close to the truth: the second period of Weber's life and work, this "quite singular life-achievement," was snatched against all odds from the problematic inner tension between a "mighty pathos" and "rigid self-discipline."[6] Sometimes Weber was able to harness this tension for productive capacity; occasionally he was not.

Our interest is not confined to the details of the alternating pattern, however. It is directed more specifically toward Weber's objectification of his experience in a cultural science. Let us ask, then, how Weber recommenced his journey along the path to this understanding.

PRESUPPOSITIONS OF INQUIRY

When he was able to resume something approaching normal work in 1902–3, Weber first turned his attention back to the foundations of the German "historical school" of political economy exemplified in the writings of Karl Knies, his late Heidelberg mentor, and Wilhelm Roscher. The result was an ungenerous and barely readable essay, a "fragment" Weber called it, stretching over three years and still unfinished, in which he attempted to set forth with painful care "emanatist" presuppositions that had become meaningless for science. In a way, this project of recovery and criticism gave Weber an opportunity to annihilate the founders of the scientific school with which he most closely identified—"truly a form of patricide" in Hennis' judgment, a repetition in the intellect of the earlier familial episode.[7] Yet in another sense the entire unfinished exercise is simply puzzling, reading now like an obsession with murky ideas attributed to long-forgotten scholars, an impression that grows as one moves on to the other subjects of Weber's "methodological" (or better: philosophy-of-science) critiques—Eduard Meyer, Rudolf Stammler, Wilhelm Ostwald.

5. *On the Genealogy of Morals*, trans. W. Kaufmann (New York: Random House [Vintage Books], 1967), 62 (Essay II, sec. 3).

6. Meinecke, "Max Weber," 145.

7. Wilhelm Hennis, *Max Webers Fragestellung: Studien zur Biographie des Werks* (Tübingen: J. C. B. Mohr [Paul Siebeck], 1987), 161, for whom the essay on Knies was best left uncompleted, against Weber's original plan, because of its disingenuous and ill-tempered argumentation.

It seems odd that though taking pride in concealing major intellectual debts, Weber should have chosen to christen his return by devoting such concentrated study to contemporaries of the second rank. Even Weber's *Archiv* coeditors, Edgar Jaffé and Werner Sombart, complained to each other, if not to Weber directly, about these obscure pursuits:

> Naturally from Weber himself I [Jaffé] would prefer ten times more to have an essay like that on the Protestant Ethic than three logical-epistemological essays on Eduard Meyer, Stammler, etc. But the situation is such that I am pleased with any contribution from Weber and can only try quite indirectly to induce him to devote his attention to more positive rather than critical work. I'll file the "message from the people" someplace where I won't forget it; perhaps it will still come in handy.[8]

Without overt prompting, Weber did in fact increasingly shift his writing interests from negative criticism to systematic topics, even failing to complete his announced continuations of the essays on Meyer and Stammler. On the other hand, he never fully surrendered the aim to explore certain categories and logical problems of thought, as in his "Basic Outline" of 1898, the "Categories" essay of 1913, or their extension in part 1 of *Economy and Society* that drove his Munich students to distraction, although in this genre it turned out to be one of his most successful texts. Nevertheless, Weber was not completely immune to collegial criticism: Why did he undertake these endeavors?

The best answer to this question, indeed the only comprehensive answer, is suggested by Löwith's observation that Weber's entire philosophy of science, including what he dares to call the "exemplary" treatise on "Roscher and Knies," intends "the radical demolition of 'illusions'" in line with the "recognition of the questionable character not merely of modern science and culture but of our present orientation to life in general."[9] Weber is fully aware of this situation, aware of the paradox residing in his attempt "to reflect on those general presuppositions on which our scientific work is based"[10] by considering the quest for knowledge as just *one* among many possible life-orientations and

8. Jaffé replying to a "message" from Sombart, 24 April 1907, NWS 17:83–84. In a letter to Sombart of 19 June 1907, NWS 17:93–94, Jaffé had increased his preference to "a hundred times more" and suggested "discretion" vis-à-vis the hypersensitive third member of the triumvirate. The "situation" was undoubtedly both Weber's fulminations against the normal frustrations of an editorial post and the precarious psychology of his labored mode of work.

9. Karl Löwith, *Max Weber and Karl Marx*, (1932), trans. H. Fantel (London: Allen & Unwin, 1982), 34.

10. *GAW*, 1; translated by Guy Oakes as *Roscher and Knies: The Logical Problems of Historical Economics* (New York: Free Press, 1975), 53.

emerging armed only with the alarming provisional conclusion that such presuppositions are groundless and "our science" thus is without grounding in any "ultimate" sense. This is, indeed, the specifically modern predicament, the divide separating Weber's post-Nietzschean view of science and its presuppositions from, say, Marx's positivist residues.

I want to suggest that Weber had no "solution" to this predicament in the sense of a final remedy, as the predicament is embedded in our culture and thus incapable of solution or even definition from an Archimedean standpoint outside that culture. Just as one cannot hope independently to invent cultural values without courting absurdity, so one cannot expect to solve such problems without the luxury of a solipsism that is "not of this world," to use the borrowed Weberian terminology. But as a contribution to understanding our plight Weber does offer an observation about the willing and choosing human agent, a proposal for inquiry or science itself (in the broadest sense of *Wissenschaft*, or pursuit of knowledge), and, most significantly, an analysis of the larger problem of Western culture.

As for the human agent and science, Weber called for clear-eyed judgment without the solace of deceptions, myths, or illusions. This was not a thought borrowed from elsewhere; it represented his own experience, and it appears at every turn in his self-observations: "I wish to be without illusions for the rest of my life" was the formulation at one moment, or at another, "I yearn for simplicity or unpretentiousness [*Schlichtheit*] and a solid grasp of realities." [11] Whether or not he personally attained these rare aspirations, Weber certainly objectified and generalized his craving for the actually existing world, the only world in which we are placed, to a conception of the modern person and the modern possibility for knowledge. As this person, one was now released to one's *own* resources for action and knowledge by a culture incapable of asserting objectively valid substantive meaning. "Objectivity" was attached to the reconstruction of "the empirically given" on the basis of "evaluative ideas [*Wertideen*]," and not to empirical things-in-themselves, which could never demonstrate the validity of such ideas. This had to be so, Weber maintained, because on the one side empirical "life in its irrational actuality and its store of *possible* meanings is inexhaustible," while on the other "the *concrete* configuration of relevance to values [*Wertbeziehung*] remains in flux, ever subject to change

---

11. Letters to his sister Lili, probably December 1915, NW 30/14:26–27; and to Hans Ehrenberg, 10 April 1919, NW 30/8:119–20.

in the dim future of human culture." The meaning of these reconstructions and of the evaluations that "anchor our existence [*Dasein*]" was now ours to create.[12] Weber's "science of reality," his *Wirklichkeitswissenschaft* with its categories, "ideal types," and value postulates, thus became the necessary counterpart to any longing for the actual, a will to knowledge for those "without illusions," snatched from the "ever changing finite segment of the vast chaotic stream of events, which flows away through time." [13]

The position Weber affirms is apparent even in the most prosaic comments. Consider, for example, one of his "positive" defenses of "Some Categories of Interpretive Sociology":

> "*Verstehende* sociology"—not understandable? . . . It is the attempt to *set aside* everything "organicist," Stammler-like, extra-empirical, valid according to *norms*, and to conceive the "sociological theory of the state [*Staatslehre*]" as the theory of purely empirical, typical *human actions*—in my view the only *way* to do it—while the individual *categories* are a question of appropriateness [*Zweckmässigkeitsfrage*].[14]

As an initial proposal for the meaning Weber attached to *verstehende Soziologie* and "empiricism" generally, it should be read as a critique of the search for "natural" entities and teleologies in favor of an orientation toward subjectively meaningful action. It was an orientation that allowed Weber to speak abstractly of the modern "state," in addition to its formal characteristics, as nothing more than a probability of action.[15] In addition, for this orientation we should not miss the subordination of the entirely formal and typical to purposes or ends of investi-

12. The important summation on the penultimate page of "Die 'Objektivität' sozialwissenschaftlicher und sozialpolitischer Erkenntnis" (literally, "The 'Objectivity' of Social-scientific and Sociopolitical Knowledge" [1904]), in *GAW*, 213; S&F, 111. Weber considered this major statement sufficiently important to cite its authority on a number of later occasions. Weber nearly always placed "objectivity" in quotation marks, as if to draw attention to the *hiatus irrationalis* separating idea from actuality. Were it not for the awkward locution, one should always speak of "that which we choose to call objectivity."
13. Ibid., *GAW*, 214; S&F, 111.
14. A reply to Hermann Kantorowicz, 29 December 1913, NW 30/11:49, who had evidently written Weber with questions about the "Categories" essay published in *Logos*, now reprinted in *GAW*, 427–74, and entitled "Über einige Kategorien der verstehenden Soziologie."
15. *WuG*, 40; *EaS*, 56; letter to Robert Liefmann, 9 March 1920, NW 30/8:76–80, where he writes: "Sociologically considered, the state is nothing more than the probability [*Chance*] that specific kinds of actions will take place, actions of particular individual persons. Otherwise it is nothing at all. I have written and taught this for years. What is 'subjective' about this is that action is oriented toward particular ideas or conceptions [*Vorstellungen*]. What is 'objective' is that we, the observers, judge the probability that such action will occur when oriented toward these particular conceptions. If it fails to occur, then the 'state' ceases to exist."

gation, whose specification is reserved for the inquiring mind. Not the general "nature of things," but rather the nature of a particular questioning determines a world. Moreover, even to utter this statement is to place oneself squarely within the dilemma of modern culture, which has itself authenticated such a statement.

Weber's reemergence into the world of scholarship and the "philosophy of science" thus led him back to the problems he had touched on previously in the first analysis of capitalist development and the general inquiry into "the fate imposed upon us." His investigations and the questions I want to raise about them are both essentially an expression of the stresses and strivings of a modern, post-Nietzschean experience that he shared, observed, and criticized. Some aspects of Weber's contribution are familiar, but much of the reference, development, inner logic, and pattern of his thought that I shall emphasize has remained concealed. That pattern unfolds beginning with an assessment of what modern, rationalist, Western culture has become, which is in turn so integrally connected with the meaning, consequences, and discontents of modernity.

THE AGE OF SUBJECTIVIST CULTURE

Can one speak of a "problem" of modern culture? And if so, what is that problem? What is its "political" content, or relation to politics? There may be countless ways of approaching such questions to make them intelligible, but for my purposes two appear especially fruitful. In the first place, the critique of emergent modern culture in its various guises (including the materialist culture of capitalism) becomes a dominant theme of Western thought from Kierkegaard and Marx, through Nietzsche, Tolstoy, and Freud, to contemporaries as diverse as Bell, Habermas, and Lyotard.[16] The theme appears in different forms: as a political revolt against the "modern"; a break with the liberal historicist outlook and moral order; a flight from politics into a "sphere" of culture, such as the aesthetic or the erotic, and sometimes back again to a "new" politics; an exercise in transcending the historically given via the return to religious belief, the enchantment of utopian vision, or the res-

16. Daniel Bell, *The Cultural Contradictions of Capitalism* (New York: Basic Books, 1976); Jürgen Habermas, *The Philosophical Discourse of Modernity: Twelve Lectures*, trans. F. Lawrence (Cambridge: MIT Press, 1987); and Jean-François Lyotard, *The Postmodern Condition: A Report on Knowledge*, trans. G. Bennington and B. Massumi (Minneapolis: University of Minnesota Press, 1984).

toration of "reason" in the dialectic of enlightenment; or as a reflection on what Freud and Nietzsche referred to respectively as humanity's "technique for fending off suffering" and asceticism's use of "life *against* life."[17] But regardless of its specific statement, the central problem appears to be the same in every case: a sense that unified experience lies beyond the grasp of the modern self and that malaise and self-conscious guilt have become inextricably intertwined with "culture." It is within *this* general problem and movement of thought that Weber's own reflections are to be located.

A second, more proximate and specific setting for the problem is found in Weber's own time in the specifically urban, aesthetic, ahistorical, and amoral *Gefühlskultur* out of which grew a special sensitivity to human feelings, psychological truths, the authenticity of emotion, and the public power of "personality" and personal style—all closely connected in the flowering of a "late romanticism." This culture encouraged such minute scrutiny of the subjective self as to propagate two dialectically connected results: "Today, two things seem to be modern," Hugo von Hofmannsthal observed in the nineties: "the analysis of life and the flight from life." Thus, he continued,

> One practices anatomy on the inner life of one's mind, or one dreams. Reflection or fantasy, mirror image or dream image. Old furniture is modern, and so are recent neuroses. . . . Paul Bourget is modern, and Buddha; splitting atoms and playing ball games with the cosmos. Modern is the dissection of a mood, a sigh, a scruple; and modern is the instinctive, almost somnambulistic surrender to every revelation of beauty, to a harmony of colors, to a glittering metaphor, to a wondrous allegory.[18]

In the name of subjectivist validation the old, the ancient, the worn-out could also be rejuvenated as a genuine artifact of modern culture. Among Weber's most perspicacious and cleverly "modern" friends, surely Simmel best understood and developed these key ideas, thinking of modernity's essence as a preoccupation with the "inner self" and the experience of decentering, dissolution, and surrender to the power of inwardness. The question for him then became, what forms of expression would follow from this "inward turn," both toward "life" and away from it, that had gathered such speed since Nietzsche?

17. Sigmund Freud, *Civilization and Its Discontents*, trans. J. Strachey (New York: Norton, 1961), 26; Friedrich Nietzsche, *On the Genealogy of Morals*, trans. W. Kaufmann (New York: Random House [Vintage Books], 1967), 120 (III, 13).
18. From an 1893 article on Gabriele D'Annunzio, quoted in *Modernism 1890–1930*, ed. M. Bradbury and J. McFarlane (New York: Penguin, 1976), 71.

At the first meeting of the German Sociological Society, Weber took up precisely this question. Replying to Sombart's speech on "Technology [*Technik*] and Culture," he began by noting that the present-day world is governed by a "technical" development that goes hand in hand with capitalist development, thus suggesting the idea that *Technik* is the "leading element in our cultural development." In this circumstance the question became whether modern "technique," or "technology," as experienced, for example, in the modern metropolis, could in any way affect "formal-aesthetic values" in such different areas as poetry, music, painting, architecture, and even science. Weber had no doubt that it could, citing "the wild dance of impressions of sound and color, the impressions that have an effect on sexual fantasies, and the experience of variations in the constitution of the soul . . . [and] all sorts of apparently inexhaustible possibilities for the conduct of life and for pleasure" characterizing the modern city. Because the self encounters such possibilities, culture now emerges as either "protest" or "adaptation," as an attempt to find "specific means of escape from this reality" through "the highest aesthetic abstractions, deepest dream-states, or most intensive kinds of intoxication," or as an effort to invent "defenses against this reality's fantastic, intoxicating rhythms." In artistic fields like music, painting, and poetry, Weber suggests, the cultural situation conditions the "search for a new unity beyond the old, fixed elements of form."[19] In short, this culture ushers in the reign of assertive subjectivity and "inwardness," or "interiority" (*Innerlichkeit*), with all their hidden and explosive potentialities for both subversion and originality.

The range of possibilities for Weber and his contemporaries can thus be most succinctly conceptualized, as suggested previously, by the revolt of a new aestheticism against the liberal historicist culture of "progress." It would be mistaken to suggest that *every* aspect of this revolt was reflected in Weber's writings. But the theme that emerges from the cultural crisis does in fact bring us into Weber's intellectual milieu, even

19. For these passages see Weber's response to Sombart's speech, "Technik und Kultur," in *Verhandlungen des ersten Deutschen Soziologentages* (Tübingen: J. C. B. Mohr [Paul Siebeck], 1911), 98–100; reprinted in *GASS*, 453–55. In Weber's well-known essay on "Value-Freedom," "Der Sinn der 'Wertfreiheit' der soziologischen und ökonomischen Wissenschaften," first presented at the Verein für Sozialpolitik in 1914, the same perspective informs his unusual analysis of the concept of "progress" used in discussions of the sphere of subjective "feeling" (*Gefühlssphäre*), or of architecture, music, painting, and the intellectual disciplines: *GAW*, 518–26; *S&F*, 27–35; and the original version, "Gutachten zur Werturteilsdiskussion im Ausschuss des Vereins für Sozialpolitik," in Eduard Baumgarten, *Max Weber: Werk und Person* (Tübingen: Mohr, 1964), 127–29.

to the heart of his most famous Viennese declaration in 1909, whose "modernist" content is unmistakable:

> We know of no scientifically demonstrable ideals. To be sure, our labors are now rendered more difficult, since we must create our ideals from within our chests in the very age of subjectivist culture. But we must not and cannot promise a fool's paradise and an easy street, neither in the here and now nor in the beyond, neither in thought nor in action, and it is the stigma of our human dignity that the peace of our souls cannot be as great as the peace of one who dreams of such a paradise.[20]

Since Weber had just seen a performance of *Faust* in the Burgtheater, one is tempted to read his soliloquy as a fin de siècle reflection on Goethe's creation, one that points toward the intensified struggle within ourselves (our "souls") occasioned by the rootless "age of subjectivist culture." The most serious modern motifs are accentuated: self-conscious creation of meaning, the psychological stigmata of an awareness of "being modern," the explosion of subjectivity, the self-limitation of post-Enlightenment science, the struggle among competing "gods," and our feeble efforts to choose among them with dignity under conditions in which the "will to truth" has become a *problem*.

Weber developed these ideas in remarks scattered throughout his major works, typified by those well-known, arresting passages in the essays on "objectivity" and "value-freedom" concerned with the "fate of an epoch of culture" that has "tasted the fruit of the tree of knowledge." As in the Viennese declaration, this fate is

> to have to know that we cannot read the *meaning* of the world in the results of its investigation, no matter how perfect, but must instead be in a position to create that meaning ourselves; that 'Weltanschauungen' can never be the product of advancing empirical knowledge; and that therefore the highest ideals, which move us most powerfully, are worked out for all time only in struggle with other ideals, which are just as sacred as ours are to us.[21]

It would be difficult to imagine more confessional statements that are simultaneously cultural analyses, quintessentially modernist in tone, conditioned by the desire of "knowing," yet bound together by a resolve to preserve the paradoxes they uncover. But these are admittedly dense

20. From Weber's remarks in the debate on "productivity," *Verhandlungen des Vereins für Sozialpolitik*, in *SVSP* 132 (1910): 585; *GASS*, 420. In *Max Weber's Vision of History: Ethics and Methods* (Berkeley: University of California Press, 1979), Guenther Roth and Wolfgang Schluchter adopt, without comment, an abbreviated version of this statement as their frontispiece motto.
21. *GAW*, 154, 507; *S&F*, 57, 18.

passages whose meaning will become clearer as the discussion unfolds. They illustrate the central question emerging from an encounter with modern culture: What stance is one prepared to take and defend vis-à-vis the new aesthetic of a culture of "sensation" and "experience"? It is this question that leads to the deeper levels of Weber's work.

WEBER'S SCIENCE OF CULTURE

As a scholar who had taken up the discipline of political economy, but who was still concerned with the subject matter of the human sciences generally, Weber chose as the starting point for his mature reflections the view that the fields of inquiry within such a domain were "sciences" in two closely related senses: they were (to use his terminology) *Wirklichkeitswissenschaften*, or literally "sciences of actuality," and *Kulturwissenschaften*, or "sciences of culture."

Undoubtedly the best-known single comment setting forth these basic claims appears in the 1904 "Objectivity" essay, presented as a statement of editorial policy for the *Archiv*, but one that is more importantly a specification of the presuppositions for inquiry in the human sciences. (The entire essay is, in fact, concerned with a critique of the untenable notion of a "science without presuppositions.") Unfortunately, Weber's original statement is distorted in the standard English translation, which ought to read:

> The social science that *we* want to promote is a *science of actuality*. We want to understand the surrounding reality of life in which we are placed *in its uniqueness*—that is, on the one hand the relationship and cultural *significance* of its individual appearance in its present configuration, and on the other hand the basis of its being historically so and not having become otherwise.[22]

Stated negatively, Weber wanted in this statement, whose subject is the "actuality" or "reality" of life, to suggest that a science of the social was not merely constructed out of general, abstract, purely logical regularities and law-like propositions. Unlike a "science of laws," which was its opposite, this science sought instead to comprehend the "peculiarity" or "uniqueness" of the historically given world, a uniqueness conceived in terms of (a) contemporary *cultural* meanings and (b) *historical* reasons that could be advanced for the presence of just this cultural "re-

22. *GAW*, 170–71; S&F, 72; cf. *GAW*, 237; S&F, 135.

ality" and not some other. The movement in thought in these sentences is absolutely crucial to understanding Weber's reasoning: science of the "actual," or "real," the "uniqueness" of a form of life, cultural meaning, and historical explanation are necessarily connected in the sense that the possibility of realizing each element is dependent on the presence of all the others.

That the conception of a science of the "actually existing" could not be separated from an attempt to establish specific cultural content was underlined even more emphatically in the little-known "Preface" also written by Weber (though unsigned) on assumption of coeditorship of the *Archiv* with Sombart and Jaffé. Contrasting the journal to other social science periodicals, Weber alluded to its distinctive contribution from 1888 to 1904 under its founding editor, the socialist Heinrich Braun, noting that

> the step which distinguished the "Archiv" from its predecessors was that it placed the problems identified under the heading "the question of labor" [*Arbeiterfrage*] in the most general context, that it grasped the "question of labor" in its *cultural significance* as the outwardly most clearly visible expression of a much larger complex of phenomena: the fundamental process of transformation experienced by our economic life and thus by our cultural existence as a whole through the advance of capitalism.[23]

And the "new direction" announced by Weber and his colleagues, starting from the ubiquitous labor question, was even more firmly anchored in the cultural problematic:

> Above all, today the research domain of the "Archiv" must be fundamentally expanded, something that until now happened only sporadically and from case to case. Our journal will have to consider historical and theoretical knowledge of the *general cultural significance of capitalist development* as the scientific problem whose understanding it serves.[24]

One cannot imagine a more concise and unambiguous statement of the specific direction charted by this new science of the "actual" as a "science of culture." The posing of familiar questions in relation to "cultural significance" and "cultural existence" gave this form of knowledge its basic claim to preeminence.

But what does a *Kulturwissenschaft*, a science of culture, presuppose? This was really the question that guided Weber's thinking and encouraged him to unleash a barrage of propositions, scattered espe-

23. "Geleitwort," *Archiv* 19 (1904): i–ii.
24. Ibid., v.

cially through "'Objectivity' in Social Science and Social Policy," which can in the interest of comprehensiveness be reinterpreted as a logical series:

First: Culture is preeminently a sphere of disagreement, value-conflict, and competing Weltanschauungen. At stake are "the regulative standards of judgment themselves . . . because the problem extends into the domain of general *cultural* questions." The more general the problem or "the more far-reaching its cultural significance," the more intensive and extensive the conflict. Culture is ruled by a thoroughgoing perspectivism. Yet paradoxically there can be no "objective" analysis of culture without such perspectivism, without "one-sided points of view." Nor can the pursuit of knowledge solve this struggle among different ideals, for it is itself a part of that struggle.[25]

Second: The very concept of culture is a "value-concept" (*Wertbegriff*), therefore its meaning and content are open to interpretation. In other words, that which is historically given becomes "culture" because we assign significance (*Bedeutung*) to a finite part of it, not because of its supposedly valid content, inherent meaningfulness, or ontological status. The assigning of significance constitutes "the intellectual ordering of the empirically given" out of the "meaningless infinity of the world process."[26] Culture is constructed on the basis of our ideas regarding significance.

Third: In social life culture represents that which is particular, unique, and individual—a level of concreteness and particularity promoted and accentuated by employing the "ideal type," whose major purpose is "to bring sharply into consciousness *not* that which is generic, but conversely the *individuality* of cultural phenomena."[27] The function of ideal-typical comparison is to achieve a consciousness of difference.

Fourth: Yet scientific knowledge, of whatever kind, is produced by culture itself and thus represents a *possible* rather than a natural, necessary, or definitive way of depicting the world: clearly, "belief in the value of scientific truth is a product of specific cultures and is not given in nature."[28] Furthermore, the concepts of a science are useful relative

25. *GAW*, 153, 170, 181; S&F, 56, 72, 81; all the quotations in these paragraphs are drawn from Weber's "Objectivity" essay, "Die 'Objektivität' sozialwissenschaftlicher und sozialpolitischer Erkenntnis."

26. *GAW*, 156, 175, 180; S&F, 59, 76, 81.

27. *GAW*, 202; S&F, 101.

28. *GAW*, 213; S&F, 110.

to problems, and problems in turn depend on culture and are altered
with the inevitable movement of culture. In Weber's imagery, "There
comes a moment when the atmosphere changes. . . . The light of the
great cultural problems moves on"; and then, quoting Goethe, "The god
sinks down, I seem forsaken; / But I feel new unrest awaken / And hurry
onward to drink his eternal light, / The day before me, and the night
behind, / The heavens above me, and the waves below." [29]

Fifth: The ultimate goal of a *Kulturwissenschaft* is knowledge of "reality in its cultural significance," and cultural significance can be established only by evaluative ideas, not by laws or empirical regularities.
But what Weber calls the "transcendental presupposition" of cultural
science is not that we find culture "valuable." It is instead that we are
"cultural beings," or *Kulturmenschen*, endowed with consciousness—
that is, with the capacity to give the world meaning. [30]

Sixth: The attempt to answer the nonempirical question, "What is
the *meaning* of culture?" belongs to science and is one of the most challenging and stimulating questions for cultural life, of which science in
the modern age is a major part. [31] This question is, in its essence, reflexively related to the activity of science as an aspect, perhaps even *the*
leading aspect, of the life of modern culture.

Each of these points not only bears on the "science of culture" as a
science of "what is," but also describes the metatheoretical foundations
of Weber's conception of knowledge. Together they show that he proposed a special conception of the cultural problem, avoiding the usual
terminology of a psychology of the modern, sociology of culture, or
Kulturkritik. Substantively, Weber favored a particular formulation of
the central question for culture: namely, how is it possible that only in
the West a certain combination or "concatenation [*Verkettung*] of circumstances" has produced "cultural phenomena" that "lie in a line of
development having *universal* significance and validity?" [32] This statement from the very first paragraph of the essays in the "sociology of
religion," penned by Weber in 1920 as a "son of the modern European
cultural world," is at once a retrospective summation and an invitation

29. *Faust*, part I, act I, sc. 4, lines 1084–88; *GAW*, 214, also 152, 207; S&F, 55,
105, 112.
30. *GAW*, 174, 176, 180; S&F, 75, 77, 80–81.
31. *GAW*, 156; S&F, 59.
32. "Vorbemerkung," *GARS* 1:1; *PE*, 13; Weber does speak of validity (*Gültigkeit*)
in this passage, not "value," as in Parsons' translation. As a causal term *Verkettung* conveys the sense of linking or chaining together in a series, hence a "concatenation of
circumstances."

for future thinkers, a bringing together of the "universal-historical problems" of culture and a call for inquiry into their significance for the conduct of life.

We must ask what specific questions or *particular* contents lie concealed in Weber's monumental inquiry into the ideal and material complex called culture. Stated somewhat differently, what is the "uniqueness" of Weber's own culture? What precisely is the thinking that stands under the sign of this Weberian science of culture?

THE MOST FATEFUL FORCE IN OUR MODERN LIFE

The answer to these questions that is closest to the inner dynamic of Weber's thought commences from the "fact" of modern capitalism, and it moves toward an interpretation of what I shall call the cultural discontents of modernity. This unfolding pattern of interpretation and argumentation takes numerous complex forms and directions. In every case, however, as Weber says, "it is a question of the specific and peculiar 'rationalism' of Western culture"[33] and the responses to it. Paradoxically, this "rationalism" is emphatically not necessarily "rational," but is persistently called into question by variations on the formula, with apologies to Hegel: what is rational is not actual, and what is actual is irrational.

Weber's first analysis of the "general cultural significance of capitalist development" is found, as I have suggested, like numerous aspects of his thought, in embryonic form in the 1890s studies of the East Elbian territories' agrarian organization of labor relations. In the context of the subsequent identification of a cultural problematic, what is important to notice about these studies is their invocation of a traditionalist world collapsing under the onslaught of new capitalist productive forces; they tell the story of fin-de-siècle sociocultural and *therefore* political dislocation. The process of capitalist rationalization not only puts an end to the multifaceted, historically articulated relations of social stratification in the East, it also creates a new propertyless class of "formally free" labor *and* dissolves the centers of authority that had previously served as carriers of culture. A change of such magnitude will reverberate throughout the social and political order, Weber maintains. But his conclusion in the early studies of the agrarian world leaves un-

---

33. *GARS* 1:11; *PE*, 26.

defined the precise character of the culture that might emerge through this "irreversible" process.

That "definition" of the cultural significance of capitalism first appears as a cornerstone to Weber's developing argument most clearly and powerfully in the essays of 1905–6—that is, in the second part of *The Protestant Ethic and the Spirit of Capitalism*, completed after his return from America, and in the essays on Russia. The central passages are well known, although Weber's meaning is obscured by the standard translation (which I have therefore altered):

> The Puritan *wanted* to work in a vocation [*wollte Berufsmensch sein*]; we *must* do so. For when asceticism was carried out of monastic cells into vocational life and began to dominate inner-worldly morality, it helped to build the tremendous cosmos of the modern economic order. This order is now bound to the technical and economic presuppositions of mechanical, machinelike production, which today determines with irresistible force the lifestyle [*Lebensstil*] of all individuals born into this mechanism, *not* only those directly engaged in economic enterprise, and perhaps will determine it until the last ton of fossil coal is burned. In Baxter's view the care for external goods should only lie on the shoulders of the saint like "a light cloak, which can be thrown aside at any moment." But fate [*Verhängnis*] decreed that the cloak should become an iron cage.[34]

The infamous "iron cage," perhaps Weber's most telling Epimethean metaphor, is formed out of the objectification of material culture and its "inexorable power," but also out of the projection of asceticism into the external world of production, labor, and, above all, "style of life" in the most extended sense conceivable. For the modern individual, action and existence are regimented by the necessities of *vocational* activity, now stripped of its sustaining structures of meaning. We are all, as it were, conscripted as unconsenting participants in a universalized vocational culture, our horizons limited to the rationalized, endless, and inwardly meaningless certainties of "vocational humanity" (*Berufsmenschentum*). To attempt to "advance" *this* culture from the standpoint of its own assumptions, as a "cultural being" (*Kulturmensch*), is only to advance farther along the path of modern discontents. The ethos of inner-worldly asceticism, the "Protestant ethic," is overcome not by its moral opponents, but by the material powers of capitalist development. This ethos creates a world that then turns against its creator and destroys it. So for Weber, as for Nietzsche, asceticism is not only our

34. *GARS* 1:203; *PE*, 181.

"fate" but our "fatality."[35] The consequences of its release into the world leave us with the demand of calling forth our own ideals from within ourselves, of transvaluing our values. In this view anything else is weakness.

In the acerbic debates with the two economic historians H. Karl Fischer and Felix Rachfahl over what he really intended to say in *The Protestant Ethic and the Spirit of Capitalism*, Weber was adamant and precise about his meaning. His questions had to do with "the analysis of the development of an ethical 'style of life'" that was "spiritually 'adequate'" for the formation of *modern* capitalism, achieving a remarkable and enduring "victory in the 'souls' of human beings."[36] This style of life embodied an ethos of vocation, of systematically disciplined inner-worldly accomplishment capable of remaking an entire "world"— the world of bourgeois society. Furthermore, the ethos had in fact extended beyond the point of local origin in ascetic Protestantism to acquire "universal" significance for the cultural history of a humanity driven to vocational specialization. "My arguments," Weber insisted, "were *explicitly and intentionally limited* to the theme of "the development of '*Berufsmenschentum*' in its significance as a component of the capitalist 'spirit'. I can't help it if careless readers think it is all right to ignore this."[37]

But the vocational ethos has now been set adrift from its spiritual moorings, or, in Weber's metaphor, it "prowls about in our lives like the ghost of dead religious beliefs," vanquished by the power of a material civilization of large-scale production and voracious consumption resting on merely "mechanical foundations." The individual's attempt

35. *Verhängnis* carries this crucial double meaning, as in Nietzsche's use of the term in *The Gay Science*, trans. W. Kaufmann (New York: Random House [Vintage Books], 1974), bk. 5, sec. 371, and in the discussion of asceticism as "our fate," "fatality" or "calamity" in *The Genealogy of Morals* (e.g., I, 11; III, 14), a text Weber knew thoroughly. See the comments in Alexander Nehamas, *Nietzsche: Life as Literature* (Cambridge: Harvard University Press, 1985), 125, and the provocative remarks on these ideas in Hennis, *Max Webers Fragestellung*, chap. 4.

36. From "Bemerkungen zu der vorstehenden 'Replik'" (1908) and "Antikritisches Schlusswort zum 'Geist des Kapitalismus'" (1910), both published in the *Archiv* and reprinted in *Die protestantische Ethik II: Kritiken und Antikritiken*, ed. Johannes Winckelmann (Munich: Siebenstern, 1968), 55, 286. Unfortunately, the partial translation by Wallace M. Davis, "Anticritical Last Word on *The Spirit of Capitalism*," *American Journal of Sociology* 83 (1978): 1110–30, does not include the entire first half of Weber's essay, in which these remarks appear.

37. "Antikritisches Schlusswort," 173. One might add that Fischer and Rachfahl were only the first in a long line of readers imputing contrary intentions to Weber's work.

to "justify" life-activity is either surrendered completely or (in what amounts to the same thing) reduced to the compulsions of "mundane passion"—the pursuit of pleasure, entertainment, self-gratification, or (in a word) money. In these respects America became overwhelmingly important for Weber, because its social order revealed the capitalist spirit's "highest freedom and emancipation [*Entfesselung*]," today, of course, stripped of any "religious or ethical meaning" and instead acquiring the "character of sport."[38] America stood as the great cultural experiment for this new humanity of vocational specialization; alternatively, it symbolized an unbound Prometheus bent on acting out "such matters in their most massive and original shape," perhaps with a fate like that of humankind's immortal benefactor. At the very least, one observed in America the potential for the "cultural contradictions" attending capitalism's life-history to be driven to their highest levels.[39]

It is the problem of the orientation toward life under modern conditions, so characteristic of Weber's interpretation of the deepest meaning of capitalism for culture, that also informs the essays on Russia and reveals their relation to his reflections on America. For historical and cultural reasons the Russian case revealed in particularly strong form the clash occurring everywhere between capitalist rationalism as an "economic inevitability" and the cultural values firmly rooted in premodern and religiously inspired traditions—in America the values of "democratic individualism," in Russia the communal and in a quite different sense "egalitarian" norms of the mir. These traditions had radically different points of reference, to be sure: in America what Weber called the "democratic traditions handed down by Puritanism" could be traced to the legacy of antiauthoritarian doctrines entrenched in ascetic Protestantism, whereas in Russia the quite different notion of democratic *Gemeinschaft* found roots in the "mystical" form of reli-

38. *GARS* 1:204; *PE*, 182; *GAW*, 605; G&M, 149; *Entfesselung* conveys the sense of a violent and destructive unleashing (literally, "de-binding"). Compare the similar general viewpoint in Thorstein Veblen, *The Theory of Business Enterprise* (New York: Scribner's, 1904), esp. chap. 9 ("The Cultural Incidence of the Machine Process"), a book Weber greatly admired.
39. For an extension of the Weberian ideas, see Bell, *Cultural Contradictions of Capitalism*, esp. 21–22, 83–84, where it is argued that modern capitalism has annihilated its self-limiting, moral "transcendental tie" or "legitimacy," while substituting "hedonism" as a justification and advancing "functional rationality"—Weber's concept of *Zweckrationalität*—as its sole cognitive standard; and at the same time "modernist culture" has deliberately subverted bourgeois society and championed modes of expression opposed to functional rationality. For Bell the "cultural contradictions of capitalism" are constituted minimally by the interplay among these elements.

gious orthodoxy. For Weber both came increasingly under attack as they were challenged by the dynamic of rationalization. In one passage he notes that

> those who live in constant anxiety lest there might in the future be *too much* "democracy" and "individualism" in the world, and too little "authority," "aristocracy" and "respect for office" or the like, may take heart; all too much care has been taken to make sure that the trees of democratic individualism do not grow to the skies. . . . It is utterly ridiculous to suppose that it is an "inevitable" feature of our economic development under present-day advanced capitalism, as it has now been imported into Russia and as it exists in America, that it should have an elective affinity with "democracy" or indeed with "freedom" (in *any* sense of that word), when the only question to be asked is: how are all these things, in general and in the long term, *possible* where it prevails? [40]

In Weber's view no one can be exempted from this final question: "Everywhere the cage for the new serfdom is ready" and every "developmental tendency" points to its perfection and permanence.

However, can the question Weber poses—the most political expression of the cultural dilemma—in principle be answered? For the moment let us say only that in Weber's view an adequate and, above all, honest answer requires in his phrase "swimming against the stream of material developments." It can have nothing to do with obediently following the course determined by the inexorable flow of "historical laws."

Weber's analysis of capitalism thus reaches its apogee in invoking the imagery of the "iron cage." But as a cultural analysis, a search for the significance of a unique process, it does not end there. Modernity is characterized not just by a kind of petrifaction and homogenization of external conditions of life, but in addition by inescapable conflict among the very contents of different value-spheres, life-orders, and life-powers (in Weber's terminology the *Wertsphären*, *Lebensordnungen*, and *Lebensmächte*) with their autonomous and internally coherent "lawfulness" (*Eigengesetzlichkeit*) that recurs at critical junctures throughout Weber's work. Not only are different value-spheres, such as the political and the ethical, or the ethical and the aesthetic, *not* identical, it is also the case that *within* a sphere of value (e.g., the ethics of personal conduct) a system of uniform rules, say, of a Kantian type, *cannot* be found that will "solve" once and for all the problems of ac-

40. "Zur Lage der bürgerlichen Demokratie in Russland," *Archiv* 22 (1906): 347; partially translated in *Selections*, 282.

tion and choice. Instead, "ultimately everywhere and always it is really a question not only of alternatives between values, but of an irreconcilable death-struggle like that between 'god' and the 'devil.' Between these there are no relativizations or compromises." [41] If the first theme— the cultural significance of capitalist development—is intertwined with Marx's problematic, then this second one—the "struggle among the gods"—is woven from materials discoverable in Nietzsche. If the implications of the first line of thought are external and political, then the implications of the second are internal and ethical; the latter touch the conduct of life itself.

It is interesting to note, furthermore, that what can be said about "ethics" can also be said about "modern culture": that is, it too is not exempted from Weber's line of reasoning, but rather becomes only a part of the "deadly struggle." This is why, according to Weber, "culture" is for the person who derives identity and life-meaning from it alone, the "cultural being" who risks treating culture as a *vocation*, never in actuality a source of personal "salvation." It must instead be associated inevitably with "guilt" or, specifically in the case of aesthetic culture, with "the persistent presence of conscience in the temple of Narcissus." [42]

The cultural significance of capitalist development thus finds final expression in the great tensions and conflicts—in a word, the discontents—of modern life. Having perceived this outcome, Weber appears on balance committed to a twofold response. On the one hand, adopting a skeptical and critical perspective, he is prepared to consider certain attempts from *within* the problematic of the culture of modernity to overcome or escape that very problematic, although for Weber it is undeniably true that all these attempts are paradoxical and questionable, whether or not they are judged to be "authentic." But on the other hand, Weber does himself draw a conclusion for the individual who stands face-to-face with such a culture, arguing in the last analysis "that every single important action and finally life as a whole . . . signifies a chain of ultimate decisions, through which the soul, as in Plato, *chooses* its own fate—that is, the meaning of its doing and being." [43] This disguised reference to the *Phaedrus* demarcates a realm of existential

41. "Der Sinn der 'Wertfreiheit,' " *GAW*, 507; S&F, 17–18.

42. Carl E. Schorske, *Fin-de-siècle Vienna: Politics and Culture* (New York: Random House [Vintage Books], 1981), 10.

43. "Der Sinn der 'Wertfreiheit,' " *GAW*, 507–8; S&F, 18.

choice, of Weberian authenticity. But the meaning and combination of both responses—the search for alternatives to the "iron cage" and the search for "the daemon who holds the fibers" of one's life[44]—are far from self-evident. How can they be understood in relation to the cultural problem that has now emerged out of the analysis of capitalism?

THE STRUGGLE OF THE GODS

The answer to the question just posed is found, I would like to suggest, at the very center of Weber's thinking in the section of *Economy and Society* on "Religious Ethics and the 'World'" and especially in the "Zwischenbetrachtung," or as it is known in English translation, "Religious Rejections of the World and Their Directions," first published in 1915 and then appended to the very end of the first volume of the *Sociology of Religion*. In theme and problem the leap from the essays of 1905–6 to these texts written after 1909 is deceptively short, for it is in the latter that Weber begins to confront the most serious responses to the threatening constraints of the "iron cage." According to Weber's notation and to Lukács' citation of the "enormous impression" it left with him,[45] at least portions of the "Intermediate Reflection" were read to Weber's Heidelberg circle before World War I and almost certainly in 1913. Marianne Weber's account of the episodes suggests that Weber intended his text partially as a reply to Lukács' and others' "eschatological hopes" for "salvation from the world" through creation of a new "socialist society founded upon an ethic of brotherliness."[46] This context announces Weber's principal intention in the "Reflection"— namely, to provide a commentary on the relentless struggles waged by those dwelling within the different life-orders and value-spheres in their attempts to cope with the historically given "world" through adaptation, rationalization, manipulation, escape. Although other aspects of the text can be deciphered, such as the influential typology of asceticism and mysticism or the implicit schema for understanding action orientations, they are subordinate in importance to the great cultural theme— the enormous tensions among the various orders of life in confronting

44. "Wissenschaft als Beruf," *GAW*, 613; G&M, 156.
45. *GARS* 1:237; letter of Lukács to Weber, mid-December 1915, in *Georg Lukács: Selected Correspondence, 1902–1920*, ed. and trans. Judith Marcus and Zoltán Tar (New York: Columbia University Press, 1986), 253.
46. *Lebensbild*, 474; Eng. trans., 466.

"the fate of our times," the search for replies and routes of escape from within culture—that builds the groundwork for Weber's entire inquiry.[47]

The "Reflection" contains not only the basic elements of a comprehensive analysis, parts of which surface elsewhere in Weber's later essays (especially the second halves of "Science as a Vocation" and "Politics as a Vocation"), of the "internal and lawful autonomy" of the familial, religious, economic, political, aesthetic, erotic, and intellectual (scientific) life-orders or spheres of life-activity and value, but it also contains the rudiments of Weber's own evaluation of each in relation to the problem of culture—modern culture in particular. In Weber's terminology, "religious" rejections of the world are characterized in terms of an "ethic of brotherliness" (*Brüderlichkeitsethik*), which is a species of an absolutist ethic of pure intentions, convictions, or "ultimate ends" (*Gesinnungsethik*). Although the ambiguous category "ethics" cannot in itself be a sphere of value with its own "lawful autonomy," Weber's entire treatment of the religious sphere of action and valuation must be interpreted as suggesting there are distinctively "absolutist ethical" paths, sharing an affinity with the ascetic religious life, that some choose to follow as a way of counteracting the dilemmas of living in this world. With respect to action claiming political standing, notably syndicalism and some variants of socialism belong here for Weber: they master the demands of inner-worldly existence by imaginatively replacing the present life-world with another world and, above all, by claiming to discipline the *self*. They represent what are in themselves apolitical ethical positions, thrust into the political realm and thus "political" in their effects, but advanced with the aim of transforming that very realm, of compelling it to be "moral."

While the sphere of absolutist ethics is thus fundamental, it is far from exhaustive; there are alternative responses to the "iron cage" as well, especially in the aesthetic, erotic, and intellectualist value-spheres. The first two, which above all others Weber treats "developmentally," tend increasingly as they become more differentiated to be absorbed into the escapist "culture of feeling" of psychological reflection, pure experience, and "inwardness." Thus, in Weber's idiom, "Art takes over the function of an inner-worldly salvation," music becomes "the most 'in-

47. Overlooking this context and the significance of Nietzsche, Rogers Brubaker, *The Limits of Rationality: An Essay on the Social and Moral Thought of Max Weber* (London: Allen & Unwin, 1984), can find Weber's treatment of the irreconcilable conflict among value-spheres "a difficult and obscure argument" (69).

ward' of all the arts," while eroticism appears as "a gate into the most irrational and thereby real kernel of life, as compared with the mechanisms of rationalization."[48] Once this has occurred, the intellectualist culture so characteristic of modernity then tends to *substitute* one sphere of value for another, one life-order for another, based upon the principle that the most subjective judgment is the most authentic and "valid." To cite Weber's example, "The refusal of modern men to assume responsibility for moral judgments tends to transform judgments of moral intent into judgments of taste ('in poor taste' instead of 'reprehensible')." The consequence of such a shift, as well as its intention, is to reinforce the transcendent claims of subjectivity, for "the inaccessibility of appeal from aesthetic judgment *excludes discussion*."[49] That is its function. With this formulation we arrive at the complete victory of aesthetic culture in the age of intellectualization.

What of the economic and political life-orders, the most soulless and diabolical of powers? In this schema they may be said to represent the paradigm cases for adaptation, the conditions of action given on the one hand by the abstract rationalism of the money economy, on the other by the "inescapable pragmatics [*Pragma*] of violence."[50] The economic sphere merely recapitulates the problem of capitalism's cultural significance: in a phrase, "Money is the most abstract and 'impersonal' element that exists in human life" and is thus for Weber, as for Georg Simmel in *The Philosophy of Money*, the source par excellence of all objectifications, human self-alienation, material gratification, and just plain misery.[51] If there is "meaning" to the acquisitive quest, then it is found simply in analogies with games and sport. Not so Weber's agonistic political sphere, where matters are more serious, both because of the threat of organized violence and because of the contradictory invasion by moral purposes and sublimated eros—the action of those who, in Weber's paraphrase of Machiavelli, love their native city more than

48. *GARS* 1:555–56, 558; G&M, 342, 345; *WuG*, 468; *EaS*, 607.
49. *GARS* 1:555; G&M, 342 (my italics).
50. *GARS* 1:549; G&M, 336; cf. *WuG*, 464; *EaS*, 600–601.
51. *GARS* 1:544; G&M, 331. In *The Philosophy of Money* (1900), trans. T. Bottomore and D. Frisby (London: Routledge & Kegan Paul, 1978), a book Weber read in 1902, Simmel comments that "Money is the representative of abstract value. From the economic relationship, i.e. the exchangeability of objects, the fact of this relationship is extracted and acquires, in contrast to those objects, a conceptual existence bound to a visible symbol. Money is a specific realization of what is common to economic objects . . . and the general misery of human life is most fully reflected by this symbol, namely by the constant shortage of money under which most people suffer" (120). Obviously similar ideas appear in Marx's writings as well.

the salvation of their own souls. Modern rebels, repelled by the de-humanized orders of acquisitiveness and the bureaucratic state, can not only flee *from* but also *into* politics. They will never find salvation there, but they may find a close second, "a pathos and a sentiment of community."[52]

We can wonder whether Weber's distinctions among truly "autono-mous" orders are intended to be comprehensive. Although evidence ex-ists on both sides of the issue, on balance the most persuasive view seems to be that any number of competing orders or value-spheres at different levels of generality may be formed out of modern experience. Indeed, the potentiality for such formations is characteristic of the mod-ern. Minimally, this is because of the differentiation and heterogeneity of our experience, which exists paradoxically alongside the standardiza-tion of consumable "mass" culture, together with a contradictory long-ing for the new, the original, the distinctive, the authentic and essential.

The crucial test for comprehensibility comes with the idea of "cul-ture" itself, in one sense merely an overarching concept with variable contents useful for referring to a particular way of life or "life-style," yet in another a quite specific object of cathexis or fetishism, employing the language of Freud and Marx, or in Weber's own terms a "holy task, a 'calling [*Beruf*].'"[53] Weber's *Kulturmensch* can be absorbed into cul-ture, orienting action in such a way as to convert culture into a unique sphere of value. Life-activity thereby becomes "meaningful," or so one believes, only through participating in and possessing the latest, most stylish and faddish forms of expression and identification, to the exclu-sion of everything else, which is denigrated as beneath oneself and be-hind the times. Using a slightly different idiom, what Octavio Paz has called "the longing for true presence" thus leads to those innumerable "triumphant gestures of mutually surpassing one another" so annoy-ingly characteristic of the avant-garde.[54] As a final irony, to pursue "cul-ture" in this sense is also to flee from its grasp, to attempt to race be-yond it in a flash of negative dialectics. Yet the endeavor is doomed, for neither the pursuit nor the flight can be expected to arrive at a deter-minate destination.

Given this interpretation of the life-orders and value-spheres and the possibilities for *directions* taken by action within them, let us consider

52. "Politik als Beruf" ["Politics as a Vocation"] (1919), *GPS*, 546; *GARS* 1:98, 548; G&M, 126, 335; *PE*, 107.
53. *GARS* 1:570; G&M, 357.
54. Quoted from Habermas, *Philosophical Discourse of Modernity*, 53, 93.

the major specific avenues of escape that open up in Weber's reflections on the uniqueness of his own modern culture, which is still ours to comprehend.

THE ETHICAL ALTERNATIVE

The most important first-order problems are those appearing on the large and differentiated terrain of ethics, serving under the heading "ethic of brotherliness" as the nodal point against which all spheres of value are placed in tension and from which, to a great extent, the various orders of life derive their meaning. The issue of "ethicism" had in fact occupied Weber on many occasions, from early critical comments on "ethical culture" to the later disputes over value-judgments and science. Keeping in mind his Vienna statement from 1909 concerning the absence of "scientifically demonstrable [ethical] ideals," one can sharpen the issue further by considering Weber's powerful challenge to Michels on the same theme, which is worth quoting in full:

> There are *two* possibilities: either (1) "my kingdom is not of this world" (Tolstoy, *or* syndicalism *thought to its conclusion*, which is *nothing more* than the sentence "the goal means nothing to me, the *movement* everything" translated into a *revolutionary-ethical, personal* statement, but one that *you* too have certainly not thought through to its conclusion. I shall probably write something about *that* sometime) *or* (2) *affirmation* of culture (that is, *objective* culture, expressing itself in *technical* and other "achievements") through *adaptation* to the sociological conditions of *all* "technique" [*Technik*], whether it be economic, political, or whatever else. (Such adaptation is embodied *most often* precisely in "collectivist societies.") In the *second* case all talk of "revolution" is a farce, *any* thought of *replacing* the "domination of man over man" by *any* kind of "socialist" society or ingeniously devised forms of "democracy" is a *utopia*. In this respect your own critique surely doesn't go far enough. Whoever wants to live as a "modern man," if only in the sense that he has his newspaper, railroads, trams, etc. every day, *renounces* all those ideals which hover darkly around you as soon as he completely *abandons* the revolutionary standpoint *for its own sake, without* any "goal," indeed without the *conceivability* of a "goal." You are a thoroughly honest fellow and will on your own (the plain statements in your article show *that*) complete the critique that has long since brought me to this way of thinking and *thereby* stamped me as a "bourgeois" politician, *so long as* the least that one as such *can* want doesn't get pushed into the limitless distance.[55]

55. Letter of 4 August 1908, AMW 59; Weber is replying to Michels' article, "Die oligarchischen Tendenzen der Gesellschaft," *Archiv* 27 (1908): 73–135, the earliest pub-

In the entire corpus of Weber's writings there is probably no more pointed statement of the either/or alternatives, pushed to their logical extremes. Most importantly, this "logic of alternatives" served as an indispensable element in his public discourse, notably in later formulations of the principle of "responsibility" in "Politics as a Vocation" and the revealing text "Between Two Laws," with its magnificent and terrifying images of the individual caught in contradiction between the demands for personal salvation on the one side and the autonomous pull of the social world conceived as "*a world of 'culture' in the here and now* [*diesseitige Kultur*], thus of creaturely beauty, dignity, honesty and greatness," on the other. Each could not be satisfied simultaneously, especially for the individual challenged to win responsibility for history, and thus for the future, in the face of the "'pragmatics of power [*Macht-Pragma*]' that rules all political history."[56]

It should be noted that the statement of alternatives is presumed valid at two levels: in the first instance one must choose, Weber insists, between two fundamentally opposed possibilities for the general conduct of life: rejection of the world or world-abnegation (*Weltablehnung*), or affirmation of the world or of its objective culture (*Kulturbejahung*). In this context "objective culture" (in contrast to "subjective culture") means for Weber exactly what it meant for Simmel, namely an autonomous order of values external to the self, although produced by it, and whose contents presuppose a process of spacial and temporal "distancing" between ourselves and the forms of our activity.[57] By selecting the former possibility of world-abnegation, one must be prepared to live with "fictions" in order to achieve ethical unity of belief. For the latter case, on the other hand, one must be prepared to live with "antinomies" or "tensions" (*Spannungen*) in order to achieve clarity about the world as it "is." Second, one must choose between value-spheres: either an absolute ethics of brotherliness that promises to end all forms of domination or acceptance of the relative conditions of political conduct. If the former, then one must be prepared to live with the maddening incongruities between "ideal" and "real." If the latter, then one must be

---

lished statement of the thesis developed at length in *Political Parties* (1911), trans. E. and C. Paul (New York: Collier, 1962). He repeated the position in a letter of 21 August, AMW 62 and NW 30/7:96: "*either—or*! an 'appeal' *or* a cool 'history.'" Weber made quite similar, but briefer comments to Professor Goldstein, in a letter of 13 November 1918, NW 30/10:125–26.

56. "Zwischen Zwei Gesetzen" (1916), *MWG*, I/15:98.

57. See Simmel, *Philosophy of Money*, 59–78, 446–48.

prepared to live with the diabolic uncertainties of responsibility for consequences of action. Weber insists on a necessary alignment among these alternatives: there is an "elective affinity," so to speak, between world-abnegation and an absolute ethics, between world-affirmation and an ethics of (political) responsibility. Efforts to recombine alternatives are the breeding ground for both intellectual confusion and practical catastrophes.

Ignoring for the moment Weber's deceptive and ironic "bourgeois" affirmation of modern culture, we can readily use his statement to delineate the most formidable world-abnegating ethical alternatives: pacificism (Tolstoy); revolutionary syndicalism, or an ethically oriented commitment to "pure democracy" (the position Michels toyed with); and a kind of "socialist" credo believing in the possible elimination of all relations of domination (the early Lukács). There was another concrete variant of ethicism as well, visible in some versions of radical feminism, as Marianne Weber acknowledged in several of her essays and in an exchange with Simmel on the possibility of an autonomous "female culture." For if feminism could be conceived as an alternative to the constraints of everyday life organized in vocational work, then it could also be thought to foreshadow a qualitatively different world. For the most part Max Weber left this fourth possibility to his wife's and Simmel's diligence,[58] but he did, as promised, grapple with the first three as "directions of world-abnegation" or as ideological ethics of "ultimate ends" or convictions.

Absolute internal consistency was the sine qua non for these ethical positions, according to Weber, and it required an unflinching determination to suppress any "compromises" with the realities of the existing world. All consistent ethical alternatives shared some postulate of absolute righteousness or justice—in effect, *fiat justitia, pereat mundus*—at the level of both collective and individual ethics. They also shared complete indifference to rational "ends," or to any rational calculation of the consequences of an act. Demonstration of the purity of moral conviction, motive, or intention qualified as the criterion of justification. In Weber's terminology the ethical escape route was always emblazoned with the characteristics of an absolute and uncompromising conviction.

58. One of Weber's few published remarks is found in the first essay on Russia, "Zur Lage der bürgerlichen Demokratie in Russland," 325–26 n. 72, where he comments on the strength of feminism among the intelligentsia.

But what does all this have to do with the cultural dynamics of capitalist development? For Weber and his contemporaries capitalist development was bound up with "technical progress," with the working out of purposive-rational (*zweckrational*) or instrumental orientations toward action, with the standardization and routinization of life-activity, with control of the conditions of existence through calculation. Compared to what Tolstoy (and following him, Weber) conceived as the "organic cycle of life," these forces created an endlessly "progressive" life of specialization, dislocation, fragmentation, and "tensions." Every ethical school of thought sought in opposition to re-create the world as an "organic and natural whole" (Tolstoy), a "totality of being" (Lukács), or an ethically "rational" unity (Michels). The spirit of these views was perfectly captured in Lukács' later observation that his pre-1917 position as summarized in *The Theory of the Novel* expressed "the hope that a natural life worthy of man can spring from the disintegration of capitalism and the destruction, seen as identical with that disintegration, of the lifeless and life-denying social and economic categories."[59] Not only must the capitalist productive system be destroyed, so must its modes of language, thought, and being. Lukács was at least sufficiently honest to see in such views "a highly naive and totally unfounded utopianism." Similarly, this kind of absolutist commitment, from which Weber himself was not entirely immune, was exemplified in an activist like Michels, "a 'moralist' from head to toe" as Weber had observed: "In his political evaluations he is so exclusively ruled by this highly personal ethos that he once completely failed to understand the distinction that I mentioned ad hoc between vocation (affairs [*Sache*]) and 'life.'"[60] Weber, on the other hand, had treated the "psychology" of the "great inner tensions and conflicts between 'vocation,' 'life' (as we like to say nowadays) and 'ethics'"[61] as a specific characteristic of inner-worldly asceticism passed on to the modern age.

59. Georg Lukács, *The Theory of the Novel*, (1916), trans. A. Bostock (Cambridge: MIT Press, 1971), 20. Weber knew this work and expressed reservations about it; like the "Zwischenbetrachtung," parts of the text may have been read to their circle of acquaintances in Heidelberg before the war: see the Weber-Lukács correspondence of 1915–16 in *Georg Lukács: Selected Correspondence*, 253–39, 263–65.

60. Letter to Gisela Michels-Linder, Robert's wife, 25 December 1909, AMW 67, with similar language in a letter of 11 January 1907, AMW 31: "Your are indeed *yourself* a 'moralist' from head to toe, of course more foresighted than the 'philistine.' Why not admit it?" Cf. my essay, "Max Weber and Robert Michels," *American Journal of Sociology* 86 (1981), esp. 1269–73. In an early feminist paper, "Das Dilemma des Weibes in der Liebe," *Die Frauenbewegung* 9 (1903): 82–84, Michels had at least seen the clear "tension" between work and family, especially for the modern woman.

61. "Antikritisches zum 'Geist' des Kapitalismus," 167.

The utopianism of a rigorous and consistent ethical alternative certainly accounted for one of Weber's objections (though perhaps the least persuasive) to ethicism. After all, a "science of actuality" was already in conception a science *of* the historically given world and not separate from it. In addition, from the standpoint of the *political* sphere utopianism meant "irresponsibility" or the complete repudiation of Weber's preferred "ethic of responsibility." On the other side of the issue, Weber could still honor the dignity of an absolutely consistent *Gesinnungsethiker* (moralist of pure intentions)—a source, no doubt, of his interest in Tolstoy, or in Lukács' apocalyptic and Michels' syndicalist convictions. But the brunt of Weber's rejoinder to ethicism lay elsewhere, in a remarkable critique, filtered through the reading of Tolstoy, of the *meaning* of modern culture under conditions of a "technical progress" promoted by what Tolstoy called "experimental science."

In Tolstoy's view, modern science had heightened the problem of "meaninglessness" by exposing denial or ignorance, epicureanism or hedonism, the destruction of life through mastery of nature or through suicide as its only "solutions." [62] Rationalist science for him had to be jettisoned in favor of an absolutist ethical stance, an unconditional embrace of the moral teaching of the "Sermon on the Mount." The essence of Weber's reflection on Tolstoy's moral critique of scientism was to show, first, that the search for meaning in "progress," "newness," and everything associated with them, engaged in by the modern "cultural being," could never from the ethical standpoint be successful: culture, "necessarily burdened with guilt," would "become ever more meaningless [*sinnlos*]." [63] However, Weber also wanted to show, secondly, that the alternative construction of "meaning" by Tolstoy's ethical escape route would just as surely prove to be an illusion; it would, in his words, "succumb in the end to the world dominion of unbrotherliness."

Why is this the case? The most interesting reasons are found toward the conclusion of the "Reflection" and "Science as a Vocation." [64] A comprehensive ethic for the totality of life-conduct presupposes a *genuine* prophecy, which, Weber insists, "is simply not there," and cannot be "for purely external reasons" given "the technical and social conditions of rational culture." (It is well known in any case that Weber rejected all forms of modern prophecy, whether stemming from Marx,

62. See esp. "My Confession" and "What Shall We Do Then?" in Tolstoy's *Complete Works* (New York: AMS Press, 1968), 13:3–90; 14:3–340.
63. *GARS* 1:571; G&M, 357.
64. *GARS* 1:569–71; *GAW*, 594–95, 609–13; G&M, 139–40, 152–56, 355–57.

Wagner, Nietzsche, Tolstoy, or even his egocentric colleague Werner Sombart.) The "conditions" Weber has in mind are clearly those of an objective, material culture that continually undermines the serious-ness of any appeal for metaphysical transcendence by challenging its grounds, questioning its motives, co-opting its effects, imitating its contents, and even propagating its messages, typically through the de-mystifying resources of science or the medium of money. Universal un-masking is matched by a universal corruptability of the "sacred."

In this situation the internal needs of subjectivity are not so much replaced as displaced onto counterfeit objects, whose frivolity is re-vealed in the incontrovertible lesson that all values, the "moral life" included, have a market price. For our modern objective culture, Weber insists, this means in one sense that ethicism has economic presupposi-tions: only among those privileged to exist outside the vocational world, to remain economically independent as rentiers or otherwise, can it become a comprehensive and consistent life-order—a clear allusion to Tolstoy and to some members of the George Circle (notably Stefan George himself), not to mention Weber's rentier existence itself. But such a charmed circle of the privileged, defined against the *Berufs-mensch*, is itself parasitic on the order it radically negates—a negation that must be self-defeating.

Finally, insofar as it aims for universality, the ethical alternative as a doctrine must founder on a social contradiction: in Weber's words, it is "*not* accessible to everybody" and therefore "definitely means aristoc-racy."[65] Ethicism then faces the unenviable and impossible task of achieving the new order of equal justice (i.e., realizing the goal of elimi-nating the "domination of man over man") through the asserted privi-leges of aristocratic domination. Once again, whatever form it takes, the ethical alternative seems to run afoul of a kind of "reality principle" embedded in capitalist development. It represents a possible choice, available to a few, capable of renewal from generation to generation, but always at the mercy of the unrelenting pressure of the "fateful" forces of culture continually calling it into question.

THE FLIGHT INTO AESTHETICISM

Weber characterizes the aesthetic and erotic value-spheres as "inner-worldly powers of life" whose fundamental essences are "arational or

---

65. *GARS*, 1:571; G&M, 357.

antirational" and that are therefore opposed on the face of it both to the acosmic "ethic of brotherliness" and to the rationalization of the world through intellectualism, technical "progress," or any of the various forces aligned with modern productive systems and instrumental rationality. In this view, which clearly precedes the intellectualization of twentieth-century art, the visual arts, music, and the aesthetic value-sphere generally develop in a peculiar relationship to the modern:

> Art becomes a cosmos of more and more consciously grasped independent values which exist in their own right. Art takes over the function of an inner-worldly salvation, no matter how this may be interpreted. It provides a *salvation* from the routines of everyday life, and especially from the increasing pressures of theoretical and practical rationalism.[66]

With such a breakthrough to a core of unique meaning, the aesthetic becomes a distinctive, autonomous sphere of value. Precisely this point appears to be the one Weber wants to emphasize, especially in relation to the expression of discontents.

It is important and instructive to notice that Weber's mode of reasoning, with its characteristic juxtapositions and dialectics, is in profound ways representative for the entire fin-de-siècle milieu. Among contemporaries engaged with the aesthetic, Simmel, for example, offers numerous representative commentaries of a similar kind, especially when evaluating specific artists. Take, for instance, the concluding synthesis in his last and most extensive essay on Rodin:

> But if one perceives salvation from the confusion and turmoil of life, the peace and reconciliation beyond life's movements and contradictions, as the essential goal of art, then one may think that artistic liberation from something disturbing or unbearable in life succeeds not only through flight into the opposite but also precisely through the most perfect stylization and enhanced refinement of life's own contents. . . . Rodin redeems us because he presents precisely the most complete image of this life. . . . He redeems us from just that which we experience in the sphere of actuality, because he allows us to experience our deepest sense of life once again in the sphere of art.[67]

"Salvation" and "redemption," "flight" and "liberation" from the unbearable through and into art, or art as the source and setting for "depth" (*Tiefe*) of personality and truly intensified "lived experience" (*Erleben*)—the language and imagery evokes a special domain of value,

66. *GARS* 1:555; G&M, 342.
67. *Philosophische Kultur* (Berlin: Wagenbach, 1983), 153.

in Simmel's as in Weber's thought, as a construction of culture. That is, the aesthetic comes to be endowed with such significance *because* it is grasped by the mind in dialectical opposition to the grinding forces of routinization and rationalization. Translated into the idiom of philosophical idealism, it henceforth stands for the positive moment in which the modern person, the cultural being, is lifted out of the shadowy cage and into the brilliant sphere of transcendental being. But the "transcendent" is now a category of aesthetic *culture*, not philosophical reflection; and "true being" is found in movement toward itself, in the activity of flight as such, not at any illuminated point of repose.

Since the aesthetic tendency was strongly noticeable in Simmel's own writings, including the essays collected in his *Sociology*, with their self-conscious orientation toward "lived experience" and "interaction," he might serve as one of the best witnesses and exemplars of aestheticism's cultural meaning and claims for autonomy, for *l'art pour l'art*. Yet among Weber's contemporaries the intrusion of aesthetic criteria into science, politics, and elsewhere was a widespread phenomenon, suggesting not simply the presence of the modern, but also aestheticism's attempted conquest of other value-spheres. That is, the important problem concerned not merely appropriation of the aesthetic as "salvation" from the world's rationalization, but instead the attempt to re-create the aesthetic as a genuine sphere of redemption bearing cosmic significance for an entire way of life. Aestheticism became a substitutive ethos. In this last sense, for Weber, it was without a doubt two areas of artistic creativity and two personalities that demonstrated the overpowering spell of the new ethos: in music the dramatic, compositional innovations and example of Richard Wagner, and among the poets the meteoric rise of Stefan George and the amazing developments in his circle, especially after its post-1904 adoption of the "Maximin" revelation, the cultic apotheosis of the teenage Maximilian Kronberger. Carried beyond the community of devotees, these flights into the consolations of high art became the original life-models for entire generations.

Within the region of the aesthetic it is music, the most "inward" form of human expression, that can conceivably set itself against moral and scientific culture even as a "diabolical" power, as the finest and highest expression of amoral and irrational interiority. Perhaps one should say that music, of all the arts, is capable of immediately awakening an inwardly authentic and plastic expressiveness, not merely in sharp contrast to the dull beat of technical rationalization and the vocational life-world, but as "a surrogate for primary religious experience," a "means to ecstasy or exorcism"![68] Or in Nietzsche's words, music became "the independent art as such, *not* offering images of phenomenality, as the other arts did, but speaking rather the language of the will itself, directly out of the 'abyss' as its most authentic, elemental, nonderivative revelation."[69]

For Weber the clearest display of these Schopenhauerian ideas and the beginning of a "modern" music, was to be found in Wagner's art, which he knew thoroughly, from acquainting his sister at an early age "with all Wagner operas" to publicly reading the text of *Die Walküre* during his last months.[70] The high point of musical expression came specifically with *Tristan und Isolde*, because of its brilliant harmonic breakthrough to atonal chromaticism, sustained throughout the score. Weber began his unfinished treatise on music with this problem, citing in his terminology the "tension" without which "no modern music could exist" between harmonic innovation (i.e., "chordal rationalization" that contains its own "irrationalities" in the chromatic scale exploited so effectively by Wagner) and the "irrationality of melody" as the musical element most dependent on inspiration.[71] Echoing Nietzsche's earlier judgments, for Weber *Tristan* offered "the kind of great experience that one very seldom has, a work of great human truthfulness and unparalleled musical beauty," and with the exception of *Die Meistersinger*, Wagner's "only truly 'eternal' work," in contrast to any intended "religious experience" in *Parsifal*.[72]

Wagner's achievement in one sense was to develop a kind of tonality, harmonic intensity, and irresolution that was a perfect vehicle for advancing certain expressive aesthetic purposes: conveying emotions of intense longing, delirious submission, boundless expansion—all of which were alluring, and questionable. Evocative of modernity's *Gefühlskultur*, Weber alluded to such aims in Baudelaire's idea of the "sacred prostitution of the soul," that is, the unconditional devotion to emotional "surrender" as a sacred end in itself, a flight from the world.[73] Above all other art forms, Wagnerian opera-drama could effect such surrender. Like Thomas Mann, who confessed "an enthusiastic

68. *GARS* 1:556; G&M, 343; *WuG*, 468; *EaS*, 607.
69. *Genealogy of Morals*, 103 (III, 5).
70. *Lebensbild*, 178, 700; Eng. trans., 168, 686.
71. *The Rational and Social Foundations of Music*, trans. and ed. D. Martindale et al. (Carbondale: Southern Illinois University Press, 1958), 10, 128 n. 7.
72. Letter to his mother, probably August 1912, NW 30/6: 161, written after attending operas in Bayreuth and Munich; also *Lebensbild*, 510; Eng. trans., 502.
73. *WuG*, 456; *EaS*, 589; *GARS* 1:546; G&M, 333.

ambivalence" for Wagner's "dilettantism raised to the level of genius,"[74] Weber admitted to both enchantment and doubts:

> I would like to get to know the great sorcerer [*Hexenmeister*] once more . . . since I am *very* much of two minds about him. Next to great admiration for his ability, I have a deep aversion for many spurious and artifical things. Now I would like to see which predominates.[75]

The truth is, both predominated—or neither did; Weber continued,

> I will probably write something about music *history*, that is, *only* about certain *social* conditions, from which can be explained the fact that *only we* have "harmonic" music, although other cultures exhibit a much finer sense of *hearing* and a much stronger musical *culture*. Remarkable! It is a product of monasticism, as will be shown.[76]

Weber remained ambivalent about the Wagnerian aesthetic, "the problem of modernism itself" in Mann's words,[77] alternately attracted to its unchallenged power of expression and suspicious of its absorption into subjectivist culture. Yet, from the "historical" perspective of Weber's acknowledged interests, Wagner stood in the tradition of *harmonic* innovation in Western music, marking a turning point in the use of aspects of harmony that like many other "cultural phenomena" lay "in a line of development having *universal* significance and validity."[78] This line of development in music would certainly not terminate with Wagner, either. His art too, in all its "modernism," was thoroughly a part of that "concatenation of circumstances" responsible for creating the modern world of culture.

As for the aesthetic of poetry, the group of devotees assembled around Stefan George transformed it into a cult, a temple of devotion, with the master himself as prophet, high priest, and savior. What was most noteworthy about George as a poet, in contrast, for instance, to the "mysticism" of Rilke, was the combining of aestheticism with the drive toward *ascetic* world-mastery. To Weber's mind George's poetry showed that he "himself steps out of the aesthetic cloister in order to renew and rule the world from which he had at first fled as an ascetic

---

74. From statements in 1933 and 1951, in *Pro and Contra Wagner*, trans. A. Blunden (Chicago: University of Chicago Press, 1985), 103, 222.

75. Letter to his sister, Lili, 5 August 1912, NW 30/6:158–59, and NW 26:45–46.

76. Ibid.; cf. *Lebensbild*, 509; Eng. trans., 501.

77. From 1909, in *Pro and Contra Wagner*, 41.

78. *GARS* 1:1–2; *PE*, 13–15; the problem is stated with respect to "technical progress" and the role of monasticism in the history of Western music in the "Value-Freedom" essay, *GAW*, 521–23; S&F, 30–32.

(with aesthetic rather than with ethical characteristics), following the pattern of so many other ascetics."[79] But the path to "ecstatic rapture" through deployment of aesthetic "forms" led not to any sort of substantive message of salvation from objective culture, judged in terms of *content*, but rather to a "purely formal prophecy" with "nothing positive to offer" except the usual platitudes concerning the (formal) need to overcome "rationalism, capitalism, and so forth." We might say, paraphrasing Simmel, that this is quintessential modernism: the dissolution of all content in the fluidity of one's soul.

The very attempt to substitute form for content then led in Weber's judgment to the undermining of original aesthetic purposes, a judgment based without doubt on his experiences with George, Friedrich Gundolf, and other members of the Circle, the "ecstatic" poets [*Ekstatiker*] as the Webers called them:

> One perceives most clearly how strongly this undermining of content affects artistic form, if one hears the poems of this genre (for instance, the introduction to "Der Teppich des Lebens") read in the artistically correct manner by a disciple of the school—that is, in a liturgical monotone that acoustically shakes one up. It is a violent and completely unartistic exertion. Here the work of art is steeped to its last pore in a purpose that lies beyond the work of art—a powerfully ironic comment on the original strict exclusion of all nonartistic purposes.[80]

Such prophetic ambitions seemed in the end to derive not from the poet's expected sources of inspiration—experience, mystical revelation, myth, memory—but rather from an inner need, "necessity," or even "arbitrary" willfulness that was essentially reactive, an agitated counterthrust against the new forces of objective culture. George's aesthetic flight was all movement and motion, as if in imitation of the very world it rejected. Instead of vanquishing the forces of rationalization, this new aestheticism spiraled back within them and became their hapless captive. The most vital of these forces was, of course, intellectualization.

As a coda to this discussion, one might observe that the process Weber sensed at work in the George Circle has continued down to our own time. Avant-garde art has begun "to function as a terrain for indepen-

---

79. From a programmatic letter on the George Circle to Dora Jellinek, 9 May 1910, reprinted with omissions and errors in *Lebensbild*, 465–67; Eng. trans., 457–59; the original typescript is in NW 30/6 : 6–8. Dora Jellinek, the daughter of Weber's Heidelberg colleague, and not Margarete Susman (as Harry Zohn suggests), is the "gifted woman" who inspired this exchange.

80. NW 30/6 : 6–8.

dent philosophical speculation," in concert with the view that "what matters is the idea" instead of the image or visible form.[81] When art actually becomes conceptual and is guided by a logic of "propositional thinking," then its intellectualization can be said to be complete. This is what the rumored "end of art" means; in Weberian terms it represents the predictable rationalization of the aesthetic sphere. In this dreary situation the choice for aestheticism does not disappear; rather it is re-directed out of high art into other areas of culture, preparing for revenge at home. Let us only add that the results of this preparation are as yet still unknown.

EROTICISM AS ESCAPE

Of all the life-forces, eros, or "sexual love," deserves for Weber to be labeled the most irrational, and in its sublimated expression as eroticism the most capable of pressing beyond the everyday to the limits of the extraordinary. The escape from the everyday is to be understood in We-ber's idiom as a perceived unfolding process of separation from an ex-istence tied to organic "natural" processes that leads finally, in the "in-tellectualist culture" of vocationally organized humanity, to a peculiar characteristic of the modern era: Eroticism becomes "a gate into the most irrational and thereby real kernel of life, as compared with the mechanisms of rationalization." From this point of view it becomes the primary source of "inner-worldly salvation from the rational," or the *only* power still binding "humankind to the natural source of all life."[82]

The choice of language for designating eroticism as a specific char-acteristic of the modern is significant in the first instance because, more so than the discussion of other value-spheres, it contains an explicit demarcation of developmental "stages" in the rationalization and intel-lectualization of *Erotik*: from Platonic eros as a "strongly *tempered* feeling" that leads the soul onto the path toward philosophy, to the tragic and honor-bound eros of feudal culture illustrated in the "Tristan

81. Suzi Gablik, *Progress in Art* (New York: Rizzoli, 1977), 8, 45–46. Weber thought one source of art's special enchantment (in contrast to science) was that although it might reveal "progress" in terms of evolving "technique," its productions did not evince "prog-ress" in the sense of lacking "completion" and thus inviting attempts to be "surpassed." Gablik's provocative application of Piagetian cognitive theory to painting does not seem to overturn this view, but instead is aimed at interpretations that approach progress in art as a question of passive and accurate "representation."

82. *GARS* 1:558, 560; G&M, 345–46.

and Isolde" narratives, to the refinements of Renaissance salon culture paying homage to eros in the "creative power of intersexual conversation" as an object of literature (e.g., Diderot, Rousseau), ending finally in the sublimated eroticism of the modern world of vocational specialization and rule by technique. This genealogy of the erotic starts from the fiction of a Tolstoyan "organic cycle of simple peasant existence" and concludes in the paradoxical "eroticism of intellectualism." Whether historically permissible or not, the fictional possibility of "organic life" borrowed from *War and Peace, Resurrection,* and other novels becomes logically appropriate as an anchor for Weber's mode of argumentation: it represents "natural" eros (and its negation, *thanatos*) without the heightened sensibility and tension of eroticism.

Given such genealogical forms, Weber's line of interpretation then proceeds to describe our timeless present through a radical opposition between the "cold skeleton hands of rational orders" and deadening "banality of the everyday" on the one side, and on the other the "natural," the "real," the "irrational," and the "truly living" (*das Lebendigste*). The latter four-part configuration, a transposition of the "organic," can be fashioned only in the crucible of the modern consciousness: eroticism is *experienced* as closest to the real and natural because eros has been reconceived as the ultimate source of "life"—that is, of life's most *irrational* force. Precisely these connections in thinking, which appear so self-evident to modern humankind, already disclose the uniquely modern conception of "life": only in the secret, inward sphere of the irrational, far beyond the banalities of routine existence in the everyday, can one directly sense life's pulsating forces. To assume its fullest meaning, "life" in this world, the only world there is, must be lived "beyond good and evil." Only under such conditions can its irrational core—eroticism—ever be imagined to offer an avenue of eternal renewal and escape. And this view of eros—Weber's view—appears itself to be fully dependent on the fin-de-siècle experience of desublimation, of promised release from repressive culture.[83]

83. Recently H. N. Fügen, *Max Weber* (Hamburg: Rowohlt, 1985), 118–22, has interpreted the passages on eroticism, containing the most extensive 1919–20 revisions in the "Reflection," as a sublimated expression of Weber's relationship with Else Jaffé-Richthofen—a plausible suggestion that must await publication of Weber's correspondence in the *Max Weber Gesamtausgabe* for fuller discussion. For biographical details, see also the interesting observations on Weber, women, and feminism in Guenther Roth, "Marianne Weber and Her Circle: Introduction to the Transaction Edition" of Marianne Weber, *Max Weber: A Biography*, trans. H. Zohn (New Brunswick, N.J.: Transaction Books, in press).

Where does the paradox lie in this last embrace of eroticism in "intellectualist culture"? Despite all rationalization under conditions of "technical progress," the "eroticism of intellectualism" in its deadly seriousness "affirms precisely the natural quality of the sexual sphere again, but consciously, as an embodied creative power."[84] The possibility of a *conscious* affirmation of the natural, a willful consciousness obstinately defying the external and material culture that is historically so and not otherwise, is the essence of this most modern of eroticisms. But as Weber well knows, modern humanity, precisely because of the sources of its identity, has lost all direct knowledge of the "natural" as an immanent creative power. Our affirming consciousness is a feat of imagination and will, and whatever meaning it can acquire is generated as a rebellious reply to negation of what we call "nature." The one attribute still reserved to humanity is self-consciousness of a refined sort—that is, a subjective realm of inwardness and heightened experience. Importantly, residing within this realm is an eroticism Weber can affirm, if only because it expresses what one might call a heroic pathos of the most personal, a pathos of *distance*, aware of repetition coupled with lost natural innocence—"again, but consciously."

Weber's attempt to grant some dignity to the life-sustaining but guilt-ridden value-sphere of eroticism emerges from the background of his experience and his deep reservations concerning the erotic *Lebenskult* of the age. From Schwabing in Munich, to Monte Verità above Ascona in Switzerland, and eventually to Heidelberg, the disciples of eros began to propagate a new Weltanschauung of liberation derived from a specific clinical practice. Weber came into contact with the new teachings at every turn: in discussions with colleagues like Simmel and Michels, among friends and acquaintances in Heidelberg and Munich, in two stays at Ascona in 1913 and 1914, even among some of the main personalities themselves, such as the renegade "Freudian" Otto Gross and his wife, Frieda, the anarchist painter Ernst Frick, the von Richthofen sisters, and Franziska Gräfin zu Reventlow, all of whom Weber knew personally and befriended at one time or another.[85]

Here as elsewhere in his encounters with the modern, there can be

84. *GARS* 1:561; G&M, 347.
85. After 1906, Weber's correspondence is peppered with comments on this theme. Some biographical details can be pursued in Martin Green, *The von Richthofen Sisters: The Triumphant and the Tragic Modes of Love* (New York: Basic Books, 1974); and *Mountain of Truth: The Counterculture Begins, Ascona, 1900–1920* (Hanover, N.H.: University Press of New England, 1986).

no doubt that Weber experienced both attraction and repulsion. But on balance, instead of the promise of sexual-personal liberation followed by a new community of "brotherliness" and "love," he foresaw among the convinced practitioners a reign of confusion, disappointment, and self-deception. One reason was that any thought, no matter how ingenious, of deducing a personal morality or practical world-view from scientific investigation was greeted with extreme skepticism. In the case of the new therapies, he observed

> that the Categorical Imperative, "Go to Freud, or to us his pupils, to learn the historical *truth* about yourself and your actions, or else you are a coward" not only reveals a kind of childish "departmental patriotism" of the psychiatrist and the modern type of professional "*directeur de l'âme*," but also totally debases itself from the ethical point of view because of the fatal admixture of purely "hygienic" motives.[86]

In addition, under the motto Know Thyself, pursuit of the erotic *as a value* ended not in unbounded human brotherhood, but rather in the exact opposite—an exclusive and incommunicable possession of the individual other: an ineradicable conflict characterized relations between these two value-spheres. No doubt the recommended therapy of freeing oneself from psychic mechanisms of "repression" in order to promote "health" (or moral traits such as honesty or strength of character) could be interpreted as a revolt against inner-worldly asceticism *tout court*. But the question was, In a positive sense could the new "freedom," based on a critique of sexuality and the erotic life, be anything more than an age-old hedonism? Only a fine line might be seen to separate the escape into eroticism from the nihilistic enjoyment of pure sensuality. Eroticism as pleasure-seeking led not to higher self-knowledge, but to those "last men who invented happiness," the "sensualists without heart" excoriated in the closing pages of *The Protestant Ethic*. In this form eroticism as a path of escape from the rational and the everyday ceased to be only humanly interesting and became tragic. Perhaps the appropriate and unfortunate symbol for this outcome was Otto Gross' dissipation and drug-crazed death at age forty-two.

The decisive characteristic of what Weber called "subjectivist culture," with its ubiquitous searches and confused arrogance, was in sum a carefully cultivated, redemptive inwardness. Modernity was charac-

---

86. Baumgarten, *Max Weber, Werk und Person*, 647; Weber, *Selections*, 386.

terized not only by technical achievements of world-historical significance, but also by reactive flights into the obscure interior spaces of the
modern subject re-presented as ascetic, aesthete, ethicist, erotic. To
chart these psychic spaces in a new soteriology of "inwardness" became
for the convinced "cultural being" a calling of the highest order, a dare
to live at what Ortega y Gasset called "the height of the times," a level
that was itself symptomatic of modern discontent and inseparable from
it. Modern culture was thus deeply divided against itself: the "objectivist" strain appeared to erode the sources of "subjectivist" inspiration,
while the latter lived in a condition of permanent hostility toward all
purely purposive-rational *Technik*. Sociologically considered, in Weber's diagnosis the deepest paradox emerged from subjectivist culture's
essential dependence on its objectivist counterpart. That is, the blos-
soming of an inwardness of cultural redemption was scarcely imaginable without the new technologies of publication and communication,
the cultural hothouse of the modern city, new possibilities for economically independent urban existence—or, in short, the complete intellectualization of even the most sacred value-spheres of subjectivity. For the
privileged creators and guardians of "subjectivist culture" this was simply a paradox that could not be resolved.

But what of Weber's own position in relation to this paradoxical end-
point? What is one to make of his cryptic, but carefully placed references to choosing one's own fate, to serving the "demands of the day,"
and to "affirming" culture through adaptation to the "conditions" of
its existence? Where did Weber's choices lie, and why?

INTELLECTUALISM: THE CALLING
FOR SCIENCE

In "Science as a Vocation" Weber denied himself the possibility of giving a comprehensive answer to the ancient question, stated anew by
Tolstoy, How should we live and what should we do?—a question
about the fate of the "soul" in a rationalized world that begged for new
prophetic solutions he considered illusory. But in confronting the critique of culture and the situation of science in our twentieth century, he
did seek clarity about the ways in which such a question might be pro-
visionally answered, given the economy of choice posed by the modern
struggles among rival value-spheres and life-orders. The dynamics of
this provisional answer were set by the heavily accentuated contrast
between the conditions of the "modern" and the cosmos of the "or-

ganic." Stating the matter boldly, choice never appeared as an issue for the latter, since meaning was prescribed by ethical unities, which were actually projections by modern memory of what might have been, had Western culture followed a different course. But for those striving for the fabrication and possession of rational knowledge and culture there was a responsibility to choose in the context of a plurality of value-spheres, none of which could be universally preeminent. This Weberian "perspectivism" rested not on metaethical or metaphysical postulates, but rather on a claim about the nature of action and experience in modern culture. No doubt it imposed a stringent discipline, for clearly in this view one *ought* to side with the historical world as it had become, with a "disenchanted" actuality from which there could be no magical escape, but from which contingently hopeful futures might emerge.

Why this particular choice, however? What reasons lie behind Weber's affirmation? In the last analysis there seem to be three kinds of answers or, if one prefers, three "levels"—psychological, political, and scientific—to a complete answer to this last and most fundamental of all questions.

First of all, Weber frequently enough expressed his *personal* choice for understanding, as he put it, "what is": "I am not an astrologer and not rash enough to attempt to satisfy those craving belief. My most decisive inner need is 'intellectual integrity': I say 'what is.'"[87] This "decisive inner need," which appears so strongly underscored in all of Weber's discussions of "vocation," from the religious to the scientific and political, certainly underlies the "pathos of distance" that characterizes his most brilliant work. But it should also be said, simply with respect to the personal conduct of life, that the values Weber objectified for himself and others, particularly the demand for "integrity" and "matter-of-factness" (*Sachlichkeit*), strove for the same kind of "distancing" effects.

No more perfect illustration of what might be called the "therapeutic" implications of such self-objectification can be found, especially in relation to the modern, than the sentence of advice Weber directed toward his sister Lili:

> What would *objectively* do her some good is the most straightforward acceptance of life and fate in the spirit that life not only wants to be lived as it is, but also again and again *deserves* to become lived, not emotionally but rather in plain sincerity with respect to persons and things, in uncomplicated

87. Letter to Elisabeth Gnauck-Kühne, 15 July 1909, NW 30/4:85–86.

simplicity with all of its "problematics"—in short, all that which lies in the opposite direction from the modern chase after "experience."[88]

The dualism operative in such a formulation—the problematics of an unpretentious directness against the emotionally alluring and exhausting search for genuine, lived experience—contains a plea and a hard strategy for fending off the demons of inwardness and subjectivism that must for cultural reasons hover around every modern individual (at least around those who are not, in Weber's words, "spiritually or inwardly dead")[89] and determine the entire problem of life's purposes. The personal significance of "integrity," of facing up to "what is," then lies in the struggle for the mastery of self within a world in which the manifold of experience, the normal testing-ground for self-expression, has come to challenge the very possibility of an "integrated" self. Weber's choice for the world that is historically "as it is" can in this sense represent a way of coping with discontent brought about by such fundamental contradiction. Only by repudiating its own presuppositions could Weber's analysis be expected to have a different character.

Beyond the personal, Weber's choice also rested on reasons having to do with his conception of politics. The affirmation of "objective culture" expressed through "technical achievements" had practical political consequences: it led, above all, to a political stance (and reputation) widely, if misleadingly, characterized as "bourgeois." But if Weber accepted the historical results of the sociocultural transformation inaugurated by ascetic Protestantism, it was not because of a secure faith in progress through technological development or a smug belief in the inherent superiority of new forms of economic rationalization and their salutary political and cultural effects. *That* would have indeed been "bourgeois." Rather, the essential rationale of his position was found in the choice favoring a "politics of responsibility" toward the future of history and in the search for a political dynamic adapted to the culture of modernity, an arrangement of powers and orders that would measure up to the fact of "bureaucratization" of institutions on the one hand and the demand for "democratization" on the other. As I shall suggest subsequently at greater length, these twin pillars of argumentation implied a politics anchored in the historical world of causes and consequences, means and ends, facts and explanations. Weber even radicalized this assessment to the point of seeing in the most plausible self-

88. Letter to a friend of hers, Lisa von Abisch, 1 January 1917, NW 30/8:8–9, in response to Lili's bouts of depression; she committed suicide in 1920.
89. *GPS*, 547; G&M, 127.

proclaimed "political" alternatives, such as revolutionary socialism, a mirror-image of the present: the call for revolution often meant merely the introduction of state socialism (i.e., the reconstruction of the state as "rational" entrepreneur) and thus a social order still encased in the constraints of the "iron cage," but now without even the "freedoms" permitted by voluntary association. Those who elected politics as a vocation, regardless of ideological persuasion, were in Weber's idiom condemned to bear the burden of action within the world as it is, informed by a "tragic" knowledge of human affairs. All attempts through politics to deny this burden altogether would predictably have precisely the reverse effect and make the state's dominion even more complete, unbearable, and unaccountable.

Finally, faced with the turn-of-the-century cultural problematic, Weber sought clarity above all in the diagnostic and critical powers of scientific reflection, or in what could be called "the sphere of intellect" and "theoretical knowledge," surely the object of his most openly expressed passion. Like the political, the aesthetic, and the erotic, knowledge or *Intellekt* was conceived in the terminology of the "Intermediate Reflection" and "Science as a Vocation" to be a particular value-sphere possessing an internal logic and a self-sustaining commitment to "intellectual integrity," which set it in opposition to any "ethic of brotherliness," but whose own presuppositions it was nevertheless ultimately prevented from justifying:

> Rational knowledge, which has followed its own autonomous and inner-worldly norms . . . has fashioned a cosmos of truths which no longer has anything to do with the systematic postulates of a rational religious ethic. . . . Although science has created this cosmos of natural causality and has seemed unable to answer with certainty the question of its own ultimate presuppositions, in the name of "intellectual integrity" it has come forward with the claim of representing the only possible form of a reasoned view of the world. Thus the intellect, like all cultural values, has also created an unbrotherly aristocracy of the rational possession of culture [*unbrüderliche Aristokratie des rationalen Kulturbesitzes*], one that is independent of all personal ethical qualities of humankind.[90]

Undoubtedly one of Weber's most fundamental choices, the flight into the "unbrotherly aristocracy" of rational scientific culture, represented a specific, permanent and comprehensive answer to the various escape routes of modern discontent.

Weber explored the substance and implications of the preference for

90. *GARS* 1:569; G&M, 355.

the life-order of *Intellekt* in several distinctive ways. In "Science as a Vocation" he deliberately and provocatively set his answer in the context of the explosive cultural debate between "life" and science (*Wissenschaft*), that gray, abstract, ascetic power. Nietzsche's question, What is the meaning of ascetic ideals for life?, was reformulated to read, What can the pursuit of (theoretical) knowledge or science contribute to "practical and personal 'life'"?—the "*inward*" question that really mattered most to Weber and his audience.[91] Against those who answered with "Nothing at all!" (as did members of the youth and reform movements in 1917 at Lauenstein Castle, where these ideas were put to the test), Weber countered with the self-referential lines from *Faust*, uttered by Mephistopheles to youthful students, enthusiasts for "life" who had declined to applaud his show of superior knowledge:

> My words appear to leave you cold;
> Poor youth, I will not be your scolder.
> Mind you, the devil, he is old;
> To understand him, best grow older![92]

This exceptional moment of Faustian identification and posing enacts a dramatic gamble for Weber, like scientific activity itself. It is both a summons and a dare to enter this contested sphere in order to grasp its limits and its instrumental powers.

For science to offer instrumental knowledge for the technical control of life, logical tools for thought, ways to calculate means with respect to a given end, and so forth, is an achievement of sorts, but not much of one. However, the wager with knowledge leads to something more significant: For if the impersonal, disenchanting rationalism of knowledge could not possibly solve the problem of its own ultimate meaning, while still remaining true to its critical premises, then it could nevertheless in its mode of "philosophical" reflection minimally fulfill the "duty of bringing about self-clarification and a sense of responsibility." The informed discussion of principles could compel the individual "to give himself *an account of the ultimate meaning of his own conduct.*" Science then stood in the service of "'moral' [*sittliche*] powers."[93] On this ground and this ground alone, Weber insisted, the pursuit of knowledge

---

91. *GAW*, 588, 607; G&M, 134, 150.
92. *Faust*, part II, act 2, sc. 35, lines 6817–18; quoted in *GAW*, 609; *GPS*, 546; G&M, 126, 152. Machiavelli's pithier reminder to Guicciardini was that "the true way of going to Paradise would be to learn the road to Hell in order to avoid it."
93. *GAW*, 608; G&M, 152.

and science could be "justified" within the total economy of human choice.

But among all the life-orders, how could science hope to join forces with ethics? What did such an alliance assume? Weber found the answer in an exceptional suggestion, declaring at the end of the key passage just quoted that moral achievements are made more likely and more secure, not the more insistently opinion is declaimed with the authority of science, but on the contrary, "the more conscientiously [a teacher] avoids attempting personally to impose or insinuate a [moral] position on the audience." The postulate of "value freedom" addressed the situation *inside* the community of science with respect to the cultural crisis over the standing of scientific knowledge, the nature of the university, educational policy, academic freedom, and numerous related issues that have become commonplace in our own time. In "The Meaning of 'Value-Freedom' in the Sociological and Economic Sciences,"[94] the controversial text prepared for the special 1914 session of the Verein für Sozialpolitik, Weber even pinpointed the target precisely: Gustav von Schmoller and his popular mainstream defense of (a) the vocational right of the teacher to propagandize, express personal preferences, and otherwise make "subjective *demands* on culture" in the name of science; (b) the exclusion of both Marxists and Manchesterites from university faculties on grounds that their approaches had been proven scientifically false;[95] (c) the view that the validity of a practical evaluation (Is a particular state of affairs desirable or undesirable?) is identical to the truth-value of an empirical proposition (Is a particular assertion true or false?); and (d) the claim that the value-sphere of ethics is synonymous with cultural values.[96]

94. Shils' and Finch's translation of *Wertfreiheit* as "ethical neutrality" is unfortunate, as it can suggest that in science Weber wanted to promote indifference, lack of involvement, or a tactic of finding the middle path with respect to moral questions. Numerous statements say precisely the opposite: for instance, "An *attitude of moral indifference* [*Gesinnungslosigkeit*] has no inner relationship with *scientific* 'objectivity' " (*GAW*, 157; S&F, 60).

95. This issue was addressed especially in exchanges with Michels, whose university career had been blocked by his outspoken socialism; see, for example, Weber's comment that "in university circles . . . there *is* the foolish opinion that the 'abominable nature' of social democracy can be and has been *scientifically* 'proven,' just as in *your party* the opinion about 'bourgeois' pseudo-science is tolerated and encouraged" (letter of 1 February 1907, AMW 35).

96. *GAW*, 492, 495, 501, 504; S&F, 4, 7, 12, 15. Probably the most prominent and powerful social scientist in his day, a beneficiary of Althoff's policies, Schmoller held sway as chair of the *Verein* from 1890 until his death in 1917. Weber's original text from 1913, "Gutachten zur Werturteilsdiskussion," in Baumgarten, *Max Weber: Werk und Person*,

Opposed to all of these positions, Weber wanted to counter them by
seizing the high ground for science and its standards of discourse, doing
so not simply to shelter the inquiring mind from violence against it or
to solve a methodological problem, but also to address profoundly disturbing cultural deficits: "Cultural consensus in the field of education
can be justified only on the condition of severe self-restraint in the ob-
servance of the canons of science and scholarship," was his defense at
one point, followed by the injunction that "if one desires this consensus,
one must put aside the idea of any sort of instruction in ultimate values
and beliefs." [97] When used without prejudice, the indispensable vehicle
for this purpose and Ranke's great Socratic invention for the modern
university, the seminar, functioned to institutionalize the authority of a
common ground for discussion and selection: there "one asks the most
inconvenient questions," Weber argued, "until clarity appears, until one
knows how to distinguish between one's opinion and one's scientific
work in such a way as to allow us to say: this is a thinker, therefore he
belongs to the community of science, no matter how absurd his personal
convictions or religious beliefs may appear to us." [98] "Freedom" in these
matters, an inexact and fragile product of culture, was the precondition
for the will to truth's moral effects: self-clarification, responsibility, integrity. And what was scientific truth itself for Weber?—"only that
which *wants* to be valid for all those who *want* the truth." [99]

Having distinguished among three kinds of reasons for Weber's
choice in the "age of subjectivist culture," it is necessary to emphasize
in the end the logical consistency and substantive unity among all three.
Again and again at every level Weber returns to the same configuration
of principles: responsibility for the self and others, intellectual integrity,
clarity of vision, the pathos of distance and objectivity toward the self
and the world, meeting the Goethean "demands of the day." With these

102–39, provides a more unguarded glimpse of the source of his position in the *Verein*
debates involving Schmoller after 1905.

97. "The Academic Freedom of the Universities" (1909), in *Max Weber on Universities*, ed. E. Shils (Chicago: University of Chicago Press, 1974), 22.

98. From one of Weber's statements at the Conference of University Teachers in Leipzig (1909), in *Verhandlungen des III. Deutschen Hochschullehrertages* (Leipzig: Verlag
des Literarischen Zentralblattes für Deutschland, 1910), 16, copy in the MWE.

99. *GAW*, 184; S&F, 84; the sense of the active will in Weber's declaration is difficult
to convey: "Denn wissenschaftliche Wahrheit ist nur, was für alle gelten *will*, die Wahrheit
wollen." Only Nietzsche had given the "problem of truth" such a radical formulation.

ideas we have touched the foundations of Weber's evaluative response to the modern age of subjectivist culture. It does not seem possible to go beyond them to anything more fundamental.

Has Weber then offered us "only a diagnosis" of culture and its discontents and not a "therapy?"[100] Is this self-imposed restraint what distinguishes him from a Hegel or a Marx? If by therapy one means a code of explicit recommendations for transforming nature and history in line with a fundamental ontology, then the distinction seems secure. However, if instead one means a practice for testing illusions, eliminating Baconian "idols of the mind," and questioning metaphysical assumptions in line with a critical teaching about the conditions for knowledge, then the important contrast appears to be between two rival corrective proposals. Weber's sociohistorical science of culture and "actuality" achieved a diagnostic understanding of the course of Western rationalism and the struggles waged among the different orders of life and value. Yet, as part of the philosophical discussion of value-positions that Weber considered integral to science, it also set forth a strategic position at three levels for facing up to the discontents embedded in our rationalist culture.

Weber's fully articulated perspective is of course open to criticism from the standpoint of other life-orders or spheres of value, but its strength lies precisely in its having accounted already for these alternatives, their assumptions and paradoxes. There are, as it were, no unanticipated surprises left to startle and derail the inquiring modern mind. Whether we can share Weber's formulation of the issues, his juxtaposition of the antinomies and ironies of existence, and his choice for science, or whether we are attracted instead to the rival claim of an alternative will depend not merely on those "daemons" who "hold the fibers of our lives," cited in the closing sentence of "Science as a Vocation," but also on our understanding and judgment of the culture that surrounds us, which is itself preeminently a task for the intellect.

However, to the extent that we continue to share the larger problem of culture and its discontents with Weber and his fin-de-siècle generation, to the extent that modernity and the adaptive maneuvers and protests provoked by it continue to pursue us, we should at least be able to

100. The terminology is from Löwith, *Max Weber and Karl Marx*, 25; and Erik Wolf, "Max Webers ethischer Kritizismus und das Problem der Metaphysik," *Logos* 19 (1930):363.

gain in understanding through recovery of an analysis prepared to heed the warning in Goethe's lines:

> Day is still upon us, while we remain active;
> But the night approaches, where none can be productive.

One would like to think that remembrance of what has gone before and might again lie ahead can provoke a modest step away from the shadows of forgetfulness and self-deception.

CHAPTER IV

The Sociology of Culture and Simmel

Although culture is indeed a completion or perfection of humanity, each such completion is in no sense really culture.

—Georg Simmel

From the circle of intellectuals who came to prominence with Weber in the decades after 1890, probably no figure is more challenging in the profundity and sheer sweep of his thought than Georg Simmel. One would be hard-pressed to locate two men from the new generation with comparable achievements during the critical formative years of modern social theory. Some of their contemporaries are remembered essentially for a single study: Tönnies' *Gemeinschaft und Gesellschaft* or Michels' *Political Parties.* Others—Werner Sombart, Ernst Troeltsch, Heinrich Rickert—have largely faded from view, while still others—Lujo Brentano, Leopold von Wiese, Heinrich Herkner—have been forgotten altogether. But the spirits of Weber and Simmel continue to command a large field of attention not only in the history and practice of sociology, but also in reflection on the Western intellectual tradition over the last century. Weber's grip on our imaginations has really never diminished, while (considering directions in recent scholarship) Simmel's is surely on the ascendant.

Given their standing nowadays and among members of their own generation, it is all the more remarkable that the important judgments of recent years remain as relevant as ever: our lack of "a thorough examination of the relationship between Simmel's work as a whole and that of Max Weber" or "the absence of systematic, comparative analysis" continues to be "one of the great unfinished pieces of business in

the analysis of the history and conceptual foundations of sociology"[1]—
and, one might add, not only sociology. Even apparently simple questions have not been satisfactorily answered: When and under what
circumstances did the exchange of views between Weber and Simmel
commence? What did they know of each other's work? What ideas did
each accept or reject from the other, and why? Can one speak of reciprocal influences, borrowings, or traces? What was the nature of their
shared involvements with the representatives and movements in modern
culture, such as the George Circle, or the nature of their activities within
the prewar scientific community, such as the German Sociological Society or the *Archiv für Sozialwissenschaft und Sozialpolitik* and *Logos*?
And these matters still leave untouched the significant theoretical problems: What did Simmel and Weber represent to each other as thinkers?
How did their seemingly quite different questions or "problematics"
develop, and in response to which intellectual currents and thematics?
What is the meaning and significance of their contributions?

It is necessary to consider these questions at three "levels"—the personal, the practical, and the theoretical—in order from the start to dis-
pel certain elementary misunderstandings that can now be corrected in
light of newly available evidence, and in order to move our investigations explicitly beyond the level of methodological comparison. From
Tenbruck's early paper to Levine's latest essays[2] the Weber-Simmel connection has been conceived exclusively in terms of methodological simi-
larities and divergences with respect to interpretation, *Verstehen*, pure
concepts, the ideal type, interaction, social action, forms of "sociation"
(*Vergesellschaftung*), the status of "general laws," value-judgments, or
criticisms of "positivism" and "historical materialism." The notion that
Weber was drawn to Simmel primarily because of the latter's "work in
epistemology"[3] has been fueled understandably by the supposition that
their association began in earnest after 1902 (one author has even

1. Quotations from David Frisby, "Introduction to the Translation," in Georg Simmel, *The Philosophy of Money* (London: Routledge & Kegan Paul, 1978), 14; Jim
Faught, "Neglected Affinities: Max Weber and Georg Simmel," *British Journal of Soci-
ology* 36 (1985): 155; Donald N. Levine, "Introduction," in Max Weber, "Georg Simmel
as Sociologist," *Social Research* 39 (1972): 157–58.
2. Friedrich H. Tenbruck, "Formal Sociology," in *Georg Simmel, 1858–1918*, ed.
K. H. Wolff (Columbus: Ohio State University Press, 1959), 61–99; Donald N. Levine,
"Ambivalent Encounters: Disavowals of Simmel by Durkheim, Weber, Lukács, Park, and
Parsons," in *The Flight from Ambiguity: Essays in Social and Cultural Theory* (Chicago:
University of Chicago Press, 1985), 89–141.
3. Levine, *Flight from Ambiguity*, 95.

claimed 1908!),[4] when Weber read *The Philosophy of Money* and *The Problems in the Philosophy of History* and used the latter in his painfully labored essay on "Knies and the Problem of Irrationality" (1905–6).

I want to show, however, that Weber was thoroughly familiar with Simmel and his work well *before* 1902, in an environment dominated by the quite distinctive sociocultural themes just mentioned that came to be reflected in the work of both authors. Our conception of the meaning of Weber's and Simmel's intellectual choices needs to be extended far beyond a discussion of method, or even of the proper foundations and purposes of social theory. For to locate Simmel with Weber in the context of their *own* discourse is to see the way in which both were caught up in a maelstrom of essentially *cultural* problems associated with "modernity": urbanization; the life of the city; the problem of labor and vocation; the fate of religious, ethical, and aesthetic life-orientations; the prospects for free individuality in the face of what Weber symbolized as the "iron cage" and Simmel called the "social-technological mechanism": and, above all, the objective and subjective consequences of capitalism and the "peculiar rationalism" of Western culture. These are most fundamentally the problems that brought Weber and Simmel together, the true sources of their shared interests and parallel questioning. I want to suggest that if we are to enter into their dialogue, it must be in relation to a sociology of culture, to an array of modern problems that are, after all, still ours to attempt to understand.

BERLIN AND THE GENERATION
OF THE NINETIES

Even more so than Weber, Simmel was a product of Berlin, born and raised in the city, like Weber completing his higher degrees in the philosophical faculty of the Humboldt University, but without ever sampling student life elsewhere. Both studied philosophy and history, the latter subject with Theodor Mommsen, among others, but Simmel (who was six years Weber's senior) combined the standard fare characteristically with unorthodox supplementary fields: art history, old Italian, and what might be called "ethno-psychology" (*Völkerpsychologie*). For dis-

4. Yoshio Atoji, "Georg Simmel and Max Weber," in *Sociology at the Turn of the Century* (Tokyo: Dobunkan, 1984), 47.

sertation and "habilitation" topics he selected aspects of Kant's philosophy, but as political economy gained in stature, so he moved gradually
in its direction (as did Weber), delivering the paper that led to his finest
study, *The Philosophy of Money*, in Gustav Schmoller's famous political economy seminar.[5] In the broad sense propagated by Schmoller and
his school,[6] Simmel's early professional interests could even be fit beneath the canopy of political economy, notwithstanding their evident
leanings toward psychological modes of thinking. Whereas Weber, coming at political economy from the direction of law, history, and politi-
al science (*Staatswissenschaft*), developed a version of it emphasizing
mainly historical and socioeconomic or "structural" factors, as the discussion of his East Elbian studies has demonstrated, Simmel elaborated
a kind of "structuralism" in the quite different sense of abstract logical
categories for the analysis of forms and constellations of interaction.[7]

These intellectual starting points and convergent and divergent directions already reveal some important clues to the mature Simmel-Weber
relationship. While both emerged from the upper-middle-class intellectual life of Berlin, Simmel's deepest commitments and mental instincts
were formed early-on in the hothouse of an aesthetic culture sensitive
to art, psychic nuance, emotive expressiveness—the kind of marginal,
particularizing, amoral *Gefühlskultur*, or emotive culture, that has been
so closely linked with the "oppositional identity" formed by Jewish intellectuals and with the milieu characteristic of the turn-of-the-century
Viennese bourgeoisie.[8] For Simmel the refined artistic atmosphere of the
household of the painter Gustav Graef served to prepare the way for his

5. "Zur Psychologie des Geldes," *Schmollers Jahrbuch* 13 (1889): 1251–64.
6. See Gustav Schmoller, "Volkswirtschaft, Volkswirtschaftslehre und -methode," in *Handwörterbuch der Staatswissenschaften*, vol. 6, ed. J. Conrad et al. (Jena: Fischer, 1894), 527–63.
7. See Birgitta Nedelmann, "Strukturprinzipien der soziologischen Denkweise Georg Simmels," *Kölner Zeitschrift für Soziologie und Sozialpsychologie* 32 (1980): 559–73.
8. See Dirk Käsler, *Die frühe deutsche Soziologie 1909 bis 1934 und ihre Entste-hungs-Milieus* (Opladen: Westdeutscher Verlag, 1984), 357–85; and Carl E. Schorske, *Fin-de-siècle Vienna: Politics and Culture* (New York: Random House [Vintage Books], 1981). Käsler's thesis (see esp. 235–57) that the new stratum of sociologists was recruited largely from the *Besitzbürgertum* and entered the *Bildungsbürgertum* in an effort to gain status and "respectability" appears better suited to account for Simmel's development than Weber's. Simmel's father and grandfather were businessmen, and the artistic tutelage of his guardian, Julius Friedländer, and the Graef household (a kind of substitute family for young Georg) began relatively late with the father's death when Georg was sixteen. In Weber's case, however, despite his father's origins in the propertied class, the milieu of the *Bildungsbürger* seems to have pervaded the immediate culture of family life, including the fraternal circle of politicians and scholars who frequented family gatherings in Charlottenburg.

later association with the artists and poets of the Berlin *Sezession*, the George Circle, and the earliest literary expression of the "culture of narcissism," the magazine *Jugend*—not to mention his attraction to Gertrud Kinel, a young painter who studied at the renowned Académie Julien and whom he married.[9] Throughout his life Simmel prided himself on cultivating such aesthetic sensibilities and attachments, using them self-consciously as sources of reflection in his own "science" and transposing them into his own version of "philosophical culture," as he entitled his major collection of essays.

Although Weber too was fascinated by aestheticism as a life-order and sphere of value, unlike Simmel he remained *personally* outside the boundaries of its charmed circle, instead cultivating an orientation that had a great deal to do with the sense of public responsibility promoted by ascetic Protestantism. But in contrast to Weber, Simmel was decidedly "unmusical" in the political sphere. Against Weber's relentless, razor-sharp political judgments, Simmel's "political" tracts of the war years, for example, must seem like hopeful and naive musings of the aesthetic consciousness, an apolitical product of the kind of sheltered "inwardness" that Weber could otherwise appreciate.[10] Yet even the culture flourishing beneath such protection could not escape Weber's Calvinist eye: whereas for Simmel culture sprang into being out of the permanent contradiction between subjective life and objective form, for Weber it was above all a sphere of value rendered "meaningless" by striving for an ever-renewable and perfectable expressiveness that could never be attained. What for Simmel was rendered "tragic" became in Weber's vision "burdened with guilt."

9. The best account is Sabine Lepsius' autobiography, *Ein Berliner Künstlerleben um die Jahrhundertwende* (Munich: Gotthold Müller, 1972), 62–65, 137–41, 179–83.
10. The dynamics of *machtgeschützte Innerlichkeit*, as it has been called, are captured appropriately in Max Horkheimer and T. W. Adorno's comment (*The Dialectic of Enlightenment*, trans. J. Cumming [New York: Continuum, 1987]) that "in Germany the failure of democratic control to permeate life had led to a paradoxical situation. Many things were exempt from the market mechanism which had invaded the Western countries. The German educational system, universities, theaters with artistic standards, great orchestras, and museums enjoyed protection. The political powers, state and municipalities, which had inherited such institutions from absolutism, had left them with a measure of the freedom from the forces of power which dominates the market. . . . This strengthened art in this late phase against the verdict of supply and demand, and increased its resistance far beyond the actual degree of protection" (132–33). Weber's underlying objection to Friedrich Althoff's skillful domination of higher education in Germany during his quarter-century tenure in the Prussian Ministry of Education (1882–1907) was based on the erosion of this "paradoxical freedom" in favor of blatantly political and economic criteria for educational policy.

It is worth noting that Simmel spent nearly his entire life in Berlin, where he could observe, celebrate, and contribute to the multifaceted aesthetic culture of modernism. Simmel was modern culture's truest servant, the peerless epicure of its many moods, possibilities, and pleasures, all of which were perfectly captured in *The Philosophy of Money*. This was not a sociological or economic treatise, but a book about the Zeitgeist. Simmel's friend and fellow philosopher Karl Joël was precisely correct when he noted that it could have been written only "in these times and in Berlin"; it had "overheard the innermost tone of modern life from the babble of the vast market place." [11] Weber heard these voices too, but as a young professor he had chosen to leave Berlin for the "freer atmosphere" of Baden. The choice seems to have stuck. Weber came to be remembered as the "myth of Heidelberg," the city symbolizing liberal-scientific opposition and protection for "rational" political culture in Bismarck's *Reich*. Weber's vocation took shape more or less around a sustained effort to defend just this cultural legacy, and to do so on the most uncompromising grounds of a deep pessimism concerning modernity's liberating potential. Weber's stance, unlike Simmel's, was *against* the spirit of the age, *against* the times, "'against the stream' of the material constellations" of interests. [12] If in this respect Simmel mirrored his environment, then Weber shattered its illusions.

Simmel was drawn to Weber, this "fighter against his time," quoting Nietzsche's words, no doubt because of his daemonic nature, possessed by a passion for science that had "tasted the fruit of the tree of knowledge" and created a world under its "rational" dominion. Weber took his stand, "in spite of all" as he liked to say, in the value-sphere of "knowledge," and he did so with a consuming thoroughness: "I want to see how much I can bear" seems to have been his identifying motto, with its unmistakable resemblance to one of Simmel's own favorite dictums: "One sees best what a man is made of by *what* he *does* in order to bear life at all." For both men the life of the inquiring mind was like performing a vivisection, complete with Nietzschean overtones, for "vivisection is a *test*: whoever cannot bear it does not belong to us." [13]

11. Quoted in Frisby, "Introduction," 8.
12. Weber, "Zur Lage der bürgerlichen Demokratie in Russland," *Archiv* 22 (1906): 348; *Selections*, 282; *GAW*, 540; S&F, 47.
13. *Lebensbild*, 690; Eng. trans., 678; Michael Landmann, "Arthur Steins Erinnerungen an Georg Simmel," in H. Böhringer and K. Gründer, eds., *Ästhetik und Soziologie um die Jahrhundertwende: Georg Simmel* (Frankfurt: Klostermann, 1976), 275; Friedrich Nietzsche, *Werke: Kritische Gesamtausgabe*, ed. G. Colli and M. Montinari (Berlin: de Gruyter, 1974), 7/2: 85; *aushalten* is the verb all three prefer.

"Yes, yes, what should one say about him?" Simmel once remarked about Weber, according to their close mutual friend, Sophie Rickert: "There is no other way to put it: he was simply a genius."[14] Marianne Weber liked to see in her husband the immortal knight of Germany's timeless past; for Simmel he could only have approximated the universal humanity of Faust.

And what did Simmel represent for Weber? There are easy answers: cultural philosopher and critic of culture, philosopher of history, and social psychologist. But Simmel was above all the modern *Kulturmensch*, or "cultural being," who figures so prominently in key passages of Weber's writing, the essentially *new* human self fully absorbed into the life-order of aesthetic modernism, the ahistorical self actualized in a world of limitless possibilities. Weber's scanty published praise of Simmel can be understood only from this angle: Simmel's theoretical contributions and stimulating insights are uniquely valuable *because* of properties intrinsic to the observing self that cannot be imitated by others. In this view any attempts to sift through Simmel's writing in search of a usable "method" would be utterly fruitless. Simmel achieved a special standing for Weber, earning a respect reserved for the very few, only because of a particular and unique mode of perception based on an unrepeatable temporal and spacial convergence of experience in "the modern." All of Simmel's "sociology"—his "sociological impressionism," as critics from Lukács to Frisby have called it[15]—is suffused with this point of view. It is precisely this viewpoint, however, that made Simmel *the* most significant contemporary for Max Weber.

But these representative sketches are not intended to overpower the historical evidence. What can be said about the earliest encounters between Simmel and Weber?

THE SIGNIFICANCE OF NIETZSCHE

We cannot be sure when Weber's and Simmel's paths first crossed, although they may well have become aware of each other at the University

14. Cited in K. Gassen and M. Landmann, eds., *Buch des Dankes an Georg Simmel: Briefe, Erinnerungen, Bibliographie* (Berlin: Duncker & Humblot, 1958), 212.

15. Georg Lukács first used the phrase in 1918 in his appreciation of Simmel, in ibid., 171–76; also David Frisby, *Sociological Impressionism: A Reassessment of Georg Simmel's Social Theory* (London: Heinemann, 1981), and, more recently, *Fragments of Modernity: Theories of Modernity in the Work of Simmel, Kracauer and Benjamin* (Cambridge: Polity Press, 1985), chap. 2, under the Hegelian sign of "modernity as an eternal present."

of Berlin in the circle of "younger political economists" and "historians" Weber mentions joining in 1887.[16] Weber's earliest explicit reference to Simmel occurs in a letter of 26 July 1894 to Marianne Weber (who was in Freiburg searching for their new apartment). The context is remarkably suggestive:

> Your letter certainly still testifies to a severe decrease in spirits, but that is good and healthy and hopefully will remain so until you return to me here in these civilized environs, so that my cerebral nerves, ill-treated by the surveys, Kierkegaard, Nietzsche, and Simmel, will at last be able to recover somewhat.[17]

In what was undoubtedly a reference to *Thus Spake Zarathustra* Weber had previously asked his wife whether she wanted additional reading material sent to her, "or is the 'Overman' tormenting you enough for the time being?" He added that "several fairly foolish moralistic tracts have arrived for you here ('The Curse of Masculinity' and similar things), which I'll send only on demand."[18] Weber also reported attending a small dinner gathering on July 25, commemorating his Freiburg appointment, attended by Simmel, Schmoller, Adolph Wagner, Otto von Gierke, August Meitzen, Heinrich Brunner, and Ernst Eck, and at which Simmel spoke in personal terms.

There can be no doubt then that Weber knew Simmel well—personally and as a scholar—by the summer of 1894, the semester in which Simmel began to lecture on "sociology" and to prepare a fall course entitled "On Pessimism," a topic out of Schopenhauer and Nietzsche. Moreover, as Lichtblau has shown,[19] this was exactly the moment in Simmel's intellectual development when, influenced by Nietzsche, he had abandoned mechanistic and evolutionary theories built on Herbert Spencer and Gustav Fechner in favor of an exploration of Nietzsche's value theory and cultural criticism. The starting point for Weber's reception of Simmel had little to do with "methodology" or "epistemology," and everything to do with an "ethical atmosphere" created by questions about the "transvaluation of values," the meaning of

16. Letter to Hermann Baumgarten, 30 September 1887, *JB*, 273.
17. NW 30/1:50. The "surveys" Weber mentions are probably those of East Elbian agricultural labor distributed by the Evangelisch-sozialer Kongress, whose preliminary results Weber had reported at the fifth annual meeting in May 1894; cf. Wilhelm Hennis, *Max Webers Fragestellung: Studien zur Biographie des Werks* (Tübingen: J. C. B. Mohr [Paul Siebeck], 1987), 172.
18. Letter of 12 July 1894, NW 30/1: 47–48.
19. Klaus Lichtblau, "Das 'Pathos der Distanz,' Präliminarien zur Nietzsche-Rezeption bei Georg Simmel," in *Georg Simmel und die Moderne*, ed. H.-J. Dahme and O. Rammstedt (Frankfurt: Suhrkamp, 1984), esp. 240–49.

"ascetic ideals," and the emergence of feminism. For Weber these themes were reinforced in a political direction by identical concerns within the Protestant social movement, the main setting of his public engagements in the nineties. In Simmel's case, on the other hand, the themes were pushed in the direction of a philosophical psychology that culminated in a *Lebensphilosophie* drawn extensively from Nietzschean categories.[20]

This triumvirate—Kierkegaard, Nietzsche, and Simmel—could only have presented an enormous challenge to Weber, just as it can suggest tantalizing possibilities for the interpreter, not the least of which is the conjecture that the texts for Weber's reading may have formed a complex relationship with one another. A hint as to the connection can be discovered in two of Weber's later remarks on the "ethical problem" in *The Protestant Ethic and the Spirit of Capitalism*. According to one passage, "the conflict between the individual and the ethic (in Soren Kierkegaard's sense) did not exist for Calvinism, although it placed the individual entirely on his own responsibility in religious matters."[21] The conflict that *did* exist for Calvinism—that between the logical and psychological consequences of predestination—then led subsequently (in sentences added in 1920) to Nietzsche, or rather to Weber's restatement of *Simmel's* interpretation of Nietzsche.[22] For psychological reasons similar to those found in Calvinism, Weber maintained, "the followers of Nietzsche claim a positive ethical significance for the idea of eternal recurrence. This case, however, is concerned with responsibility for a future life which is connected with the active individual by no conscious thread of continuity, while for the Puritan it was *tua res agitur*," a thing to turn over in one's mind.[23] Precisely this ethical content—specifically, the ethic of responsibility—was at the core of Simmel's positive evaluation of the potentially most "metaphysical" aspect of Nietzsche's teachings, which Weber had encountered in the last chapter of *Schopenhauer and Nietzsche*.

---

20. Bryan S. Turner, "Simmel, Rationalisation and the Sociology of Money," *Sociological Review* 34 (1986): 108, has similarly observed that "the impact of Nietzsche's problem of the devaluation of values in a nihilistic culture had a significant set of common theoretical consequences for both Simmel and Weber which have yet to be systematically assessed." The comments that follow can be considered an attempt at such an assessment.
21. *GARS* 1:101; *PE*, 109.
22. See Georg Simmel, "Nietzsche und Kant" (1906), in *Das Individuum und die Freiheit* (Berlin: Wagenbach, 1984), 41–47; on the "eternal recurrence," see his *Schopenhauer und Nietzsche: Ein Vortragszyklus* (Leipzig: Duncker & Humblot, 1907), 246–61, and the English translation by Helmut Loiskandl et al. (Amherst: University of Massachusetts Press, 1986), 170–79; cf. Lichtblau, 260–61.
23. *GARS* 1:111 n. 4; *PE*, 232 n. 66.

In other words, Kierkegaard's and Nietzsche's probing of consciousness, as Weber would have understood, came to view the self as a recording of possibilities and intangibles, created by choices and by "dread," in contrast to Calvinism's assertion of a unity to life, vocation, and moral duty. Against the somber background of the latter world of certainties, Weber encountered the problem of the modern "self," or, rather, the self became a problem for him through the agency of the devastating questioning of what had gone before. (Surely Weber's fascination with Calvinism's balancing of accounts—self-responsibility and providence, loneliness and grace—had something to do with these modern perceptions of irreversible fragmentation.) For this problem and all others like it the line of thought for the generation of the nineties led principally and invariably through Nietzsche. The central question has to be, What was Nietzsche's early significance for Weber and Simmel?

The briefest answer to this deceptively simple question must be sought for *both* of these representatives of the Berlin milieu in the writings of Simmel, for it is these writings that in an important way mediate and disclose Weber's own understanding of Nietzsche, as well as that of a generation of contemporaries.[24] In addition, although Weber's explicit comments on Nietzsche are rare and cryptic, Simmel's are profuse and profoundly revealing, from four articles beginning in 1895 to the influential 1907 study *Schopenhauer and Nietzsche*, a book now most remembered, it would seem, for Weber's marginalia in his personal copy. (Parenthetically, Simmel's earliest reference to Nietzsche occurs in his 1890 review of Julius Langbehn's notorious *Rembrandt als Erzieher*.) By inquiring into Simmel's accessible interpretation of Nietzsche, one is able to say a good deal about Weber's enigmatic image of this philosophical apostate. The basic design of Simmel's and Weber's depictions, even down to specific items, is actually quite similar.

Simmel's argument, which developed as a riposte on the one hand to

---

24. As representative examples, one could cite Thomas Mann, Emil Hammacher, and Georg Lukács. "Is not Georg Simmel correct when he claims that after Nietzsche, 'life' became the key concept of all modern world views? In any case, Nietzsche's entire moral criticism stands under the sign of this idea," writes Mann, *Reflections of a Nonpolitical Man* (1918), trans. W. Morris (New York: Ungar, 1983), 58, neatly summing up the thoughts of an entire generation. For Weber's own reception of Nietzsche and relationship to him, see the suggestive discussion in Hennis, *Max Weber's Fragestellung*, chap. 4; also Georg Stauth and Bryan S. Turner, "Nietzsche in Weber oder die Geburt des modernen Genius im professionellen Menschen," *Zeitschrift für Soziologie* 15 (1986), 81–94; in addition, Robert Eden, *Political Leadership and Nihilism: A Study of Weber and Nietzsche* (Tampa: University Presses of Florida, 1984), is useful, although his formulation of central questions based on American political thought renders the discussion somewhat awkward.

the self-appointed Nietzscheans (including the group around Elisabeth Förster-Nietzsche) and on the other hand to the critics of the "Nietzsche cult" (including Tönnies), can be reduced to three claims: Nietzsche was not a decadent or egoist, but rather a moralist whose teachings centered on the problem of "morality"; he was neither a cynic nor a philistine, but rather a critic of the age, of its "modernity" and incipient nihilism; and he was to be understood not as a prophet or poet, as many of his "disciples" believed, but as a master psychologist of human existence.[25] In his reply to Tönnies Simmel particularly stressed a conception of responsibility for the self, the Nietzschean "will to self-overcoming" and "hardness" toward the self placed in service to the "increase of life." Indicative of what Simmel called the "objective value" of the morality of "nobility," these ideas were combined in the third essay of the *Genealogy of Morals*, "What Is the Meaning of Ascetic Ideals?," one of the most remarkable of Nietzsche's expositions, with an "astute sensitivity, a depth of causal analysis, an accuracy of expression never before reached in German psychology."[26] Friedrich Nietzsche, moralist and psychologist, would have been the heading for all of Simmel's critical thinking on this topic.

Weber's understanding of Nietzsche appears to have followed precisely the same course. It is most improbable, for instance, that Weber could have pursued the twists and turns in the momentous career of asceticism in the "sociology of religion" without Nietzsche's achievements in the *Genealogy*, that "brilliant essay," quoting Weber's words,[27] that must be credited with turning the practice of the "ascetic life" into

25. For these views, see Georg Simmel, "Elisabeth Försters Nietzsche-Biographie," *Berliner Tageblatt*, 26 August 1895, 481; "Friedrich Nietzsche, Eine moralphilosophische Silhouette," *Zeitschrift für Philosophie und philosophische Kritik* 107 (1896): 202–15; his review of *Der Nietzsche-Kultus*, by Ferdinand Tönnies, *Deutsche Litteraturzeitung* 42 (1897): 1645–51; and his "Zum Verständnis Nietzsches," *Das Freie Wort* 2 (1902): 6–11. Compare Thomas Mann's similar confession of Nietzsche's early influence in the nineties: "If, however, this same basic mood made me into a psychologist of *decadence*, then it was Nietzsche to whom I looked as master, for from the start he was not so much for me the prophet of some kind of vague 'superman,' as he was for most people when he was in fashion, as rather the incomparably greatest and most experienced psychologist of decadence" (*Reflections*, 54–55).

26. Simmel's review of Tönnies' *Der Nietzsche-Kultus*, 1649; referring to Tönnies' work, Wolfgang J. Mommsen writes, "The few biographical references we have suggest that Max Weber's understanding of Nietzsche was strongly influenced by Ferdinand Tönnies' extremely successful book on Nietzsche" ("Introduction," in *Max Weber and His Contemporaries*, ed. Mommsen and J. Osterhammel [London: Allen & Unwin, 1987], 15). But surely this is not the case, for on the contrary, it is precisely the elements that Tönnies *missed* in Nietzsche, and that Simmel recovered in his Tönnies critique, that Weber also claimed for his own. In these matters Simmel, not Tönnies, was Weber's authority.

27. *GARS* 1:241; *G&M*, 270.

a world-historical *problem* that could be addressed beyond the boundaries of "psychology." It is not without accident that Nietzsche's presence
through citation, imitation, and criticism is felt most strongly in this
part of Weber's work, and invariably in those places (such as the last
three pages of *The Protestant Ethic and the Spirit of Capitalism*) where
his thought breaks through to a synthetic judgment of our "modern
fate." (It is just at these moments too that Weber repudiates the "prophetic" Nietzsche of the epigones.) Furthermore, like Simmel, Weber
did explicitly stress that not the "biological trimmings" but rather the
"morality of nobility" was to be considered the contribution from
Nietzsche that had "permanent value."[28] This contribution more than
any other can be seen as responsible for the sharpening of Weber's critical rhetoric circa 1894–95, as in his assault on a facile eudaemonism
and his defense of a view of life as a perpetual, "hard struggle," expounded with unrestrained vigor in the Freiburg "Inaugural Address"
of 1895.

These observations help establish a certain parallelism in Simmel's
and Weber's interpretation and interests: in Nietzsche both see the same
driven and uncompromising spirit, the same demands for unyielding
toughness with oneself and the world. If any single idea is taken over
from Nietzsche it is the problem of "meaning" within "subjectivist"
culture, or, in a somewhat different terminology, the problem of a modern "perspectivism." Despite its curiously individualized language, a
passage in the last chapter of Simmel's *Philosophy of Money* captures
one version of the matter:

> The subjectivism of modern times has the same basic motive as art: to gain
> a more intimate and truer relationship to objects by dissociating ourselves
> from them and retreating into ourselves, or by consciously acknowledging
> the inevitable distance between ourselves and objects. When confronted with
> a stronger self-awareness, this subjectivism inevitably leads to an emphasis
> upon our inner nature, while on the other hand it is associated with a new,
> deeper and more conscious modesty, a delicate reticence towards expressing
> the ultimate.[29]

To Simmel's mind what Nietzsche perceived in such an inward turn,
a preoccupation with the psychic self, was a searching for a concept
of "lived experience" (*Erleben*) or of "life" as an "end in itself."

28. This important statement is found in the concluding paragraph of Weber's critique
of Otto Gross's essay submitted to the *Archiv*, dated 13 September 1907, in Eduard Baumgarten, *Max Weber: Werk und Person* (Tübingen: J. C. B. Mohr [Paul Siebeck], 1964), 648.
29. *The Philosophy of Money* (1900), trans. T. Bottomore and D. Frisby (London:
Routledge & Kegan Paul, 1978), 475.

Nietzsche's critique succeeded in showing to Simmel's satisfaction that for us moderns "life itself becomes the purpose of life." [30] Appropriately, art turns into the model for "experience," for the dissociated subject driven back upon itself. If Nietzsche condemned such subjectivist leanings, then Simmel responded by building a vitalist philosophy of life on them. Having praised the "brilliant images [Bilder]" [31] in Simmel's last chapter of the *Philosophy of Money*, Weber may be understood to have pushed these consequences of modern self-consciousness to a conclusion by resolving to preserve distance, to hold out against various convenient modern escapes. Like Simmel's comments, the entire meaning of Weber's melancholy meditations on the "modern soul" presupposes the paths in thought traversed by Nietzsche.

But parallels and agreements concerning cultural significance do not demonstrate identity. What separated Weber's Nietzsche-reception from Simmel's were two disagreements—one philosophical, the other political. For Weber chose to question Simmel's "philosophy of life" with its apparent suspension of "judgment," or, what is the same thing, its passive acquiescence in the "modern." Probably nothing was greeted with greater skepticism by Weber than the obsessive absorption with the experiencing self: "What is hard for modern man, and especially for the younger generation, is to measure up to *workaday* existence. The ubiquitous chase for 'experience' stems from this weakness; for it is weakness not to be able to countenance the stern seriousness of our fateful times," intoned the warning of "Science as a Vocation." [32] If such renunciation brought Weber closer than Simmel to the spirit of Nietzsche's "pathos of distance," then his "political" criticism thrust him farther apart: Nietzsche's politically tinted reflections on "will," as Simmel set them forth in *Schopenhauer and Nietzsche*, displayed none of the "sensitivity" encountered elsewhere in his work, but rather the commonplace generalizations of the philistine—a failing Simmel but not Weber tended to overlook or discount. [33] But the omission was characteristic, for Simmel's cultural prowess was gained at the price of his political innocence. His version of Nietzsche was poorly suited to political combat.

30. *Schopenhauer und Nietzsche*, 5; altered from the English translation, 6.
31. *GARS* 1:34 n. 1; *PE*, 193 n. 6.
32. *GAW*, 605; G&M, 149.
33. See Wolfgang J. Mommsen, *Max Weber: Gesellschaft, Politik und Geschichte* (Frankfurt: Suhrkamp, 1974), 261–62 n. 125, for commentary on Weber's marginalia in his copy of *Schopenhauer und Nietzsche*, now housed in the library of the Max-Weber-Arbeitsstelle, Munich.

THE PROBLEM OF PSYCHOLOGISM

There is a second major source for Weber's pre-1900 reception of Simmel's work: the immensely important *Basic Outline of Lectures on General (Theoretical) Political Economy* of 1898 (*Grundriss zu den Vorlesungen über allgemeine* [*"theoretische"*] *Nationalökonomie*), its privately printed first book (out of a projected six), and Weber's unpublished handwritten notes for the project. In this ambitious treatise, a systematic historical-critical exposition of everything having to do with the science of "political economy" in his day, Weber proposed to treat Simmel under the heading "The Concept of Society and Social Science" as the author of *On Social Differentiation* (1890) and "The Problem of Sociology" (1894), the earliest version of the famous first chapter of Simmel's *Soziologie*, published in 1908. The outline and the notes prepared for it give a revealing glimpse into the obverse side of Weber's appreciation of Simmel, the one that has heretofore attracted attention: not the connection to Nietzsche and the problem of the "modern," but rather the route to "sociology" and the problem of knowledge is highlighted in these texts. These are not heterogeneous problems, however. One must be prepared to see that the two sides of the relationship cannot be separated, for reasons that will soon become evident. The question to bear in mind is not, How did Simmel "influence" Weber's reflections on "methodology?" but rather, What did it *mean* for Simmel to choose to write "sociology" and "epistemology" at the turn of the century?

The key to understanding Weber's treatment of Simmel within the confines of the "science of society," or "sociology" (which, it must be emphasized, was only one small segment of the vast *Grundriss* subject matter), is to be found in the juxtaposition of fundamental theoretical categories. In the first place, the orientation of political economy (*Nationalökonomie* or *Volkswirtschaft* for Weber) is distinguished from that of sociology, or *Gesellschaftswissenschaft* ("science of society," the term Weber prefers at this point). Second, in Weber's text and notes each of these orientations is divided for historical-analytic purposes into "schools" that look approximately as follows:

I. Political economy
   A. The individualist school: classical liberalism
      (Adam Smith, David Ricardo)
   B. Scientific socialism (Karl Marx)
   C. The historical school

1. Older (Wilhelm Roscher, Karl Knies)
2. Younger (Gustav Schmoller)
3. Youngest (Weber)
    D. Marginal utility (Karl Menger)
II. Sociology
    A. Rationalism or positivism (Auguste Comte)
    B. Psychologism (Georg Simmel)

While greatly simplifying Weber's presentation in the *Grundriss*, this outline remains true to his most basic categories and facilitates two quick observations: first, by the mid-1890s Weber was reading Simmel as a theorist who had broken from the confines of political economy and as a major writer worth noting for a unique orientation; and, second, in Weber's schema Simmel's version of sociology gained special meaning in contrast to the preceding rationalist stage-theory of Comte with its belief in history as a progressive movement according to "laws" and "uniformities." According to Weber, Simmel's alternative then swung far in the opposite direction and became in spirit an ahistorical "psychological" sociology emphasizing the general properties of social interaction and the typical categories of inner experience. The label "psychologism," reappearing as a central criticism in Weber's later essay on "Roscher and Knies" (1903–6), is already used in 1898. Since it is without a doubt the term that unifies his evaluation of Simmel's version of the science of "sociology," let us ask what Weber meant by it. What can be said for and against Simmel's distinctive alternative?

Of course, Weber expressed as little admiration as did Simmel for the rationalistic attempt to establish "historical laws" under the aegis of evolutionary "progress," an undeniable similarity in outlook that can encourage the superficial view that Weber agreed with Simmel on fundamentals.[34] But in Weber's published comments on Simmel two characteristics are invariably emphasized, both of which become the basis for criticism: Simmel's "psychologistic language," or "way of formulating" questions, and his uniquely personalized "style."[35] Consider for the former a typical example from Weber's Knies essay, in which the reference is to the conception of "understanding" (*Verstehen*) in Simmel's *Problems of the Philosophy of History*:[36]

34. As suggested in Tenbruck, "Formal Sociology," 80–83.

35. *GAW*, 94; *Roscher and Knies: The Logical Problems of Historical Economics*, trans. Guy Oakes (New York: Free Press, 1975), 153.

36. *Die Probleme der Geschichtsphilosophie: Eine erkenntnistheoretische Studie*, 2d, rev. ed. (Leipzig: Duncker & Humblot, 1905), 28; *The Problems of the Philosophy of History*, trans. Guy Oakes (New York: Free Press, 1977), 64.

Simmel articulates this in his psychologistic language as follows. "Through the spoken word, the mental processes [*Seelenvorgänge*] of the speaker . . . are also produced in the listener." In this process the thoughts themselves are "excluded." Only the content of speech remains, which the listener understands by comparison with his own speech.[37]

Weber proceeds to call this proposed description of *Verstehen* "imprecise." The grounds for the complaint consist in Simmel's repeated use of *Seelenvorgänge*, literally pre-occurrences of the *soul*, the deepest, most inward, and inaccessible recesses of personality. The choice of terminology deliberately emphasizes a distinction between mind and soul, *Geist* and *Seele*. Mere "mental process" in the English translation is hardly what Simmel had in his mind in this kind of formulation, which is a perfectly representative use of the language of "interiority" and the metaphors of "depth" that appear in his writings from beginning to end. Only on the basis of such a distinction (and, parenthetically, a dubious theory of language) could it make sense to speak of excluding "thoughts" from understanding, leaving just the primal stratum of meaningful speech "contents."

Choice of language is usually internally related to mode of thought, and so it is with Simmel to a remarkably striking degree. Every reader of Simmel's sociological essays and avowedly philosophical works cannot possibly avoid the impression of a mind driven to consciously heightened sensibility, to the refinement of nuance and the brilliant aperçu. Weber even begins his 1908 "fragment" on Simmel with such observations: "brilliant," "subtle observations," "a wealth of stimulation"— in short, "a mode of exposition . . . [which] attains results that are intrinsic to it and not to be attained by any imitator," notwithstanding its "strange" and "uncongenial" qualities.[38] We must be clear about this: These are curious terms of praise, a distanced and ironic sizing-up of Simmel's self-asserted "place" in the pantheon of cultural heroes, and not at all pieces of evidence for Simmel's "methodological" or "epistemological" influence on Weber. For in Weber's view Simmel never had (or even wanted to have) an impersonal "method of inquiry" that with proper housekeeping might have been made available in principle to all comers. The problem of knowledge in Simmel's sense was never exclusively a problem of mental operations, of a Cartesian working out of practical rules for "knowing"; it was a problem of *expression*.

    37. *GAW*, 94; *Roscher and Knies*, 153.
    38. Max Weber, "Georg Simmel as Sociologist," trans. D. N. Levine, *Social Research* 39 (1972): 158; cf. Levine, *Flight from Ambiguity*, 95.

Weber did not miss this fact: Simmel's "as always, refined and artistically formed theses" was the quasi-laudatory language of "Roscher and Knies," followed by acknowledgment of his "exquisite" observations with "their uncommonly sensitive character."[39] The laudatory term was always *fein* or *Feinheit*, that is, the obligatory sign for exquisite, artistic, refined, discriminating, elegant, sensitive *aesthetic* judgment. The precise intention of Weber's language is unmistakable: for Simmel, the aesthetic personality of insight and intuition, knowledge at its deepest level of "understanding" could only be the result of an authentic grasping of processes internal to the individual soul. This is what "psychologism" ultimately had to mean.

In a somewhat more familiar idiom, Simmel's "psychological" sociology could be summed up as having to do with (a) his opposition to the possibility of establishing "historical laws"; (b) a belief that in modern life the complex and manifold character of "social" objects of knowledge made a "psychology" indispensable; (c) a conviction that a certain psychological method was a presupposition for knowledge of "reciprocal action" or "interaction" (*Wechselwirkung*) and "sociation" (*Vergesellschaftung*), which was, pari passu, in combination with (d) an interest in probing the deeper, subjective meaning for individuals of objective social forms, *the* subject matter of sociology. Weber encountered all these convictions early in Simmel's work—convictions that essentially remained unchanged. Already in "The Problem of Sociology" Simmel insisted that "primary psychological process must be presupposed" in order to understand primary phenomena like love and hate, competition and cooperation, egoism and altruism; or that "the methods according to which the problems of sociation are to be investigated are the same as those in all comparative psychological sciences."[40] Given statements like these, the direction of Weber's interpretation of Simmel's antipositivist sociology seems fully warranted.

Importantly, the characteristics Weber perceived as "psychologism" are really at one with Simmel's attraction to Nietzsche and enchantment with the modern. Simmel himself was alert to the connection: "For the essence of the modern is above all psychologism," he once remarked; it is "the experiencing and interpretation of the world according to the reactions of our inner selves . . . the dissolution of stable contents in the fluid element of the soul, from which all substance has been emptied

39. *GAW*, 97, 101, 124; *Roscher and Knies*, 258, 259, 272.
40. "Das Problem der Soziologie," *Schmollers Jahrbuch* 18 (1894): 275–76.

out, and whose forms are only forms of movements."[41] Although the phrasing is typically Simmelian, the meaning remains within reach: Simmel personally wanted to penetrate to this level of subjectivity, to touch the fluctuations of *Innerlichkeit* resonating within modernity. His turn to sociology, the modern science of reciprocal action and experience, is conditioned by this very project of grasping the world of essential phenomena. Sociology *cum* psychologism becomes for Simmel, without apologies, the instrument for coping with the unsettling fluidity of the world and the self. And if this is so, then the problems opened up by Nietzsche—moral, cultural, psychological—provide the materials out of which knowledge of sociation, interaction processes, and their subjective effects is in Simmel's style to be generated.

CULTURE AND SOCIOLOGY

Both Weber and Simmel were fascinated by the stirrings of modern culture, by what some have called "the specific characteristics of the modern" or, more grandly, the "metaphysics of modernity."[42] Reading Marianne Weber's biography of her husband, one is led to see this fascination as the major aspect of Weber's and Simmel's friendship and shared intellectual interests, from discussions about aesthetics and the circle of poets around Stefan George to an engagement with music or with the "woman question." No doubt the friendship matured through these exchanges, just as it grew to include Marianne and Gertrud Simmel.

The controversy over Stefan George provides one appropriate illustration: after a decade of close and intense involvement with the George circle, Simmel, like Weber (who was a much more recent interlocutor), became disturbed by George's substitution of prophetic for poetic impulses.[43] The Simmels, Weber reported to his wife in 1910, had arrived at conclusions similar to their own: "He and *she* also, who clearly knows George quite well, basically judge George's substantive side no differently than ourselves. They also believe his desire to become a prophet is an alien intrusion," that is, a violation of artistic purpose.[44]

41. *Philosophische Kultur* (Berlin: Wagenbach, 1983), 152; originally published in 1911.

42. Nedelmann, "Strukturprinzipien," 561; Turner, "Simmel, Rationalisation and the Sociology of Money," 108.

43. For the details of this involvement, see Michael Landmann, "Georg Simmel und Stefan George," in Dahme and Rammstedt, *Georg Simmel und die Moderne*, 147–73.

44. Letter of 16 January 1910, NW 30/1 : 152–53; at this late date Gertrud was personally closer to George than was her husband.

Similarly, with respect to music there are glimpses of the kind of empathic understanding Simmelian sociology would have appreciated: Simmel is "obviously very musical," observed Weber after a performance both attended in Berlin; "the music visibly went through his body in spirals"[45]—an uncannily appropriate image, given the deep significance of the "spiral" figure for Simmel's thinking *and* style of visually conveying his ideas through dramatic gestures and body language.

Weber's insight into Simmel's character was also sufficiently penetrating to allow imitation of his senior colleague's prose style, but only in private correspondence with Marianne that until now has not found its way into print:

> The many dark green, gray-green, olive green, and gray tones that supply everything with background and intensifying hues carry over the tones of late autumn with their quiet melancholy into the spring, which then rests just like a bridal wreath at a silver wedding anniversary upon the brow of mature beauty. A youthful soul and a cheerful heart in a body no longer young, trim and dapper is also worth something, perhaps more than the thoughtless raging of youth that is nothing more than youthful. But I'm becoming almost Simmelian, and it's surely a much too beautiful day for that.[46]

If Weber turned this experiencing of the arrival of spring (he was vacationing in France after the exhausting labor required to complete *Agrarverhältnisse im Altertum*) into a private joke, then he also disclosed a serious appreciation for Simmel's aestheticism—his highly developed sense of color, tone, light, sound, rhythm, metaphor, the nuances of meaning in life and its forms—and for the conditions of aestheticism's realization. Simmel "needs not simply a 'public,'" Weber commented on another occasion, "but rather the feeling of warmth and understanding."[47] Perhaps an intimation of envy and regret with respect to his own expressive impulses escaped from between Weber's unpolished lines as well.

This shared curiosity about innovation in different spheres of modern culture became manifest not only in their personal relationship, but also in Weber's and Simmel's initial efforts within the German Sociological Society. Both had always thought of the "science of society," or the study of what Weber once referred to as "the peculiar image [*Gebilde*]

---

45. Letter to Marianne of 22 January 1911, NW 30/1 : 194–95; cf. *Lebensbild*, 504; Eng. trans., 496.

46. 2 April 1908, NW 30/1 : 132.

47. Letter to Marianne of 16 January 1910, NW 30/1 : 152–53; in these comments Weber also had Gertrud Simmel in mind, who "could evidently tolerate Simmel's manner once again," he observed.

that we call society,"[48] as a "science of culture"—Weber most emphatically, as we have seen, in central passages in his 1904 essay on "Objectivity," and Simmel through the exploration of a variety of cultural complexes and questions in numerous texts, including his treatise *Sociology*, compiled in large part from essays first published in Weber's coedited *Archiv für Sozialwissenschaft und Sozialpolitik*. To conceive of "sociology" as a "cultural science" was for both not so much to call attention to choosing topics for investigation based on an interpretation of culture or on one's cultural assumptions, as it was a matter of directing inquiry toward questions of cultural significance and meaning. If sociology set forth the nature of general, external, impersonal, "objective forms" of association, then it was in order to address the problem of their meaning for subjective life within a *particular* culture.

Substantively, in the new Sociological Society such convictions nurtured an attempt to shore up what Weber referred to in a moment of exasperation as "this confounded science" and Simmel in a similar state of mind called the "precarious position of sociology" by promoting topics for discussion and research devoted to major cultural problems.[49] The record of proposals, negotiation, misunderstanding, and actual research with respect to these matters is complicated and bewildering, but read from Simmel's and Weber's points of view it suggests an uninterrupted pursuit of the cultural thematic. Having delivered the opening salvo at the very first session in October 1910, with a spirited defense of "sociability" as a culture's "playful and inventive form [*Spielform*] of sociation,"[50] Simmel proceeded over the next two years to support those efforts directed toward the substantive cultural problematic and away from "formal" disputations. For example, with respect to the second meeting in 1912, in advice that still sounds timely, he expressed reservations about purely abstract conceptual topics and supplied an alternative (unsuccessfully, as it turned out):

In my opinion for meetings where discussion is expected one should avoid everything that can or even must lead to a quarrel over concepts and defini-

48. In his printed letter of invitation: "Einladung zum Beitritt zur Deutschen Gesellschaft für Soziologie," 1909, 2 (copy in NWS 18b:1–4).
49. Weber in a letter to Franz Eulenburg, 10 October 1910, NW 30/6:22; and Simmel writing to the society's Executive Committee, 10 June 1912, NWS 18b:86. My discussion is based in part on correspondence regarding the early history of the German Sociological Society found in no. 18b of the Sombart papers, to my knowledge the most extensive documentation available, containing numerous letters from Simmel and Weber between 1909 and 1914, addressed either to the seven-member Executive Committee (to which both belonged) or to Hermann Beck in Berlin as corresponding secretary.
50. "Soziologie der Geselligkeit," in *Verhandlungen des Ersten Deutschen Soziologentages* (Tübingen: J. C. B. Mohr [Paul Siebeck], 1911), 4.

tions. In sociology we have in this regard suffered to the point of suffocation, and a discussion about what folk, nation, or race "actually are" would be deadly for our session. . . . What do members think of the theme, the relations of handicraft industry to individual spheres of culture, that is, to political organization, to art, to relationships with foreign countries, to the nature of the family, etc.?[51]

For the delivery of the inaugural lecture for this session Simmel threw his support behind one of the up-and-coming proponents of *Kultursoziologie*, Alfred Weber, who could address questions of "nation and economy," or, should he decline, then his older brother Max, who could discuss the topic "nation and culture."[52] (The assignment actually went to Alfred, who in fact spoke on "The Sociological Concept of Culture.") Simmel's interventions were in some sense strategic: by emphasizing the "sociology" of different spheres of culture, he hoped to enlist the best and most promising work and avoid squeezing the entire field into a uniform conceptual or systematic definition. In Simmel's vision of scientific inquiry, innovation and openness or variety were interdependent. As he argued in one exchange, the promotion of "men, not measures" ought to be the association's overriding goal.[53]

Weber's stance on these problems was, if anything, even more clearcut than Simmel's. For instance, at the first sociology meetings he took it upon himself to identify the specific problem of modern culture as the relationship between the technologies and form of objective culture on the one hand and the subjective "conduct of life" on the other, while for the second session he continued to urge, as he put it, that "the theme: culture" be included in the definition of a thematic focus.[54] But more importantly, Weber was largely responsible for rechanneling the sprawling first list of possible directions for the society's inquiries into essentially two culturally relevant research topics: the sociology of "associational life" and, in particular, the ambitious inquiry into the cultural significance of the modern press. The latter effort was truly Weber's brainchild: he defined and organized the tasks, raised the funds, and commissioned the research. As Hennis has shown in detail, the survey of the sociology of the press was conceived as a cultural tour de force, an investigation of the effects of the press on the modern "con-

51. Letter of 10 November 1911, NWS 18b:56.
52. Minutes of the Executive Committee meeting, 2 March 1912, NWS 18b:62–63.
53. Letters of 26 March and 10 June 1912, NWS 18b:80–81, 86.
54. See his comments on Sombart's lecture, "Technik und Kultur," in *Verhandlungen des Ersten Deutschen Soziologentages*, 95–101; *GASS*, 449–56; and letter of 8 November 1911, NWS 18b:55.

duct of life" and "subjective individuality."[55] The language in Weber's
various reports said as much: "In the last analysis," he intoned, "an
inquiry into the press must focus upon the great cultural problems of
the present."[56] As the "last questions" placed before his colleagues in
the Sociological Society, Weber proposed, "What does the press contribute to the formation of modern humanity?" and "What kinds of
mass beliefs and hopes, of 'feelings toward life' [*Lebensgefühle*] as one
says today, of possible points of view will be destroyed forever or created anew" by it?[57]

For Weber a parallel cultural concern informed his contemporaneous
participation in the heated debates over national educational policy, reform of the system of higher education, and standards for university
teaching—debates that actually began in the German Conference of
University Teachers and spilled over into the Sociological Society and
the Association for Social Policy (Verein für Sozialpolitik).[58] What could
be asked of the press concerning the "formation of modern humanity"
could also be asked of the emergent modern university. In the sphere of
knowledge it was a question of the subjective consequences of institutional arrangements and standards for inquiry with respect to the "intellectual integrity" and "the self-discipline and moral [*sittlich*] outlook
of the young person."[59] The entire weight of Weber's conception of the
scientific vocation and its postulate of "value-freedom" was thrown into
the *cultural* task of rescuing education from pressures that would lead
to "an extraordinary narrowing of the student's intellectual horizon"
by turning the university into an arena for technical training, status legitimation, political dispensations, and careerism.[60] Weber's relentless

55. *Max Weber's Fragestellung*, 50–53.
56. Weber's "Vorläufiger Bericht über eine vorgeschlagene Erhebung über die Soziologie des Zeitungswesens" [1910–11], 1; typescript in NWS 18b:200–210.
57. "Geschäftsbericht der Deutschen Gesellschaft für Soziologie," in *Verhandlungen
des Ersten Deutschen Soziologentages*, 51; GASS, 441.
58. Weber spoke at meetings of the professors' association in 1909 and 1911, attacking the "Althoff System" and the bureaucratization of education, while defending his own
controversial view of the scientific vocation.
59. "Gutachten zur Werturteilsdiskussion im Ausschuss des Vereins für Sozialpolitik"
(1913), in Baumgarten, *Max Weber, Werk und Person*, 105; "Der Sinn der 'Wertfreiheit'
der soziologischen und ökonomischen Wissenschaften" (1917), in GAW, 491; S&F, 3.
60. "Denkschrift an die Handelshochschulen" (7 November 1911), from a typescript
copy in MWE. Given the current spate of writing on the crisis in education, Weber's pre-
World War I fears concerning the fate of American and European universities seem pre-
scient and sobering. In his view, the source of the coming American crisis would be a shift
away from (a) the classic pattern of an education aiming "at the formation of character
through the experience of holding one's own in the society of similarly situated students,
at the formation of adult citizens, and at the development of an outlook which serves as

attacks on the "Althoff system" that ruled the professoriate had to do precisely with the corrupting effects of the Prussian minister's entrepreneurial norms and policies, which produced not educators and scholars, but academics like "the type of American who is active on the stock exchange."[61] In short, the transformation wrought by this system was leading to the demoralization and colonization of *Kultur* by the power of money. Need one add that today, with the state's complicity, everywhere the conquest has become complete?

Such questions about the "subjective meaning" of "objective" social "forms" were typical of what Weber and Simmel had in mind for a sociology of culture. However, in the case of the Sociological Society their vision of the new organization's intellectual mission and field of research really never took hold, as the two prewar meetings of 1910 and 1912 became immobilized by disputes over "value-judgments" and what would nowadays be called "sociobiology." Of course, Weber himself must share responsibility for the former controversy, the misunderstandings surrounding its cultural import, and the failure to find a more persuasive defense for a science of "what is" oriented toward the historically established cultural world. He resigned from the German Sociological Society promptly at the conclusion of the second meeting, caustically citing temperamental incompatibilities and impatience with the *salon des refusés* the association had become:

> I resigned from the executive committee of the "sociologists." In a struggle in permanence my nerves aren't a match for such pesky insects as Herr [Rudolf] Goldscheid—for his "services" in good faith and his "idealism" too! Now I am only still trying to organize the *scientific* activity as best I can. May these gentlemen, *none* of whom can stifle the impulse (for that's what it is!) to importune the public with his subjective "valuations," all infinitely uninteresting to me, and *everyone* of whom *must* otherwise still turn his lectures into hard cash (this does *not* occur in the Verein für Sozialpolitik!) kindly stay in their own circle. I am absolutely fed up with appearing time

---

the foundation of the American governmental and social systems," and toward (b) a universal emphasis on formal qualification and trained expertise to the exclusion of everything else. For the maturing universities, Weber could express only the "hope that they will be in a better position to protect their independence, and that they will be better placed to protect their most sacred values than the German universities" ("American and German Universities," a speech at the *Deutscher Hochschullehrertag*, 1911, in *Max Weber on Universities*, ed. E. Shils [Chicago: University of Chicago Press, 1974], 24). How empty the hope has become today can be seen in virtually every discussion of these matters, where "independence" and "sacred values," when encountered at all, are little more than slogans or cause for embarrassment and misunderstanding.

61. "American and German Universities," in *Max Weber on Universities*, 27.

and again as a Don Quixote of an allegedly "unfeasible" principle and of provoking "embarrassing scenes."[62]

Weber's revealing comparison with Cervantes' hero, the perception of a disconcerting slide from the sublime to the ridiculous, show from his point of view how far the experiment with a scientific founding had gone awry. Furthermore, his sociology of academic culture revealed that sociology itself, as a new science, had attracted an underprivileged stratum of untenured and unsalaried scholars for whom the struggle for survival placed a premium on personal display and subjective value-judgments. Paradoxically, the very structure of sociology and its publics worked against the vocational self-restraints Weber wanted to see confirmed.

Simmel followed Weber's exit a year later, candidly pleading other and incompatible intellectual commitments: "In the course of the years my interests and the direction of my work have turned so completely toward pure philosophy and have alienated me from sociology with a radicalism that has surprised even me, that my remaining in a leading position of the Society seems inwardly dishonest." Characteristically, Simmel cited not so much public reasons, but rather subjective feelings stemming from "so to speak, having to swim against an inner stream."[63] But in any case, with expectations disappointed and the collectively supported cultural projects each had hoped to promote at a standstill, Simmel and Weber continued on the independent courses they had already established in the previous decades.

FEMINISM AS CULTURAL CRITICISM

The question of women's social status and political rights and the larger issues of "feminism" came early to the attention of both Simmel and Weber. Simmel's first essay on the subject appeared in 1890, simultaneously with On Social Differentiation. Applying sociopsychological categories from the latter sociological work, this first philosophical essay attempted to develop an argument for woman's "unique being" or gender-determined "difference" on the rather unpromising ground of a relative "lack of differentiation in the feminine life of the soul [Seelen-

62. Letter to Michels, 9 November 1912, AMW 102; portions of this letter appear in Lebensbild, 430 (Eng. trans., 424–25), but with errors, omissions, and lack of citation. Weber's "official" letter of resignation is from 22 October 1912, NWS 18b:122.
63. Letter of 11 October 1913, NWS 18b:183.

lebens]."[64] Filtered through the early Nietzsche discussions, where Simmel encountered "a priori" assumptions about women running counter to Nietzsche's well-known assertions,[65] and through his own evolving theory of culture, this argument from "difference" became much more rigorous (and, incidentally, much less loaded with uncritical patriarchal assumptions) by the time it reemerged in the important major essays of *Philosophical Culture.*

Notwithstanding a lifelong preoccupation with the philosophy and sociology of gender, Simmel could not be called a feminist; his interests were, as always, guided by an intriguing sociocultural and intellectual problem, rather than by practical concerns for political justice. By contrast, Weber did avow politically informed support for a kind of "liberal" feminism that was in line with his reformist stance on the "social question" and with his generational revolt against the men of 1871. Glimpses of his position appear in the 1890s, as with the recording of "a conversation with a Swiss woman that turned immediately and naturally to—the 'women's question.' She was certainly no 'homebody,' and clearly more radical than I am."[66] It was not fortuitous, then, to find Weber supporting the organizational efforts of early liberal feminists in Friedrich Naumann's Protestant reform movement, especially the *Evangelisch-sozialer Kongress*; encouraging the first women doctoral candidates in German universities (specifically his wife, Marianne, at Freiburg, and Else von Richthofen at Heidelberg); or defending women, like his protégé, Marie Baum, who tried to enter the male domain of work along the one path available to professional women at the time—as factory inspectors.[67] Culturally, the depiction of androgynous figures

64. "Zur Psychologie der Frauen," in *Schriften zur Philosophie und Soziologie der Geschlechter*, ed. H.-J. Dahme and K. C. Köhnke (Frankfurt: Suhrkamp, 1985), 36.

65. See esp. "Elisabeth Försters Nietzsche-Biographie," in which Simmel explicitly questions Nietzsche's view of women. The topic's importance in the nineties is suggested by Hedwig Dohm's insightful feminist critique, "Nietzsche und die Frauen," *Die Zukunft* 25 (24 December 1898): 534–43.

66. Letter to Marianne, 30 July 1898, NW 30/1:62. Shortly thereafter Weber mentions rereading *Faust* and sampling *Madame Bovary*, though Flaubert could not hold his interest!

67. Weber's reservations about Naumann's attempt to found a new party (see *GPS*, 26–29) had to do not just with his lack of a political following, but also partly with his handling of feminist issues: "Monday in Erfurt Naumann botched things badly by presenting a platform from which he had excluded the women's question and opposition to the large [East Elbian] estate owners. The result was that I resolutely attacked him and the entire 'party,' saying that along this path they would become politically spineless old men" (letter to Marianne, 23 November 1986, NW 30/1:56). For Weber's defense of Marie Baum, who had succeeded Else von Richthofen as a factory inspector in Baden, see "Zur Stellung der Frau im modernen Erwerbsleben," *Frankfurter Zeitung*, 13 Au-

and of an unconventional, "freer" woman surely drew the Webers in the 1890s to Klinger's etchings. Perhaps the bold experimentation with female eroticism even helps account for the fin-de-siècle fascination that Weber shared with the avant-garde for the *Salomé* of Oscar Wilde and Richard Strauss: "The audience left the hall crushed and as though caught red-handed," Weber reported after witnessing a performance of the opera, "Six people and I applauded."[68]

For these two close observers of the age modern feminism represented many things: a protest against patriarchalism and male privilege, a demand for meaningful occupations among middle-class women, a force for political democratization. But at its deepest level it was a movement of cultural protest against the limits and obsessions of the contemporary "masculine" world of "vocational humanity." Like modern socialism, it stood for a possibility, an alternative, a qualitative leap out of history, but now conceived in terms of a uniquely gender-specific "being." In his finest essay on the subject, which was not without a deliberately complex dialectic, Simmel probed the meaning of this cultural equivalent of a path toward salvation, starting from the assertion that "with the exception of a very few areas, our objective culture is thoroughly male" and then searching in feminism for "the creation of objectively new values."[69] Could there be "specifically female *forms*" of art, medicine, literature, historical knowledge, science, politics, or other spheres of culture? Simmel found he could not answer this question, except in the conditional tense in which it was asked. Perhaps a developing "cultural history" would point toward "an objective female culture parallel to the male and thereby annulling and transcending [*aufhebend*]" the latter's imposition on our historically given world:

> The female form of existence would present itself as a different form, autonomous on the basis of its ultimate essence, incommensurable on the basis of the standard of the male principle, and with contents that are not formed in the same way. Thus its meaning would no longer turn on an equivalence

gust 1906, 22; and "Die badische Fabrikinspektion," *Frankfurter Zeitung*, 24 January 1907, 24.

68. Letter to Marianne, 24 January 1911, NW 30/1:195–96; cf. *Lebensbild*, 504–5; Eng. trans., 497, where Marianne curiously fails to include the last and most important testimonial sentence from her husband. The combination of beauty, horror, and the erotic in *Salomé* was a typical fin-de-siècle motif, as in Franz von Stück's paintings of the subject.

69. "Weibliche Kultur," in *Philosophische Kultur*, 208–9; "Female Culture," in *Georg Simmel: On Women, Sexuality, and Love*, trans. Guy Oakes (New Haven: Yale University Press, 1984), 66–67.

within the general form of objective culture but rather on an equivalence between two modes of existence that have a completely different rhythm.[70]

This outcome would have to be the most radical extension of all experience based on the assumption of *difference*.

Max Weber himself never wrote an essay in response to Simmel's reflections on feminism, but his wife certainly did in a thoroughgoing critique that has unfortunately but predictably escaped notice.[71] What is remarkable about Marianne's essay, viewed with our cultural problem in mind, is the way in which it incorporates, reworks, and extends some of her husband's ideas in the direction of a feminist reply to Simmel's clear juxtaposition of an "objective culture" created by male achievement to the prospects for alternative cultural forms based on "woman's being." Her critique turned essentially on two claims. First, just as Max in his "Categories" essay rejected Simmel's deliberate combining of "subjectively intended" and "objectively valid" meaning,[72] so Marianne questioned the synthetic meshing of psychological description with metaphysical speculation, or the derivation of normative claims from alleged "essential being." For her, Simmel's "psychological analysis and normative philosophical thinking are . . . so closely bound together that one finds a prescription for woman's destiny contained within the description of her being," and "psychology is interlaced with a metaphysics of gender."[73] Second, like her husband, Marianne Weber wanted to insist that the great "antinomies," "tensions," and "dualisms" of life (and especially *modern* life) were not avoidable according to any Simmelian claim of unity for "feminine being." In the Weber family view, "woman" did not represent an autonomous life-order or value-sphere. According to Marianne,

---

70. "Weibliche Kultur," 240; "Female Culture," 100–101.

71. Marianne Weber's essay, "Die Frau und die objektive Kultur," (1913), in *Frauenfragen und Frauengedanken: Gesammelte Aufsätze* (Tübingen: J. C. B. Mohr [Paul Siebeck], 1919), 95–133, was originally published in the same volume of *Logos* as her husband's well-known "Categories" essay, "Über einige Kategorien der verstehenden Soziologie" (1913), *GAW*, 427–74 ("Some Categories of Interpretive Sociology," trans. Edith Graber, *Sociological Quarterly* 22 [1981], 151–80). Marianne's essay has been ignored for decades and was recovered only recently by Suzanne Vromen, "Georg Simmel and the Cultural Dilemma of Women," *History of European Ideas* 8 (1987), esp. 574–76.

72. "Über einige Kategorien der verstehenden Soziologie," *GAW*, 427 n. 1, ("Some Categories of Interpretive Sociology," 179 n. 1), written at the time Marianne was working on her Simmel critique; also *EaS*, 4.

73. "Die Frau und die objektive Kultur," 98–99.

The creation of her own essence through culture also forces woman into the struggle, the tension, the choice among the different, conflicting possibilities for the formation of her external and internal life. She too cannot become a cultural self without leaving behind the natural unity of being. *Every* step beyond the circle of the natural forces her into the dualism between being and idea, into the choice between one value and another value.[74]

Thus, whereas for Simmel the notion of an "objective female culture" suggested an intriguing *possible* outcome, for the Webers such a culture could only be part of the gender-free experience of modern life as a whole. It could not be an autonomous life-order or sphere of value governed by its own rules, for in this view culture was everywhere culture, and choice in the modern epoch was everywhere subjected to the same constraints.

In a sense Marianne's criticisms pinpointed the dangers inherent in a feminism based on gender difference, *especially in its naturalistic form*, for "difference" could be compatible with claims for uniqueness, but also with patriarchal arguments for subordination. Nevertheless, she too wanted to acknowledge woman's unique, if limited task within the total economy of a modern culture threatened, as she said in language recalling the final passages of *The Protestant Ethic and the Spirit of Capitalism*, by "ending in paralysis and specialization of humanity [*Fachmenschentum*]" through the "monstrous mechanism of a know-how [*Wissen*] that no individual can control any longer." The task was authenticated by women's special social and therefore personal history, not in a separate life-order, but within shared objective forms: "Perhaps woman can succeed better in unifying the dissonances between knowledge and action, between higher intellectual culture and more modest moral [*sittliche*] culture."[75] Yet this hesitant "perhaps" could not be converted into a certainty through argument alone.

For Marianne Weber the final corrective to Simmel's enthusiasms had to be sought in an experienced distancing of woman's "self" from the coercive force of the purely private and subjective: "For countless women creative participation in something objective [*Sachlichen*] . . . comes as a salvation, as a way to 'get beyond oneself' [*über sich selbst hinauszukommen*],' and that always means to arrive at a higher form of her self, to strive for a means for inner harmonization."[76] To reach for

74. Ibid., 113.
75. Quotations from "Die Beteiligung der Frau an der Wissenschaft," *Frauenfragen und Frauengedanken*, 9.
76. "Die Frau und die objektive Kultur," 114.

this level of authentic selfhood was thus to move onto a new plane of public acknowledgments.

And how did Simmel respond to her collegial refutation? With chivalric renunciation he thanked Marianne "like an Austrian soldier" for the "gracious punishment,"[77] and then dedicated his book on Goethe to her.

THE SEARCH FOR MEANING

Both Simmel and Weber were preoccupied throughout their lifework with the problem of meaning. Simmel, however, was interested in a "world," a totality, a form put together out of infinite multiplicity. What this totality claimed was universality, but at the expense of historicity; Simmel's version of modern culture was simply not endowed with historical consciousness. In an important sense the "methods" Simmel selected for emphasis were admirably suited to these characteristics: the logic of relations among "things," the frequent use of analogies, the focus on "reciprocal action" or "interaction," and the concern for details of "lived experience" served as perfect categories for his purposes. They were without specific content, emphasized the variability of spacial and temporal connections, and, especially in the case of the last two, actually became the categories through which personality, society, and sociology were constituted.

Weber's work, by contrast, revealed an interest at a different level of analysis in worlds that by their very plurality came to be defined and limited through history. Appeals to what "all historical experience shows" emerge like a leitmotif through his thought. What caught his historically conditioned attention most was the vast divergence through time and within culture in life-orders, value-spheres, and general patterns for the conduct of life. Not totalities, but rather the great "tensions" and "antinomies" emerging from among these orders and spheres lay at the very center of his most inspired and engaging writing, including that found in the voluminous comparative-historical studies. The manageability of the entire tableau depended on clear and precise concepts, including a favored use of "ideal types" as logico-historical and heuristic devices for clarification of given realities.

To put it another way, Weber wanted to know how the world, our world in its "characteristic uniqueness," had come to be what it is—this

77. Gassen and Landmann, *Buch des Dankes an Georg Simmel*, 132.

"reality in which we are placed" and the basis of its being "historically
so and not having become otherwise." Thus, it is quite in keeping with
the seriousness of his mood to find Weber appealing for "intellectual
integrity," confessing a need to "say what is," and condemning the *sac-
rificium intellectus*. But Simmel wanted to know the world in its infinitude, as it just might possibly become; differentiation and ever more
differentiation, rather than rationalization, was his central theme. On
this matter Lukács has reported Simmel's striking and characteristically
revealing complaint: "There are not enough categories, just as there are
not enough sexes."[78] Because of such a contrast, Weber could speak of
tragedy *in history*, Simmel of the tragedy *of culture*. To be sure, for both
men our world had become a world of calculability, pure functionality,
and the instrumental rationality of means: in Weber's words, "One can,
in principle, *master* all things by *calculation*" in the present-day, while
for Simmel instrumental culture tended to view the "world as a huge
arithmetical problem."[79] However, Simmel's imagination was ignited
by certain possibilities he perceived in modern culture, by a vision of
"freedom" as "negative sociation." Weber instead warned darkly of the
"iron cage," of domination by Nietzsche's "last men" who had "invented happiness."

   Yet both Weber and Simmel raise a similar question about the "fate
of our times"—that is, about the nature of human experience in the
"age of subjectivist culture." This is the final and undoubtedly the most
important question in their "sociologies of culture." For Simmel the
"specific problem" is established by the great clashes in psychological
time between "life" and "form," between the subjective experience of
individuals on the one hand and the increasing contents of objective
culture on the other, which then provoke awareness of "the insignificance or irrationality of the individual's share" of modern, material culture.[80] Weber's "cultural being" also resides within this problematic,
caught by the great conflicts in historical time among life-orders and
value-spheres. The problem appears identical: The "cultural being [*Kulturmensch*], placed in the midst of the continuous enrichment of culture
by ideas, knowledge, and problems, may become 'tired of life' but not
'satiated with life,'" so that by its very progressiveness "the life of culture [*Kulturleben*] as such is meaningless" or its "every step forward
seems condemned to lead to an ever more devastating senselessness."[81]

78. Ibid., 174.
79. *GAW*, 594; G&M, 139; *Philosophy of Money*, 444.
80. *Philosophy of Money*, 449–50.
81. *GAW*, 594–95; *GARS* 1:570; G&M, 140, 357.

This language is merciless: possibilities are counterbalanced by trivialization, choices by disenchantment. In the end we are trapped by the culture we have created and of which we are a part, but which we can no longer master.

The reasons for Simmel's and Weber's relentless probing of cultural significance can be found in the situation of intellectual questioning (and the new science of sociology) at the margins in a double sense— that is, at the frayed edges of the social order and community of science, and at the boundary between a traditionalist-patriarchal social order and a capitalist order determined by technical rationality and characterized by rapid changes in the division of labor, time and space, rhythm and distance, and social stratification. This is really the world after Marx and Nietzsche, characterized by "disenchantment." And Weber's and Simmel's question is simply, What comes next? Should we expect affirmation of modern culture, adaptation to its many modes, an exhaustive search for alternatives, a call for new prophets, a return to old religions, the persistence of familiar wisdom ("meeting the demands of the day"), individual inventiveness ("creating ideals from within our chests"), or simply nothingness?

That question still defines the modern predicament. It leads us next toward the politics of Weber's standpoint, and beyond that to the most explicit discussion of modernity and its discontents in the Weber Circle.

CHAPTER V

Politics in the Age of Subjectivist Culture

And then the political . . . it is my old "secret love."
—*Max Weber*

Few subjects in the Weberian heritage are more controversial than Max Weber's political views and his general conception of politics. The understanding of what he considered the "internal and lawful autonomy" of the political life-order or value-sphere and his own engagements in the public life of Wilhelmian Germany prompted considerable debate from the very beginning. If the "daemon" holding the fibers of Weber's life guided him into the sphere of the intellect, then it also urged him to enter the gates of politics, but under the Dantesque sign of an austere realism: "*lasciate ogni speranza*." For within these gates loomed not the "dream of peace and human happiness," Weber insisted, but rather the "'pragmatics of power' that rules all political history."[1] Desiring an altogether different "history" against the agonies of this century, posterity has sometimes had difficulty coming to terms with Weber's outspoken insistence, much less approving or accepting his matter-of-fact political standpoint, no matter how much "truth" it might contain.

Several characteristics rooted in Weber's thought and evident in his public persona help account for these political controversies. Surely one operative in Weber's own day was his deserved reputation as "an incorruptible, relentless speaker of the truth, a man of superior knowledge and unsurpassed brilliance [*Geist*]" (in the words of the *Frankfurter*

---

1. From passages written in 1895 and 1916: *GPS*, 12; *MWG* I/15:98; "The National State and Economic Policy (Freiburg Address)," *Economy and Society* 9, (1980): 437.

Zeitung), whose political skills emphatically did not include patience, tact, and flattery. His wartime essays, for instance, many of which were first published in the popular press, were instead marked by a strident, hypercritical, uncompromising tone that the English-language audience can only imagine, as these essays still cannot be read in translation from beginning to end. Such "intellectual ruthlessness" might have had few long-term disadvantages in the world of science, but in politics it tended always to provoke immediate and strong reactions, positive and negative, including after a speech in the January 1919 national election campaign "something of a brawl with chair legs swung about."[2] Verbal brawls were equally common then and have continued down to the present.

In the years since the violent birth of the Weimar Republic, however, the source of provocation has come to be located more especially in the aura of enigma and paradox thought to characterize Weber's position on some large and popular topics in the politics of our century: liberalism, democracy, and "constitutionalism." We should be as clear as possible about the issue: Weber's actual comments about any member of this triumvirate conceived as bourgeois ideology, political principle, institutional arrangement, sociohistorical doctrine, or economic theory are few, scattered, and fragmentary. Weber chose not to engage in a significant discussion, much less to write a major treatise on any of these matters with respect to their theories, meanings, major advocates, or historical achievements. To be sure, in *Economy and Society* he did set forth a certain clarification of terminology, calling a constitution "the modus of distribution of power which determines the possibility of regulating social action"; and "democracy" those practices committed to (1) maintaining "universal accessibility of office" and (2) expanding "the sphere of influence of 'public opinion' as far as possible."[3] In political essays after 1917 and as a member of Hugo Preuss' select committee for drafting the Weimar Constitution he also defended a specific institutional "distribution of power" for postwar Germany. Furthermore, in many settings he commented insightfully on the "modern fate" of "democratic" phenomena. But typically, according to the sharpest criticism of Weber, all this was done with sufficient ambiguity and quali-

---

2. *Frankfurter Zeitung*, 23 December 1917; *Nordbayrische Zeitung*, 15 January 1919, reporting on Weber's speech in Fürth.
3. *WuG*, 249, 725; *EaS*, 330, 985.

fication to justify at the very least a charge of contradictory, nationalist, or illiberal thinking encased within an "antinomian structure."[4]

We should recognize that the very *problem* posed by "democracy" or a "liberal" politics as we have come to accept it in the late twentieth century—attempting to articulate coherent "foundations" for various "theories," or trying to balance accounts between "elitist" and "pluralist" conceptions of democracy, or seeking to criticize the relationship between a given "theory" and certain political "realities"—was simply not Weber's starting point, nor even a part of his central concerns. Interestingly, early formulations of these respective "problems" were developed by Weber's good friend and colleague, Georg Jellinek, and by his sometime protégé, Robert Michels, and both received Weber's commendations—and criticisms. Jellinek's magisterial *Allgemeine Staatslehre* (1900) and the shorter *Verfassungsänderung und Verfassungswandlung* (1906), works of constitutional-political theory, brought to Weber's attention the development of the "theory of the state" from Aristotle to Montesquieu and J. S. Mill, as well as the more recent French, British, and American literature, including writers like Albert Venn Dicey, James Bryce, Sidney Low, Moisei Ostrogorski, and Woodrow Wilson. Weber praised the latter treatise as "very congenial" to his viewpoint, a serious "beginning to a *scientific* treatment of 'politics' " in its discussion of "constitutional" change, in which Jellinek makes a distinction between "legal change" and "*political* transformation."[5] But Weber also objected to the narrowly legalistic and formalistic assumptions characterizing Jellinek's method of political analysis: "As

---

4. Wolfgang J. Mommsen is almost entirely responsible for triggering and then sustaining this polemic for nearly three decades, although he has moved from seeing Weber as a dangerous nationalist who managed somehow to soften up the German audience preparatory to its reception of fascism, to viewing him more sympathetically as the last great "liberal in the borderline situation" or "in despair," or finally as a thinker who attempted to hold contradictory positions in "dialectical combination" in order to achieve an "open" social and political order—all interpretations residing within the boundaries of the "problem of liberalism": *Max Weber and German Politics, 1890–1920*, trans. M. Steinberg (Chicago: University of Chicago Press, 1984), originally published in 1959; *Max Weber: Gesellschaft, Politik und Geschichte* (Frankfurt: Suhrkamp, 1974), 21–43; *The Age of Bureaucracy: Perspectives on the Political Sociology of Max Weber* (Oxford: Blackwell, 1974), chap. 5; "The Antinomian Structure of Max Weber's Political Thought," in *Current Perspectives in Social Theory*, vol. 4, ed. Scott G. McNall (Greenwich: JAI Press, 1983), 289–311. This last terminology recalls Lukács' critique of the "antinomies" of bourgeois thought, directed presumably at Weber and Simmel, but without any positive "pluralist" implications. David Beetham, *Max Weber and the Theory of Modern Politics* (London: Allen & Unwin, 1974), adopts a line of criticism similar to Mommsen's earlier views.

5. Letter of 17 August 1906, NJ 31.

good as its intentions are, it is typical for the manner in which *legal scholars* treat *political* things. The more intelligent they are, the more they are blinded by formalism."[6] For a corrective, Weber advocated a mode of discourse that was sociocultural, comparative, and historical.

Michels avoided the pitfall of legal formalism in *Political Parties*, originally entitled *Zur Soziologie des Parteiwesens* (1911), but stumbled into another difficulty. Praising this study as an "act of *great* moral courage and moral self-discipline that does not avoid the face of reality, no matter how it looks,"[7] Weber nevertheless objected to its conclusion that "democratic" authority was impossible to achieve in complex, organized orders or in situations characterized by representation, administration, or leadership. He was prepared, contra Michels, to see "democratization" (i.e., minimally the "leveling" of traditional status differences and the extension of "rights" to formerly underprivileged social strata) as a "developmental tendency" in modern societies, just as he was able to characterize the German Social Democratic Party studied by Michels as "strictly disciplined and centralized" but "within democratic forms."[8] The drawback to Michels' "Rousseauian" investigations, simply put, was obscurity in the concept of "domination" (or, roughly speaking, "authority") rooted in the radical conviction that authority as such was universally "undemocratic." "The *concept* of 'domination' [*Herrschaft*] is not clarified in your work," Weber wrote. "Your analysis [of it] is too *simple*."[9] The typology of "legitimate domination" and its partial elaboration in *Economy and Society* became Weber's own well-known alternative.

Weber's quite different approach to such issues and his "omissions" undeniably represent not a mere oversight, but a deliberate choice and a judgment about politics. They have to do with his early turn toward political economy and the larger project of a "science of culture" ori-

6. Letter to Alfred Weber, 22 May 1907, NW 30/7:18, replying specifically to Georg Jellinek, "Bundesstaat und parlamentarische Regierung," *Neue Freie Presse* (Vienna), reprinted in *Ausgewählte Schriften und Reden*, 2 vols. (Berlin: Häring, 1911), 2:439–47, an article written in connection with a dispute between Gustav Schmoller and Alfred Weber, conducted in the Vienna press, over the question of insuring the accountability of the executive vis-à-vis legislative authority in the German *Reichsverfassung*. Generally speaking, the Weber brothers supported a strong form of parliamentarism in this controversy.
7. An undated letter to Michels, probably written in late 1911, with detailed criticism of *Political Parties*, AMW 126.
8. *MWG* I/15:530; *EaS*, 1445.
9. AMW 126; see my paper, "Max Weber and Robert Michels," *American Journal of Sociology* 86 (1981): 1269–86, for a fuller discussion of these issues.

ented toward the problems of the modern culture of capitalism in the largest sense: the formation of a type of humanity under the compulsion of specialized and routine labor (*Berufsmenschentum*), the "rationalized" world of vocational specialization and bureaucratization, the "depersonalization" of the political order, the "iron cage" and the tormented searches for ways of escaping its constraints that are so characteristic of modern life. It is only in relation to *these* primary problems, the "thematic" of social modernity, that the entirely ancillary matters on the plane of what *we* choose to call "liberal-democratic theory" and "constitutionalism" enter Weber's field of vision at all, and even then only as a "disenchanted" portion of the modern. That is, although the old "world images" of another, better political condition have survived, they will now take the form of inconvenient and fictional ideals. The force of modern sociocultural development should have jolted us awake from our Lockean slumbers and Rousseauian reveries. This awakening also heralds the death of utopia as social criticism rather than as mere fantasy.

From this point of view, second-level political issues surface in two ways in Weber's work. First, there are the relatively straightforward practical constitutional questions governing his proposals for Germany's "new political order" and discussed in thorough detail in his longest and most significant tract during the war, "Parliament and Government in a Reconstructed Germany," and in numerous other essays and speeches: plebiscitary versus parliamentary governance, proportional versus plurality electoral principles, federal versus unitary rule, bureaucratic order versus party leadership, and so forth. In one sense these issues are time-bound, potentially remote, and consequential primarily for the historian of the "German question" and Weimar's failure. But in another sense they can be abstracted and relocated in the ongoing contemporary debates in the West, usually hedged in by national peculiarities, over the actual (and desirable) relationship between political "forms" and material outcomes, formal and substantive rationality, efficiency and equality, competence and fairness, leadership and participation. Herein resides one version of the politically "relevant" Weber, speaking with foresight about the strengths and dangers of plebiscitary rule, the effects of bureaucratic usurpation of political decisions, or the political consequences of proportional representation.

Second, there is the equally urgent and contentious subject of Weber's critical standpoint on the "values" of "individualism," "freedom of conscience," and the "natural rights" doctrines from the eighteenth-century Enlightenment. In one place where he addressed these matters directly, the first essay on Russia, Weber openly identified with the "'individualists' and supporters of 'democratic' institutions," but not from the self-congratulatory standpoint of their inevitable ascendancy. In his view the "old-fashioned" and "outmoded" ideals of Western culture, taken for granted just "as black bread is to the man who has enough to eat," are in fact battling for survival. Their formation presupposed "a certain conjunction of unique and unrepeatable conditions": the success of European expansionism, the socioeconomic structure of early capitalism, the conquest of the world of everyday life by science, and an "ethos" propagated by the inner-worldly religious asceticism of the Protestant sects.[10] These ideals represented not an autonomous and self-sustaining problematic for Weber, but rather an important late survival of the once heroic, a "self-evident possession" from the "school of hard asceticism"—ideals that had "impressed their particular stamp on the 'ethical' character and the 'cultural values' of modern humanity."[11]

The meaning of Weber's affirmations in these passages should not be difficult to ascertain, although it seems to have proven exceptionally elusive. At the very least, for him the central political *problems* could lie only beyond these inherited dogmas and forms, beyond the decline of "bourgeois liberalism" and the nineteenth century's historicist culture of progress. The "beyond" in this case signified the mechanical and material foundations of present-day instrumentally oriented civilization and its accompanying psychologically inclined culture of "feeling" and "experience." For Weber this was a "subjectivist culture" in relation to politics, most importantly in the sense that it validated a standard of *judgment* based on the state of the "inner" self, the life of the psyche, the authenticity of subjective experience. Weber's autonomous political life-order or value-sphere is conceived against this culture and in response to it. What remains significant to us in Weber's reflections is the

10. "Zur Lage der bürgerlichen Demokratie in Russland," *Archiv* 22, (1906) 347–48; *Selections*, 282–83. If one insists on classifying Weber's thinking in relation to liberalism, it makes sense to view these passages as evidence for its "voluntaristic" character: see the argument in Wilhelm Hennis, *Max Webers Fragestellung: Studien zur Biographie des Werks* (Tübingen: J. C. B. Mohr [Paul Siebeck], 1987), 220–22.

11. Letters on this theme to Adolf von Harnack, 12 January 1905 and 5 February 1906, copies in MWE; in the latter, Weber comments, "That our nation never went through the school of hard asceticism in *any* form is the source of everything that I find hateful in it *as well as in myself*," suggesting that to proclaim these ideals "self-evident" is not to say they should be taken for granted.

character of politics and its calling in the midst of subjectivist culture, for this culture is still ours to experience and comprehend, and its "politics" will be with us for some time to come.

CULTURE AND POLITICS

In the preface to "Parliament and Government in a Reconstructed Germany," revised for publication in 1918 under the subtitle "Toward a Political Critique of Officialdom and Political Parties" from *Frankfurter Zeitung* articles of the previous year, Weber confronted the problem of his political subject matter and critical approach. Addressing the constitutional questions facing his audience, he surmised that "one may perhaps complain that such bourgeois and prosaic things" are taken up in his discussion "with deliberate self-limitation and exclusion of all of the great *substantive* cultural problems facing us." [12] Regrettably, "technical changes in the form of the state" had become a public topic, Weber added and then called his contribution a "minor occasional writing merely intended to 'serve the times.'" And serve the times it does, with more than ample reasoning on the immediate constitutional problems going back to 1871, broached by Jellinek and others (including Weber himself) in the debates after 1906, and now assaulting public consciousness as a result of the war. But clearly Weber had misgivings about these prosaic pursuits, for in his scheme of intellectual values, both in politics and in science, considerations of a formal kind were always derivative and dependent on the contents of the "actuality of life" in its historical and sociocultural bearing. Constitutionalism was to political life what methodology was to scientific activity: a merely instrumental means to a superior substantive and practical end.

What of the more permanent questions—the "great substantive cultural problems" Weber chose to postpone? The writing from 1917 and 1918 typically has difficulty toeing the line he had drawn for himself, especially in several important asides about the meaning of "bureaucratization." As a matter of fact, Weber had taken up the cultural problems previously in two quite different settings: in "The Suffrage and Democracy in Germany" ("Wahlrecht und Demokratie in Deutschland"), a

12. *MWG* I/15:436; *EaS*, 1384; this longest of Weber's wartime essays was originally published in five installments in the *Frankfurter Zeitung* in 1917; all but the last section is translated as an appendix in *EaS*, 1381–1469.

1917 text that starts from what he called the "far-sighted problem of democracy" (and for decades the only one of the wartime political essays available in partial translation), and well before that in some of his prepared remarks at the German Sociological Society's inaugural sessions. Both exemplify an effort to peer beneath the surface of contemporary political affairs in order to consider their cultural foundations.

Taking the ubiquitous "problem of democracy" as a point of departure, it becomes apparent that what Weber otherwise identifies as a democratization *process* is treated in two ways: as a formal inquiry into comparative constitutional arrangements, and as a cultural "problem" having to do with the formation of a collective "ethos" for entire political communities. Reflecting the central thematic of *The Protestant Ethic and the Spirit of Capitalism*, it is obviously the latter idea that achieves greatest significance, for it governs what Weber at one point refers to provocatively as the "'spirit' of a future German politics"[13]—or any politics, for that matter. Moreover, this particular weighting of concerns must prevail because of what he saw (with Simmel) as the intensive and extensive quality of a modern culture characterized by rapid innovations of baffling variety that reach into all social strata, become "mass" phenomena, and exercise broad political effects. Such essential characteristics are apparent in many spheres of culture, some of which Weber considers: the modern media of communication, the latest monumental "public" art, and modern associational activity.

Consider Weber's comments on the effects of the modern newspaper, which are worth quoting in full: "Before going about their daily business," he suggests, "modern humans have become accustomed to sampling a ragout, to being forced into a kind of chase through all spheres of cultural life, from politics to the theater to everything else imaginable." On the printed page a nonfictional world appears that is marked by "incessant changes," "tremendous shifts in public opinion," and "universal and inexhaustible possibilities for viewpoints and interests"—all of which "weigh enormously on the characteristic features of modern humanity" and encourage "powerful dislocations in the pattern and entire manner the modern individual uses for receiving outside views." Employing the language of the day, developed among oth-

13. "Wahlrecht und Demokratie in Deutschland" [The Suffrage and Democracy in Germany] (1917), *MWG* I/15:351; only about a fourth of this important essay has been translated under the heading "National Character and the Junkers," in G&M, 386–95 (corresponding to *MWG* I/15:381–92).

ers by Weber's brother, Alfred, the general "feeling for life" (*Lebens-gefühl*) comes to be deeply affected by this artifact of objective culture.[14]

Similar ideas appear in connection with Weber's surprising commentary on the development and democratization of a national *Geschmacks-kultur*, or "culture of good taste" and "refinement" in art, conceived partly as an ironic and trendy decorative embellishment, as in Nietzsche's denunciation of "merely decorative culture," but also as a serious standard for civilized achievement. Revealing the state of the public in visible form, this culture's contemporaneous feats were not reassuring, from Berlin's commemorative victory boulevard, victory column, and "monstrous Bismarck memorial" to the "hollow theatrics and bad taste of the 'terza Roma' " with the pretentious and flashy memorial on the Capitol to Victor Emmanuel II. In Germany, Weber asserted, "the only adequate monumental structure" was the Bismarck memorial of the Hamburg patriciate. Otherwise one had either to return to the "classical" European models of secure "aristocratic" tradition and their "democratic" extension in cities like Munich, Zurich, and Vienna or to seek out the "intimate circles" of artistic creativity and "aesthetic development" typically found in France.[15] For Weber, observation shows that "our greatest art is intimate and not monumental," and if we attempt "to 'invent' a monumental style in art, such miserable monstrosities are produced as the many monuments of the last twenty years." The artistic *Geschmackskultur* contains a report to ourselves that "precisely the ultimate and most sublime values have retreated from public life."[16] It visibly authenticates the crisis in citizenship and political education that so exercised Weber's critical powers.

14. From Weber's 1910 report to the German Sociological Society, "Geschäftsbericht der Deutschen Gesellschaft für Soziologie," *Verhandlungen des Ersten Deutschen Soziologentages* (Tübingen: J. C. B. Mohr [Paul Siebeck], 1911), 50–51; *GASS*, 440–41; Alfred Weber, "Der soziologische Kulturbegriff," in *Verhandlungen des Zweiten Deutschen Soziologentages* (Tübingen: J. C. B. Mohr [Paul Siebeck], 1913), for whom "the task of the sociological reflection on culture is . . . to clarify the origin and dynamic significance of the feeling for life" (15).

15. "Wahlrecht und Demokratie," *MWG* I/15:375–76; and a characteristic aside in a letter to Michels (20 June 1915, NW 30/14:13–14), who became an Italian citizen in 1911 and had already entered the press campaign from Basel against German wartime policy: "I am going to excuse the Italians' barbaric bad taste in the artistic realm, above all the ostentatious mark of infamy on the Capitol [in Rome], compared with which our victory boulevard [in Berlin] is child's play." Weber added, "The fact that Sombart can *never* keep quiet and must always have the 'dernier cri' doesn't mean that everyone must do likewise." Michels simply could not follow Weber's recommendation of "silence" for reasons of "dignity and good taste," and Weber broke with him in the fall (letters of 9 September and 21 October, 1915, NW 30/14:15–16, 24).

16. "Wissenschaft als Beruf" [Science as a Vocation] (1919), *GAW*, 612; *G&M*, 155.

With respect to public life as it does exist under the shadow of the modern state in the activity of associations, clubs, and sects, Weber thought it also revealed everything important for understanding the formation of cultural ideals and a type of character, habit of mind, or world-view—a *Gesamthabitus*—for the modern individual. Associations imposed external and internal constraints, serving as mechanisms of "selection" for assigning "business, political, or any kind of authority [*Herrschaft*] in social life," and as social forms for molding the modern "self." The questions Weber then posed are self-explanatory: "How, under what conditions, according to which (I would like to say) 'rules of the game' does the selection of leaders come about?" "How does membership in a particular kind of association affect the inner person, the personality as such?" "What specific ideal of 'manliness' is cultivated consciously and intentionally, or unconsciously and traditionally in a German fraternity on the one hand, or in an English athletic club or American student association on the other?" In the face of external influences, "how does the individual come to terms with his *own self-esteem* and need to be a 'personality'?"[17]

Expressed most famously in sections of "The Suffrage and Democracy in Germany," but dating actually from the 1890s, Weber's follow-up critique of the politically consequential alliance in civil society between the state bureaucracy, the Junkers, student fraternities, parvenu culture, and the "feudalization" of public norms was intended to locate the atavistic sociocultural hegemony of a distinctly unheroic, plebeian ideal. Weber hammered away at this destructive configuration: It propagated a mentality that knew only the "corporal's form of power," he complained to Friedrich Naumann: "Give commands, fall in line, stand at attention, show off with big talk."[18] Popularized by the leadership above and embraced by citizens below, such a widespread ethos demonstrated a political incapacity that had to be considered "a factor of first-order 'world-political' significance."[19] It was not merely an innocuous or charming cultural "attitude."

A less familiar and more daring exemplification of Weber's views is

17. Weber's "Geschäftsbericht," 55–56; *GASS*, 443–45.
18. Letter to Naumann, 12 November 1908, MWE; the loosely translated terminology ("*Kommando, Parieren, Strammstehen, Renommage*") comes appropriately from dueling, which for Weber represented the institutional anchorage for this mentality.
19. Letter to Naumann, 14 December 1906, MWE; also discussed in my paper, "Max Weber's Politics and Political Education," *American Political Science Review* 67 (March 1973): 128–41.

found in his comments on those remarkable instances where political effects are least anticipated, such as in the choral society and the subjectivist culture it inspires. Every human association, even one that is voluntary and artistic, has content relevant to a Weltanschauung and ordered pattern of living. In this case, Weber noted for his Sociological Society colleagues,

> A person who is daily accustomed to having powerful emotions flowing out of his chest and through his larynx, without any relation whatsoever to his action, without having the catharsis of the expressed and powerful feeling result in correspondingly powerful actions—and that is the essence of the choral society's artistry—that is a person, briefly stated, who quite easily becomes a "good citizen" in the passive sense of the word.[20]

Artistic performance *is* life-conduct for this aesthetic ideal, which can then be widely disseminated in a culture given over to the "singing club" and affirmed by the devotees of "order," in accordance with the expectation: "Where people sing, they settle down quietly." Such conduct and the ethos contained within it is the essence of that process Weber criticized as *passive* democratization.

Other kinds of associational processes have similar effects on practical conduct and the "inner bearing" with respect to life. One revealing modern case is the sect-like association formed on the basis of particular "mental" products or "theories." Drawing on his own experience, Weber considered the George Circle, united in an aesthetic ideal and belief in the ideal's "incarnation of the sacred," one instance of such dynamics. So too, he thought, was a tendency at work among certain followers of Freud, "a famous Viennese psychiatrist" in Weber's words, where the enthusiasts appeared to be "on the road toward the formation of a sect." For them it could be said that "the object of this sect's activity is the human being ideally 'free of complexes' [*der 'komplexfreie' Mensch*] and a conduct of life through which this ideal human being can be created and preserved."[21] In this instance a medical or psychiatric "theory" thus became, like the inner-worldly asceticism of the Protestant ethic, the authoritative source for a systematic regulation of *practical* activity, only with a precisely opposed result: "crass hedonism," as Weber once called it.[22]

20. "Geschäftsbericht," 57; *GASS*, 445.
21. "Geschäftsbericht," 58; *GASS*, 446.
22. In a letter to Michels, 11 January 1907, AMW 31, attacking the Bund für Mutterschutz und Sexualreform, an association Weber had in fact joined at first, but then repudiated when its leadership began to advocate the therapeutic benefits of free love.

In the end, Weber asserted, a "tragic" fate awaits the associational life of the modern enthusiasts, much like the "tragedy of culture" Simmel identified. For as initially inspiring ideals and "great *Weltanschauungen*" are appropriated for intellectual purposes, used to attract an audience, translated into everyday practice, and, especially, are then made subjects of entrepreneurial activity, propaganda appeals, and public persuasion, so the mechanisms of routine control must inevitably take over. The association's apparatus becomes "objectified and occupied by *vocational* and specialized humanity [*Berufsmenschentum*]," Weber maintained, while at the same time it creates "the *pecuniary* basis for people's livelihood."[23] The obvious and disturbing example of the systematic, organized exploitation of the erotic life, its transformation from a natural sphere into what Weber terms "an awkward and delicate problem," and which today as a pornography industry must be seen as much more than that, demonstrates the lengths to which this tendency can be pushed.

But what do these examples drawn from modern culture reveal about the "spirit" of politics? Why have the "most sublime values" withdrawn into the intimate circle of private life? What happens when this occurs, and what implications can it have for a politics of culture? Clearly, in Weber's comments the most revealing answer lies in the contradiction between the inexhaustible possibilities and excitement of a culture in which "everything is permitted"[24] and the constraints of a culture of unavoidable vocational specialization. As for the latter, in "The Suffrage and Democracy in Germany" Weber went out of his way to restate his thesis from *The Protestant Ethic and Spirit of Capitalism* that *modern* "capitalism" had nothing to do with a simple desire for "profits" or "booty," which had existed everywhere and under all sorts of conditions, but instead was based on a "rational ethos": In his words, "The ethic of duty and honor in one's vocation produced and maintains that

---

"What are you doing in the same camp with these wild philistines?" Weber demanded of Michels, who had just published a racy article in their journal, a kind of comparative sociology of the erotic life in Paris, Italy, and Germany: "This specific *Mutterschutz* gang is an utterly confused bunch. I quit after the babble of [Helene] Stöcker, [Walther] Borgius, etc. Crass hedonism and an ethic as the goal for women that would benefit only *men*—that is simply nonsense" (also cited without attribution in *Lebensbild*, 376; Eng. trans., 373, revised according to the original). Michels wrote quite extensively on feminism and sexuality, and discussed these topics at every opportunity with Weber.

23. "Geschäftsbericht," 57; *GASS*, 445.
24. "*Pánta moi éxestin*," cited in connection with the "radical *anomism*" of chiliastic prophecy: "Zwischenbetrachtung," *GARS* 1:554; G&M, 340.

iron cage, through which economic activity nowadays acquires its special character and fate." A systematic and continuous "profitability" (*Rentabilität*) then nourished an economic order "dominating the everyday fate of humanity."[25] Hence, we are trapped in the paradox of a subjectivist culture of incessant stimulation and change on the one side and the objectivist constraint of the iron cage on the other. It is peculiarly the case that whichever side of the paradox is embraced—and it is essential to see that the modern individual must embrace *both*—those "sublime values" of "publicness" are driven from the stage in full retreat.

This emphasis is developed by Weber partly to advance an unrestrained critique, one of the most sarcastic and ill-tempered in all his writings, of the "romantic fantasies," "absurd nonsense," and plain avoidance of "the specifically *modern* problematic situation" so characteristic of the efforts of the "literati" to transform our "fate."[26] At first glance the criticism appears straightforward, but in actuality it contains important complexities, both personal and political, and in some measure because Weber himself was not immune from the literati's conceit. In one extraordinarily blunt exchange, for example, Weber warned Robert Michels, as perfect an exemplar of the type as one could find, of "the fate awaiting you given the way you work and conduct your life." Weber's words were, among other things, a thinly veiled exercise in self-criticism:

> You have "cut back" on working at *night*? And *that* is supposed to help? You are traveling to *Paris* "for convalescence"(!!) and *that*—curing your fatigue through new *stimuli* [*Reize*]—helped *not at all* (how astonishing!) Believe me, I am *quite well* acquainted with the bohemian *temptation* [*Reiz*], so to speak, of your intense way of life. But whoever wants to continue to live that way at *your* age must stand alone in the world and be able to leave it at a moment's notice, voluntarily or not, without owing an explanation to anyone, when the inevitable collapse comes. Give up *all* foreign lecture tours and *all* work under pressure for a year; go to bed at 9:30 *every* (*every*!!) evening; take an extensive summer vacation *without books* (without *any* books) in the secluded German forest . . . and *then* after a year you will know *what* you have left in capacity for work. You will recover the healthy security of your self-esteem and be able to work successfully, especially to *know* exactly *how much* you can work. But *only* then. And since you aren't

25. *MWG* I/15:356–57.
26. Ibid., 358, 366, 371.

doing *that at all, partial* concessions are completely useless and will simply cause depression.[27]

Michels was driven to experience both the compulsions of vocation and the allure of new enticements. This is what it means, existentially, to be caught in the paradox of a modern culture divided against itself.

In politics the problem of rescuing "fate" from the grasp of cultural paradox reemerged in Weber's wartime essays, from comments on the intellectuals' attempt to appropriate the "German classics" to remarks about their rediscovery of a kind of moral *Sonderweg*, an exceptional path, in traditions of "nobility." Weber found all such maneuvers misguided: "The modern problems of parliamentary government and democracy, and the essential nature of our modern state in general, are entirely beyond the horizon of the German classics."[28] The "aristocratic" and "noble [*vornehm*]" traditions are in fact counterfeit; they are those of the parvenu, lack any "civil [*bürgerlich*]" character, and cannot be "democratized."

It would be mistaken, however, to assume that Weber's aims were exclusively critical, for in crucial passages in "The Suffrage and Democracy" and elsewhere they issued in an appeal for "distance" against the "emotionalism" of the subjectivist culture of feeling, as well as in an appeal for meeting the "demands of the day" against the temptations of eschatological politics. Weber drew the lines of debate and the paradox in culture as he did, not only for critical purposes, but also to sharpen the distinctions and render the alternatives more precise and compelling. "Democratization" might indeed be able "to free the path for the development . . . of 'genuine' and noble values [*vornehme Formwerte*]," even though it remains true that such values "can no more be 'invented' than can a style."[29] They must be supplemented with an understanding of "responsibility" in the face of "history."

But these ideas already belong to the final phase of Weber's thinking. Having said this much about selected aspects of "culture" in their bear-

27. Letter of 12 May 1909, AMW 66. One sense of the meaning of these comments is suggested by Lukács' fin-de-siècle appreciation of the German forests as "homely and inviting," able to "suffer patiently whatever may happen inside them," and suitable for writing "poetic songs of longing," appropriately in his 1911 essay on Charles-Louis Philippe, entitled "Longing and Form," in *Soul and Form*, trans. A. Bostock (Cambridge: MIT Press, 1974), 91.
28. "Wahlrecht und Demokratie," *MWG* I/15:390; G&M, 394.
29. *MWG* I/15:389; G&M, 393.

ing on a modern politics, let us before entering that phase move to reflections on the political sphere that are most relevant to our theme.

THE POLITICAL LIFE-ORDER

As one of the orders of life, politics is considered by Weber under the
category of adaptation to the historically given world; according to his
thinking, it is "inescapably bound" to the conditions of worldly existence and to the "objective pragmatism" of power and its uses.[30] In
"The Religious Rejections of the World and Their Directions" (the
"*Zwischenbetrachtung*") and its first version in *Economy and Society*,
the particular political mode of adaptation is played out in an unusual
way in relation to a religious "ethic of brotherliness," conceived, as we
have seen, not as a kind of theological dogma, but rather as an absolutist ethic of pure conviction, a *Gesinnungsethik*. Weber identified
"ethical action" in this way partly to highlight the unique "lawful
autonomy," or *Eigengesetzlichkeit*, of politics and the contradictory
demands that pervade its sphere. These are action-related contradictions that stand no chance of being resolved or transcended within the
compass of any postulated, hypothetical totality.

The conception articulated in these texts from the sociology of religion is noteworthy because of the absence of explicit commentary at the
surface of politics in favor of a discussion of the deep "tensions" generated by ethical demands and what can be called the developmental expressions such tensions assume as politics is rationalized through the
agency of the modern state. I use the term "developmental" in order to
point toward the specifically historical, comparative, and sociological
character of Weber's account. His reflections on politics become interesting and understandable only at this developmental level, rather than
with respect either to practical pronouncements or to an allegedly
grounded "theory" of politics.

The problems and dilemmas posed within the political order have a
permanent and thematic core, which might be dramatized in austere
language: power is always "diabolic" and never neutral or benign.
But the problems of politics have also been altered historically, or,
more precisely, the tensions between the "demand for brotherliness" or
"love" (in today's parlance) and the "pragmatics of power" have been
heightened with the emergence and growth of the *modern* state. In We-

30. "Zwischenbetrachtung," *GARS* 1:547, 552; G&M, 334, 339.

ber's view, "The more rational the political order became, the sharper the problem of these tensions became."[31] Today they have reached their furthest point of development, and this fact in turn illuminates the essential characteristics that give the political order of life its peculiarly modern coloration or tone. The most important can be briefly ✓ summarized:

First: The modern state is characterized by impersonality. Unlike the patriarchal system Weber studied in the East Elbian territories, where the "estate" existed to ensure personal rule carried out on the basis of personalized authority relationships, the modern state apparatus functions "in a matter-of-fact manner, 'without regard to the person,' *sine ira et studio*, without hate and therefore without love." The *homo politicus*, like the *homo economicus*, performs "without personal predilection and therefore without grace, but sheerly in accordance with the impersonal duty imposed by his calling, and not as a result of any concrete personal relationship. He discharges his responsibility best if he acts as closely as possible in accordance with the rational regulations of the modern power system."[32] In the terms of the "Sociology of Law" discussion in *Economy and Society*, this is to say that a gain in the formal rationality of codes and rules, hence in "fairness" defined as "following the rules," is achieved at the expense of substantive rationality— that is, of "justice" conceived as the realization of an absolute or "ultimate" value.[33]

Second: The modern state is an order based on law, or in Weber's terminology, "The use of force internal to the political community increasingly objectifies itself in the order of the '*Rechtsstaat.*'" This state based on rule of law has come about through the "expropriation" of the means of finance, warfare, and administration. For Weber such historical processes mean that "the modern state is a compulsory association which organizes domination [*anstaltsmässiger Herrschaftsverband*]." Its rational-legal institutions, including elections and parties, constitute the basis for "the modern rational form of governmental policy- or will-formation [*staatliche Willensbildung*]" and the forma-

---

31. *GARS* 1:546; G&M, 333.
32. *GARS* 1:546; G&M, 333–34; *WuG*, 463–64; *EaS*, 600.
33. *WuG*, 60–61, 506–7; *EaS*, 85–86, 655–57. Under the heading of "substantive [*materiale*] rationality" Weber includes "ethical imperatives or utilitarian or other expediential rules [*Zweckmässigkeitsregeln*] or political maxims." The term *zweckmässig* more literally suggests suitability with respect to achieving an announced purpose, result, or end-state, as in the radically egalitarian distributive maxim from Marx's *Critique of the Gotha Program*: "From each according to his ability, to each according to his needs."

tion of "public opinion," often guided by party leaders and the press or other media.[34]

Third: The modern state is a bureaucratic state, and its bureaucratic mode of action represents the triumph of purposive-rational technique, of "mind objectified [*geronnener Geist*]" in public life. With respect to continuity and permanence, it functions as "the rationally transposed counter-image of patriarchalism." For Weber "the future belongs to bureaucratization" to the extent that even "modern parliaments are primarily representative bodies of those ruled with bureaucratic means."[35] Yet administrative action is condemned to a kind of alienation and unaccountability, to a separation between humans and their means of action that Hannah Arendt once appropriately called "rule by Nobody."[36] Weber maintained, "In today's 'state'—and this is essential for its conceptualization—the 'separation' of the administrative staff, the administrative officials, and workers from the material means of the administrative enterprise [*sachliche Betriebsmittel*] is completely carried through." Revolutionary politics thus attain a specific meaning: "Here the most modern development begins and attempts before our eyes to inaugurate the expropriation of this expropriator of the political means and therewith of political power."[37] The putatively new revolutionary state does not alter the course of modern development, but merely extends and rationalizes it further.

Fourth: The modern state, especially because it must operate within the system of sovereign nation-states and therefore face up to the "primacy of foreign policy," finds that its full range of policies must be oriented toward "reason of state." This is the case notwithstanding all social welfare legislation or *Sozialpolitik*, which is itself justified in terms of the "objective pragmatism of reason of state," hence in terms of the state's claims to "legitimacy," to territorial sovereignty, and to a monopoly on the "legitimate means of violence."[38] For the modern state, regardless of its hegemonic ideology, "legitimation" thus becomes an inescapable and continuous *problem* that must be confronted through state action. Today such action often takes the form of an ap-

34. "Wahlrecht und Demokratie," *MWG* I/15:368; "Politik als Beruf" [Politics as a Vocation] (1919), *GPS*, 499; *WuG*, 464, 721; G&M, 82; *EaS*, 600, 980.

35. "Parlament und Regierung," *MWG* I/15:462, 464, 472; *WuG*, 832; *EaS*, 1111, 1401–2, 1407.

36. Hannah Arendt, *Crises of the Republic* (New York: Harvest, 1969), 137.

37. "Politik als Beruf," *GPS*, 499; G&M, 82.

38. "Zwischenbetrachtung," *GARS* 1:547; "Politik als Beruf," *GPS*, 494; *WuG*, 464; G&M, 78, 334; *EaS*, 600–601.

propriation of nonpolitical spheres, such as the scientific or cultural, for purposes of legitimation.

Fifth: In extraordinary circumstances, such as in time of war or revolutionary upheaval, the modern state and its symbols can directly supplement or replace religious ethics and become an alternative source for "a pathos and a feeling of community" as a "mass phenomenon." In this borderline and generally short-lived case, the politicized state order appears similar to the exclusive "salvation aristocracies" of religious movements, only now, paradoxically, its impersonal order becomes an object of inclusive devotion and is endowed with the qualities of a charisma that is otherwise typically attached only to *personal* gifts and prophecy.[39] Obviously this tendency will be accentuated if the state is commanded by a genuinely charismatic movement.

Sixth: Politics in the modern state is dominated by new vocational types, many of whom live "off of" rather than "for" politics: the lawyer, the journalist, the intellectual, the technocrat, the administrative specialist. These types of actors and their claims to authority, responsibility, knowledge, and competence based on expertise and specialized training supply modern political phenomena with their distinctive human and mental culture.

These are important "developmental" generalizations, revealing Weber's vital concerns with the nature of politics as a part of human historical experience. Yet it is equally the case that his deepest interest resides in tracing the "rationalization" of the political sphere *in relation to the ethics of human action.* Parallel to his discussion of the other life-orders, such as the aesthetic or erotic, the understanding achieved is thus really guided by the question, What are the typical responses, the flights into and away from the impersonal, objective, "soulless" order governed by the "pragmatics of power?"—especially since today this political order has long since shown itself adapting to the "iron cage" of vocational specialization, or more alarmingly bent on preparing "the cage for that bondage of the future" as an alliance between bureaucracy, economy, and a hierarchy of social status.[40] Had Weber never delivered "Politics as a Vocation," as was his original intention, the significance of this organizing question might have been more apparent. But, in any case, his influential definitions of politics and the state, as well as his juxtaposition and reconciliation of the "two ethics," are all viewed under the perspective of such questioning.

39. "Zwischenbetrachtung," *GARS* 1:548; G&M, 335.
40. "Parlament und Regierung," *MWG* I/15:464; *EaS*, 1402.

Generally considered, the perspective suggested by these remarks works itself out in spiraling interactions between social and aesthetic modernity, or, in Weber's own words, between the "rational autonomy" of the modern political life-order and "an increased tendency toward flight into the irrationalities of apolitical emotionalism or feeling [*apolitischen Gefühls*] in different degrees and forms."[41] The latter tendency increases *because* of the progressive "rationalization of [legitimate] force [*Gewaltsamkeitsrationalisierung*]" away from a "personalistic attitude" concerning sociopolitical relationships and toward domination by the abstract, impersonal relations of the modern "rational" state. It represents an aesthetic sensibility in revolt.

The resulting tensions cannot be canceled, but they can be alleviated somewhat, Weber suggests, if the "vocational ethic of inner-worldly asceticism" predominates in a culture, for only this ethic is "inwardly adequate" with respect to the entirely "problematic" objectification of a "power structure [*Gewaltherrschaft*]" in the state. Why should this plausibly be the case? Because of its matter-of-fact clarity about the self and the world, asceticism oriented toward the here-and-now is better able than other-worldly or mystical alternatives to work out an acceptable *modus vivendi* with the existing order. But correspondingly, we may say, to the extent that a form of asceticism like the Protestant ethic loses its cultural moorings, a process long underway, the field of political forces will be both increasingly polarized around objective and subjective symbols and opened up to disputes about its boundaries. A modern questioning will then read, Should politics promote deliberation *or* inspiration? Is terror simply another in a long list of *political* means?

To speak of the state we have described as "rational" is neither to voice approval of it nor to deny the irrationalities embedded in its instrumentally rational practices. It is precisely perceptions of the latter that will fuel any politics in search of inspiration and the extraordinary, a modern response that can be expected to take numerous forms: in Weber's words, "a flight into mysticism and an acosmic ethic of absolute 'goodness' ";[42] or retreat into an "extra-religious sphere of feeling [*Gefühlssphäre*], above all, eroticism"; or the possibility he unwittingly bequeathed to contemporary discussion, where it has been notoriously cheapened—namely, acquiescence to "charisma." This last re-

41. See the striking and dense discussion in *WuG*, 464; *EaS*, 601. Arendt's comment expresses these ideas more directly: "The greater the bureaucratization of public life, the greater will be the attraction of violence" (*Crises of the Republic*, 178).

42. *WuG*, 464; *EaS*, 601.

turn of the oldest form of rule—domination as *personal* devotion—usually in the name of the modern age's greatest enthusiasm, revolution, suggests the impersonal, rational state's vulnerability to charismatic appearance and "style" as a promise of that authenticity and immediacy of communal relations lost in the "rationality" of the modern political order.

Clearly, all such courses of action are guided by a promise of heightened experience and reconciliation with the self and the world. The question must become, How should their promises be assessed?

SALVATION THROUGH POLITICS

Weber's discussion of politically relevant responses to the order of life that modern politics represents is woven like a connecting thread through his political writings and into other texts, such as "Science as a Vocation" and "The Meaning of 'Value-Freedom' in the Sociological and Economic Sciences." Many of these responses are in Weber's view inherently *apolitical* and thus likely to crumble under unavoidable pressure from the "internal and lawful autonomy" of the political sphere. Their source, indeed, as the Burg Lauenstein meetings of 1917 demonstrated, was located in an intellectualized cultural romanticism, expressing itself in "the chase after 'lived experience [*Erlebnis*],'" that primary analytic category of Simmelian sociology, and a mode of being that had now in reality become "all the rage in present-day Germany." For Weber it was "a product of diminishing strength inwardly to withstand the 'everyday'" and realized itself in "that publicity, which the individual increasingly feels the urge to give to his 'lived experience.'" In our sensuous, visual, self-absorbed culture it meant "a loss of the sense of distance [*Distanzgefühls*] and thus of propriety and dignity."[43] One hardly needs to add that this pattern has not been confined to Weber's Germany. Today its signs are everywhere.

At Lauenstein, Weber dueled personally with various representatives of the new romanticism and culture of sensation: organizer and publisher Eugen Diederichs, the mercurial Max Maurenbrecher, the idealistic socialist Ernst Toller whom "God in a fit of rage had made into a politician," and in general the "principled politicians" (*Gesinnungspol-*

43. "Der Sinn der 'Wertfreiheit' der soziologischen und ökonomischen Wissenschaften" [The Meaning of "Value-Freedom" in the Sociological and Economic Sciences] (1917), *GAW*, 519; S&F, 28; "Wissenschaft als Beruf," *GAW*, 605; G&M, 149.

itiker), right and left, in the patriotic "Society of 1914," in the youth movement, and among the revolutionaries.[44] These debates sharpened arguments that were reworked in "Science as a Vocation," delivered shortly thereafter in November 1917, and again fourteen months later in January 1919, in "Politics as a Vocation." The same *Gesinnungspolitiker*, or politicians motivated by absolute conviction and pure intention, reappear toward the very end of the latter speech, held in revolutionary Munich, where Weber revealed the overriding problem of his cultural-political critique: not principally what kind of exceptional person one must *be* in order "to put one's hand on the wheel of history"—a question he had long had in mind—but rather, "what in the inward meaning of the word will have 'become' " of those who "feel themselves genuine *'Gesinnungspolitiker'* and take part in the intoxication [*Rausch*] this revolution signifies." What choices will be made in the "hard and clear atmosphere," the "polar night" that Weber repeatedly insisted to his audiences *is* the political condition.[45] Will those who avoid complete collapse retreat into "bitterness," "philistinism," "dull acceptance of world and occupation [*Beruf*]," or "mystic flight from the world" as an expression of the latest "style"? Will their disenchantment take the form of a "psychic proletarianization" and devitalization of the soul in the interest of collective power?[46] Or will they confront and reenter the ordinary political life-order with a defiant "in spite of all!"?

An answer to these questions rests with probably the most famous distinction in all of Weber's work: that between an ethic of absolute conviction or pure intention (*Gesinnungsethik*) and an ethic of respon-

---

44. *MWG* I/15:701–7. With respect to the Lauenstein meetings, Marianne Weber noted, "The basic theme of the discussions was to be the linking of cultural questions with political ones. The main organizer [Diederichs] hoped for more—namely, that the meetings would promote the evolution of a new German spirit, one that was anchored in religion" (*Lebensbild*, 608; Eng. trans., 597); see p. 673 (Eng. trans., 661) for the characterization of Toller Marianne attributes to her husband. On the general context and import of these discussions, consult Gangolf Hübinger, "Kulturkritik und Kulturpolitik des Eugen-Diederichs-Verlags im Wilhelminismus, Auswege aus der Krise der Moderne?" *Troeltsch-Studien* 4 (1987): 92–114.

45. "Der Nationalstaat" (1895), "Zur Gründung einer national-sozialen Partei" (1896), and "Politik als Beruf," in *GPS*, 25, 28, 547–48; "The National State," 448; G&M, 127–28; also similar phrasing in Weber's election campaign speech on "Die Wiederaufrichtung Deutschlands" (reported in the *Heidelberger Zeitung*, 3 January 1919), delivered almost four weeks before "Politics as a Vocation."

46. In "Politics as a Vocation" Weber speaks of *Entseelung* and *geistige* or *seelische Proletarisierung*, suggesting an ironic riposte to Marx's immiseration thesis (*GPS*, 532, 545; G&M, 113, 125).

sibility (*Verantwortungsethik*).[47] The distinction's meaning has often seemed clear-cut, as if to pose an easy choice between agitated catharsis and calm rationality. But Weber's evident preference for a politics of "responsibility" concealed an important complexity in his judgments.

On the one hand he despaired at the consequences of attempting to achieve "the salvation of the soul" for oneself and others by following the path of politics: the "daemon of politics lives in an inner tension with the god of love . . . that can erupt in irreconcilable conflict at any time."[48] The difficulty with any eschatological or millenarian politics was that it deliberately and necessarily denied this rule of experience, which, stated in more general terms, signified "that an everlasting tension exists between the world and the irrational metaphysical [*hinterweltlich*] realm of salvation."[49] So to imagine our actually existing historical world as a setting for salvation invited an elaborate, if understandable self-deception. It overlooked the import of that ancient truth of Hellenic pessimism, "in the midst of life we are overtaken by death," not to mention the additional grounds catalogued in great detail for modernity from Nietzsche to Freud. Furthermore, the prospects for changing an established faith in pure intentions seemed impossibly remote to Weber: "An argument with convinced socialists and revolutionaries is always a troublesome affair. In my experience one never convinces them."[50] In this respect the *Gesinnungsethik* defined the boundaries of sensible political discourse.

It is also true, however, that Weber was prepared to honor the dignity of the absolutely consistent *Gesinnungspolitiker*—undoubtedly a major source of his friendships and interest in activists like Lukács, Michels, Ernst Toller, Erich Mühsam, Paul Ernst, Paul Göhre, Otto Neurath, and countless others in the Schwabing and Ascona counterculture, in various experimental cultural and political movements of the day, and among the Heidelberg contingent of Russian and Eastern European expatriots. While the experience of these circles showed that unswerving

47. The standard translation of *Gesinnungsethik* as an ethic of "ultimate ends" can mislead by implying that it is ends-oriented; for Weber, however, this ethic deliberately refuses to think in "rational" means-ends categories: for example, "'The Christian does rightly and leaves the results with the Lord'" (*GARS* 1:553; *GPS*, 539; G&M, 120, 339). Like the word *Stimmung*, *Gesinnung* has "emotive" connotations that cannot be precisely conveyed in English.
48. "Politik als Beruf," *GPS*, 545; G&M, 126.
49. "Zwischenbetrachtung," *GARS* 1:554; G&M, 340.
50. "Der Sozialismus" (1918), in *MWG* I/15:633; complete translation in *Max Weber: The Interpretation of Social Reality*, ed. J. Eldridge (London: Joseph, 1970), 219.

consistency to an "ultimate value" could not be maintained, except by the rare saint, the one contribution attributable to "pure conviction" alone was the sense that politics was not exhausted, as Weber put it, by "the 'art of the possible,' " but completed itself only when "one reached for the impossible that lies beyond it."[51] This is why, at the conclusion of "Politics as a Vocation," a reconciliation between conviction and responsibility provides the foundation for the only fully acceptable *political* answer to our questions.

Understood in this way, Weber's two "political ethics" have received considerable attention with respect to their logical coherence, political applicability, and moral consequences.[52] But it should also be said that a politics guided by absolute conviction was additionally one of subjectivist culture's most visible claims to a new world projected outside the "ordinary" and beyond "history," a claim made explicit in two converging discourses evident in Weber's reflections: one was biblical, chiliastic, millenarian, eschatological, with reverberations of Tolstoyan ennui and longing, while the other was steeped in modernist yearning. Simply consider Weber's sublime language for describing this politics of sacred sentiments: "excitation," "intoxication," "romantic sensation," "the flame of pure intentions," "the thirst for the 'deed,' " "romanticism of the intellectually interesting," "cosmic-ethical 'rationalism,' " and most significantly a belief that either "love" will conquer violence or "*ultimate* violence" will "eliminate *all* violence."[53] As we have seen from Dostoyevski's metaphysical rebels and Georges Sorel's syndicalists onward, it would be difficult to concoct in word and deed a more potent combination of ageless, mythical "religiosity" and modern, pragmatic "idealism."

This combination and its language characterized more than a political ethic. It became the new political aesthetic, sufficiently powerful and compelling to have instigated those otherwise baffling reversals of allegiance among the déclassé, "free-floating" intelligentsia and "true believers," which Weber found so characteristic of revolutionary Russia and his own generation at home. The uncertain and dubious quality of

51. "Der Sinn der Wertfreiheit," *GAW*, 514; "Politik als Beruf," *GPS*, 548; S&F, 23–24; G&M, 128.

52. For example, Wolfgang Schluchter, "Value-Neutrality and the Ethic of Responsibility," in Guenther Roth and Wolfgang Schluchter, *Max Weber's Vision of History: Ethics and Methods* (Berkeley: University of California Press, 1979), chap. 2; originally published in 1971.

53. "Politik als Beruf," *GPS*, 533–34, 540–41, 547; "Zur Lage der bürgerlichen Demokratie in Russland," 322; G&M, 115, 121, 127–28.

a politics oriented exclusively toward ultimate values, pure convictions, and "last things" was thus not merely the search for salvation along the wrong path, which was at least still a moral-political problem, but in addition a subjugation of the entire question of the relations between ethics and politics to *aesthetic* criteria and standards of judgment.

Having begun with an either/or alternative germane to the political sphere and its distinctive concerns, those who defined the modern situation of choice now threatened to substitute for that evaluative standard another of an entirely heterogeneous type. With such a transformation and substitution the requirements of responsible and accountable action had themselves come under siege, as had Weber's own carefully crafted thinking about the alleged autonomy of the political life-order. But before we consider the line of thinking appropriate to this challenge, it is worth following our thread of argument one final step into the complexities of socialism.

SOCIALISM AS CULTURAL CRITICISM

Socialism represented a special case for Weber, and it could not be dismissed as merely an absolutist ideology. Of course, for some Weber was mainly a "Marx of the bourgeoisie," his leading political slogan was "dynamic capitalism instead of bureaucratic socialism," and his main scientific purpose was to forge the weapons of "bourgeois sociology" in order to slay the dragon of "historical materialism." Beyond Weber's mounting of this campaign, a critic has declared, "there seems to be little room left for socialism" in Weber's thought.[54] I want to propose, however, that far from being a marginal phenomenon viewed with "bourgeois" disdain, socialism intrigued Weber from the beginning to the end of his life because of its explosive mixture of potentially contradictory elements—organizational imperatives, allegedly "scientific" principles, prophetic moral vision, criticism of the "alienated" culture spawned by unrestrained capitalism—and because he understood that it was a *cultural* movement with a proposed alternative to the "iron cage" of capitalist rationalism.

As early as 1892 he suggested that modern socialism resulted not only from "definite social conditions," but from "a particular psycho-

54. Albert Salomon, "Max Weber," *Die Gesellschaft* 3 (1926): 144; Mommsen, *Age of Bureaucracy*, chap. 3; Gert H. Mueller, "Socialism and Capitalism in the Work of Max Weber," *British Journal of Sociology* 33 (1982): 151.

logical effect that is brought about by the peculiarities of *urban* existence, namely a withering away of certain aspects in the normal human life of the mind and soul."[55] And years later he spoke of the choice to promote proletarian "interests" not in the sense of "empirically given endeavors, but in the sense of that which is *most inward* and humanly highest."[56] Critique of *both* the material culture of capitalist production and the subjectivist culture of the modern was the vital source of socialism's power and appeal, even as it proposed alternative objective *forms* of production and exchange to the prevailing market economy.[57]

Weber obviously was not alone in this view. Socialists themselves, particularly those influenced by Lassallean and revisionist ideas, such as Heinrich Braun, David Koigen, Eduard Bernstein, and Max Adler, were attracted to the notion of modern socialism expressing a general problem in culture. For Bernstein "the most comprehensive understanding of socialism always remains the cultural, which conceives socialism as a cultural problem and places its function as a factor or carrier of culture in the foreground." And in Vienna, Adler pronounced it "no longer paradoxical to assert that socialism is not fundamentally a workers' movement, but a cultural movement," whose meaning "is that socialism will attain a new culture through the working-class movement." Even for an astute and sympathetic observer like Durkheim, socialism was essentially a form of cultural protest, "not a science, a sociology in miniature," but "a cry of grief, sometimes of anger, uttered by men who feel most keenly our collective *malaise*," in the words of his most famous statement on the topic.[58]

Weber took up the problem of socialism as cultural criticism at the first meeting of the German Sociological Society in the context of his commentary on modern culture as a whole. Socialism was not simply an organization in the process of being transformed from a party with a Weltanschauung into an electoral machine; it was also and above all a proletarian "cultural community" (*Kulturgemeinschaft*) whose "most magnificent" task lay in promoting "the rapturous hope of from within

55. "'Privatenquêten' über die Lage der Landarbeiter," *Mitteilungen des Evangelisch-sozialen Kongresses* 6 (1 July 1892): 2.
56. Letter to Tönnies, 9 May 1909, NW 30/7:124.
57. Considered by Weber in *WuG*, 78–82; *EaS*, 109–13.
58. Bernstein's remark from 1903, as quoted in Emil Hammacher, *Das philosophisch-ökonomische System des Marxismus* (Leipzig: Duncker & Humblot, 1909), 690; Adler, *Socialism and the Intellectuals* (1910), quoted in *Austro-Marxism*, ed. T. Bottomore and P. Goode (Oxford: Clarendon, 1978), 262; and Emile Durkheim, *Socialism and Saint-Simon* (1895–96), ed. A. Gouldner (London: Routledge & Kegan Paul, 1959), 7.

itself opposing the bourgeois world with completely new values in *all* areas" of culture. "That was for us the most interesting aspect of this movement," or one of "the most important inquiries we can be concerned with," Weber declared. Although the new cultural community had not created unique concepts of cultural or aesthetic "form" (*Formwerte*), it had opened up previously ignored subjects and raised a question about the significance and standing of "culture" that "belongs specifically to a future discussion of the materialist interpretation of history."[59] In the hands of others from Lukács to Herbert Marcuse, a discussion of this sort did in fact evolve in Western Marxism around the question, What can be the approach and content of a Marxist aesthetics?

It was the view of socialism as a "cultural community" that Weber incorporated into his most specific proposals for an empirical sociology of culture—namely, those research projects mentioned in Chapter 4 that were developed in 1909–10 and channeled through the Sociological Society: the inquiry into the modern press and the meaning of associational life in modern society—especially the former. The contemporaneity of these proposals is striking. Considering the press "a component in the *objective* peculiarity of modern *culture*," as we have seen, and "as one of the means for forming the *subjective* character of modern *humankind*," Weber wanted, among other things, to investigate the extent to which the socialist press contributed to the development of a particular mentality within its audience, and thereby to the definition of a specific kind of cultural community on the Left.[60]

Although the press project yielded few results, Weber characteristically never quite let his questions about socialism and culture die, reviving them among the themes for the monumental *Outline of Social Economics*. The man he approached for the task was probably the best critical observer of social democracy at the time: Robert Michels. In the essays written preparatory to *Political Parties*, Michels had of course emphasized the undermining of democratic purpose by organizational necessities in the socialist movement, partly in reply to Weber's persistent questioning. But when Weber recruited Michels to write an article

59. [Diskussionbeitrag in der Debatte über Werner Sombart, "Technik und Kultur"], in *Verhandlungen des Ersten Deutschen Soziologentages*, 97–98; *GASS*, 450–51.
60. Quotes from Weber's eleven-page "Vorläufiger Bericht über eine vorgeschlagene Erhebung über die Soziologie des Zeitungswesens" (Preliminary report on a proposed inquiry into the sociology of the press), undated but probably from late 1910 or early 1911, in NWS 18b:200–210.

on "the international socialist movement" for the *Outline of Social Economics*, as he had attempted to recruit him previously for a study of the socialist press, it was with the understanding that he instead give priority to the problem of culture:

> I assume that you will analyze . . . the position of Social Democracy or the socialist movement above all as a party of *culture* [*Kulturpartei*]. The movement certainly wanted to create and *believed* it *had* created *not* only its own *social* outcomes, but also its own *cultural* content. *What* content? From which *ultimate* ethical or other standpoints? It *wanted* a substitute for *religion*, even to be a religion itself. In what *sense*? Is this still the case? Why no longer in most cases? Why *not* in some countries, in others less than previously?[61]

Despite his critical proclivities, Michels remained too much the participant to follow these questions to their conclusion.

Certainly for Weber, however, not merely party programs and organizational forms, but the deeper "spirit of socialism" mattered most in what he called "a universal history of culture." In effect, his proposal called for nothing less than a study of socialism parallel to his own earlier cultural investigations of the "spirit of capitalism." As became evident in those other inquiries, were socialism in general to lose its peculiar "spirit," conjured by capitalism's revolutionizing of actually existing culture, then it would likely also lose its uniquely attractive and critical powers and prowl about "in our lives like the ghost of dead religious beliefs."[62]

What might have gone into a study of this kind remains open to speculation, for Weber did not complete a work on the subject or even the preliminary 1920 Munich lectures on socialism. However, in those scattered passages where his own questions are addressed a clear line of argument emerges: as a movement of cultural criticism socialism is both a specific product of the forces that have produced modern culture and a willful negation of those forces. Thus, as it moves seriously to implement its critique, it undercuts the conditions for its own existence and appeal. But this formal paradox, although interesting, is less significant than socialism's actual rationalization of the substance of economic life. For to the extent it adapts to "technical progress," *any* style of social-

---

61. Weber to Michels, 30 May 1914, AMW 116a; Weber's urgings along these lines in fact date from February 1910 (see AMW 70, 71, 72), with a proposed deadline of 1 November 1911!
62. *GARS* 1 : 10, 204; *PE*, 23, 182.

ism, regardless of "ethical" or "historical" overtones, will tend to reify the forces of industrialization unleashed by capitalism into everyday culture.

In this regard Russia represented for Weber "the great experiment," partly because of the unusual convergence there, for cultural reasons, of a modern "socialist" *ideology* with an "'unmodern' agrarian communism," or "the historic village communism of the *mir*."[63] This convergence gave socialism a source of popular appeal, while usefully concealing its modernizing intentions. Yet in such experiments, Weber argued, "it is the dictatorship of the official, not that of the worker, which for the present at any rate is on the advance"[64]—and, one might add, not only for the present! Thus, quoting Habermas,

> Max Weber took up this critique [of the relationship between civil society and state] and sharpened it; he has been proven correct in his prognosis that the destruction of private capitalism would by no means signify a bursting of the iron cage of modern industrial labor. In "really existing socialism" the attempt to dissolve civil society [*bürgerliche Gesellschaft*] into political society actually had only its bureaucratization as a result; it only expanded economic constraint into an administrative control pervading all realms of life.[65]

Combined with "submissive attitudes" and "spiritual apathy," resulting partially from the abortive "eschatological" politics of the movement,[66] the subsumption of civil society within the state seems in Weber's eyes a ready-made formula for multiplying the constraints of vocational life. Far from offering a solution to the paradoxes of the present, the politics of this particular revolutionary socialism becomes a prescription for more of the same within the confines of the "iron cage."

Weber's perspective on socialism involved a questioning of its prospects and future: What can become of the project to put an end to the "domination of human beings over human beings" under modern conditions? Weber found this a fascinating project, even an admirable one if lived out consistently, but a hopeless exercise in self-deception if com-

---

63. "Zur Lage der bürgerlichen Demokratie in Russland," 320–21.
64. *MWG* I/15:621, 628; "Socialism," 209, 215.
65. *The Philosophical Discourse of Modernity: Twelve Lectures*, trans. F. Lawrence (Cambridge: MIT Press, 1987), 70; an identical view is expressed by Albrecht Wellmer, "Reason, Utopia and The *Dialectic of Enlightenment*," in *Habermas and Modernity*, ed. R. Bernstein (Cambridge: MIT Press, 1985), 43.
66. Phrases from "Zur Lage der bürgerlichen Demokratie in Russland," 349; *Selections*, 283.

promised under the exigencies of modern political and social life. He feared that *modern* revolution was different from what it claimed to be. As he maintained in the second essay on Russia,

> Like the modern military engagement, stripped of the romantic charm of knightly combat, so it is also with modern "revolution": it represents itself as a mechanical operation between the products of mental labor in laboratories and industrial plants, objectified as instrumental things, and the cold power of money, together with a perpetual tension placed on the strength of *nerve* of the leader as well as the hundreds of thousands of followers. Everything is—at least for the eye of the spectator—"technique" and a question of iron steadfastness of nerves.[67]

That is perhaps Weber's single most important statement about the material and psychological conditions for a modern revolutionary politics. The formula for revolutionary success might read, mastery of technique (including the social technique of "organization") plus strength of ideological commitment; the formula already represents a purposive rationalization of "spontaneous" consciousness and an overcoming of all "developmental laws." The genealogy of revolution after Marx thus leads to the "instrumentalization" and "scientization" of revolution, or in the Hegelian terms borrowed by Weber, "the return of Spirit to itself"—that is, the rationalization of revolutionary technique through deliberate self-reflection.[68] To the extent that it too had become rationalized, revolutionary politics promised only to reaffirm and reify state domination and the general conditions of industrial, technological civilization.

In sum, what socialism has in fact brought forth (which is all to the good) is new subjects and problems for culture. But it has not and will not ever create new cultural *forms*, for to do that would require renouncing the world of "objective," purposive-rational culture it desires to inherit. As a positive movement, socialism is set against itself, trapped in what Weber (following Sombart) once called "the 'two-souled character' " of Marxism.[69] It is at its best as cultural critic.

---

67. "Russlands Übergang zum Scheinkonstitutionalismus," *Archiv* 23 (1906): 396.
68. "Zur Lage der bürgerlichen Demokratie in Russland," 283, 348; *Selections*, 282.
69. "Zur Lage der bürgerlichen Demokratie in Russland," 282; Werner Sombart, *Socialism and Social Movement* (London: Dent, 1909), 69.

RESPONSIBILITY FOR HISTORY: THE
CALLING FOR POLITICS

Two sets of categoric distinctions establish the dialectic of Weber's political thinking: external versus internal, the everyday (or ordinary) opposed to the extraordinary.[70] It is a measure of Weber's deepest interests that his finest discussion of the calling for politics (and science, too) begins with external factors and then moves to what really matters most: the internal "conditions" for a way of leading one's life or a specific kind of conduct "within the total life of humanity."[71] This overriding concern for "inner meaning" and not some prissy reservation about the *Rechtstaat* (the constitutional state) or passionate attachment to nationalist rhetoric accounts for Weber's contention that the "form of government" is always an "objective [*sachliche*] question," since a "technical change" in these forms can never in itself "make a nation vigorous or happy or valuable."[72] Only considerations at the level of the political vocation and its bearing on culture can address such fundamental issues.

The conduct of life in *any* of its many orders follows a pattern of alternation between the continuous and long flow of typicality and the sudden, brief moments of transcendence. Weber makes the point through Thomas Carlyle: "'Thousands of years must pass before you enter into life and thousands more wait in silence.'" In thought and art the breakthrough to originality, passion, inspiration, or "delirium," to a Platonic *manía* of the "soul,"[73] is followed always by painstaking calculation, slow mastery of rational technique, the dull repetition of practice. So also in politics the spells of charismatic ascendence are followed by the patient, routine "strong, slow boring of hard boards." Weber insists that politics is a "hard business" that transpires in "the cold and clear air"; its "essence" is "struggle" conjoined in the modern constitutional state to "compromise"; it is "made with the head, not with

---

70. In Weber's terminology, *aüsser* and *inner*; *alltäglich* and *ausseralltäglich* (or *ausserordentlich*).

71. "Politik als Beruf," *GPS*, 493; "Wissenschaft als Beruf," *GAW*, 595; G&M, 77, 140.

72. "Parlament und Regierung," *MWG* I/15:435–36; *EaS*, 1383–84.

73. "Der Sinn der 'Wertfreiheit'" and "Wissenschaft als Beruf," *GAW*, 508, 589, 591; S&F, 18; G&M, 135–36; Weber's reference is to *Phaedrus* 244–45, where Plato proposes that "in reality, the greatest blessings come by way of madness, indeed of madness that is heaven-sent."

other parts of the body or the soul." Yet politics too is "certainly not *only* made with the head," and its deliberative practice requires "passion and perspective," devotion and distance, intellect and soul.[74] All the problems and "tensions" of politics in its *inner* meaning follow from these dialectic combinations that Weber purposely establishes. They are combinations, furthermore, that are built into the very conception of politics.

Now the question must become, What position is one prepared to take and defend in light of the abuse of the political life-order, its invasion from one side by the tedium and banality of "impartial" administration, from the other by the new aesthetic of a culture of "sensation" and heightened experience? On the one hand and notwithstanding his national pathos, for Weber the popular nationalism of the age did not represent an acceptable stance—this "hollow, empty, and purely zoological nationalism" that in his judgment "necessarily leads to an unprincipled attitude with respect to all the great problems of culture."[75] Suffering from an arrogant blindness, it disclosed unrivaled irresponsibility and destructive potential. Much the same could be said for claims made generally in the name of power. For although power in and for itself could generate what Weber called "strong effects," "glamour," and "enjoyment," the achievements of the mere power politician were externally meaningless and inwardly weak and empty, revealing the "purely personal self-intoxication" of an actor taken with appearances.[76] On the other hand, despite invoking those "individualists and supporters of democratic institutions," himself among them, as a touchstone of political judgment, Weber thought unqualified and exclusive reliance on this test could yield only superficial results. Thus, "'Democ-

---

74. Phrases used from 1895 to 1919: "Der Nationalstaat," "Zur Gründung," and "Politik als Beruf," *GPS*, 25, 28, 534, 546, 548; "Wahlrecht und Demokratie" and "Parlament und Regierung," *MWG* I/15:367, 537; "The National State," 448; *EaS*, 1450; G&M, 115, 127–28.

75. Letter to his Freiburg Colleagues, 15 November 1911, NW 30/6:98–102. Reflecting on his understanding of the autonomous life-orders, Weber continued, "A critique of particular *political* ideals, no matter how high they may be, as a subversion of *moral* powers must certainly call forth justified protest. In 'ethics' the pacifists have it 'over' us without a doubt. In my Freiburg Inaugural Address, even though immature in many respects, I already put forward in the most relentless way the sovereignty of national ideals in the sphere of practical politics and in so-called social policy [*Sozialpolitik*], at a time when the great majority of my colleagues were falling for the swindle of the so-called 'social monarchy.' But back then I quite intentionally emphasized that politics is not, nor can it ever be, a profession based upon morality."

76. "Politik als Beruf," *GPS*, 534–35; G&M, 116–17, suggesting a criticism of *The Prince* that Machiavelli may well have shared.

racy' was never an end in itself," but became defensible because of its "internal" import and effects. This is why the political writings devote such considerable attention, which is otherwise so inexplicable, to the "democratization" of civic learning and "politically worthwhile social forms or values."[77]

Setting aside these possible competitors *within* the political value-sphere, Weber turned to a conception of responsibility or accountability as a vocational *ethos* for the answer to our question. This was a political answer because responsibility from its earliest appearance in Weber's language of action was meaningful not merely for the person, but for the future, in relation to subsequent generations and "*in the face of history*," an "expression full of pathos," Weber said, and the link to the "what is" of his science of culture.[78] In conventional terms responsibility required a consideration of "consequences," including perceptive understanding of the long-term course of historical development:

> A national politician will surely direct his gaze toward those universal developmental tendencies that will have control in the future over the external regulation of the life-fate of the masses. . . . If he proceeds differently, then he is one of the literati and not a politician. Then he should interest himself in eternal truths and stick to his books, but not appear on the battlefield of current political affairs.[79]

With sights set unusually high in these concluding remarks from "Politics and Government in a Reconstructed Germany," Weber urged upon his "leaders" a clear-sighted assessment of the "fate" of our "disenchanted world." And he maintained the same level of discourse in far less conventional remarks on this demanding political ethos governed by "distance."

The most penetrating solution to the dilemmas in the political order of life, including "becoming conscious of its ethical paradoxes and one's responsibility for what can become of *oneself* under their impact,"[80] is located in an idea of *Distanz*, of the "pathos of distance" toward the self, others, and the world. In Weber's thinking this form-creating

---

77. For the last phrase, Weber speaks of *gesellschaftliche Formwerte*; quotations from "Zur Lage der bürgerlichen Demokratie in Russland," 347; "Das preussische Wahlrecht" [The Suffrage in Prussia] (1917), and "Wahlrecht und Demokratie," *MWG* I/15:234, 389; *Selections*, 282; G&M, 393.

78. "Der Nationalstaat" and "Politik als Beruf," *GPS*, 24, 537; "Zwischen zwei Gesetzen" [Between Two Laws] (1916), *MWG* I/15:95; "The National State," 447; G&M, 118.

79. "Parlament und Regierung," *MWG* I/15:595–96.

80. "Politik als Beruf," *GPS*, 545; G&M, 125.

power had nothing to do with either the "misconceived 'prophecies' which go back to Nietzsche" and heighten "the 'aristocratic' contrast between one's self and the 'all-too-many'" from *Zarathustra*, or with the intellectuals' heroic display of authenticity in "their urge to brag about and to print their personal 'experiences'—erotic, 'religious,' or whatever they might be." Instead, its basis was an "attitude of inner *distance* and *reserve*," and its proving ground was located in history, in the developmental tendencies of a "democratization" that might yield genuine and worthy cultural values. In Weber's idiom, "Perhaps the necessity of holding one's own inwardly in the midst of a democratic world can serve as a test of the genuineness of distance."[81]

Just as Nietzsche had proposed the paradox of "life against life" to account for the origins of morality, so Weber proposed to turn his revision of Nietzsche against the misguided Nietzsche-cult in order to find a resource for preserving and mastering the daemon of politics through "responsibility" and a "pathos of distance." The borrowed figure of thought was transposed into the modern and democratic setting, transformed, and rendered practical. Even in his later political appearances, including the campaign speeches of 1919 for the German Democratic Party, Weber did not miss the opportunity to follow through with this solution, repudiating a "politics of feelings" and defending political action oriented toward the future, guided by dignity and *Distanz*, strengthened "in spite of all" against the coming "polar night of icy darkness and hardness."[82] Such a politics would be an inoculation against the all-too-modern dangers of "psychic proletarianization,"

81. "Das preussische Wahlrecht" and "Wahlrecht und Demokratie," *MWG*, I/15: 231, 389–90; G&M, p. 393; cf. the passage added in 1917 to "Der Sinn der 'Wertfreiheit,'" *GAW*, 519; S&F, 28; *Selections*, 93, where *Distanzgefühl* is misleadingly translated as "sense of privacy" or "feeling of detachment"! In Weber's words, one "should not overlook the fact that the chase after 'experience [*Erlebnis*]'—the really fashionable thing to do in present-day Germany—may in large measure be the product of diminishing strength inwardly to withstand the 'everyday,' and that the publicity which the individual feels the increasing need to give to his 'experience' can perhaps be evaluated as a loss in the sense of distance [*Distanzgefühl*] and therefore in the sense of appropriate style [*Stilgefühl*] and dignity." For Nietzsche's "Viel-zu-Vielen," see "Thus Spake Zarathustra," *The Portable Nietzsche*, ed. W. Kaufmann (New York: Viking, 1954), 156–57; the "pathos of distance" appears in *On the Genealogy of Morals*, trans. W. Kaufmann (New York: Random House [Vintage Books], 1967), 26, 125 (I, 2; III, 14); and *Beyond Good and Evil*, trans. W. Kaufmann (New York: Random House [Vintage Books], 1967), 201–2 (pt. 9, "What is noble?," sec. 257).

82. "Deutschlands weltpolitische Lage" and "Die Wiederaufrichtung Deutschlands," speeches reported in *Münchner Neueste Nachrichten*, 28 October 1916; *Heidelberger Neueste Nachrichten* and *Heidelberger Zeitung*, 3 January 1919.

whether under the auspices of either arid administration or "'sterile' excitation."[83]

Weber's earliest recorded encounters begin with politics, and then with the most political of sources, the most fervent advocate of the "autonomy" of the political life-order: Machiavelli and *The Prince*, read in 1876. We might say they come to a conclusion in 1919 in the same atmosphere, with Machiavelli's Florentine citizens, cited in the closing pages of "Politics as a Vocation," whose "love of their native city stood higher than fear for the salvation of their souls."[84] Their exemplary pathos of devotion and distance led them to seize responsibility for their own fate. Their commanding "genius or daemon" of politics may not have been Weber's only passion, but it was without a doubt his oldest and greatest "secret love." Like all sublimated eros, it created a purified and acute ethos, a calling for politics with a sense of responsibility for history, which is to say a personal accountability for all the orders of life. "This rare freedom," Nietzsche called such responsibility, "this power over oneself and over fate."[85] It was the conception Weber took as his own, as if to say that the political life-order can offer nothing more exceptional, nothing more sublime in the modern age of subjectivist culture.

83. "Politik als Beruf," *GPS*, 533, 545–46; G&M, 115, 125, 127; Weber attributes the phrase "'sterile' excitation," describing "a certain type of Russian intellectual," to Simmel.

84. According to Weber's very first letter, 21 August 1876 (to his mother), in *JB*, 3; *GPS*, 546; *GARS* 1:98; G&M, 126; *PE*, 107; paraphrasing *The History of Florence*, bk. 3, chap. 7, and Machiavelli's letter to Vettori, 16 April 1527. Cf. Hennis, *Max Webers Fragestellung*, 120, 230, 235, where the connection to Machiavelli is suggestively conceived as an education in the "power of judgment" (*Urteilskraft*).

85. *Genealogy of Morals*, 59–60 (II, 2).

CHAPTER VI

The Weber Circle and the Problem of Modern Life

And we may well heave a sigh of relief at the knowledge that it is given to a few individuals to bring up easily out of the maelstrom of their own feelings the deepest insights, toward which the rest of us have to find our way with tormenting uncertainty and restless groping.

—*Sigmund Freud*

In the years just before the guns of August shattered the peace of Europe, an important debate over "culture" and "modern life" developed among the writers and scholars grouped around Max Weber. The cultural issues that emerged in what some of its Heidelberg members later designated the "Weber Circle" were broad indeed: the problem of ethical conduct in an age increasingly dominated by "technical progress" and "instrumental rationality"; the opposition between socialism and middle-class society; the partial sociologies of aesthetic spheres of life, such as music or poetry; the politics of cultural movements with apocalyptic convictions; and the controversy over what Paul Honigsheim called the "causal relationship between the economy and the life of the mind [*Geistesleben*]" or religious life.[1] The dialogue over these issues was given shape in Marianne's "jours" at the Webers' Ziegelhäuser Landstrasse residence, in public settings like Heidelberg's Café Häberlein, at the first two sessions of the German Sociological Society in 1910 and 1912, to an extent (at least for Max and Alfred Weber) at the meetings of the Association for Social Policy (Verein für Sozialpolitik) and the German Conference of University Teachers (*Deutscher Hochschullehrertag*), in publications by this very literary group of intellectuals,

---

1. Paul Honigsheim "Der Max-Weber-Kreis in Heidelberg," *Kölner Vierteljahrshefte für Soziologie* 5 (1926): 274.

and naturally in countless informal contacts and exchanges. These discussions swirling around Max Weber did not achieve unanimity of viewpoint, nor did they produce anything like a "school" of thought, but they did create something even more notable, as the participants later acknowledged: an atmosphere of intensely engaged thought and a sense of having lived in close contact with the crucial issues and the elusive spirit of the emerging modern age.

The debate over modern culture that started to take shape among Max Weber's contemporaries and within his immediate circle of colleagues before 1914 was hardly a unified, clear, and theoretically unambiguous exchange, and perhaps for that reason all the more vigorous and instructive. These discussions were not unprecedented, either, and can be traced to three sources. In the first instance members of the Weber Circle continued the much older nineteenth-century discussion of the problem of labor and the "social question," with its usually explicit critique of the Dickensian world created by industrial capitalism, a critique reaching across the spectrum of opinion from romantic nationalists to utopian socialists. As we have shown, the problem of labor also figured prominently in Weber's early writings on East Elbia, just as it pushed him toward the study of political economy.

Closer to home, the circle revived and augmented the debate initiated in the 1890s over the new, modernist literary and aesthetic movements and their respective cultural-political import: that is, the questioning of modern life in the work of writers like Kierkegaard, Tolstoy, and Dostoevski; the directions taken by composers and poets in the aftermath of Wagner and Mallarmé; or the controversies provoked by the break with artistic tradition in innovations like *Jugendstil*.[2] It is not without reason that Max Weber wanted to write on the Russian novelists and did write on the sociohistorical development of a Western harmonic and melodic aesthetic. Nor is it surprising that he and his Circle were attracted to many important figures of cultural innovation, such as Charles Baudelaire, Auguste Rodin, Émile Zola, August Strindberg, Henrik Ibsen, Oscar Wilde, Maurice Maeterlinck, Charles-Louis Philippe, Stefan George, Rainer Maria Rilke, Ricarda Huch, Leopold von Andrian, Richard Strauss, Gerhart Hauptmann, Paul Ernst, Arnold Böcklin, Max Klinger, Peter Behrens. Symptomatic of this interest are

2. For an appropriate early example among Weber's acquaintances, see Carl Neumann, *Der Kampf um die neue Kunst* (Berlin: Walther, 1897).

the references to these figures and their work that appear recurrently in Weber's own personal correspondence.[3]

Finally, an equally fundamental source of questioning was to be located in parts of Marx's work and, as we have noted previously, especially in Nietzsche. It may appear odd to mention these two monumental critics in the same breath—thinkers, after all, who are in the most obvious and important ways so radically opposed—but in one respect an area of convergence attracted the attention of the turn-of-the-century generation: their critique of the "soulless" and alienating power of capitalism. Thus, eclectic socialists like Max Maurenbrecher, with whom Weber tangled at Lauenstein Castle, took it upon themselves to develop a synthesis of the two thinkers, attempting to appropriate Nietzsche's "new man" ("*ein neuer Typus Mensch*" in Maurenbrecher's phrase) for revolutionary socialist purposes.[4] Others among the philosophers and sociologists, such as Simmel and Tönnies, produced their own paradoxes trying to use both these nineteenth-century minds for social criticism. Typically, Weber promoted a rather different orientation that instead led him to formulate those "ideal types" of what he called "capitalist culture"—that is, the logical "utopias" created from a selection according to criteria of cultural significance from among the "individually present, diverse characteristics of modern material and intellectual culture in its uniqueness."[5] For him both Marx and Nietzsche resided within this particular sphere of interest in the objective and subjective culture of the modern world.

The three sources of debate for the Weber Circle converged on a

---

3. In Weber's case I have in mind especially the references in Marianne Weber's partial transcriptions of letters, most of which were subsequently lost in the original, catalogued as hundreds of items in No. 30/1 through 30/14 of the Nachlass Weber. One representative example is Weber's report on Philippe's 1904 novella of the erotic life, *Marie Donadieu*, which he read in French at Ascona and found "magnificently written, and with profundity [*Tiefe*] and sensitivity [*Feinheit*]" (letter to Marianne, 14 April 1913), and then followed with Lukács' essay on the subject ("Longing and Form," in *Soul and Form*.) Upon completion he loaned the book to Frieda Schloffer Gross in exchange for the recently published work of another Ascona resident, Countess Franziska zu Reventlow's indiscreet autobiographical *roman à clef* of Schwabing, *Herrn Dames Aufzeichnungen oder Begebenheiten aus einem merkwürdigen Stadtteil*, featuring Andrian, Stefan George, Karl Wolfskehl, and Ludwig Klages in a cast drawn from Munich's bohemia. Of course, Simmel and Lukács published essays on a significant number of the representatives of modern culture.

4. See Maurenbrecher's *Die Gebildeten und die Sozialdemokratie* (Leipzig: Leipziger Buchdruckerei, 1904), esp. 18.

5. "Die 'Objektivität' sozialwissenschaftlicher und sozialpolitischer Erkenntnis" [literally, The 'Objectivity' of Social Scientific and Sociopolitical Knowledge] (1904), *GAW*, 192; S&F, 91.

philosophical and sociological inquiry into modernity, for which our initial question must read: What kind of thematic issue does reflection on life under modern conditions reveal, and why should modern life—or simply "the modern"—present a *problem* at all?

THE CENTRAL QUESTION OF THE MODERN

Like most major questions, the central question of the modern is not one that can be answered quickly or with a single voice, and the discussion that follows will return to it often in a kind of dialogue of oppositions between Weber and those among his circle of contemporaries who address the question in important ways. Nevertheless, as a supplement to what has already been said specifically about Weber, a general preliminary answer is worth attempting, if only as a rough guide to the contested terrain that lies ahead. In part that answer can be sought in Marx's critique of political economy and the new world of property and productive forces, a body of writing motivated not only by a perception of social injustice and human self-alienation, but also by the demonstrably disruptive effects of capitalism with respect to *existing* culture and social relations, and by the unstable and unadmirable sociocultural substitutes produced by advanced capitalism itself. The message of cultural criticism is undeniably present in Marx, even in central passages in the *Manifesto*, and it helps account for the interest in his work from revisionists like Weber's acquaintance Eduard Bernstein to contemporary modernists like Marshall Berman, still long after its economic predictions had been declared dead and buried.[6]

But there is another more specific place to look for an answer as well: in an interpretation of the significant ideas expounded in Nietzsche's *On the Genealogy of Morals*, the text that came to the attention of Weber, Simmel, Tönnies, and others because of its endlessly troubling central questions about the cultural and sociopsychological meaning of ascetic ideals.[7] Stated somewhat schematically, Nietzsche's approach lo-

6. Marshall Berman, *All That Is Solid Melts into Air: The Experience of Modernity* (New York: Simon & Schuster, 1982), for whom Marx is "the first and greatest of modernists" (129), and esp. chap. 2.

7. Among the later "others" notably Heinrich Rickert, "Lebenswerte und Kulturwerte," *Logos* 2 (1912): 131–66, who unfortunately devotes major attention to Nietzsche's "biologism," which Weber and Simmel correctly regarded as the weakest aspect of his thought; also Emil Hammacher, *Hauptfragen der modernen Kultur* (Leipzig: Teubner, 1914), 248–70.

cated asceticism's meaning paradoxically in the deployment of "nature against something that is also nature," or using terms I have cited previously, in the psychological interplay of "life *against* life" that is a "provisional formulation . . . an artifice for the *preservation* of life."[8] It turns out that to adopt this point of view is to suggest that the self-contradictory promotion of life against itself, the repression of "life" in order to obtain "culture," occurs in response to suffering, unhappiness, the desire "to be in a different place" or to get free of one's self. But culture represents only an alternate form of life, and, located as we are in its determinate, finite world of the here-and-now, we can never eliminate existential discontent or satisfy such radical desires. Instead, our reason assigns blame, redirecting the stream of betrayed life inward: in Nietzsche's accusation the self-negation of nature is carried out by ourselves as cultural beings, for we "alone are to blame for it—*you alone are to blame for yourself.*"[9] This is the gateway to asceticism's great achievement as a "yes-creating life force": it protects life against itself, cultural form against vital powers upon which culture ironically must depend, by constructing a conscious self opposed to the self's natural inclinations and dedicated to "the purpose of self-discipline, self-surveillance, and self-overcoming."[10]

Now what do these seemingly obscure ideas from Nietzsche's masterful third essay, "What Is the Meaning of Ascetic Ideals?," have to do with the problem of *modern* life? The connection is made more accessible than it otherwise might be (and unintentionally so) in a recent comment by Nehamas concerning the *Genealogy's* key passages: for "in blaming suffering on the sufferer himself and on features that cannot possibly be eliminated," Nietzsche's conception of asceticism

> does not promise to accomplish what cannot be accomplished: it does not promise to eliminate suffering itself, at least during the course of this life. . . . But it does promise that suffering may decrease if one distances oneself as far as possible from the features asceticism takes to be responsible for it. But . . . we cannot do away with these features; to want to do away with them is to want to do away with ourselves. This is why Nietzsche insists that the ascetic ideal, "this horror of the senses, of reason itself, this fear of hap-

8. From *The Will to Power*, sec. 228, as cited by Alexander Nehamas, *Nietzsche: Life as Literature* (Cambridge: Harvard University Press, 1985), chap. 4; *On the Genealogy of Morals*, trans. W. Kaufmann (New York: Random House [Vintage Books], 1967), 120 (III, 13).
9. *Genealogy of Morals*, 128 (III, 15).
10. Ibid., 128 (III, 16).

piness and beauty, this longing to get away from all appearance, change, becoming, death, wishing, from longing itself—all this means—let us dare to grasp it, *a will to nothingness*, a counter-will to life, a rebellion against the most fundamental presuppositions of life." [11]

If we accept this reasoning as psychologically compelling and sound, then the question for post-Nietzschean thought and culture is, What if modern objective, external, material culture were to be assigned responsibility for our suffering? Should we not then expect the same mechanism of *distancing* to take hold in the name of "promoting life," in the belief that not personality or character but rather the external conditions of our suffering could be controlled? Should we not suppose that an inward pursuit of subjective culture—of beauty, happiness, sensuality—would offer a resolution to our discontents, a will to something, a return to "life," at the very least *"une promesse de bonheur"*? [12] As Weber and Simmel would have appreciated, achieving "distance" is the crucial step: "one distances oneself as far as possible" from the sources of discontent, and in taking this step one enters a slightly altered moral and political terrain, marked by a "transvaluation" of asceticism in the service of what are thought to be "the most fundamental presuppositions of life." For this is the problem of modernity: How is it possible for us to rebel against the world, the culture, the civilization *we* have created, yet to do so in the name of our ideals of life? What does it mean for us to subvert ourselves, to counter culture with culture? And is this agonistic rebellion and subversion merely an extravagant exercise in self-deception?

What I have referred to as the "thematic issue" of the modern and especially modern *culture* is stated with directness and perspicacity (and in a way that sums up and places in perspective Nietzsche's challenge) in Emil Hammacher's *Main Questions of Modern Culture* of 1914, which in Thomas Mann's view "seemed to sum up recent Germany," [13] a work from the edges of the Weber Circle by a young interpreter of Nietzsche and Marx, a philosopher, member of the German Sociological Society, and contributor to Weber's *Archiv für Sozialwissenschaft und Sozialpolitik* whose life was cut short on the Western Front in No-

11. Nehamas, *Nietzsche*, 123; quoting the *Genealogy*, 162–63 (III, 28).
12. Stendhal's famous definition of beauty: Nietzsche, *Genealogy of Morals*, 104 (III, 6); and Georg Simmel, *The Philosophy of Money*, trans. T. Bottomore and D. Frisby (London: Routledge & Kegan Paul, 1978), 328.
13. *Reflections of a Nonpolitical Man*, trans. W. D. Morris (New York: Ungar, 1983), 173.

vember 1917. Hammacher is careful to recognize two contrasting definitions of culture: "domination of nature and its powers" and what he
calls "autonomous spirituality [*autonome Geistigkeit*] and realization
of values."[14] Modern culture can be understood to set one against the
other in an especially sharp and relentless way or, in plainer words, to
pose the question of an "antagonism between rationalism and life." In
Hammacher's view, "The most efficacious factor in our culture, and
that which distinguishes it from the past, is undoubtedly (as a consequence of its extent) the rationalistic spirit, that is, the vigorous will to
create a new *Weltanschauung* and practice of life through the independent reflections of mind."[15] The forces of what Weber called "intellectualization" and "rationalization" constitute a new "form of life" that
is calculating, abstract, mechanistic, instrumental. These forces are
identified directly with a capitalist system of production "that dissolves
inherited social relationships and puts ever renewed agitations in their
place . . . that replaces all substantiality with causality, all certainties
with relations," so that "one wants to flee from oneself, one hunts for
new, unheard-of possibilities and satisfactions of longing, surely in the
end to feel even more strongly the inner emptiness and impermanence
of all pleasures." This socioeconomic system creates a new kind of freedom and a heightened consciousness, but Hammacher's central question is, With what human costs? "In a word, what does it mean that we
really live more consciously?"[16] The suspicion is that any "meaning" in
such circumstances is a counterfeit claim, that like modern culture itself
it can leave us with nothing more than "an enormous question mark,"
or in a language Nietzsche would have willingly called his own, with a
longing to flee from ourselves.

Appropriately, Hammacher's tour of "modern culture" does itself
conclude with unanswered questions, or perhaps equally fitting, with
the "modern" thought that the "only hope" for the future of a culture
of "autonomous spirit" under current conditions is "the deepening of
personality through its felt opposition to the ruling powers"[17]—a hope,
to be sure, but a slim one. However, Hammacher's purpose was essentially to survey, describe, define, report, and not to offer a comprehensive philosophy or sociology of modern life and its discontents. For that
further attempt we must turn to the main figures and debates of the
Weber Circle.

14. *Hauptfragen der modernen Kultur*, 79–80.
15. Ibid., 97.
16. Ibid., 8, 9, 3.
17. Ibid., 295.

CULTURE BETWEEN LIFE AND FORM: SIMMEL

Of all the classical sociologists, Simmel is the major figure who can be said not only to have contributed to the sociology of culture, but to have self-consciously developed a "theory" of modern life and culture in the sense of an interconnected conceptual language and a perspective for ordering, understanding, and judging our experience. Simmel sought to elaborate and perfect this theory throughout his lifework, often giving it different forms and emphases, but always with the intention of illuminating the modern subject's inner response to the external, humanly created world of material culture. The peculiar and ingenious effect of his thinking was achieved by setting material alongside immaterial properties, or, using one of his examples, by combining "the money principle with the developments and valuations of inner life," thereby considering money's "effects upon the inner world—upon the vitality of individuals, upon the linking of their fates, upon culture in general." [18] The originality, comprehensiveness, and deep attraction of Simmel's purpose recommend him as the foundational thinker in these matters. (It was for good reasons, after all, that students arriving in Berlin from St. Petersburg were rumored to head straight for Simmel's lecture hall before disposing with the trivia of everyday life.) Moreover, as Lukács pointed out, "a sociology of culture, as it was taken over by Max Weber, Troeltsch, Sombart, and others [including Lukács himself], surely became possible only on the basis established by Simmel." [19] Starting from what has already been said about Simmel's and Weber's sociologies of culture, let us pursue the theoretical issues one step further in relation to the problem of the modern.

Modern culture poses a question for Simmel, one that first achieves a mature expression in the important last chapter of *The Philosophy of Money*, where Weber found such "brilliant images." The question comes to a focus around the perceived contradiction between a simultaneous "increase" in material or objective culture and "decrease" in individual or subjective culture: whereas in the modern age the former becomes more and more refined, complex, sophisticated, expansive, comprehensive, and domineering, the latter in relation to it becomes cruder, simpler, more trivial, limiting, fragmentary, and anarchic. Un-

---

18. *Philosophy of Money*, 54.
19. "Georg Simmel" (1918), in *Buch des Dankes an Georg Simmel*, ed. K. Gassen and M. Landmann (Berlin: Duncker & Humblot, 1958), 175.

der these conditions Simmel speaks of "the fragmentary life-contents of individuals" and "the insignificance or irrationality of the individual's share" of objective culture.[20] The culture we have created is set against ourselves and against human purposes; we lose control of it, are assaulted and overwhelmed by it, and can respond only with rebellion. This insight into the duality of culture, its "two-faced" character, presents Simmel with his sociological and philosophical problem: not only how is it possible, but what does it mean for *life*?

The sociology of cultural contradiction is rather easy to imagine: objectification has its causes in such "solid" facts as the "division of labor"—that is, the specialization of tasks and functions in the economic order, which spreads everywhere and "brings about a growing estrangement between the subject and its products" and then "invades even the more intimate aspects of our daily life."[21] Not surprisingly, some have found the hand of Marx in passages like these, but it is a hand made largely invisible by Simmel's added insistence that the fetishism of objects is of a piece with the fixation of *psychological* dependence on fashion, on "a pace that mirrors [our] own psychological movements," on change and motion in and of themselves—in a word, we might say, on *style*. And the primacy of style, which for Simmel "is in itself one of the most significant instances of distancing,"[22] is merely one indication of increasing consciousness of the growing distance between the self and objects, the self and others, that has resulted from aesthetic culture's "inward turn" and absorption into the entirely fluid realm of psychological experience. This absorption is indeed what it means in Simmel's perceptive phrasing "to construct a new storey beneath historical materialism such that the explanatory value of the incorporation of economic life into the causes of intellectual culture is preserved, while these economic forms themselves are recognized as the result of more profound valuations and currents of psychological or even metaphysical pre-conditions."[23] Simmel has, as it were, subverted Marx with Nietzsche.

The more troubling question of the "meaning" of modern culture for "life," which in its Nietzschean formulation places a strain on any tidy Kantian dualism, is left unresolved in *The Philosophy of Money*— unresolved but not unnoticed, for Simmel returns to it in his own

20. *Philosophy of Money*, 449.
21. Ibid., 459.
22. Ibid., 461, 473.
23. Ibid., 56.

acutely self-conscious "style" in the later essays. As always, the approach is "philosophical," which is to say in Simmel's idiom that it rests on the possibility "of finding in each of life's details the totality of its meaning."[24] The logical point of departure is "dualistic," now in a twofold sense—"person" versus "world," subject versus object:

> Humans, unlike the animals, do not allow themselves simply to be absorbed by the naturally given order of the world. Instead, they tear themselves loose from it, place themselves in opposition to it, making demands of it, overpowering it, then overpowered by it. From this first great dualism springs the never-ending contest between subject and object, which finds its second tribunal within the realm of spirit [Geist] itself.[25]

The violent and agonistic diremptions then reveal themselves as a process of objectification:

> The spirit engenders innumerable structures [Gebilde] which keep on existing with a peculiar autonomy independently of the soul [Seele] that has created them, as well as of any other that accepts or rejects them. Thus, the subject sees itself confronting art as well as law, religion as well as technology, science as well as custom. Now it is attracted, now repelled by their contents, now fused with them as if they were part of itself, now estranged and untouched by them. In the form of stability, coagulation, persistent existence, the spirit becomes object, places itself over against the streaming life, the intrinsic responsibility and the variable tensions of the soul. Spirit . . . experiences innumerable tragedies over this radical contrast [Formgegensatz]: between subjective life, which is restless but finite in time, and its contents, which, once they are created, are fixed but timelessly valid.[26]

This dense passage with its exotic language of "spirit" and "soul" amounts to Simmel's version of the Hegelian objectification of mind: The human appearing as subject, with a subjective being and life, is opposed to the objective "natural world," and in this opposition creates a content and form for "life" and its "objects." The most fundamental dualism between human consciousness and "world," which also lies at the root of Weber's genealogy of religious ethics, resolves itself into a contradiction between subjective life and the contents of life. While the former is transient, finite, fluctuating, relative to subjects, inward, and immediately experienced, the latter is permanent, timeless, static, objec-

---

24. Ibid., 55.
25. *Philosophische Kultur* (Berlin: Wagenbach, 1983 [1911]), 183; "On the Concept and Tragedy of Culture," in *The Conflict in Modern Culture and Other Essays*, trans. K. Peter Etzkorn (New York: Teachers College Press, 1968), 27.
26. *Philosophische Kultur*, 183; "Concept and Tragedy of Culture," 27.

tively valid, external, and mediated by distance. And the "idea of culture," declares Simmel, "dwells in the middle of this dualism."

What can this daring assertion, barely hinted at in Simmel's earlier account in *The Philosophy of Money*, possibly mean? Essentially two senses of culture seem to follow from these remarks. The first elaborates the metaphor of culture "as the path of the soul to itself," a kind of counterplay against Nietzsche's critical conception of the ascetic view of life "as a wrong path on which one must finally walk back to the point where it begins."[27] Against the one-sided interpretation of asceticism as life-denying, Simmel's idea of culture suggests expression, development, and fulfillment of that which is essentially human: Culture becomes, quite directly,

> the completion of the soul . . . in which it takes the detour through the formations of the intellectual-historical work of the species [*Gattungsarbeit*]: the cultural path of the subjective spirit traverses science and the forms of life, art and state, vocation and knowledge of the world—the path on which it now returns to itself as higher and perfected spirit.[28]

Yet "life" must also be something formed, and the activity of culture can offer it a "unity of the soul"—that is, the enticing prospect of a "solution to the subject-object dualism" through the promise of setting the preconditions for qualities that could be designated self-development and personality. In Simmel's view, we appear to embody a "bundle of developmental lines," all having varied potentialities; but that is only appearance, for "man does not cultivate himself through their isolated perfections, but only insofar as they help to develop his indefinable personal unity." In Simmel's translation of his peculiar language, "Culture is the way that leads from closed unity through unfolding multiplicity to unfolding unity."[29] Or what comes to the same thing, "culture exists only if man draws into his development *something that is external to him*. . . . The perfection of the individual . . . is consummated in a unique adjustment and teleological interweaving of subject and object."[30] In sum, culture is necessarily dualistic, necessarily objec-

27. *Genealogy of Morals*, 117 (III, 11).

28. "Die Krisis der Kultur" (1916), in *Das individuelle Gesetz: Philosophische Exkurse*, ed. M. Landmann (Frankfurt: Suhrkamp, 1968), 232.

29. "Kultur ist der Weg von der geschlossen Einheit durch die entfaltete Vielheit zur entfalteten Einheit": *Philosophische Kultur*, 185; "Concept and Tragedy of Culture," 29.

30. "Vom Wesen der Kultur" (1908), in *Das Individuum und die Freiheit [Brücke und Tür]* (Berlin: Wagenbach, 1984), 87; "Subjective Culture," in *On Individuality and Social Forms: Selected Writings*, ed. D. Levine (Chicago: University of Chicago Press, 1971), 230.

tive and subjective, and it makes possible the *process* of forming the self (this "unfolding unity") through reciprocal action between the objective and the subjective.

This sense of culture is rich with paradox, for on the one hand culture requires an unresolved dualism, while on the other hand it proposes to mediate or synthesize the two poles of existence. On one plane it assumes unresolved gender-specific difference (the subject is "man" and his choices), whereas on another it urges development through mediative inclusion of the other (that is, "woman" and her being). Subjective life, driven toward perfection of its identity, "cannot by itself reach the perfection of culture," yet culture "is always a synthesis" of subjective life and the contents of life that "presupposes the divisibility of elements as an antecedent." Modernity accounts for such otherwise incomprehensible tension and potential confusion: "Only in an analytically inclined age like the modern could one find in synthesis the deepest, the one and only relationship of form between spirit and world."[31] It would be most accurate to speak of the *longing* for synthesis or what one later critic of the age has called the "hunger for wholeness."[32]

The clearest depiction of a second sense of culture comes at the end of Simmel's thinking on the subject in "The Conflict of Modern Culture," where he decides to speak of culture not so much whenever it functions through mediation, but rather

> whenever life produces certain forms in which it expresses and realizes itself: works of art, religions, sciences, technologies, laws, and innumerable others. These forms encompass the flow of life and provide it with content and form, latitude [*Spielraum*], and order. But although these forms arise out of the life process, because of their unique constellation they do not share the restless rhythm of life, its ascent and descent, its constant renewal, its incessant divisions and reunifications. These forms are cages [*Gehäuse*] for the creative life that, however, soon transcends them. They should also house the imitative life, for which, in the final analysis, there is no space left. They acquire fixed identities, a logic and lawfulness of their own [*eigene Logik und Gesetzlichkeit*]; this new rigidity inevitably places them at a distance from the spiritual dynamic which created them and which makes them independent.[33]

In Simmel's formulation it is not capitalism, vocational specialization or instrumental rationality, but rational culture itself that becomes the

31. *Philosophische Kultur*, 186, 192–93; "Concept and Tragedy of Culture," 30, 35.
32. Peter Gay, *Weimar Culture: The Outsider as Insider* (New York: Harper & Row, 1968), chap. 4.
33. "Der Konflikt der modernen Kultur" (1918), in *Das individuelle Gesetz*, 148; "Conflict in Modern Culture," in *Conflict in Modern Culture*, 11.

new "iron cage," with an "internal and lawful autonomy" of the kind
Weber assigns the different life-orders and value-spheres. As a distinctive supralife form, culture is in this way of thinking set squarely against
the forces of (creative) life. Simmel has thus restated Nietzsche's depiction of "life against life": culture is not merely the path to self-
recognition, but also the dwelling place of repressive order. In one sense
culture suggests movement and possibility, in another rigidity and
limitation.

Simmel's theory raises this quality of culture that he refers to variously as a paradox, crisis, conflict, or tragedy to the conscious level, not
in order to abolish or transcend it as Heinrich Rickert supposed, for
that would destroy culture *and its sources in life,* but in order to view it
as a moment in its own development.[34] Like all of human life, culture
has a history, too, which shows that in the modern present "we are
experiencing a new phase of the old struggle," in Simmel's words; it is
"no longer a struggle of a contemporary form, filled with life, against
an old, lifeless one, but a struggle of life against form as such, against
the principle of form."[35] The peculiar "increasing 'formlessness' of
modern life" is the hallmark of the present, and, in agreement with
Weber, Simmel believes it has accompanied, since Nietzsche, all sorts of
exaggerated expressions of life: endless searches in the avant-garde for
originality and heightened experience, strivings for a "new ethic" or a
"new religiosity," attempts to sanctify the soul in blasé and cynical personal styles. "Thus," Simmel maintains, "arises the typical problematic
situation of modern man, his feeling of being surrounded by an innumerable number of cultural elements that are neither meaningless to
him nor, in the final analysis, meaningful. In their mass they depress
him, since he is incapable of assimilating them all, nor can he simply
reject them, since, after all, they do belong potentially within the sphere
of his cultural development."[36]

34. Rickert's unsympathetic critique, *Die Philosophie des Lebens: Darstellung und
Kritik der philosophischen Modeströmungen unserer Zeit* (Tübingen: J. C. B. Mohr [Paul
Siebeck], 1920), esp. 64–72, suffers from the assumption that Simmel sought a "solution," whatever that might mean, to the paradoxes of "life" and its "forms." In any case,
the polemical intent here and elsewhere (e.g., "Urteil and Urteilen," *Logos* 3 [1912]:
230–45) seems to have been to subordinate discussion of substantive problems of culture
to "logic," a curious argument that succeeds mainly in revealing Rickert's own panglos-
sian view of the world and talent as a logician, but deficiency as a philosopher.
35. "Der Konflikt der modernen Kultur," 150–51; "Conflict in Modern Culture,"
12.
36. *Philosophische Kultur,* 204; "Concept and Tragedy of Culture," 44.

However, in Simmel's view it was not always so, for a brief history of cultural development will show that at the center of culture, from antiquity to modernity, has been a movement from an assumed "unity of being" (Greek philosophy), to "god" (Christianity), "nature" (the Renaissance), the "self" (the Enlightenment), "society" (the nineteenth century), and finally "life" (modernity), a schematic developmental process that has parallels in Weber's concise critique of the illusory meanings Western culture has assigned to "science" as the path to "true being" (Plato), "true art" or "nature" (the Renaissance), "true God" (the Reformation), and "true happiness" (the Enlightenment).[37] Just as Weber's modern science has now become disabused of its innocent pretense, so Simmel's modern culture has surrendered the delusion of unitary meaning. For Western thought to move from Kant to Nietzsche has meant precisely to replace the universal individuality of a transcendental ego, situated in a single and generalizable world of mechanistic properties, with the unique individuality of a determinate subject, dispersed into multiple and particularizing worlds of qualitative variation.[38] This historic diagnosis of modern culture's paradoxes and tragedies is given an immediacy it would otherwise lack because now our experience has driven the tension between "life" and its "forms" (most importantly including science among them) to the greatest extreme yet attained.

In his lifework Simmel responds to the contemporary state of affairs in three important ways. In the first place he is intrigued by the many social forces, organizations, interactions, or processes of sociation and sociability, or *Geselligkeit*—such as socialism, the secret society, and the feminist movement—that aim "to subordinate the whole of life to a meaningful order" which will serve "that deepest longing of the soul to mold everything that is given in its own image."[39] All of this subject matter for Simmel's special version of sociology might be understood as modern attempts to recover a lost unity to culture, to find a way of

37. "Der Konflikt der modernen Kultur," 152–53; "Conflict in Modern Culture," 13–14; "Wissenschaft als Beruf" [Science as a Vocation] (1919), *GAW*, 595–98; G&M, 140–43.

38. This is the subject of Simmel's concluding discussion in *Kant: Sechzehn Vorlesungen* (Leipzig: Duncker & Humblot, 1904), chap. 16; revised as an example of "philosophical sociology" in the *Grundfragen der Soziologie (Individuum und Gesellschaft)* (Berlin: Göschen, 1917), chap. 4; English version in *The Sociology of Georg Simmel*, trans. and ed. K. Wolff (New York: Free Press, 1950), 58–84.

39. "Rodins Plastik und die Geistesrichtung der Gegenwart" (1902), in *Ästhetik und Soziologie um die Jahrhundertwende: Georg Simmel*, ed. H. Böhringer and K. Gründer (Frankfurt: Klostermann, 1976), 234–35.

overcoming the paradoxical juxtaposition of life and form. A healthy metaphysical skepticism often prevents Simmel from doing more than honoring such attempts as humanly understandable and significant efforts from within culture to "solve" the crisis of culture. But for Simmel, as for Weber, "real" solutions lie in the far-distant future, beyond our history, so to speak. Attempts in the meantime will lead to further fragmentation and differentiation, to a continuing proliferation of cultural forms, to further tensions between objective and subjective culture.

A second response becomes apparent in the realm of aesthetics, through the experience of "salvation through art" and the conduct of one's life as a "work of art." Simmel's writing on art and artists, such as Goethe, Rodin, and George, his own authorial experimentation with poetry and the subjectivist essay *sub specie aeternitatis*, and surely in addition the strong aesthetic components of his sociology, are all inclined in this direction.[40] Some of the most provocative formulations appear in this connection, to wit:

> The problem that afflicts us in all areas, namely, how purely individual existence can be unified, how one can reject consideration of general norms . . . without descending into anarchy and rootless caprice—this problem has been solved by Rodin's art as art always solves spiritual problems: not in principle, but in individual perceptions [*Anschauungen*].[41]

The closest Simmel ever came to a personal answer to the problem of culture was also in his own "individual perceptions," not in a definitive, principled "solution" to the conflict and "tragedy" his analysis disclosed. No such solution existed, for to say the cultural problem can be resolved only aesthetically is to say it can and must persist.

But if Simmel was attracted to the light of the aesthetic life as a source of warmth and illumination, as he most certainly was, then he was also in calmer moments pulled in the direction of "cool reflection." Simmel was self-divided, and necessarily so. As Weber chose to bind himself to the sphere of knowledge, so Simmel at these points in his

40. Cf. Weber's remark on Goethe taking "the liberty of trying to make his 'life' into a work of art": "Wissenschaft als Beruf," *GAW*, 591; G&M, 137. The route to understanding this dimension of Simmel's work is provided by Wittgenstein's remarks in the *Tractatus Logico-Philosophicus* (London: Routledge & Kegan Paul, 1961 [1921]), 149 [6.45]): "To view the world *sub specie aeterni* is to view it as a whole—a limited whole [*begrenztes Ganzes*]. Feeling the world as a limited whole—it is this that is mystical." It can be said that this perspective on world as "limited" separates Simmel from notions of comprehensive totality.

41. "Rodins Plastik," 233.

thought chose intellect over enchantment, realism over latent possibility. In one of his very last comments on the subject, he reasoned that

> it is a philistine prejudice that believes all conflicts and problems exist in order to be solved. Both have additional tasks in the economy and history of life, tasks that they fulfill independently of their own solution. Thus they exist in their own right, even if the future does not replace conflicts with their resolutions, but only replaces their forms and contents with others. In short, the present is too full of contradictions to stand still. This itself is a more fundamental change than the reformations of times past. The bridge between the past and the future of cultural forms seems to be demolished; we gaze into an abyss of unformed life beneath our feet. But perhaps this formlessness is itself the appropriate form for contemporary life. Thus the blueprint of life is obliquely fulfilled. Life is a struggle in the absolute sense of the term which encompasses the relative contrast between struggle and peace, whereas that absolute peace which might encompass this contrast remains an eternal secret to us.[42]

This Nietzschean passage, discovering form itself in the formless present, may vouchsafe Paul Ernst's casting of Simmel as a "tragic figure"[43] completely absorbed within the dynamic of modern culture, unable to penetrate those "eternal secrets" that might lead us into another world. In this respect Simmel remained a cultural being, his imagination attuned solely to the rhythms of culture.

However, for Simmel the barrier to finding definitive solutions and a new world, when it arose, was not inability but unwillingness: the other worlds, the alternatives, were still a part of that unprecedented modern culture he had so carefully dissected in all of its complexity and contradiction. In his critical judgment of those alternatives Simmel surely shed the alleged "ambivalence" that has haunted his reputation as philosopher, sociologist, and, above all, modernist. But he did reserve the right to pass over some proposed solutions in silence.

For can it ever be the case, to speak with Wittgenstein, that "the solution of the problem of life is seen in the vanishing of the problem?"[44] Or is this only to say that the "solution" is seen in the vanishing of life? We might then prefer to think that the very search for solutions lies at the root of our difficulties.

---

42. "Der Konflikt der modernen Kultur," 173; "Conflict in Modern Culture," 25.
43. Paul Ernst to Lukács, 23 March 1916, in *Georg Lukács Briefwechsel 1902–1917*, ed. E. Karádi and E. Fekete (Stuttgart: Metzler, 1982), 370.
44. *Tractatus*, 149 (6.521).

THE WORLD AS ORGANIC WHOLE:
SOMBART

Having considered Weber's critique of the life-orders and traced the contours of modern culture and its discontents in Simmel's work, we are in a position to consider more precisely the range and types of responses to modernity that appear within the Weber Circle. These are representative responses of the intellectuals, of course, and they bear all the imprints of contemporary intellectualism: abstraction, heightened consciousness, reflexivity, literary stylishness, self-reference, and occasional self-indulgence. For precisely these reasons they often unintentionally reveal the deepest dynamics at work in reflections on "the modern."

There can be hardly any doubt that the problem of modern culture dominated Werner Sombart's writings not later than his sprawling two-volume treatise, *Der moderne Kapitalismus*, at the center of which was a portrait of capitalist activity as "a complicated psychological process" requiring organizational, calculative, and rationalistic norms and abilities.[45] As the fully modern and "soulless" power, capitalism's most decisive quality—"rational" calculation or calculability (*Rechenhaftigkeit*), a concept Weber also usefully modified and applied—was even described by Sombart as a "talent" or "disposition" of the soul (*Seelenveranlagung, Seelenstimmung*) and one that became more pronounced with the spread of the capitalist mode of production. In Simmelian terminology this quality represented to Sombart the mandatory "subjective presupposition" of modern capitalism.[46]

While contemporaries like Weber and Simmel also tracked down the "psychological" determinants of entrepreneurship, they did not miss the popularization of a cultural theme implicit in Sombart's approach to modern capitalism. Indeed, it would have been difficult to overlook. With respect to *Der Bourgeois*, Weber suspected the study was about him![47] Or concerning Sombart's *Die Juden und das Wirtschaftsleben*,

---

45. *Der moderne Kapitalismus*, 2 vols. (Leipzig: Duncker & Humblot, 1902), 1:195–99. On these themes generally, see Arthur Mitzman, *Sociology and Estrangement: Three Sociologists of Imperial Germany* (New York: Knopf, 1973), pt. 3, the only readable discussion of Sombart in English.

46. Werner Sombart, *Gewerbewesen* (Leipzig: Göschen, 1904), esp. 58–61.

47. Weber's comments in Munich were reported posthumously by Else Jaffé-Richthofen in a letter to Sombart, 10 September 1921, NWS 10a, 788–89: "I still remember quite well how in the summer of 1919, on the occasion of reediting the 'Spirit of Capitalism,' he [Weber] borrowed 'The Bourgeois' from Edgar [Jaffé] (his library had still not arrived) and half in jest, half in annoyance said: Sombart thinks I am also a 'bourgeois,' you know."

Weber's most memorable sentence was simply, "I thought 'nearly every word was wrong,' insofar as religion was concerned"—a typically devastating and unrestrained swipe at self-indulgent pandering to the fad-conscious "modern" public under the guise of "science," touched off no doubt partly by Sombart's insistence that his later investigations were provoked by Weber's "Protestant ethic" studies.[48] What Weber came to understand as an essentially "aesthetic" achievement was echoed in Schumpeter's retrospective conclusion that *Modern Capitalism* exhibited primarily an "artistic quality."[49] Sombart would have been hard pressed to deny the charge, had he wanted to. In *Liebe, Luxus und Kapitalismus*, for example, provocatively subtitled *The Origins of the Modern World from the Spirit of Extravagance*, he went so far as to advance the thesis that capital formation in the modern world was brought about by "luxury," which was in turn brought about by "illegitimate" sexual relations between upper-class males and courtesans, a ribald interpretation of capitalism sufficiently bizarre to shock even the worldly historians.[50] If one popular explanation of capitalism grew stale and trite, Sombart was always willing to try another.

All the most serious problems for Sombart's mature thought are to be found in the aesthetic tendency. The evidence is everywhere: Sombart participated directly through speeches, writings, and public forums in the mushrooming turn-of-the-century debate over art, personality, and culture. In 1902 he helped found the Deutsche Gartenstadtgesellschaft

48. Letter of 2 December 1913, NWS 4k:3–4; Werner Sombart, *Die Juden und das Wirtschaftsleben* (Leipzig: Duncker & Humblot, 1911), v; and *Der Bourgeois: Zur Geistesgeschichte des modernen Wirtschaftsmenschen* (Leipzig: Duncker & Humblot, 1913), 1–10.

49. Weber's most relevant remark is found in a letter to Sombart, 2[0] December 1913, NWS 4k:5–6: "*For a long time* in writing and *publicly* in discussions I have said the same thing about your book on the Jews [and economic life]—and I can *prove* it: '*perhaps not a word* is correct concerning Jewish religion; nevertheless, I would have been pleased to have written the book myself'—aesthetically, that is to say"—a backhanded compliment if there ever was one! In his *History of Economic Analysis* (New York: Oxford University Press, 1954), Schumpeter notes that *Der moderne Kapitalismus* "shocked professional historians by its often unsubstantial brilliance. They failed to see in it anything that they would call real research—the material of the book is in fact wholly second-hand—and they entered protests against its many carelessnesses. Yet it was in a sense a peak achievement of the historical school, and highly stimulating even in its errors" (816–17 n. 14); and again: "It is a vision of the historical process that has an artistic quality. . . . It is a *histoire raisonnée*, with the accent on the reasoning, and systematized history with the accent on system in the sense of a succession of frescoes of social states" (818).

50. Georg von Below, review of Sombart's two-volume *Studien zur Entwicklungsgeschichte des modernen Kapitalismus*, which included *Liebe, Luxus und Kapitalismus* and *Krieg und Kapitalismus*, in *Jahrbücher für Nationalökonomie und Statistik* 105 (1915): 396–402.

and joined its first executive committee. The aim of the "garden communities," such as Hellerau outside Dresden, was to use architectural design and urban planning to promote a symbiosis of art, "natural" community, leisure, and vocational activity to overcome the specialization and alienation of life in the industrial age. A cascade of publications on work, art, fashion, handicrafts, class, and social policy revealed the sociocultural theme: *Wirtschaft und Mode* (1902); *Die gewerbliche Arbeiterfrage* and *Gewerbewesen* (1904); *Warum interessiert sich heute jedermann für Fragen der Volkswirtschaft und Sozialpolitik?* (1904); *Das Proletariat* (1906); and *Kunstgewerbe und Kultur* (1908). Characteristically, Sombart recorded sending one of these studies, *Das Proletariat* (published, incidentally, as the first volume in Martin Buber's lengthy cultural tour de force, "Die Gesellschaft"), not only to colleagues like Tönnies and Michels, but to feminist factory inspectors and activists—Marianne Weber, Else Jaffé-Richthofen, Lily Braun—and to the Viennese modernist writers Hugo von Hofmannsthal and Arthur Schnitzler.[51] By 1907 Sombart had achieved a standing in the pages of the Berlin press as "a voice in the desolate wilderness of the metropolis," a reputation he sought, promoted, and relished.[52] Sombart's mature scientific production fully depended on, even derived from, such cultural engagements; his vocation became a captive of the need for stylish public acclaim, the flashiness of the feuilleton, the narcissistic radiance of *Jugendstil*. All this is sufficient to account for the reserve and distance, even the barely concealed *ressentiment*, that crept into the Weber-Sombart relationship and encouraged Weber to stress with Sombart "the very different 'spirit' in which you and I engage in 'science.'"[53]

The cultural issues in Sombart's fin de siècle reflections came to a head significantly in a series of public lectures on "cultural problems of

51. According to Sombart's list in NWS 4c:18.
52. "Ein Prediger in der Steinwüste der Großstadt" is the German phrase; see the reports on two of Sombart's speeches in Berlin: "Kulturprobleme der Gegenwart" and "Kultur und Persönlichkeit," in the *Vossische Zeitung*, 25 January and 6 December 1907.
53. Letter of 20 December 1913, NWS 4k:5–6; Weber attributed the "*ressentiment*" that soured their exchanges to the way "someone had always played me off against you" in arguments Sombart had now "repeatedly put to paper" in *Der Bourgeois*, criticizing Weber's "spirit of capitalism" thesis. Weber never published a proposed reply, perhaps at Sombart's request—"Very well," he wrote, "I am going to *abandon* the review [of *Der Bourgeois*] and only reply indirectly on another occasion"—but in correspondence at the time he made clear that Sombart's knowledge of the issues and sources was incomplete, "second-hand," and uninformed on "precisely the decisive matters." The "other occasion" eventually turned out to be the 1920 footnote revisions for *The Protestant Ethic and the Spirit of Capitalism*, especially in the "'Spirit' of Capitalism" chapter, where *Der Bourgeois* was called "a book with a thesis in the worst sense": see *GARS* 1: esp. 38–41, 56–58; *PE*, 194–98 n. 12, 200–203 n. 9.

today" and "economy and culture" delivered in Berlin shortly after his appointment to the School of Economics. In these presentations the central phenomenon of modern culture became technology or technique (*Technik*)—and that really meant "the technical" as opposed to "nature"—an overpowering technology to which a lengthy list of modern ills could be attributed, from the "destruction of the family" to the withering away of the sources for "our spiritual and artistic culture."[54] The most urgent question had to be, "What does modern culture do for us, how does it affect the personality?" Sombart's answer was served up as strong medicine for the complacent and optimistic:

> Modern culture has alienated us from nature, has put a layer of asphalt between ourselves and nature so that nature can at best be merely an object of aesthetic enjoyment.... It is true that modern technology creates phenomenal achievements, but all its inventions and discoveries mean nothing more than that unhappiness, misery, and distress will be hindered a little bit. All the possibilities that the daemon of inventiveness has given us dissolve into nothing if we ask the question, What do they really bring us? To what end do we need so much light in the world? ... Why do we need to fly around in the air? What do we need the telephone for? What meaning can the invention of the gramophone have for us? An age with good taste would punish the inventor of the gramophone with a life-term in prison.[55]

Sombart's impassioned account of these crimes against culture was greeted by the Berlin audience with approving laughter and applause. (One can only regret missing the spectacle of Sombart and his audience confronting the inventor of the electric guitar and its consequences for music.) As a careful student of Marx, perhaps he had remembered the *Manifesto*'s evocative images of dissolution and fantastic transformation. In any case his peroration reached its climax: "Modern culture has achieved nothing for our inner life, for our happiness, our well-being, our profundity [*Tiefe*]."[56]

The vast remainder of Sombart's writing, including his continuing forays into political economy and sociology, was a working out of these problems and themes, an attempt to slay the two-headed dragon, the

---

54. "Kulturprobleme der Gegenwart," *Vossische Zeitung*, 25 January 1907.

55. "Kultur und Persönlichkeit," *Vossische Zeitung*, 6 December 1907; cf. Sombart's talk at the German Sociological Society in 1910, "Technik und Kultur," *Verhandlungen des Ersten Deutschen Soziologentages* (Tübingen: J. C. B. Mohr [Paul Siebeck], 1911), esp. 82, dismissed by Weber as a "feuilleton" (letter to Eulenburg, 27 October 1910, NW 30/6:27–28).

56. Apropos this language, Simmel reportedly once opened a doctoral examination with the question, "*Was ist tief?*" (literally, What is deep?), a perfectly sensible and significant query from the perspective of cultural criticism: Gassen and Landmann, *Buch des Dankes an Georg Simmel*, 33.

"two most powerful adversaries of our time: capitalism and modern technology."[57] The engine driving both was *Technik*, which he defined for his colleagues as "all procedures, all means, all complexes, all systems of means for achieving a specific purpose," and which surely represented in its cultural effects *the* central problem.[58] Sombart backed up his assertion, against Max Weber's protest, by extending Marx to read: the economic base of society is a function of technology (major premise); the cultural superstructure is a function of economic relations (minor premise); therefore, culture is a function of technology (conclusion)—and not for the better either (value judgment)![59] "The noise, haste, speed, and tempo of our lives, the transactions with a thousand impressions that external life offers us—naturally all of that determines the formation of personality to an extraordinary degree and is a direct result of *Technik*."[60] Technology for Sombart has had this extensive effect in all spheres of "intellectual" and popular culture: science, art, poetry, music, entertainment, the news media, the culture of the "home," transportation, dress and fashion, and on and on—all are chained to the necessity of "technical achievements." All teach the same lesson we have seen before: "A wild chase after eternally new forms begins, whose tempo quickens as the technology of production and commerce improves . . . an unbroken succession of perpetual revolutionizing of taste, consumption, and production results."[61] What can be said for "fashion" can be said for anything—modern science included. All aspects of modern culture are equally questionable and open to challenge.

As the Proteus of political economists, Sombart is never at a loss for proposals concerning this state of affairs—many of them, kaleidoscopic and fragmentary in form, as if to mirror the world he analyzes and to which he belongs. (Perhaps Narcissus is the better prototype.) In his own words, "Life in society has become problematic. . . . Why is that

57. Sombart, *Kunstgewerbe und Kultur* (Berlin: Marquardt, 1908), 68.

58. "Technik und Kultur," 63–64.

59. In his reply Weber objected not so much to the value-judgment, but rather to (a) the idea that any factor, such as *Technik*, could be the "ultimate cause" of any other factor in human life; and (b) the historical evidence supporting Sombart's thesis. Weber thought a history of culture would show that "artistic intent" or purpose often functioned autonomously and was often responsible for the development of "techniques": see [Diskussionbeitrag], in *Verhandlungen des Ersten Deutschen Soziologentages*, 95–101; in *GASS*, 449–56.

60. "Technik und Kultur," 75.

61. *Wirthschaft und Mode: Ein Beitrag zur Theorie der modernen Bedarfsgestaltung* (Wiesbaden: Bergmann, 1902), 22–23.

so? Is it inevitable? Is there no way out?"[62] Sombart's thinking often reads like a catalogue of options for finding the escape route, for rescuing the personality: Socialism as a cultural tour de force, deployment of technology to overcome technology, the new feminism, salvation through art and the artist, a "defensive" strategy reminiscent of the youth movement (*Jugendbewegung*) built on the trinity of "nature, work, and love." All are more or less tested, some are savored, and some are eventually rejected (or rather replaced by more inspirational candidates), *except* those possessing a nostalgic urge for rediscovering the old verities, for embodying what Sombart called the "homogeneous organic creative process" or the "organic unity of artistic creation."[63] And who are the new pathfinders and culture heroes? Principally the artistic and poetic spirits, perhaps a political economist or two, even "woman" in her proper place. But the quite special nature of Sombart's pleading is revealed in his treatment of women, especially against the background of feminism, the movement for women's suffrage, and the kind of inquiry exemplified by Marianne Weber's exchanges with Simmel. For in his public lectures Sombart was given to concluding with an "appeal to women" to surrender their modern ambitions and return to the home where only they, he insisted, could fulfill the cultural task of combating alienation and homelessness.

With Sombart, then, we encounter an antimodernist modernism firmly embraced and without apologies, a return to the old in the name of the new. His thought unexpectedly confirms that for the organic worldview Novalis' reminder still holds, and its "philosophy is really homesickness, an urge to be at home everywhere." Unfortunately, however, to be at home everywhere, were that even possible, is never to be at home at all. But Sombart remains undaunted, his "postmodern" world securely cast in the images of a late romanticism.

THE WORLD AS ETHICAL UNITY: TÖNNIES AND MICHELS

As Weber foresaw in his discussion of the life-orders, an alternative major response to the problem of "modern culture" took its stand in the potentiality of "ethics" and the truly "moral" perspective. Among the actual defenders of an "ethical" standpoint in the Weber Circle, Tönnies

---

62. *Warum interessiert sich heute jedermann für Fragen der Volkswirtschaft und Sozialpolitik?* (Leipzig: Dietrich, 1904), 10–11.
63. *Kunstgewerbe und Kultur*, 80, 118.

and Michels deserve our most serious attention, for at one time or another both offered extensive and exemplary defenses of the absolutist
Gesinnungsethik of the "cosmic-ethical 'rationalist,' " often in a critical
dialogue with Max Weber. Not coincidentally, both also developed
their views in the context of a sustained engagement with socialism in
one of its variants—Tönnies beginning as an advocate of a fraternal
Gemeinschaft that he tended to conceive as the core of all socialist ideals, Michels starting from a commitment to the new communal moral
order that he understood as the revolutionary raison d'être of Marxist
socialism. In the face of what Weber understood as the inescapable
"ethical irrationality of the world," both typically responded with a disclaimer—"The world is stupid and base, not I"[64]—followed by a riposte: The world ought to be unified through moral "rationality."

Tönnies' mature thinking on this theme appears in the work translated as *Custom* (originally *Die Sitte*, a remarkably flexible term not
only for "custom," but also for habit, manners, mores, morality, or
specifically traditional morality), which, like Simmel's *Die Religion* and
Sombart's *Das Proletariat*, was published in Martin Buber's popular
series and addressed to a *problem* in modern culture. Tönnies begins
his study by identifying that problem as "philosophical," as a search for
"the unity of custom, the general and essential" in the development of
the "content of custom" out of its "form."[65] Custom is defined simply
as "social will" (*sozialer Wille*, or what was for Rousseau the *volonté
générale*) in contrast to "individual will," and social will emerges in
turn from that "secret essence," the "people." Supplementing Rousseauian populism with Burkean organicism, *das Volk* turns out in Tönnies' formulation to be a natural *Gemeinschaft* unifying the generations—living, dead, and unborn. The circle of social life is thereby
completed: custom is enclosed within community.

It becomes clear by the end of the essay, however, that Tönnies' classic framework of concepts has merely concealed the real issue: namely,
is a "unity of custom" or "customary morality" possible any longer in
modern society and in the presence of the modern state? Or framed in
other terms, what does a search for "unity of custom" presuppose?
Tönnies ends his thinking, as a knowledgeable student of Nietzsche
would, where it actually began: not with Rousseau but with the prob-

---

64. "Politik als Beruf" [Politiks as a Vocation] (1918), *GPS*, 546; G&M, 127.
65. *Die Sitte* (Frankfurt: Rütten & Loening, 1909), 16; *Custom: An Essay on Social
Codes*, trans. A. Borenstein (New York: Free Press, 1961), 41, unfortunately a translation
that suffers from imprecision.

lem in Nietzsche's reflections on the "concept of morality of custom [*die Sittlichkeit der Sitte*]," a long passage in *Daybreak* that prepares the way for the *Genealogy*'s inquiry into the origins of morality. The source of questioning for Nietzsche is sharply stated:

> In comparison with the mode of life of whole millennia of mankind we present-day men live in a very immoral age: the power of custom is astonishingly enfeebled and the moral sense so rarefied and lofty it may be described as having more or less evaporated. . . . The free human being is immoral because in all things he is *determined* to depend upon himself and not upon a tradition.[66]

Yet in such a situation what we moderns, smitten by individualism, *choose* to call "morality" in fact becomes nothing other than renunciation of that which is usual, standard, customary.

Translated into Tönnies' language, the problem of custom takes shape in the opposition between custom and those modern forces of "progress" that make up the province of sociology:

> As the subject and bearer of style [*die Mode*], society [*Gesellschaft*] stands in a certain necessary opposition to custom. Society is modern, cultured, cosmopolitan. . . . Business and trade, urban life, growth of the metropolis, the power of money, capitalism, separation of the classes, in general a burgherly nature and striving for cultivation—all these aspects of the same development of *civilization* promote style and damage custom. . . . The entire social civilization [*gesellschaftliche Zivilisation*] possesses something opposed to the artistic spirit that is based upon tradition and fidelity. This society and its products are superficial, external, thin, facile, artificial, uniform, and monotonous.[67]

And the basic contradictions symbolized by society and custom congeal in a pattern of domination:

> Thus the present age dominated by style and society becomes supreme with respect to the preceding age dominated by custom and a peasant-bourgeois-noble culture, which still resides within the present. Proof is found in the rush and noise of perpetual renewal, the fluidity of everything, the fact of permanence only in change. There is a tendency toward idealization: the ancient becomes modern. One longs to return to nature, rummages around in the old throw-aways, glorifies and nurses along old forms of life and custom, takes a fancy to religion once again, or discovers genuine artistry in

66. Nietzsche, *Morgenröte*, in *Werke in drei Bänden*, ed. K. Schlechta (Frankfurt: Ullstein, 1979–84), 1019 [I, 9]; *Daybreak: Thoughts on the Prejudices of Morality*, trans. R. J. Hollingdale (Cambridge: Cambridge University Press, 1982), 10. See also Tönnies, *Die Sitte*, 94; *Custom*, 145.

67. *Die Sitte*, 86–87; *Custom*, 133–35.

simple and homely styles. Idealization of the old repeats itself rhythmically from time to time. Industry exploits it just like anything else. But the spirit of society remains the same: it cannot spring over its own shadow.[68]

The language of this passage, so reminiscent of comments by Simmel, Hofmannsthal, and others at the turn of the century, yields a remarkable insight into Tönnies' position as a sociologist of the modern, with the polarities set in his mind between culture represented through "custom" and all the subversive and paradoxical processes and forces of modern life ("civilization," "society"), even when they do not *appear* modern. A quite similar tripartite juxtaposition of the mechanical process of civilization, evolutionary social process, and the creative "cultural movement" actually became the cornerstone for Alfred Weber's entire sociology of culture, whose primary task was to account for culture's emergence from the "feel for life" (*Lebensgefühl*).[69] However, Tönnies' tracing of these processes and forces does not end with this threesome, but continues on to the "state," which from his viewpoint works to undermine the strength of custom analogously to "society." This must be the case, because like all modern social forces the state "serves progress and the development of free personalities, but at the cost of the people [*das Volk*] and its communal and cooperative *life*."

Now Tönnies' instinctive allegiance is never in doubt: true being resides in communal and cooperative life. The question, of course, is, What is to be done? Since "the spirit of custom is communistic,"[70] he contends, the relevant modern question must become, How can this spirit's "communal" basis be restored? Or in Tönnies' familiar and classical terminology, how can *Gemeinschaft* be recovered and *Gesellschaft* transformed?

An answer has to lead down the path of knowledge, and it is a path strewn with traps and deceptions, most of which Tönnies does not avoid. His answer is nevertheless interesting and perhaps all the more revealing for its daring. Much of the response depends on asserting that "the possibility of transformation lies in society's forward movement," which will apparently bring (a) replacement of "capitalism" and its culture with something better, the precise nature of which is completely unclear, and (b) growth in what might be called social intelligence—

68. *Die Sitte*, 87; *Custom*, 135–36.
69. "Der soziologische Kulturbegriff," in *Verhandlungen des zweiten deutschen Soziologentages* (Tübingen: J. C. B. Mohr [Paul Siebeck], 1913), 15; "Prinzipielles zur Kultursoziologie," *Archiv* 47 (1920): 1–49.
70. *Die Sitte*, 88–89; *Custom*, 136–39.

that is, in Tönnies's phrasing, a "growth in reason [*Vernunft*]" and "joy in knowledge [*Erkenntnis*]."[71] So, in this view, to want more of the same, to choose what Weber called "technical progress" when alternatives are scarce, is to make a virtue of necessity. At least consistency is maintained: society is not being asked to leap over its own shadow.

But severe difficulties badger this line of reasoning anyway, and even Tönnies in his enthusiasm recognizes them: they have to do with nothing less than the conception of science, morality, and reason. For the relationship of rational science to custom is negative, Tönnies asserts; nevertheless, science must overcome its ingrained purely critical stance by recognizing the important social *function* of custom that "spares the will labor" and perceiving "reason [*Vernunft*] not only in that which is rational [*vernünftig*] in form."[72] What might the latter be? The "unconscious creative power in human, social, and individual spirit" is Tönnies' answer. Reason needs to understand, in other words, that custom not only is "useful," but has intrinsic moral and *aesthetic* value: "That which is fully ethical has aesthetic value, while that which is fully aesthetic has ethical value"![73] In sum,

> We need a new code of morality [*Sittlichkeit*] that is not tied to custom. The freer we become *from* custom and *in* custom, the more we require a conscious ethic, i.e., the recognition of that which makes us human: the self-affirmation of reason. In this way reason must really cease to be an essentially analytic power; it must develop itself into a joyous creating of *Gemeinschaft*. Only then will it prove to be or really become "the highest human power."[74]

This is Tönnies' barest, most unpretentious, most hopeful answer to the age of subjectivist culture.

It is not an answer that Weber could accept, for it gains plausibility only insofar as "believing" and "knowing" are conflated; or in other words, it reduces to a restoration of our "enlightened" faith in what Weber called the illusion of science as "the way to true nature."[75] But significantly, Tönnies is not quite trapped in the Enlightenment: his solid hymn to "reason" is interrupted by the dissonance of a modernist

71. *Die Sitte*, 88; *Custom*, 136.
72. *Die Sitte*, 92; *Custom*, 143.
73. *Die Sitte*, 93; *Custom*, 144.
74. *Die Sitte*, 94–95; *Custom*, 146.
75. "Wissenschaft als Beruf," *GAW*, 597; G&M, 142. Weber makes the first of these points in letters to Tönnies, 19 February 1909 and 29 August 1910 (NW 30/6:15–16; 30/7:109–12), the latter related directly to ideas in *Die Sitte*, which he had just read; cf. Eduard Baumgarten, *Max Weber: Werk und Person* (Tübingen: Mohr, 1964), 398–99, 670 n. 1.

concern for the unconscious, the aesthetic, the hidden vitalist forces of creative organic life and the "natural will" (*Wesenswille*). This is a concern and associated language, already present in *Gemeinschaft und Gesellschaft*, that Tönnies never abandons. Indeed, it could not be abandoned, since for him an authentic "ethics" had to be more than merely instrumentally rational, more than a matching of means with ends; it had to spring forth from the substratum of creative individual powers and communal engagements. It had to express not simply rational consciousness—for (to speak with Hammacher) what can it really mean that we live more consciously?—but also the "beauty" and grandeur of emotion. Tönnies' vocation seemed to demonstrate, despite suspicions of contradiction, that a longing for communal solidarity could be combined with an undivided faith in the healing power of knowledge. The secret was this: It turned out that what appeared contradictory to ethics or science in themselves could be reconciled on the plane of aesthetics. It was as if Nietzsche's well-known dictum—"for it is only as an *aesthetic phenomenon* that existence and the world are eternally *justified*"[76]—had been accepted as a road to the truly moral life.

Ethics and aesthetics were also closely connected in Michels' thought—or to be more precise, he seemed to interpret an aesthetic tendency manifest in virtually every aspect of his thinking as "ethical" in content. The results were in any case close to Tönnies' position, despite Michels' rather different roots in Cologne's Catholic patriciate and his early political affiliations with Hubert Lagardelle, Sorel, other Parisian and Italian syndicalists, and various anarchists scattered across Europe. Like Tönnies' views, Michels' ethical stance grew out of and was justified by a particular reading of Marxist socialism as a *moral* struggle, whose "scientific turn" was supported by a moral critique of exploitation and the ethically rational power of the "ultimate demands" for socialization of productive means and democratization.[77] Even more so than Tönnies, however, Michels deliberately set aside the "materialist" foundations of Marx's thought in favor of a concern for "justice." His answer to the fiercely contested question of the age—What is the relationship between morality and socialism generally?—was quite unequivocal: they are identical. But a curious instability threatened this answer, precisely because its intense moralism could be attached at will

---

76. *The Birth of Tragedy: or, Hellenism and Pessimism*, trans. W. Kaufmann (New York: Random House [Vintage Books], 1967), 52 (sec. 5).

77. See "'Endziel', Intransigenz, Ethik," *Ethische Kultur* 11 (1903): 393–95, 403–4; and "Was bedeutet uns Karl Marx?" *Mitteldeutsche Sonntags-Zeitung*, 15 March 1903.

to different and conflicting political objects. It is not, therefore, coincidental that, given this starting point, Michels could end as an authoritarian and fascist, but still in the name of pure idealism.

With respect to science as a vocation, Michels typically wrote as if there were no significant distinctions between ethical judgment and empirical knowledge, as if cultural questions could be settled by science, or the "ends of life" settled by analysis of the world. He was another of Weber's prototypical firm believers in the world's ultimate "ethical rationality," convinced that "the concrete *intentio* of the single act determined its value." Or as Weber pointed out, he was "a 'moralist' from head to toe" for whom "the separation between vocation and 'life'" made no sense at all, a *Gesinnungspolitiker* wedded to the conviction that for the revolutionary situation the "ethics" of the strike and not its politics were all that mattered.[78] Or in the sphere of knowledge, Michels seemed a *savant* for whom it was possible "to decide 'scientifically' the value of French and German culture." For Weber, on the contrary, "here, too, different gods struggle with one another, now and for all times to come."[79]

Michels' canonical and most political statement of the modern problem was his critique of bureaucratization in *Political Parties*, executed in part under Weber's tutelage. But as in Tönnies' exploration of the lost world of "community," Rousseauian images of fraternal equality danced through the pages of this book and pointed toward the ideal condition Michels regretted losing and hoped to regain. In Michels' case, however, it is really the dozens of apparently marginal and peripheral essays, as well as lengthy studies like *Sexual Ethics* (published in 1914 by Havelock Ellis, the guardian of modern sensibility), that reveal the complexity of his at times desperate search for a path away from the life-denying forces of bureaucratization and economic rationalization. Michels flirts with many of the culturally available and politically defined alternatives: the class struggle as a "moral" imperative, the politics of *action directe* and the general strike against hypocritical parliamentarism, the fresh currents of feminism and the women's movement, the healing aesthetic symbolism of "Italy," and even the possibilities of

78. GARS 1:113; PE, 116, where appropriately for Michels it is defined as "the Catholic ethic"; letter to Gisela Michels-Lindner, 25 December 1909, AMW 67; on "strike ethics" see the letters of 17 August 1908 and 12 May 1909, AMW 61 and 66.

79. GAW, 604; G&M, 148. Weber delivered this central message from "Science as a Vocation" directly to Michels, in a comment on one of Michels' many essays: "*No one can prove who ought not to remain 'true' to his 'nation,'* just as no one can *prove* who *ought* to be '*true*' to his *class*" (11 August 1908, AMW 60). Weber's argument seems to have had a marginal effect.

eroticism—in obvious ways the sorts of value-spheres and life-orders Weber probes in the "Intermediate Reflection," or the kinds of choices Simmel also perceives in modern "subjective" culture. Michels, however, was not satisfied with their assertions of differentiation and autonomy of the life-orders; he sought instead to reunify these orders under an "ethical" heading.

How might reunification be accomplished? Throughout Michels' sociocultural engagements and journeys of the intellect there is a profound, overriding attraction for the aesthetic as a route into ethical understanding and judgment. Sometimes the settings are obviously political and the commentary is intended to convey a political message: Thus, attending the Socialist Party Congress at Imola in 1902, Michels pronounced it not a tactical or organizational step forward, but rather an aesthetic triumph, an enchanting, harmonious, and therefore ethically admirable and "correct" vision of the "future state of socialism."[80] Or having been enchanted by Italian culture, he could write that "ethics in the political life of Italy is closely related to aesthetics. Frequently the beauty of the form in which one speaks or acts is what confers effectiveness on good deeds and good words. And the aesthetics of form does not remain without effect on a people composed of artists."[81] (Given Michels' passionate attachment to "things Italian," it is not difficult to detect the self-referential origins of such views.) On other occasions the aesthetic-ethical standard is invoked where one expects it least, as in Michels' unself-conscious report of his customary practice with his wife upon returning to Germany of enthusiastically greeting the first pair of startled lovers caught in an open and public love, a display of affection whose openness made it a distinctive cultural achievement: Such "fearless sensuality, almost proud of itself and meant for display, appeared to us like something original, healthy, powerful, portentous for the future, despite all the gray in gray of social relations in Germany," and it "gave us the strong pleasant feeling of something great."[82]

80. "Ein Blick in der 'Zukunftsstaat,'" *Mitteldeutsche Sonntags-Zeitung*, 8 March 1903.

81. "Der ethische Faktor in der Parteipolitik Italiens," *Zeitschrift für Politik* 3 (1909): 88.

82. "Erotische Streifzüge: Deutsche und italienische Liebesformen—aus dem Pariser Liebesleben," *Mutterschutz* 2 (1906): 366. As for the urban erotic life of the streets, Michels went on to defend the amazing thesis that "prostitution in France is morally superior to prostitution in Germany" because of the Latin Quarter's "*grisette*" type, depicted in *La Bohême*, a nice try at relativizing immorality that provoked a retort about "moral confusion" from Weber (letter of 11 January 1907, AMW 31); Mitzman, *Sociology and Estrangement*, esp. 305–6, interprets these quirks as evidence of Michels' incurable "romanticism."

What unifies such apparently disparate remarks on aesthetics, ethics, and eros in Michels' work is the idea that experiencing the sublime and the magnificent is the motive force behind all élan vital, ethical judgment, the quest for knowledge, great action, even behind the "creative" mode of existence Michels applied to himself and that Weber chided as a self-indulgent "aversion to a rationally disciplined way of life."[83] It is as if Michels wanted to release that most primitive and elemental life-force, eros, and place it in the service of sociocultural renewal, a tendency of syndicalism and "vitalist" thought generally. His interest in the entire range of modern subjects from revolution to sexual morality is unified, therefore, by a concern with the fate of eros abandoned to a social system that distorts its effects. Stating the idea somewhat idiosyncratically, even prostitution (several times a subject for Michels' sociology) thus has a "political" side to it: prostitutes are repressed revolutionaries, and the revolutionary society will eliminate prostitution and restore woman to dignity and citizenship.

In this respect we see a fundamentally *Platonic* outcome in Michels' work, with a similarly apolitical emphasis. Yet in Plato's classical formulation a kind of "divine mania," the love of beauty, *eros*, was the motive impulse lifting the "soul" upward onto the path toward love of knowledge, toward perception of the good, toward *episteme*. Viewing both Michels and Tönnies from a distance, one can say the classical formula remains intact as an ideal, but the unity of conception binding together eros, aesthetics, and ethics now becomes a mere possibility whose fate is to dwell unrequited in a modern social system distorting the grounds for its realization. Release of pure and absolute ethicism offers a solution of sorts to the problem of modern "rationalist" culture, but at best it can only be suprapolitical, above and beyond the Weberian oppositions among spheres and the Simmelian dualisms of subjective and objective culture. In the end, to see the world as an "ethical unity" is to view it through Platonic lenses with distortions identical to those observed originally: the enchantment of utopian vision as a painless inoculation against modern discontent.

THE WORLD AS AESTHETIC TOTALITY: LUKÁCS

A last important position on the problem of modern life and culture that became fully conscious of the possibilities for aesthetic transcen-

83. Letter to Michels, 15 October 1907, AMW 49.

dence was articulated by those exceptional "eschatological" metaphysicians, as they were sometimes called,[84] men like Georg Lukács and Ernst Bloch, who frequented Weber's circle of friends and colleagues in Heidelberg and on occasion attended Simmel's Berlin seminar. The young Lukács was the main representative of these views, an aesthetician of mercurial intellectual and political fortunes who was closely attuned to the cultural dilemmas of the day and capable of giving them a precise and refined philosophical expression. Indeed, Lukács had studied with Simmel and in his early writing displayed an analytic terminology and central problem of modern culture derived largely from *The Philosophy of Money.*

Following Simmel's ideas, Lukács' early philosophy of the modern emerged out of the assumption of a decisive conflict between subjective and objective culture, between expressive life and constraining form. Yet his metaphysical stance also embraced the concept of a self-creating "concrete totality" that was deeply challenged by modern life, and it was a stance that certainly surpassed the intensity of longing his erstwhile mentor expressed for such a totality's return.[85] Similarly, he sanctioned Simmel's crucial first sense of culture as "the unity of life, the life-enhancing, life-enriching power of unity." But rather than proceeding to Simmel's second sense, to the idea of culture as a repressive form, he then proclaimed that "all culture is the conquest of life, the unifying of all life's phenomena with a single force . . . so that whatever part of the totality of life you look at, you always see, in its innermost depths, the same thing. In an authentic culture," Lukács added, "everything becomes symbolic"—representative, that is, of the unifying concrete whole.[86] In short, according to this view, "meaning" and "totality" presuppose each other and are made possible by "culture." In the inauth-

84. In an interview with Gaston Riou of the Parisian daily *Figaro,* Weber himself cited Lukács as representing "*one* of the types of German 'eschatologism' and as the opposite pole to Stefan George" (letter to Lukács, 6 March 1913, NW 30/11:25–26; printed in *Georg Lukács: Selected Correspondence, 1902–1920,* ed. and trans. Judith Marcus and Zoltán Tar [New York: Columbia University Press, 1986], 221).

85. See Silvie Rücker, "Totalität als ethisches und ästhetisches Problem," *Text und Kritik* 39/40 (1973), esp. 52–55 on the relationship to Simmel; among the most recent literature, Eugene Lunn, *Marxism and Modernism: An Historical Study of Lukács, Brecht, Benjamin and Adorno* (Berkeley: University of California Press, 1982), chap. 4; and Martin Jay, *Marxism and Totality: The Adventures of a Concept from Lukács to Habermas* (Berkeley: University of California Press, 1984), chap. 2.

86. Quoted from the Hungarian text, "Aesthetic Culture," written in 1910 and published in 1913, in György Márkus, "Life and the Soul: The Young Lukács and the Problem of Culture," in *Lukács Reappraised,* ed. A. Heller (New York: Columbia University Press, 1983), 4.

entic and alienated culture, by contrast, the tragic and irresolvable Simmelian paradoxes reign supreme.

In Weber's view, Lukács' writings on literature and art could be understood as the contribution of a "modern aesthetician" who proceeded on the basis of culture's actual existence and accordingly asked the question, "How is that (meaningfully) possible?"[87] Following the direction then taken by Lukács' cultural criticism, one may suggest further that for his early thought the central problem became, In what respect is culture as a "totality" in the above sense any longer possible? What are the prospects for achieving and retaining an "authentic" culture, and what can such authenticity possibly mean?

All of Lukács' early writings, including the difficult and unfinished *Aesthetics*, parts of which were read to the Weber Circle at the time Weber presented his "Intermediate Reflections" on the "religious rejections of the world," involved an attempt to clarify the meaning of these claims about culture, to elaborate their applications, and to find an answer to his question.[88] For Lukács, building on Simmel's conceptions, "form" became a configuration of relations within the bourgeois-capitalist world of alienation, fragmentation, "objectification of life," and what he called the "dissolution" or "detachment of personality."[89] The key word for this generalized cultural phenomenon was "individualism" of the kind one could see, for example, in modern drama: "The new drama is the drama of individualism, and this with a power, intensity and exclusiveness we have never seen before. . . . Present-day culture is bourgeois [*bürgerlich*] culture. . . . Thus every drama is bourgeois, because the cultural forms of life today are bourgeois, and because the form in which life manifests itself will be determined by those forms."[90] This type of "individualism" became a modern form of

87. "Wissenschaft als Beruf," *GAW*, 610; G&M, 154.

88. See Weber's reference to "what you read to us then [i.e., before the war] from the splendid building blocks of your *Aesthetics*" (letter of 14 August 1916), in *Georg Lukács Briefwechsel*, 372; English translation in *Georg Lukács: Selected Correspondence*, 264 (translation altered). Weber's allusion to "your sudden turn to Dostoevsky" suggests the text in question had affinities with *The Theory of the Novel*, which Lukács also called his "aesthetics of the novel," and that Weber disliked for its "essayistic" abandon.

89. "Zur Soziologie des modernen Dramas," *Archiv* 38 (1914), in *Schriften zur Literatursoziologie*, 4th ed. (Neuwied: Luchterhand, 1970), 287.

90. Ibid., 284; for Lukács' *Kulturkritik* and discussion of "individualism" generally, consult Andrew Arato and Paul Breines, *The Young Lukács and the Origins of Western Marxism* (New York: Seabury, 1979), chaps. 2–3. The authors read too much from Lukács' later arguments in *History and Class Consciousness* (1921, 1923) into the view that he was "using Marx to correct Simmel" (15); more to the point is the certainty that Lukács' acclaimed discoveries and anticipations concerning alienation owed their inspiration to Simmel's writings on the same topic.

life, and not an admirable one, either, as it was stranded in the realm of everyday conventionality, meaningless atemporality, and senseless repetitions. In Lukács' dialectically sensitized view, it lacked "development" and therefore lacked a "higher" conception of life. Given this peculiar meaning, "individualism" exemplified human life in Weber's age of vocational specialization, but, ironically, Lukács' response to it also authenticated Weber's offhand comment: "What is hard for modern man, and especially for the younger generation, is to measure up to *workaday* existence."[91] This comment could have been written expressly with Lukács' dissatisfactions in mind.

What was "life" in the "highest" sense? Lukács really seemed to give two kinds of answers, both of which led in the same direction. The first emerged out of a critique of aesthetic culture. It placed the "lived experience" of Simmelian sociology in the realm of pure subjectivity and interiority (*Innerlichkeit*), insisting that "life lived to its fullest [*das lebendige Leben*] lies beyond the forms."[92] In this evocative language "life is an anarchy of light and dark: nothing is ever completely fulfilled in life, nothing ever quite ends; new, confusing voices always mingle with the chorus of those that have been heard before. Everything flows, everything merges into another thing, and the mixture is uncontrolled and impure; everything is destroyed, everything is smashed, nothing ever flowers into real life." Life then becomes associated with a "longing" that "destroys all form, so overpowering that one cannot express it except by stammering."[93] We have encountered these ideas before: they have to do with the reception of Nietzsche through Simmel, with the idea of a "formless" modern present. In Lukács' thinking, they lead quite directly to the conception of a world that can only be grasped aesthetically, which is nowhere more apparent than in his radical judgment that "the good is not an ethical category." It is "fanatical passion [*Besessenheit*]; it is not gentle, refined, quietistic, but instead savage, terrible, blind, and adventuresome."[94] In this idiom, life in the highest sense promises to lead onto the path toward a "redemption" from subjectivity that lies, paradoxically, "beyond the forms."

For a second answer Lukács, in *The Theory of the Novel*, written in

91. "Wissenschaft als Beruf," *GAW*, 605; G&M, 149.
92. "Von der Armut am Geiste: Ein Gespräch und ein Brief," *Neue Blätter* 2 (1912): 72, the meditation on Irma Seidler's death that so impressed the Webers: *Lebensbild*, 474; Eng. trans., 466; *Georg Lukács Briefwechsel*, 292.
93. *Soul and Form*, trans. A. Bostock (Cambridge: MIT Press, 1974), 91, 152–53, from essays published in German in 1911.
94. "Von der Armut am Geiste," 75, 78.

1914–15, went behind the modern texts, as Nietzsche had done before him, to an interpretation of Greek philosophy in relation to modernity. What he found in antiquity, naturally enough, was the original model of an integrated culture, a "homogeneous world" and concept of "totality" from which the Dionysian seems to be absent:

> Totality of being is possible only where everything is already homogeneous before it has been contained by forms; where forms are not a constraint but only the becoming conscious, the coming to the surface of everything that had been lying dormant as a vague longing in the innermost depths of that which had to be given form; where knowledge is virtue and virtue is happiness, where beauty is the meaning of the world made visible."[95]

The fate of this interpretation of the Greek ideal returned at the level of reality Lukács connected with those "great moments" of "an essential life, a meaningful process," or a "pure experience of self."[96] In *The Theory of the Novel* the application was literary: such moments described the highest achievement of Tolstoy's art and set the stage for a breakthrough to a new world of unified experience.

Returning to Lukács' most fundamental question, one sees that from his standpoint the higher life of an authentic culture can gain viability only in a "new world," only with a *vita nuova* that creates a heretofore merely imagined form of artistic expression lying beyond the epic and thus beyond Tolstoy's novels. The new aesthetic totality must transcend what Weber, borrowing from Tolstoy, had called the "organic cycle of life." In Lukács' highly symbolic language, itself a reflection of the quest for authenticity, Dostoevski is destined to become the new Dante:

> This world is the sphere of pure soul-reality in which man exists as man, neither as a social being nor as an isolated, unique, pure and therefore abstract interiority. If ever this world should come into being as something natural and simply experienced, as the only true reality, a new complete totality could be built out of all its substances and relationships. It would be a world to which our divided reality would be a mere backdrop, a world which would have outstripped our dual world of social reality by as much as we have outstripped the world of nature.[97]

Lukács' language is the language of transcendence, or *Aufhebung*, not in the retrospective sense championed by Tönnies or Sombart, but as a *Gemeinschaft* from above bent on overcoming all the inherited "du-

95. *The Theory of the Novel*, trans. A. Bostock (Cambridge: MIT Press, 1971), 34; first published in German in 1916.
96. Ibid., 151; *Soul and Form*, 156.
97. *Theory of the Novel*, 152.

alisms" that constituted Simmel's thought and world—dualisms that Simmel wanted to leave intact. But not Lukács: to recover the Greek world meant to revive a conception of knowledge as a "way to true being," citing the language of Weber's "Science as a Vocation," and to pursue this conception as a way out of the dilemma of "individualism" (read: subjectivism) posed by the modern.

That the actually existing modern world was not prepared to accede to Lukács' enchantments made all the difference to his revolutionary "eschatologism." Recognizing this fact, his next and in some ways final leap of the mind was to discover a point of rest, a home in one of the proven sacramental establishments: Marxism. Appropriately, Weber composed the epitaph for the choice of this renegade aesthetician: "The arms of the old churches are opened widely and compassionately for him. After all, they do not make it hard."[98] The Marxism of Lukács' *History and Class Consciousness* testified to the renewal of hope. Most significant of all, it took on the task of shoring up that concrete totality and structure of meaning the young Lukács had so earnestly labored to find, protect, and make his own.

What general conclusions can we draw after having followed the twists and turns of the debate over culture and modern life within the Weber Circle? The main contours of our theme take shape around a politically relevant critique of the driving forces of our rationalized objective culture—differentiation, specialization, and, particularly, intellectualization—and the troubling paradoxes hovering around these forces and the reactions they provoke. The debate has a bearing on politics in the sense that it confronts the technological and scientific orders placed at the disposal of the modern state and then calls into question the affiliated character of public life and its constructions of individuality. It is also a debate marked by the predominance of culture in the sense that a particular intellectual and spiritual condition is visualized as characterizing and at the same time reproducing and sustaining modernity. The situation of this culture is said to be disunified and paradoxical.

One important paradox that is perceived from Simmel to Lukács involves the aesthetic sphere of value. On the one hand, progressive differentiation in the division of labor and specialization of knowledge

---

98. "Wissenschaft als Beruf," *GAW*, 612; G&M, 155.

have given what Weber called the internal and lawful autonomy of different life-orders not only a certain plausibility, but also a fixity and finality in the modern world. They tend to appear impenetrable except in their own terms. But on the other hand, aestheticism seems to have invaded everywhere, now threatening to subordinate independent orders, such as the ethical or political, to its own standards and forms. Aesthetic indifference to "substance" and an overriding concern with the perfection of "form" encourage a kind of action and judgment oriented toward impression, rhythm, tempo, gesture, symbolization—in a word, toward style. Imitating and borrowing from the model of art, our public life thus comes to be defined in terms of its visual imagery, manipulation of feelings, calculation of audience effects, deployment of managerial styles—in sum, the mastery of a certain kind of method and technique. Aesthetic modes of action and categories of judgment then start to offer a deeply attractive way of deflating problems arising elsewhere, providing apparently agreeable and innocuous "solutions" and "answers" through symbolic manipulation and resort to entertainment. Such solutions may be painless, but they are not harmless. The new aestheticism promotes exactly those deceptions Weber wanted to foreswear.

At a different level of abstraction there appears to be widespread agreement among these writers on a second large paradox residing in modernity itself. For now as the external life-world becomes more objectified, functionally coordinated, and aligned with the imperatives of instrumental rationality, so the sense of an individual self becomes more inward, psychologically inclined, and connected to a search for validating subjectivity. The latter gives new meaning to the old Augustinian view, cited by Weber, that genuine belief is constrained precisely because it is opposed to reason: "*Credo non quod, sed quia absurdum est.*"[99] On the one hand culture authorizes increasing personal "freedom," while on the other it harbors increasing "homelessness" as a longing to flee from our instrumental selves into nonrational wholeness. Restated in more comprehensive terms, such tensions pit social against aesthetic modernity: that is, the socioeconomic and technological world of production and what Weber and his contemporaries called "technical progress" against the cult of the self, the call of interiority, and (in our

99. "Wissenschaft als Beruf," *GAW*, 611; "Zwischenbetrachtung," *GARS* 1:566; G&M, 154, 352.

stylish language of today) the "longing for true presence." The two sides of modernity become differentiated and set against each other in a struggle for our allegiance.

In the end these paradoxes point toward an existential impasse and spiritual dilemma—or to speak philosophically, an aporia—at the apparent center of modernity and its culture. Having considered representative responses to this state of affairs in the Weber Circle, let us turn finally to reflect on Weber's own "disenchanted" reply and the thought that lies beyond it.

CHAPTER VII

The Fate of Our Times

The tension between actuality and idea, between the establishment of the world and the world as it could be, is so manifest that the language which wants to indicate this tension succeeds only in underscoring its own superfluity. Everyone is taught a lesson, yet everything remains as impenetrable as ever.

—Max Horkheimer

From the beginning of his work, Max Weber sought to understand the historical forms and actual conditions of life he increasingly referred to as the "fate" of our culture and civilization. To the extent that his thought possesses a degree of unity, it must be located in this intention. Investigating the general condition or organization of labor and its transformation in the 1890s, he became convinced that "we will *never be asked* whether we want a given historical development"[1]—never be asked by history, that is, which consists of "inconvenient facts," produces unintended results, and defiantly teaches its own hard lessons. In his last reflections he also spoke of the unexpected "concatenation of circumstances" and "tragic" teachings "fundamental to all history." One of the most important of these teachings was the knowledge of human action whose outcome typically "stands in completely inadequate and often even paradoxical relation to its original meaning."[2] The peculiar circumstances leading to the rationalism characterizing the capitalist system and the fateful consequences of this kind of rationalism for our modern world exemplify the disjunction between beginning and end, intention and result. Any history worthy of the name regards such

1. In his response to Karl Oldenberg, *Verhandlungen des 8. Evangelisch-sozialen Kongresses* (Göttingen: Vandenhoeck & Ruprecht, 1897), 108.
2. "Politik als Beruf," [Politics as a Vocation] (1919), *GPS*, 535; G&M, 117; cf. *GARS* 1:1, 82; *PE*, 13, 90, including the specific example of the Reformation's "unintended consequences."

paradoxes, contradictions, and disappointments as the rule and never the exception.

Considering the association of fate with history, it seems entirely fitting that Weber should have once expressed a desire to linger forever at the very center of paradoxical historical phenomena having permanent and universal significance for all of civilization: Rome. "I could live there a lifetime," he wrote from renaissance Florence. "The historical imagination is the main thing." [3] The city that served in Freud's invention of civilization as a metaphor for the archaeology of the mind symbolized to Weber the possibility of excavating and recovering our sociocultural development, the layers of our construction of the modern. Let us ask how Weber's historical imagination recreated our "fate" and "fatality." What *is* the fate of our times?

WEBER'S DISENCHANTED WORLD

In passages especially in his later writings Weber makes a number of claims about modern life that we have encountered previously: it is rationalized, driven by purposive-rational or instrumental orientations, divided into opposed life-orders and value-spheres, without genuinely new prophetic truths, yet racked by endless searches for absolute experience and spiritual wholeness. Its discontents are brought together under the heading "capitalism" and economic "rationalism." But the most elemental and significant reality taught the historical imagination in the modern age is the fateful *Entzauberung*, or (literally) de-magification of life, which becomes the focus for a kind of summing up of all that Weber wants to say on the theme of modernity: "The fate of our times is characterized by rationalization and intellectualization and, above all, by the 'disenchantment of the world.'" [4]

The "world" in Weber's phrase requires emphasis: it means the temporal course of everyday affairs, the space of action and appearance, the humanly constructed environment of the life-world and culture that religious asceticism and mysticism both turned against and sought to

3. Letter from Florence to Helene Weber, 14 April 1902, NW 30/4:84, after arriving from Rome: "Here [in Florence] one sees for the first time what an ugly dump Rome really is, and yet I could live there a lifetime, here only with difficulty. The historical imagination is the main thing, and whoever doesn't have it shouldn't go to Rome. You have that imagination, thanks to Gervinus and the atmosphere of old Heidelberg." (On the complicated relationship between Weber's mother and this historian and family friend, see *Lebensbild*, 21–26; Eng. trans., 19–24.)

4. "Wissenschaft als Beruf," [Science as a Vocation] (1919), *GAW*, 612; G&M, 155.

master. Following the path of salvation religions, members of the Weber Circle and the fin-de-siècle generation longed to redefine and re-create this world ethically, aesthetically, and politically, or, in Marx's lyrical phrasing, to appropriate "the human essence" and solve "the riddle of history."[5] But for Weber the historical world, our phenomenal life-world that "is," simply can no longer subsist as the object of enacted wholeness. On the contrary, today this world itself, that *we* have cre-ated, resists and opposes reenchantment, while our own "bearing" or human condition "has been disenchanted and denuded of its mythical but inwardly genuine plasticity." Herein lies the "great problem of *life*,"[6] Weber asserts, recalling the mythic "natural" and "organic cycle of existence" anchoring the meaningful unfolding of the aesthetic and erotic life-orders. We may have chosen or become a plurality of "pros-thetic gods," to speak with Freud, but we have done so at the expense of our vivid, deep, and distinctive humanity. And "fate," Weber adds, "certainly not 'science,' holds sway over these gods and their struggles." Why and how, then, has our "mythic plasticity" been lost?

Weber provides a remarkable, yet elusive answer to this important and equally elusive question. It proceeds as a contrast and interplay between the "grandiose rationalism of the ethical-methodical conduct of life," especially the "grandiose pathos" of a Christian ethics, embod-ied powerfully in Puritanical inner-worldly asceticism, and the devel-opmental tendency of the "world," which is to say the life-world of *everyday* experience. On the one hand "our eyes have been blinded for a thousand years" by the moral pathos of a religiously sanctioned worldview, armed and defended by monotheistic theological rational-ism, capable of denying or mastering the world. But on the other hand that world has slowly developed and begun to call forth its own powers, orchestrated by a religiously "unmusical" and religiously indifferent sci-entific rationalism. Having been placed fortuitously at the historic con-juncture of these competing forces, Weber still acknowledges his voca-tional imperative as *amor fati*: as he wrote to Tönnies, "Really I am religiously absolutely 'unmusical' and have neither the need nor the ability to erect within myself any psychic 'structures' of a religious char-acter. It's simply impossible, and I reject it." But the love of fate was also a fatality, for he added tersely, "In this respect I feel myself a

5. "The Economic and Philosophical Manuscripts" (1844), in *The Marx-Engels Reader*, 2d ed., ed. R. Tucker (New York: Norton, 1978), 84, 99.
6. "Wissenschaft als Beruf," *GAW*, 604; G&M, 148; the latter translates *mythisch* as "mystical"; but it is important to preserve Weber's original and literal meaning.

cripple, a deformed human being, whose inner fate is to have to answer honestly for this."[7]

The confession provides one clear measure, at the personal level, of the limits and costs of scientific rationalism, as well as the distance separating Weber from the poets of the George Circle and the metaphysicians like Lukács and especially Ernst Bloch, whose thinking veered toward a rejuvenated political theology. But to speak only of mere limits or personal costs is misleading, for the imposition of restraint achieves a general meaning as a precondition for "knowing" and "integrity." Considered from the perspective of intersubjective understanding, there is only the choice between knowledge on the one side, which in Weber's idiom is historical, untimely, and troubling, and on the other the "sacrifice of the intellect" as either a leap to faith or a submersion in dialectical totality.

From the standpoint of knowledge that is historical, the two "rationalisms"—the theological and the scientific—were once held together in a tense and auspicious union; however, in the ages after Galileo, Bacon, and Jan Swammerdam the latter has differentiated itself, and typically with a fierce struggle, under the protective defense of *empirical* mastery of the world. But the standpoint of "empirical reflection" and "pure experience," Weber agrees with J. S. Mill, leads to a kind of "polytheism."[8] In the terms of this richly symbolic language, the unifying moral pathos of Christianity is thus seen as coming to an end. Weber states the conclusion in different ways: "In fact, whoever exists in the 'world' (in the Christian sense) can experience in itself [*an sich*] nothing other than the struggle among a plurality of value-series [*Wertreihen*], each of which appears binding when viewed for itself [*für sich*]."[9] In such circumstances "many old gods, disenchanted and hence in the form of impersonal powers, ascend from their graves, strive for control over our lives and resume their eternal struggle with each other." Or most concisely and significantly of all, "Today the routines of 'everyday life' challenge religion," and the "everyday" becomes "religious."[10]

7. Letter of 19 February 1909, NW 30/7:110–11.
8. "Der Sinn der 'Wertfreiheit' der soziologischen und ökonomischen Wissenschaften" [The Meaning of 'Value-Freedom' in the Sociological and Economic Sciences] (1917), "Wissenschaft als Beruf," GAW, 507, 603; "Zwischen zwei Gesetzen," [Between Two Laws] (1916), MWG I/15:98; G&M, 147; S&F, 17.
9. "Zwischen zwei Gesetzen," MWG I/15:98.
10. "Wissenschaft als Beruf," GAW, 605; G&M, 149; Weber's last sentence—"Heute aber ist es religiöser 'Alltag' "—defies translation; it suggests both of these interpretations. It hardly needs to be added that this entire line of thinking amounts to Weber's reflection on Nietzsche's fated announcement of humankind's complicity in the "death of God."

These Weberian formulations open onto a number of possible lines of thought. In the first place, rumors of extraordinary, prophetic challenges at the periphery have been heard before; but now, Weber seems to suggest, a different kind of entirely ordinary, even trivializing challenge has swept across culture to its common core and has become insistent and unavoidable. The very definition of the disenchanted world is in religious terms to eliminate "*magic* as a means to salvation," but more generally and essentially to sustain a culture that devalues all "mysterious incalculable forces" in favor of the grounded knowledge "that one can, in principle, *master* all things by *calculation*."[11] As the specific mechanism of disenchantment, this proven "calculability" conceals a Simmelian paradox, for its extension throughout culture as a possibility to be applied only "in principle" is accompanied by the *individual's* diminishing knowledge and control over all the conditions of life. We can interpret this to mean that each of us comes to be surrounded by and dependent on myriad complex "processes," from economic transactions to nuclear fission, affecting the immediately experienced world and the prospects for continuation and transformation of that world, which we individually cannot possibly comprehend, much less control. In the absence of individual comprehension, the likelihood of achieving genuinely collective and public control becomes increasingly remote. There is a deep pessimism to this view, recalling Weber's earliest reflections, and balanced, it would seem, only by the hope that can come from a matter-of-fact judgment of our condition.

If the desire for mystery and mystification survives, as indeed it does, then it typically becomes attached either to the plain, repetitive routine of the everyday (*der Alltag*), which itself becomes a functional metaphysic, or to the means and effects of calculation itself—to "sacred" science, to "quantitative bigness" conjoined, for example, with what Weber appropriately designates the "romanticism of numbers" pervading American culture in particular, and not excluding obeisance to "public opinion."[12] Numbered among the latest modern "mysteries" would be all those peculiar and exceptionally publicity-conscious spiritual fads of our time, indulged in by those who want to prove their "deeper spirituality," and normally served up as an ad hoc version or a

---

11. *GARS* 1:114; "Über einige Kategorien der verstehenden Soziologie" (1913), "Wissenschaft als Beruf," *GAW*, 473–74, 594; *PE*, 117; "Some Categories of Interpretive Sociology," trans. Edith Graber, *Sociological Quarterly* 22 (1981), 178–79; G&M, 139. Cf. G&M, 148, and *PE*, 105, 149; the passages on "disenchantment" in *PE* were added in the 1920 revisions and are unfortunately obscured by Parsons' translation.
12. For American culture, see *GARS* 1:54; *PE*, 71.

bizarre mixture of Eastern mysticism, native Indian lore, the occult, popular psychology, science fiction, and astrological nonsense, more often than not manufactured by an active or defrocked priest from the literati who has a book contract. These ersatz "prophecies" are by now cultural rituals and corporate enterprises run for profit, made available for public consumption by the media, and otherwise fully integrated into the dominant structure of material interests.

Calculation is, of course, the province of intellect or intellectualization, abstract mind or *Geist*, the subversive driving forces of the modern that come to penetrate everywhere. For the modern there is, as it were, a superfluity of "mind" over the "soul," an hegemony of abstract, objective intellect released on the world in its many forms: in politics bureaucratization as "mind objectified"; in science the victory of specialized knowledge over Faustian universality; in the aesthetic or erotic life-orders the triumph of "technique" and the "sensualists without heart"; in economic life the dominion of a human type formed by specialization and a vocational ideal "that prowls about in our lives like the ghost of dead religious beliefs," and driven by a pursuit of wealth that becomes a "purely agonistic passion" having the "character of sport."[13] No order of life is left untouched by the ingenuity of mind's soulless potency.

But to speak of disenchantment as world-mastery through calculation rather than through spiritual powers is above all to speak particularly of its modern representative in organized, specialized, vocational, authoritative science. Although the problem of science's "inner" meaning provoked Weber's most passionate reflections, in this connection we should not overlook his explicit sociology of its "external" features. For his writings on modern education and his involvements with university reform were motivated throughout by concern for the cultural effects of this disenchanting power, magnified and made "irreversible" through its *institutionalization*. They were also motivated by the conviction that in the self-referential modern age any corrective to the dependency on impersonal forces and to the intoxicating lure of surrender to the incalculable and mysterious would have to be sought reflexively, so to speak, within the sphere of knowledge itself.

The picture Weber sketches in "Science as a Vocation" and elsewhere has the hidden charm of a Max Beckmann painting. For Weber the meaning of disenchanting science in institutionalized form is contained

---

13. *GARS* 1:204; *PE*, 182; Weber makes clear that he is thinking especially of the United States, where the vocational spirit has been "unleashed" to the greatest extent.

within universities that have become "'state capitalist' enterprises," directed by a "captain of industry" (in the Germany of his day the minister of education, in America the university president) and "managed" for purposes external to learning for its own sake. "Freedom" of inquiry has given way, Weber suggests, following the economic analogy, to the production of knowledge useful to the state for technical and economic reasons, or, more abstractly, for purposes of legitimating state authority. As size, costs, and competition over resources and "workers" increase, so individual autonomy is replaced by a kind of alienation or "separation" of scholars and researchers from their "means of production" in libraries and laboratories. The contractual "freedom" of members really licenses "a policy of relentless selection," unintentionally encouraging careerism and "academic 'operators,'" and leading Weber to assert that there is "hardly any career on earth where chance plays such a role." The struggle for survival in an entrepreneurial environment also encourages specialization, which in turn ensures the paradox of knowing more and communicating less. And this specialized knowledge cannot even have the satisfaction of perfection and durability, for it is "chained to the course of progress" and "*asks* to be 'surpassed' and outdated."[14]

The entrepreneurial spirit works against traditional principles of collegiality and tends to displace them, and in that sense contributes to an "Americanization" of the world of intellect: "German university life is being Americanized, as is German life in general," according to Weber's assessment. But this spirit is complicated and overlaid in countervailing ways by bureaucratization of the educational and scientific "enterprise," which Weber argues "has increased greatly in the United States" and, along with "the growing appreciation of degrees," contributes to the "Europeanization which is affecting all American life."[15] Convergence everywhere around modern norms of efficient management and "standardization," an idea Weber found in Veblen,[16] further erodes differences that have obstructed the complete domination by a single mechanism. Forced into this mold, we might choose with Freud to treat science as a "deflection" providing solace, or more radically to see it

14. For these ideas, see *Max Weber on Universities*, ed. E. Shils (Chicago: University of Chicago Press, 1974), esp. 25, 33; and *GAW*, 584–85, 592–93; G&M, 131–32, 137–38.

15. "Wissenschaft als Beruf," *GAW*, 584; G&M, 131; *Weber on Universities*, 23, 29, 37.

16. *The Theory of Business Enterprise* (New York: Scribner's, 1904), chap. 2.

with Nietzsche "as a means of self-narcosis." But to pursue science for
its own sake in the entrepreneurial environment is actually no comfort
at all, for to do so only means we are committed to disenchanting the
world further. The price of the *will* to knowledge is paid with disenchantment. Or in Nietzsche's phrasing, "Creative work as enchantment
brings with it a disenchantment in relation to everything that is already
there." [17] To engage in science under such conditions also means to assume what we do is worthwhile and valuable, irrespective of its consequences, as is seen powerfully, Weber suggests, in a field like modern
medicine, with the technologies it contributes to controlling life itself.
Here clear answers to moral problems are always one step behind "technical progress," their very clarity challenged by the autonomy of objectified intellect. Indeed, the problems are posed *because* of science's advance, which cannot answer them in its own terms. Science can preserve
life, but not answer whether the quality of the life preserved is worth
having.

Finally, we might interpret Weber to be suggesting that modern science itself in the broadest sense of "inquiry" or the "pursuit of knowledge" is an order of life and a cultural artifact that is an effect of "disenchantment," as well as its cause. Science tends to develop either as a
formal scheme, an elaboration of categories or as the abstract theoretical imagination supporting the authority and propagation of the mathe-
matical model of analysis and its standards of precision, parsimony, and
quantification. Models of explanation in natural science then legislate
and enforce standards for all of human inquiry, and, in the most abstract theoretical disciplines of the human sciences, content gives way
to form and technique. The light of science is turned against itself, and
its presuppositions and methods are scrutinized. Rather than addressing
an external world, science increasingly addresses itself. But the inward
turn seems entirely justified because our life-world is now uniquely a
product of abstract mind. "Disenchanted science" thus becomes the
mirror image of the world it has created and now comes to represent.

Such are the contours of Weber's overall argument for the disenchantment of the world as the fate of our times. But to write about
"fate" is a daunting choice. What can the choice signify? We may justifiably ask whether his thought is an antiprophetic prophecy, a prophecy
(or if one prefers, a metaphysical speculation) about modern fate that
denies it is one.

17. *Werke: Kritische Gesamtausgabe*, vol. 7/1, ed. G. Colli and M. Montinari (Berlin:
Gruyter, 1977), 527, from the "Nachgelassene Fragmente" (emphasis omitted).

As attractive as it may seem, this description in fact falls short of the mark and remains superficial. For Weber's writing stakes a claim on humanity's historical experience, on the sociocultural world that has come through time to be as it is, and on the type of humanity now dwelling in that world. His work is thus a major step along the path toward clarification and specification of the "what is" announced by Hegel in the momentous "Preface" to his *Rechtsphilosophie*, taken up in a different way by Marx, and treated subsequently in philosophy down through Heidegger's reflections.[18] But in Weber's hands the clarification comes without teleological or historicist underpinnings, without immanent "reason," without the recovery of "essence" and the transformation to "true presence," and therefore (Weber also insists) without the kinds of illusions and self-assertive pronouncements that have plagued modernity about what might have been or what might come to be. It was thus not without purpose for Weber to interject, almost as an aside, a certain disclaimer and warning in his concluding 1920 reflections on the "universal-historical problems" of culture raised by *The Protestant Ethic and the Spirit of Capitalism* and the successive comparative-sociological studies of the world religions: "Whoever yearns for 'seeing [*Schau*],'" or a show or a display of feeling, "should go to the cinema," and "whoever wants a 'sermon' should go to a conventicle." The observer of history, furthermore, who cannot fail to be "shocked" by the "course of humanity's fate," "will do well to keep his small personal commentaries to himself . . . unless he knows himself to be called and gifted to give them expression in artistic or prophetic form."[19] Historical knowledge requires distance, not as a denial of sensitivity or empathetic understanding, but as a repudiation of that modish aesthetic culture that can only end in "dilettantism."

In short, Weber's clarification of the "science of actuality" becomes discontinuous with the philosophical project; it branches off on a different route toward understanding the modern. The knowledge of disenchantment seems to impose a disciplined renunciation: Perhaps we can celebrate a gain in intellectual sobriety, regret the attendant imperative

18. "To comprehend what is, this is the task of philosophy, because what is, is reason," writes Hegel, *The Philosophy of Right* (1821), ed. T. M. Knox (London: Oxford University Press, 1967), 11; and Heidegger begins "The Age of the World Picture" (1938) with the assertion, "In metaphysics reflection is accomplished concerning the essence of what is and a decision takes place regarding the essence of truth," in *The Question Concerning Technology and Other Essays*, trans. W. Lovitt (New York: Harper & Row, 1977), 115.
19. *GARS* 1:14; *PE*, 29.

loss of metaphysical solicitude, but nevertheless find the challenge for our inquiries in the "great problem of life" Weber has posed.

CRITIQUE: TOWARD A POLITICS OF
MODERN CULTURE

As an epilogue to our inquiry into culture, politics, and modernity in Weber's thought, let us ask where the discussion of our theme stands today. What judgments can be made about flights from the "iron cage" in our own time? Are there grounds for questioning Weber's reading of our history? Have we remained like Weber's dreaded *epigoni*, or have we begun to redefine the alternatives left by his legacy and to create the conditions for our own thinking?

It would be foolish to suppose that anything more than a provisional sketch for an answer can be given to questions of such magnitude—questions that really demand another inquiry equivalent to the present study. From Heidegger to Habermas far too much has occurred in Western thought in the generations since Weber's last words in 1920 to warrant any glib conclusions about advances in our thinking, new solutions to formerly intractable problems, the progress of scholarship, and other similar self-congratulatory turns of phrase. I shall of necessity limit my comments to several partial judgments and spare propositions, an approach that will not satisfy the desire for unequivocal conclusions, even where none can be expected, but that may serve the modest purpose of orienting us to the present situation and its prospects.

Three initial observations suggest themselves as a starting point with respect to Weber's contributions to understanding the conditions prevailing in our modern age. First, the material culture and the life-orientation that encouraged its formation have continued to slip farther and farther away from the actually existing ethos of what some have called a "slackening" and others a "self-absorption" characterizing contemporary culture. Weber's "ghost of dead religious beliefs" haunts the "culture of narcissism" of the critics at every turn. It inscribes the nightmares and cultural bad conscience otherwise known as the "cultural contradictions" of capitalist development. Second, the characteristic Weber conceived as an internal and lawful autonomy of the different life-orders and value-spheres has continued to be played out in terms of self-contained and self-regulating systems that are now, in our au courant language, "decoupled" from the world of everyday life and set in motion in opposition to it. Among the literati, fears arise that autonomous processes tend increasingly to shrink the sphere of personal autonomy. But among the technocrats a systems "theory" is hailed without regrets as the perfect instrument for bringing order to the messy life-world. Protests are locked with denials in a struggle for the soul of modernity. Third, the purposive-rational or instrumental action-orientation, Weber's *Zweckrationalität*, has become even more dominant as a mode of thought and action. The modern world and modern thought appear to take this form of rational calculation for granted, often simply assuming it to be synonymous with "rationality" itself.

Probably the most important of these generalizations is the last, partly because it incorporates aspects of the other two and partly because it has attracted universal assent. Purposive or instrumental rationality and its standards have been extended into every conceivable domain, including those spheres of action and association where it might be least expected (not to mention least wanted): family relations, child-rearing, love and friendship, art and aesthetic experience, knowledge and the inventions of mind, to name some of the most prominent. We have witnessed a series of continuing assaults on the sociocultural world by means-specific instrumentalities that have their true source and rationale in the production of technologies and in economic modes of action. Social problems tend to be addressed not in terms of their context, history, intrinsic nature, or unique character, but with a quick resort to generalizable and transferable formulae or recipes for "success." So-called success is in turn judged not according to achieved results, but in relation to efficiently deployable means. What can be said for social relations applies with equal force to personality and private relationships: prefabricated technique has priority. Furthermore, in the larger public world art becomes conceptual, while science achieves practicality. For modern painting, we are told, artistic production functions only as a procedure to illustrate the written word, the literary text, or the preexistent and most valorized interpretation of itself.[20] In a similar vein the province of knowledge can now be described as reduced to know-how, then transformed into "an informational commodity" that becomes indispensable both in economic production and in "the worldwide competition for [political] power."[21] Everywhere, it seems, rationality has been reduced to instrumental properties.

It is tempting to say that this development at the level of abstract

20. I take this to be the main argument in Tom Wolfe, *The Painted Word* (New York: Bantam, 1975).

21. Jean-François Lyotard, *The Postmodern Condition: A Report on Knowledge*, trans. G. Bennington and B. Massumi (Minneapolis: University of Minnesota Press, 1984), 5, as good an authority as any on the rationalization of modern science.

forces and relationships has occurred with a finality exceeding even Weber's expectations. If anything, he seems to have underestimated the
potential for the rapid extension and dominion of purposive-instrumen-
tal rationality, which has received a large assist from the development,
differentiation, and diffusion of new technologies of communication
and information "processing." The so-called technical progress of Weber's fin-de-siècle world has gone wild, creating novel possibilities about
which considerable disagreement prevails: for some, the promise of un-
impeded discussion leading to a revitalized public; for others, systematically controlled and distorted communication resulting in a desiccated
and depoliticized public sphere. At the present moment the realists seem
to have carried the day. With respect to Weber's most political application of his argument, there even appears now to be general agreement
from left to right that the most obvious concrete embodiment of instrumentally rational action, the new bureaucratic state, which has set out
to "rationalize" society with the best of intentions, has succeeded
mainly in disrupting social communication and overpowering associa-
tive activity. Thus, when we are told that "many current debates in the
United States are cast in terms implicitly structured along the lines suggested by Weber,"[22] this must mean not so much that we face a relatively uncomplicated "dilemma of rootless freedom versus oppressive
tradition," but rather that our public discourse is framed by purposive-
instrumental rationality and its far-reaching consequences versus the
criticisms, the alternatives, the putative other ways of conceiving what
is "rational."

What, then, can be said about these alleged alternatives, about the
responses to this state of affairs? In one sense the main lesson of the
present is that the flights from the cage of vocational specialization have
been popularized. Much of what used to characterize the margins of
culture has now been absorbed at the center, relabeled "counterculture"
or a suitable variant (such as "postmaterialism"), celebrated as a "life-
style," consumed as a commodity, reintegrated as a set of attitudes, and
along the way rendered harmless and trivial. We have learned to revel
in anticipation of approaching dilemmas of choice and aporias of
thought. Forms of "distancing" that used to provide badly needed perspective as a prerequisite for revolt have now been turned into attributes

22. These evaluations are made by David Kolb, *The Critique of Pure Modernity:
Hegel, Heidegger, and After* (Chicago: University of Chicago Press, 1986), 16–17; I say
uncomplicated, because if this is the dilemma, it will sooner or later be resolved in favor
of "freedom," whatever its form.

for being modern—that is, unattached, self-referential, capable of being remade at a moment's notice, always on the road to post-something-or-other. Marginalia have been overwhelmed by the bright glare of attention, distance suffocated in the embrace of lost convictions.

However, there are other, more serious constructions of modernity, "projects" for the modern in our upbeat imagery of design and the drawing board, that fill in the sketch of our theme and give it substance. The modern project of aesthetics must count as one significant response. For some social critics the influential standing of the "culturati" in the modern age is the reverse side of the expanding power of instrumental rationality. According to Daniel Bell, their high position may on the one hand signify that "culture has become the most dynamic impulse of our civilization," having an "unprecedented mission" that is "an official, ceaseless search for a new sensibility."[23] Of course, culture in this sense means not the material achievements of "technical progress," but on the contrary the aesthetic culture of the avant-garde, whose journey in search of the new, once it becomes socially legitimated, "serves to institutionalize the primacy of culture in the fields of manners, morals, and, ultimately, politics."[24] On the other hand such a perceived "primacy" can suggest to Jürgen Habermas that in our time "the potency to create meaning . . . has largely retreated into aesthetic precincts."[25] In either case, the obvious common message of these two observers of modernity, Bell and Habermas, who are in many other ways so radically opposed, is that Weber's "ethical atmosphere" of bourgeois culture as an authentic way of life, as the very "last of our heroisms," has been vaporized in the hothouse of aesthetic culture. Or stated in the recent language of a self-appointed "postmodernism," which is really aesthetic modernity with a prefixed afterthought, the "grand narratives" of the bourgeois epoch—reason, enlightenment, progress, dialectics of the spirit—have lost their competing powers of legitimation, leaving a vacuum of social

23. *The Cultural Contradictions of Capitalism* (New York: Basic Books, 1976), 33–34.
24. Ibid., 34.
25. Jürgen Habermas, *The Philosophical Discourse of Modernity: Twelve Lectures,* trans. F. Lawrence (Cambridge: MIT Press, 1987), 321. It should be remembered that Nietzsche's later, post-Wagnerian views were never so sanguine, as in his biting comment that ascetic ideals mean "*nothing whatever*" in the case of the artist. "Let us, first of all, eliminate the artists," he continues; "they do not stand nearly independently enough in the world and *against* the world for their changing valuations to deserve attention *in themselves*! They have at all times been valets of some morality, philosophy, or religion" (*On the Genealogy of Morals,* trans. W. Kaufmann [New York: Random House (Vintage Books), 1967], 102 [III, 5]).

illegitimacy that the purveyors of a new aesthetic have been eager to fill. Their art must lead the way for life—and to life.

The heroes of aesthetic culture have not reached this lofty goal, however. One impediment, according to the latest thinking, is that the search for the new has become exhausted, whether as a far too isolated and haughty "adversary culture" with respect to social modernity or as the overextended and self-defeating philosophy of subjectivism that has swept every objection before it across the plain of aesthetic culture. All the clamorous striving has only led into a cul-de-sac, and to uncertainty. But exhaustion is a strong term and a condition difficult to assess. These negative judgments are really premature expressions of optimism, for their proponents would like to hasten the departure of the project of aesthetics in favor (speaking for Bell and Habermas, respectively) of the past verities of a "liberal public philosophy" we may have thought we once had, but did not, or of the future truths of "communicative reason" we may think we want to attain, but can not.

Even if we set aside such deficits, an additional risk challenging the hopes for aesthetics, as found for instance in the later Theodor Adorno and Herbert Marcuse, lies in the undeniable threat that *any* generalizable aesthetic that is thought to open onto grand and novel vistas, cannot be commensurate with the actual condition of the aesthetic life-order, which has already been transformed under the tutelage of instrumental rationality as the handmaiden of social modernity. In the apt, if eccentric description of an envoy from the avant-garde, "Eclecticism is the degree zero of contemporary general culture. . . . This realism of the 'anything goes' is in fact that of money; in the absence of aesthetic criteria, it remains possible and useful to assess the value of works of art according to the profits they yield. Such realism accommodates all tendencies, just as capital accommodates all 'needs,' providing that the tendencies and needs have purchasing power."[26] The critics of the Weber Circle knew this decades ago: it is no longer a matter of *l'art pour l'art*, but of art for money's sake.

If aesthetics should by some extraordinary feat ever compete seriously with the grand narratives, then, like all its predecessors, it would also be subject to what could be called the different, but commensurable project of universal unmasking. The temperament of this project is perfectly captured in young Marx's immodest "ruthless criticism of everything existing," carried forward today with a Nietzschean skepticism

26. Lyotard, *Postmodern Condition*, 76.

about dialectical and all other forms of historicist science. Culminating in our own time with the work of Michel Foucault, it has become the critique of that "specific and peculiar rationalism of Western culture" located at the very heart of Weber's comparative-historical studies. Its special response to modernity has been to sift through our genealogical tables in order to show that our rationalism is indeed peculiar and suspect because it conceals its own negation: the will to power. What has been called rationalism is unmasked as the progeny of unmediated subjectivity: the gratification of ego, the pursuit of interest, the urge to dominate, the desire for revenge, the craving for spectacle, the yearning for ecstatic transcendence, and so on. It appears nothing can be excluded from the abode of a reason molded by the interest of usurping the rationality of world-domination.

One possibility for extending such criticism and rendering it concrete and "structural," so to speak, exists in a sociology of cultural institutions—the press and other media, universities, religious sects, art establishments, parties, voluntary associations, factories, the state—that was glimpsed by Weber himself in various parts of his work from the 1890s onward. Yet aside from the universal lessons about power, what such investigation reveals today is that in the ballyhooed long march through these institutions either "professionalism" or the "payoff" have been declared the winners, and certainly not the adversary culture of the avant-garde or the tough-minded proponents of a great alternative, at least not in the United States. There is no reason to believe, however, that the victorious powers cannot co-opt and exploit the usual ritualistic incantations about change—sweeping away worn-out traditionalism, conceiving every event in our unhistorical present as an epochal "crisis," pursuing the strategy of "mutually surpassing" one another and "overtrumping" every new lead, or using any means available to stay one step ahead of the "language of the tribe."

But does a positive telos lie concealed within this harsh order of critique? For some among the intelligentsia the passage to criticism and Weltschmerz does indeed indicate principally a desire to migrate to a different place, whether it be a reinvented unmodern past, a simpler non-Western or more humane non-"logocentric" culture, or a philosophically secure homeland of reasonable and responsible discourse. Like much else, universal unmasking is also the product of ennui and *ressentiment*, an opportunity for the displaced mind's revenge and relocation.

Today the most prominent version of a positive rejoinder to modernity's discontents is the project for a reconstruction of the everyday, which is essentially the invention of Habermas and his followers. There are numerous complex aspects to this particular renewal of modernity's emancipatory aims, but from our point of view its most striking attribute is also the least expected: the attempt to ground the promise for a rationalism that is conceived to be more comprehensive and richer than instrumental rationality in nothing more than "the communicative practice of everyday life."[27] This practice is identified with "the telos inscribed into communication in ordinary language" that can be brought forth in a very hopeful "step-by-step testable" critique of the "specific and peculiar rationalism" Weber granted to Western culture. The thesis is nothing if not daring, appearing as it does after endless modern expositions of breakdown in our communicative competence and the sinister deployment of language as power. Yet, according to this view, since Nietzsche the subjectivist philosophers of the "extraordinary" have registered little other than contempt for the everyday lifeworld and sought transformation instead in the logic of their own enthusiasms and their "need for the ineffable," as it has been called.[28] But their energies were misdirected by 180 degrees. The way out of the dead end of subjectivism lay before their eyes from the very beginning: in the rational procedures and forms of communicative action in the everyday world, made evident in "the model of unconstrained consensus formation in a communication community standing under cooperative constraints." Whatever such rare phrases may signify, for Habermas they contain the elements that were presupposed by all previous steps toward "de-differentiation," that is, toward reconciliation of the lifeorders of ethics, aesthetics, and science according to an ideal of unified experience.

To delve further into Habermas' "philosophical discourse," including his own self-criticism of communication in ordinary language as "a risky mechanism" for rational consensus formation that in modern times is easily replaced by *money*, would lead far beyond my objective. But even such a small admission reveals that the new project for everyday practice has not escaped the categories and strictures of social mo-

27. Habermas, *Philosophical Discourse of Modernity*, 311; *Alltagspraxis* is the key term. He also asserts that "reason is by its very nature incarnated in contexts of communicative action and in structures of the lifeworld" (322). For other representative statements of the ideas in this paragraph, see 295, 311, 314–16, 322–23, 339–41, 344–48.
28. Richard Rorty, "Habermas and Lyotard on Postmodernity," *Habermas and Modernity*, ed. Richard J. Bernstein (Cambridge: MIT Press, 1985), 174.

dernity. Indeed, how could it? Any honest assessment of instrumental rationality will show that it has led not only to new forms of domination, from which none of us are exempt, but also to a momentous separation between the contemporary bureaucratic state and the critics' sense of culture as the intellectual, spiritual, and aesthetic condition characterizing a way of life. There is a political response nourished in the ground of culture in this sense that has become distinctive of modernity, and of which Habermas' argument is exemplary.

Yet all of the three projects I have discussed, notwithstanding their obvious differences, seem to share an understanding of culture in its various modes as the source of political potentialities. What seems to be underway in modernity is the generation of political positions and sociopolitical movements in the cultural sphere that become publicly engaged at the boundaries between that sphere and the bureaucratic state with its administered societal counterparts. It is for this reason that even critics operating with divergent assumptions can speak of institutionalizing the "primacy of culture" in the field of politics; or suggest that having conquered manners, customs, and morals, culture can proceed to gain hegemony over politics, as if moving through stages of a continuum; or assert that "it is no accident that social movements today take on cultural-revolutionary traits."[29] My sense of such remarks and the development they disclose is that conflicts at the boundary between culture and system (using a simplified terminology) have become the substance of both normal, everyday politics and the most marginal groping toward unforeseen transformation. Even our thought and scholarship that are most modern have followed this lead by discovering the political import of sociocultural history and the cultural criticism of manners, morals, and the mission of civilization itself.

What, then, are the prospects for guidance by these projects? Do they only retrace the aimless wanderings of subjectivity in a rationalized world? Can they set the modern consciousness on a purposeful course, or must they, like Plato's painted surface, maintain "a most majestic silence" when questioned? Can they conceive a politics beyond both instrumental rationality and aesthetic experience?

Much depends on whether we are prepared to qualify or surrender a matter-of-fact orientation toward the self and the world. The issue is not Weber's reading of our history, whose basic themes have remained

29. Bell, *Cultural Contradictions of Capitalism*, 34, and passim; Habermas, *Philosophical Discourse of Modernity*, 365.

very much intact, but rather our own intellectualism. It is not a question of *whether we can* imagine responses or alternatives (which are never lacking), but of *how and why we should choose* to do so. The questioning of modernity is not only a philosophical discourse; it is also a wider discourse with historical, sociological, and psychological subtexts. What we now need is not so much seductive "grand narratives" and enticing routes of escape, but rather temporally bounded, self-restrained, and specific inquiries that bring our history back into view and retrieve the concrete and particular, the locally expressed, the individually experienced, the detailed. We should aim to plot a specific course through the elements that compose the necessary clash between the subjectivism of aesthetic culture and the impersonal forces of existing material culture. If we can learn to play off one against the other, then it should not be with the goal of finding a single point of reconciliation or a way of abolishing the warring elements, for neither is possible in the actual historical world, but rather with the quite modest aim of advancing our education—learning to comprehend the substance of material culture in order to appropriate it for our own purposes and uses.

Stated somewhat differently, the configuration of thought and action I have chosen to call the politics of modern culture can at its best become a form of self-creation, a practice of bringing into subjective consciousness and, in this quite specific and limited sense, "under control" those elements of abstract objectivity existing independently of individual mind. This contemporary adventure is a precondition for freeing the modern subject from the subversive tyranny of our modernized environment, although it is not yet that elusive and hard quality called "freedom" or "emancipation." But as the original alternative to repeated flights from ourselves, it is on the path toward that quality.

Perhaps this is all that can honestly be said about modernity and a politics of culture today. The discussions of our century, to which Weber contributed in a significant way, reveal the problem of the modern as a politically aware critique of the rationalist cultural forms associated with our disenchanted life-world. This multifaceted critique includes a range of adaptive responses to discontents generated by those driving forces of our modern world and its impersonal material culture. Any modern politics sustained by criticism of culture must be included against its will in the workings of these forces, and thus it is a politics always threatened with extension into the concise and violent syntax of romantic rebellion or into other ironies of escape.

Ironic willfulness is already a way of underscoring our own distance and superfluity, our sense of transience and insignificance in relation to a history and a culture increasingly governed by the process of disenchantment underway in Western culture at least since Plato's discovery of the power of writing and recorded conceptual thought. The sense of expansive discrepancy, of an increasingly radical tension between this world and the thought-to-be-inviolable self seems to be at the basis of our most serious and austere responses to a disenchanted fate. Yet there comes a moment when even the adventures of criticism have run their course, when the idea of a truly transparent world shows itself as the need for solace in the face of our fatalities and the unknown—the kind of reassurance that the most astute critique can never satisfy.

We should not want to deny the consolation that lies beyond the world and beyond critique, but neither should we want to sacrifice responsibility for our history, our world, our knowledge, or the fate of our times. Our response to modern culture should aspire to realize at least that purpose.

Bibliography of Works Cited

A. WORKS BY MAX WEBER

The authoritative bibliography of Max Weber's writings in German is the *Prospekt der Max Weber Gesamtausgabe*, published by J. C. B. Mohr (Paul Siebeck) in Tübingen. This bibliography is used as the basis for the publication of Weber's collected works that is now in progress. The chronological listing that follows includes only works cited in my text and is not meant to be comprehensive.

1. In German

Die römische Agrargeschichte. Stuttgart: Enke, 1891.
"Zur Rechtfertigung Göhres." *Die Christliche Welt* 6 (24 November 1892): 1104–9.
"'Privatenquêten' über die Lage der Landarbeiter." *Mitteilungen des Evangelisch-sozialen Kongresses*, nos. 4–6 (1892).
Die Lage der Landarbeiter im ostelbischen Deutschland. 1892. Part I, vol. 3 (cited I/3) of *Max Weber Gesamtausgabe*. Edited by Martin Riesebrodt. Tübingen: J. C. B. Mohr (Paul Siebeck), 1984.
"Die Evangelisch-sozialen Kurse in Berlin im Herbst dieses Jahres." *Die Christliche Welt* 7 (3 August 1893): 766–68.
"Die Erhebung des Vereins für Sozialpolitik über die Lage der Landarbeiter." *Das Land* 1 (1893): 8–9, 24–26, 43–45, 58–59, 129–30, 147–48.
"Die ländliche Arbeitsverfassung." *Verhandlungen des Vereins für Sozialpolitik*. In *Schriften des Vereins für Sozialpolitik* 58 (1893): 62–86.
[Diskussionsbeitrag in der Debatte über die ländlichen Arbeiterverhältnisse.] *Verhandlungen des Vereins für Sozialpolitik*. In *Schriften des Vereins für Sozialpolitik* 58 (1893): 128–33.

"Entwicklungstendenzen in der Lage der ostelbischen Landarbeiter." *Archiv für soziale Gesetzgebung und Statistik* 7 (1894): 1–41.

"Entwicklungstendenzen in der Lage der ostelbischen Landarbeiter" (1894). In *Gesammelte Aufsätze zur Sozial- und Wirtschaftsgeschichte*, edited by Marianne Weber, 470–507. Tübingen: J. C. B. Mohr (Paul Siebeck), 1924. Revision of the preceding essay.

"Was heisst Christlich-Sozial?" *Die Christliche Welt* 8 (17 May 1894): 472–77.

"Zum Preßstreit über den Evangelisch-sozialen Kongress." *Die Christliche Welt* 8 (12 July 1894): 668–73.

"Argentinische Kolonistenwirthschaften." *Deutsches Wochenblatt* 7 (1894): 20–22, 57–59.

Review of *Die Rechtsverhältnisse der Fremden in Argentinien*, by B. Lehman. *Zeitschrift für des gesammte Handelsrecht* 42 (1894): 326–27.

"Die deutschen Landarbeiter." In *Bericht über die Verhandlungen des 5. Evangelisch-sozialen Kongresses*, 61–82, 92–94. Berlin: Rehtwisch & Langewort, 1894.

"Der Nationalstaat und die Volkswirtschaftspolitik, Akademische Antrittsrede" (1895). In *Gesammelte Politische Schriften*, 2d ed., edited by Johannes Winckelmann, 1–25. Tübingen: J. C. B. Mohr (Paul Siebeck), 1958.

"Die Börse" (1895–96). In *Gesammelte Aufsätze zur Soziologie und Sozialpolitik*, edited by Marianne Weber, 256–322. Tübingen: J. C. B. Mohr (Paul Siebeck), 1924.

"Die Ergebnisse der deutschen Börsenenquete." *Zeitschrift für das gesammte Handelsrecht* 43–45 (1895–96): 83–219, 457–514; 29–74; 69–157.

"Die sozialen Gründe des Untergangs der antiken Kultur" (1896). In *Gesammelte Aufsätze zur Sozial- und Wirtschaftsgeschichte*, edited by Marianne Weber, 289–311. Tübingen: J. C. B. Mohr (Paul Siebeck), 1924.

"Zur Gründung einer national-sozialen Partei" (1896). In *Gesammelte Politische Schriften*, 2d ed., edited by Johannes Winckelmann, 26–29. Tübingen: J. C. B. Mohr (Paul Siebeck), 1958.

"Agrarverhältnisse im Altertum." In *Handwörterbuch der Staatswissenschaften*, edited by J. Conrad, 1–18. Jena: Fischer, 1897.

[Diskussionsbeitrag zum Vortrag Karl Oldenberg, Über Deutschland als Industriestaat.] In *Verhandlungen des 8. Evangelisch-sozialen Kongresses*, 105–13, 122–23. Göttingen: Vandenhoeck & Ruprecht, 1897.

"Grundriss zu den Vorlesungen über allgemeine ('theoretische') Nationalökonomie." Heidelberg, 1898. Manuscript.

"Die begrifflichen Grundlagen der Volkswirtschaftslehre: Erstes Buch." Heidelberg, 1898. Manuscript.

"Agrarverhältnisse im Altertum." In *Handwörterbuch der Staatswissenschaften*, 2d, rev. ed., edited by J. Conrad, 1:57–85. Jena: Fischer, 1898.

"Geleitwort." *Archiv für Sozialwissenschaft und Sozialpolitik* 19 (1904): i–vii.

"Die 'Objektivität' sozialwissenschaftlicher und sozialpolitischer Erkenntnis" (1904). In *Gesammelte Aufsätze zur Wissenschaftslehre*, 3d ed., edited by Johannes Winckelmann, 146–214. Tübingen: J. C. B. Mohr (Paul Siebeck), 1968.

"Der Streit um den Character der altgermanischen Sozialverfassung in der deutschen Literatur des letzten Jahrzehnts" (1904). In *Gesammelte Aufsätze zur Sozial- und Wirtschaftsgeschichte*, edited by Marianne Weber, 508–56. Tübingen: J. C. B. Mohr (Paul Siebeck), 1924.

"Roscher und Knies und die logischen Probleme der historischen National-ökonomie" (1903–6). In *Gesammelte Aufsätze zur Wissenschaftslehre*, 3d ed., edited by Johannes Winckelmann, 1–145. Tübingen: J. C. B. Mohr (Paul Siebeck), 1968.

"Zur Lage der bürgerlichen Demokratie in Russland." *Archiv für Sozialwissenschaft und Sozialpolitik* 22 (1906): 234–353 (supplement).

"Russlands Übergang zum Scheinkonstitutionalismus." *Archiv für Sozialwissenschaft und Sozialpolitik* 23 (1906): 165–401 (supplement).

"'Kirchen' und 'Sekten' in Nordamerika." *Die Christliche Welt* 20 (1906): 558–62, 577–83.

"Zur Stellung der Frau im modernen Erwerbsleben." *Frankfurter Zeitung*, 13 August 1906, 222.

"Die badische Fabrikinspektion." *Frankfurter Zeitung*, 24 January 1907, 24.

"Bemerkungen zu der vorstehenden 'Replik'" (1908). In *Die protestantische Ethik II: Kritiken und Antikritiken*, edited by Johannes Winckelmann, 44–56. Munich: Siebenstern, 1968.

"Agrarverhältnisse im Altertum" (1909). In *Gesammelte Aufsätze zur Sozial- und Wirtschaftsgeschichte*, edited by Marianne Weber, 1–288. Tübingen: J. C. B. Mohr (Paul Siebeck), 1924.

"Einladung zum Beitritt zur Deutschen Gesellschaft für Soziologie" (1909). Zentrales Staatsarchiv Merseburg, Nachlass Sombart 18b: 1–4.

"Antikritisches zum 'Geist' des Kapitalismus" (1910). In *Die protestantische Ethik II: Kritiken und Antikritiken*, edited by Johannes Winckelmann, 149–86. Munich: Siebenstern, 1968.

"Antikritisches Schlusswort zum 'Geist des Kapitalismus'" (1910). In *Die protestantische Ethik II: Kritiken und Antikritiken*, edited by Johannes Winckelmann, 283–345. Munich: Siebenstern, 1968.

[Diskussionsbeiträge auf dem 3. Deutschen Hochschullehrertag.] In *Verhandlungen des III. Deutschen Hochschullehrertages*, 6, 16–17, 20–21, 41–42, 47. Leipzig: Verlag des Literarischen Zentralblattes für Deutschland, 1910.

[Diskussionsbeiträge in der Debatte über die Produktivität der Volkswirtschaft.] *Verhandlungen des Vereins für Sozialpolitik*. In *Schriften des Vereins für Sozialpolitik* 132 (1910): 580–85, 603–7, 610–11, 614.

"Geschäftsbericht der Deutschen Gesellschaft für Soziologie" (1910). In *Verhandlungen des Ersten Deutschen Soziologentages*, 39–62. Tübingen: J. C. B. Mohr (Paul Siebeck), 1911.

[Diskussionsbeitrag in der Debatte über Werner Sombart, "Technik und Kultur"] (1910). In *Verhandlungen des Ersten Deutschen Soziologentages*, 95–101. Tübingen: J. C. B. Mohr (Paul Siebeck), 1911.

"Vorläufiger Bericht über eine vorgeschlagene Erhebung über die Soziologie des Zeitungswesens" (1910–11). Zentrales Staatsarchiv Merseburg, Nachlass Sombart 18b: 200–210.

"Über einige Kategorien der verstehenden Soziologie" (1913). In *Gesammelte Aufsätze zur Wissenschaftslehre*, 3d ed., edited by Johannes Winckelmann, 427–74. Tübingen: J. C. B. Mohr (Paul Siebeck), 1968.

"Gutachten zur Werturteilsdiskussion im Ausschuss des Vereins für Sozialpolitik" (1913). In *Max Weber: Werk und Person*, edited by Eduard Baumgarten, 102–39. Tübingen: J. C. B. Mohr (Paul Siebeck), 1964.

"Zwischen zwei Gesetzen" (1916). In *Zur Politik im Weltkrieg: Schriften und Reden, 1914–1918.* Part I, vol. 15 (cited I/15), 95–98, of *Max Weber Gesamtausgabe.* Edited by Wolfgang J. Mommsen and Gangolf Hübinger. Tübingen: J. C. B. Mohr (Paul Siebeck), 1984.

"Der Sinn der 'Wertfreiheit' der soziologischen und ökonomischen Wissenschaften" (1917). In *Gesammelte Aufsätze zur Wissenschaftslehre*, 3d ed., edited by Johannes Winckelmann, 489–540. Tübingen: J. C. B. Mohr (Paul Siebeck), 1968.

"Das preussische Wahlrecht" (1917). In *Zur Politik im Weltkrieg: Schriften und Reden, 1914–1918.* Part I, vol. 15 (cited I/15), 224–35, of *Max Weber Gesamtausgabe.* Edited by Wolfgang J. Mommsen and Gangolf Hübinger. Tübingen: J. C. B. Mohr (Paul Siebeck), 1984.

"Wahlrecht und Demokratie in Deutschland" (1917). In *Zur Politik im Weltkrieg: Schriften und Reden, 1914–1918.* Part I, vol. 15 (cited I/15), 347–96, of *Max Weber Gesamtausgabe.* Edited by Wolfgang J. Mommsen and Gangolf Hübinger. Tübingen: J. C. B. Mohr (Paul Siebeck), 1984.

"Parlament und Regierung im neugeordneten Deutschland: Zur politischen Kritik des Beamtentums und Parteiwesens" (1918). In *Zur Politik im Weltkrieg: Schriften und Reden, 1914–1918.* Part I, vol. 15 (cited I/15), 432–596, of *Max Weber Gesamtausgabe.* Edited by Wolfgang J. Mommsen and Gangolf Hübinger. Tübingen: J. C. B. Mohr (Paul Siebeck), 1984.

"Der Sozialismus" (1918). In *Zur Politik im Weltkrieg: Schriften und Reden, 1914–1918.* Part I, vol. 15 (cited I/15), 599–633, of *Max Weber Gesamtausgabe.* Edited by Wolfgang J. Mommsen and Gangolf Hübinger. Tübingen: J. C. B. Mohr (Paul Siebeck), 1984.

"Wissenschaft als Beruf" (1919 [orig. 1917]). In *Gesammelte Aufsätze zur Wissenschaftslehre*, 3d ed., edited by Johannes Winckelmann, 582–613. Tübingen: J. C. B. Mohr (Paul Siebeck), 1968.

"Politik als Beruf" (1919). In *Gesammelte Politische Schriften*, 2d ed., 493–548, edited by Johannes Winckelmann. Tübingen: J. C. B. Mohr (Paul Siebeck), 1958.

Gesammelte Aufsätze zur Religionssoziologie. 3 vols. Tübingen: J. C. B. Mohr (Paul Siebeck), 1920.

Gesammelte Aufsätze zur Sozial- und Wirtschaftsgeschichte. Edited by Marianne Weber. Tübingen: J. C. B. Mohr (Paul Siebeck), 1924.

Gesammelte Aufsätze zur Soziologie und Sozialpolitik. Edited by Marianne Weber. Tübingen: J. C. B. Mohr (Paul Siebeck), 1924.

Jugendbriefe. Edited by Marianne Weber. Tübingen: J. C. B. Mohr (Paul Siebeck), 1936.

Gesammelte Politische Schriften. 2d ed., edited by Johannes Winckelmann. Tübingen: J. C. B. Mohr (Paul Siebeck), 1958.

Gesammelte Aufsätze zur Wissenschaftslehre. 3d ed., edited by Johannes Winckelmann. Tübingen: J. C. B. Mohr (Paul Siebeck), 1968.
Zur Politik im Weltkrieg: Schriften und Reden, 1914–1918. Part I, vol. 15 (cited I/15) of *Max Weber Gesamtausgabe.* Edited by Wolfgang J. Mommsen and Gangolf Hübinger. Tübingen: J. C. B. Mohr (Paul Siebeck), 1984.

2. English Translations

From Max Weber: Essays in Sociology. Edited by Hans Gerth and C. Wright Mills. New York: Oxford University Press, 1946.
The Methodology of the Social Sciences. Edited by E. A. Shils and H. Finch. New York: Free Press, 1949.
"The Social Causes of the Decay of Ancient Civilization." *Journal of General Education* 5 (1950): 75–88.
The Protestant Ethic and the Spirit of Capitalism. Translated by Talcott Parsons. New York: Scribner's, 1958.
The Rational and Social Foundations of Music. Translated and edited by D. Martindale et al. Carbondale: Southern Illinois University Press, 1958.
General Economic History. Translated by F. Knight. New York: Collier, 1961.
Economy and Society. 3 vols. Edited by G. Roth and C. Wittich. New York: Bedminster, 1968.
"Socialism." In *Max Weber: The Interpretation of Social Reality,* Edited by J. Eldridge, 191–219. London: Joseph, 1970.
"Georg Simmel as Sociologist." Translated by D. N. Levine. *Social Research* 39 (1972): 158–63.
Max Weber on Universities. Edited by E. Shils. Chicago: University of Chicago Press, 1974.
Roscher and Knies: The Logical Problems of Historical Economics. Translated by Guy Oakes. New York: Free Press, 1975.
The Agrarian Sociology of Ancient Civilizations. Translated by R. I. Frank. London: NLB, 1976.
Max Weber: Selections in Translation. Edited by W. G. Runciman. Cambridge: Cambridge University Press, 1978.
"Anticritical Last Word on *The Spirit of Capitalism.*" Translated by Wallace M. Davis. *American Journal of Sociology* 83 (1978): 1110–30.
"Developmental Tendencies in the Situation of East Elbian Rural Labourers." Translated by Keith Tribe. *Economy and Society* 8 (1979): 177–205.
"The National State and Economic Policy (Freiburg Address)." Translated by Keith Tribe. *Economy and Society* 9 (1980): 428–49.
"Some Categories of Interpretive Sociology." Translated by Edith Graber. *Sociological Quarterly* 22 (1981): 151–80.

B. OTHER WORKS

Alexander, Jeffrey C. *The Classical Attempt at Theoretical Synthesis: Max Weber.* Berkeley: University of California Press, 1983.
Antonio, Robert J., and Glassman, R. M., eds. *A Weber-Marx Dialogue.* Lawrence: University of Kansas Press, 1985.

Antoni, Carlo. *From History to Sociology: The Transition in German Histori-cal Thinking.* Translated by H. White. London: Merlin, 1962.

Arato, Andrew, and Breines, Paul. *The Young Lukács and the Origins of West-ern Marxism.* New York: Seabury, 1979.

Arendt, Hannah. *Crises of the Republic.* New York: Harvest, 1969.

Aron, Raymond. "Max Weber and Power Politics." In *Max Weber and Soci-ology Today,* edited by O. Stammer, 83–100. New York: Harper & Row, 1972.

Atoji, Yoshio. "Georg Simmel and Max Weber." In *Sociology at the Turn of the Century,* 47–95. Tokyo: Dobunkan, 1984.

Baier, Horst. "Die Gesellschaft—Ein langer Schatten des Toten Gottes: Fried-rich Nietzsche und die Entstehung der Soziologie aus dem Geist der Deca-dence." *Nietzsche-Studien* 10/11 (1982): 6–22.

Baumgarten, Eduard. *Max Weber: Werk und Person.* Tübingen: J. C. B. Mohr (Paul Siebeck), 1964.

Baumgarten, Hermann. *Der deutsche Liberalismus: Eine Selbstkritik* (1866) Frankfurt: Ullstein, 1974.

Beetham, David. *Max Weber and the Theory of Modern Politics.* London: Allen & Unwin, 1974.

Bell, Daniel. *The Cultural Contradictions of Capitalism.* New York: Basic Books, 1976.

Below, Georg von. Review of *Studien zur Entwicklungsgeschichte des moder-nen Kapitalismus,* by Werner Sombart. *Jahrbücher für Nationalökonomie und Statistik* 105 (1915): 396–402.

Bendix, Reinhard. *Max Weber, An Intellectual Portrait.* 2d ed. Berkeley: Uni-versity of California Press, 1977.

Bendix, Reinhard, and Guenther Roth. *Scholarship and Partisanship: Essays on Max Weber.* Berkeley: University of California Press, 1971.

Berman, Marshall. *All That Is Solid Melts into Air: The Experience of Mo-dernity.* New York: Simon & Schuster, 1982.

Bernstein, Richard J., ed. *Habermas and Modernity.* Cambridge: MIT Press, 1985.

Böhringer, H., and Gründer, K., eds. *Ästhetik und Soziologie um die Jahrhun-dertwende: Georg Simmel.* Frankfurt: Klostermann, 1976.

Bottomore, Tom, and Goode, P., eds. *Austro-Marxism.* Oxford: Clarendon Press, 1978.

Bradbury, Malcolm, and McFarlane, James, eds. *Modernism 1890–1930.* New York: Penguin, 1976.

Braun, Heinrich. "Zur Einführung." *Archiv für soziale Gesetzgebung und Sta-tistik* 1 (1888): 1–6.

Brentano, Lujo. "Die Volkswirthschaft und ihre konkreten Grundbedingun-gen," *Zeitschrift für Sozial- und Wirthschaftsgeschichte* 1 (1893): 77–148.

Brubaker, Rogers. *The Limits of Rationality: An Essay on the Social and Moral Thought of Max Weber.* London: Allen & Unwin, 1984.

Burckhardt, Jakob. *Griechische Kulturgeschichte.* 2 vols. Berlin: Spemann, 1898.

Burger, Thomas. *Max Weber's Theory of Concept Formation: History, Laws, and Ideal Types.* 2d ed. Durham: Duke University Press, 1987.

Clausen, L., and Pappi, F., eds. *Ankunft bei Tönnies*. Kiel: Mühlau, 1981.

Cohen, G. A. *Karl Marx's Theory of History: A Defence*. Princeton: Princeton University Press, 1978.

Collins, Randall. *Weberian Sociological Theory*. Cambridge: Cambridge University Press, 1986.

Curtius, Ludwig, *Deutsche und Antike Welt: Lebenserinnerungen*. Stuttgart: Deutsche Verlags-Anstalt, 1950.

Dahme, H.-J., and Rammstedt, O., eds. *Georg Simmel und die Moderne*. Frankfurt: Suhrkamp, 1984.

Dibble, Vernon K. "Social Science and Political Commitments in the Young Max Weber." *Archives européennes de sociologie* 9 (1968): 92–110.

Dohm, Hedwig. "Nietzsche und die Frauen." *Die Zukunft* 25 (24 December 1898): 534–43.

Durkheim, Emile. *Socialism and Saint-Simon*. Edited by A. Gouldner. London: Routledge & Kegan Paul, 1959.

Eden, Robert. *Political Leadership and Nihilism: A Study of Weber and Nietzsche*. Tampa: University Presses of Florida, 1984.

Faught, Jim. "Neglected Affinities: Max Weber and Georg Simmel." *British Journal of Sociology* 36 (1985), 155–74.

Finley, Moses I. *The Ancient Economy*. Berkeley: University of California Press, 1973.

———. *Ancient Slavery and Modern Ideology*. New York: Viking, 1980.

———. *Economy and Society in Ancient Greece*. London: Chatto & Windus, 1981.

Fleischmann, Eugène. "De Weber à Nietzsche." *Archives européennes de sociologie* 5 (1964): 190–238.

Förster, Friedrich Wilhelm. *Politische Ethik und politische Pädagogik; Mit besonderer Berücksichtigung der kommenden Aufgaben*. 3d ed. Munich: Reinhardt, 1918.

Freud, Sigmund. *Civilization and Its Discontents* (1930). Translated by J. Strachey. New York: Norton, 1961.

Friess, Horace L. *Felix Adler and Ethical Culture: Memories and Studies*. Edited by F. Weingartner. New York: Columbia University Press, 1981.

Frisby, David. "Introduction to the Translation." In *The Philosophy of Money*, by Georg Simmel, 1–49. London: Routledge & Kegan Paul, 1978.

———. *Sociological Impressionism: A Reassessment of Georg Simmel's Social Theory*. London: Heinemann, 1981.

———. *Fragments of Modernity: Theories of Modernity in the Work of Simmel, Kracauer and Benjamin*. Cambridge: Polity Press, 1985.

Fügen, H. N. *Max Weber*. Hamburg: Rowohlt, 1985.

Gablik, Suzi. *Progress in Art*. New York: Rizzoli, 1977.

Gassen, Kurt, and Landmann, Michael, eds. *Buch des Dankes an Georg Simmel: Briefe, Erinnerungen, Bibliographie*. Berlin: Duncker & Humblot, 1958.

Gay, Peter. *Weimar Culture: The Outsider as Insider*. New York: Harper & Row, 1968.

Glockner, Hermann. *Heidelberger Bilderbuch: Erinnerungen*. Bonn: Bouvier, 1969.

Gluck, Mary. *Georg Lukács and His Generation, 1900–1918*. Cambridge: Harvard University Press, 1985.

Green, Martin. *The von Richthofen Sisters: The Triumphant and the Tragic Modes of Love*. New York: Basic Books, 1974.

———. *Mountain of Truth: The Counterculture Begins, Ascona, 1900–1920*. Hanover, N.H.: University Press of New England, 1986.

Habermas, Jürgen. *Toward a Rational Society*. Translated by J. Shapiro. London: Heinemann, 1971.

———. "Simmel als Zeitdiagnostiker." In *Philosophische Kultur*, by Georg Simmel, 243–53. Berlin: Wagenbach, 1983.

———. *Der philosophische Diskurs der Moderne*. Frankfurt: Suhrkamp, 1985.

———. *The Philosophical Discourse of Modernity: Twelve Lectures*. Translated by F. Lawrence. Cambridge: MIT Press, 1987.

Hammacher, Emil. *Das philosophisch-ökonomische System des Marxismus*. Leipzig: Duncker & Humblot, 1909.

———. *Hauptfragen der modernen Kultur*. Leipzig: Teubner, 1914.

Hegel, G. W. F. *The Philosophy of Right*. Edited by T. M. Knox. London: Oxford University Press, 1967.

Heidegger, Martin. *The Question Concerning Technology and Other Essays*. Translated by W. Lovitt. New York: Harper & Row, 1977.

Hennis, Wilhelm. *Max Webers Fragestellung: Studien zur Biographie des Werks*. Tübingen: J. C. B. Mohr (Paul Siebeck), 1987.

Heuss, Alfred. "Max Webers Bedeutung für die Geschichte des griechisch-römischen Altertums." *Historische Zeitschrift* 201 (1965): 529–56.

Honigsheim, Paul. "Der Max-Weber-Kreis in Heidelberg." *Kölner Vierteljahrshefte für Soziologie* 5 (1926): 270–87.

———. *On Max Weber*. Translated by J. Rytina. New York: Free Press, 1968.

Horkheimer, Max, and T. W. Adorno. *Dialectic of Enlightenment* (1944). Translated by J. Cumming. New York: Continuum, 1987.

Hübinger, Gangolf. "Kulturkritik und Kulturpolitik des Eugen-Diederichs-Verlags im Wilhelminismus: Auswege aus der Krise der Moderne?" *Troeltsch-Studien* 4 (1987): 92–114.

Hughes, H. Stuart. *Consciousness and Society: The Reorientation of European Social Thought, 1890–1930*. New York: Random House (Vintage Books), 1958.

Jaspers, Karl. *Max Weber: Eine Gedenkrede*. Tübingen: J. C. B. Mohr (Paul Siebeck), 1926.

Jay, Martin. *Marxism and Totality: The Adventures of a Concept from Lukács to Habermas*. Berkeley: University of California Press, 1984.

Jellinek, Georg. *Allgemeine Staatslehre*. Berlin: Häring, 1900.

———. *Verfassungsänderung und Verfassungswandlung*. Berlin: Häring, 1906.

———. *Ausgewählte Schriften und Reden*. 2 vols. Berlin: Häring, 1911.

Käsler, Dirk. *Einführung in das Studium Max Webers*. Munich: Beck, 1979.

———. *Die frühe deutsche Soziologie 1909 bis 1934 und ihre Entstehungs-Milieus*. Opladen: Westdeutscher Verlag, 1984.

Knapp, Georg F. *Die Bauern-Befreiung und der Ursprung der Landarbeiter*. Leipzig: Duncker & Humblot, 1887.

————. "Die ländliche Arbeiterfrage." *Verhandlungen des Vereins für Sozial-politik.* In *Schriften des Vereins für Sozialpolitik* 58 (1893): 6–23.

————. *Die Landarbeiter in Knechtschaft und Freiheit: Gesammelte Vorträge.* 2d ed. Leipzig: Duncker & Humblot, 1909.

König, René, and Johannes Winckelmann, eds. *Max Weber zum Gedächtnis.* Cologne: Westdeutscher Verlag, 1964.

Kolb, David. *The Critique of Pure Modernity: Hegel, Heidegger, and After.* Chicago: University of Chicago Press, 1986.

Landmann, Michael. "Arthur Steins Erinnerungen an Georg Simmel." In *Ästhetik und Soziologie um die Jahrhundertwende: Georg Simmel.* Edited by H. Böhringer and K. Grunder, 272–76. Frankfurt: Klostermann, 1976.

————. "Georg Simmel und Stefan George." In *Georg Simmel und die Moderne.* Edited by H.-J. Dahme and O. Rammstedt, 147–73. Frankfurt: Suhrkamp, 1984.

Lash, Scott, and Whimster, Sam, eds. *Max Weber: Rationality and Modernity.* London: Allen & Unwin, 1987.

Leichter, Käthe. "Max Weber als Lehrer und Politiker." In *Max Weber zum Gedächtnis,* edited by R. König and J. Winckelmann, 125–42. Cologne: Westdeutscher Verlag, 1964.

Lepsius, Sabine. *Ein Berliner Künstlerleben um die Jahrhundertwende.* Munich: Gotthold Müller, 1972.

Levine, Donald N. Introduction to "Georg Simmel as Sociologist," by Max Weber. *Social Research* 39 (1972): 155–58.

————. *The Flight from Ambiguity: Essays in Social and Cultural Theory.* Chicago: University of Chicago Press, 1985.

Lichtblau, Klaus. "Das 'Pathos der Distanz,' Präliminarien zur Nietzsche-Rezeption bei Georg Simmel." In *Georg Simmel und die Moderne,* edited by H.-J. Dahme and O. Rammstedt, 231–81. Frankfurt: Suhrkamp, 1984.

Löwith, Karl. *Max Weber and Karl Marx* (1932). Translated by H. Fantel. London: Allen & Unwin, 1982.

————. "Die Entzauberung der Welt durch Wissenschaft." *Merkur* 18 (1964): 501–19.

Lukács, Georg. *Soul and Form* (1911). Translated by A. Bostock. Cambridge: MIT Press, 1974.

————. "Von der Armut am Geiste: Ein Gespräch und ein Brief," *Neue Blätter* 2 (1912): 67–92.

————. *The Theory of the Novel* (1916). Translated by A. Bostock. Cambridge: MIT Press, 1971.

————. "Georg Simmel" (1918). In *Buch des Dankes an Georg Simmel,* edited by K. Gassen and M. Landmann, 171–76. Berlin: Duncker & Humblot, 1958.

————. *History and Class Consciousness* (1923). Translated by Rodney Livingstone. Cambridge: MIT Press, 1971.

————. *Die Zerstörung der Vernunft.* Berlin: Aufbau-Verlag, 1955.

————. *Schriften zur Literatursoziologie.* 4th ed. Neuwied: Luchterhand, 1970.

————. *Georg Lukács Briefwechsel, 1902–1917.* Edited by E. Karádi and E. Fekete. Stuttgart: Metzler, 1982.

————. *Georg Lukács: Selected Correspondence, 1902–1920.* Edited and translated by Judith Marcus and Zoltán Tar. New York: Columbia University Press, 1986.

Lunn, Eugene. *Marxism and Modernism: An Historical Study of Lukács, Brecht, Benjamin and Adorno.* Berkeley: University of California Press, 1982.

Lyotard, Jean-François. *The Postmodern Condition: A Report on Knowledge.* Translated by G. Bennington and B. Massumi. Minneapolis: University of Minnesota Press, 1984.

Mann, Thomas. *Reflections of a Nonpolitical Man* (1918). Translated by W. D. Morris. New York: Ungar, 1983.

————. *Pro and Contra Wagner.* Translated by A. Blunden. Chicago: University of Chicago Press, 1985.

Marcuse, Herbert. "Industrialization and Capitalism." In *Max Weber and Sociology Today,* edited by O. Stammer, 133–51. New York: Harper & Row, 1972.

Márkus, György. "Life and the Soul: The Young Lukács and the Problem of Culture." In *Lukács Reappraised,* edited by A. Heller, 1–26. New York: Columbia University Press, 1983.

Marx, Karl. *Capital* (1867). Vol. 1. New York: International Publishers, 1967.

————. *Das Kapital: Kritik der politischen Ökonomie.* Vol. 3. Edited by F. Engels. Hamburg: Meissner, 1894.

Marx, Karl, and Friedrich Engels. *Werke.* Berlin: Dietz, 1973– .

————. *The Marx-Engels Reader.* 2d ed. Edited by R. Tucker. New York: Norton, 1978.

Maurenbrecher, Max. *Die Gebildeten und die Sozialdemokratie.* Leipzig: Leipziger Buchdruckerei, 1904.

Meinecke, Friedrich. "Max Weber" (1927), Review of *Max Weber: Ein Lebensbild,* by Marianne Weber. In *Max Weber zum Gedächtnis,* edited by R. König and J. Winckelmann, 143–47. Cologne: Westdeutscher Verlag, 1964.

Merleau-Ponty, Maurice. *The Primacy of Perception and Other Essays.* Edited by J. M. Edie. Evanston: Northwestern University Press, 1964.

Meyer, Eduard. *Kleine Schriften.* 2d ed. 2 vols. Halle: Niemeyer, 1924.

Michels, Robert. "Das Dilemma des Weibes in der Liebe." *Die Frauenbewegung* 9 (1903): 82–84.

————. "'Endziel', Intransigenz, Ethik." *Ethische Kultur* 11 (1903): 393–95, 403–4.

————. "Ein Blick in der Zukunftsstaat." *Mitteldeutsche Sonntags-Zeitung,* 8 March 1903.

————. "Was bedeutet uns Karl Marx?" *Mitteldeutsche Sonntags-Zeitung,* 15 March 1903.

————. "Erotische Streifzüge: Deutsche und italienische Liebesformen—aus dem Pariser Liebesleben," *Mutterschutz* 2 (1906): 362–74.

————. "Die oligarchischen Tendenzen der Gesellschaft." *Archiv für Sozialwissenschaft und Sozialpolitik* 27 (1908): 73–135.

————. "Der ethische Faktor in der Parteipolitik Italiens." *Zeitschrift für Politik* 3 (1909): 56–91.

————. "La société allemande de sociologie et sa premier congrès," *Revue internationale de sociologie* 18 (1910): 810–15.

————. *Political Parties* (1911). Translated by E. and C. Paul. New York: Collier, 1962.

————. *Probleme der Sozialphilosophie*. Leipzig: Teubner, 1914.

————. *Sexual Ethics: A Study of Borderland Questions*. London: Walter Scott, 1914.

————. *Bedeutende Männer: Charakterologische Studien*. Leipzig: Quelle & Meyer, 1927.

Mitzman, Arthur, *The Iron Cage: An Historical Interpretation of Max Weber*. New York: Knopf, 1970.

————. *Sociology and Estrangement: Three Sociologists of Imperial Germany*. New York: Knopf, 1973.

Mommsen, Wolfgang J. *Max Weber: Gesellschaft, Politik und Geschichte*. Frankfurt: Suhrkamp, 1974.

————. *The Age of Bureaucracy: Perspectives on the Political Sociology of Max Weber*. Oxford: Blackwell, 1974.

————. "The Antinomian Structure of Max Weber's Political Thought." In *Current Perspectives in Social Theory*, vol. 4, edited by Scott G. McNall, 289–311. Greenwich: JAI Press, 1983.

————. *Max Weber and German Politics, 1890–1920*. Translated by M. Steinberg. Chicago: University of Chicago Press, 1984.

Mommsen, Wolfgang J., and Osterhammel, Jürgen, eds. *Max Weber and His Contemporaries*. London: Allen & Unwin, 1987.

Mueller, Gert H. "Socialism and Capitalism in the Work of Max Weber." *British Journal of Sociology* 33 (1982): 151–71.

Naumann, Friedrich. "Der evangelisch-soziale Kursus in Berlin." *Die Christliche Welt* 7 (2 and 23 November; 21 December 1893): 1083–88, 1151–54, 1249–51.

Nedelmann, Birgitta. "Strukturprinzipien der soziologischen Denkweise Georg Simmels." *Kölner Zeitschrift für Soziologie und Sozialpsychologie* 32 (1980): 559–73.

Nehamas, Alexander. *Nietzsche: Life as Literature*. Cambridge: Harvard University Press, 1985.

Neumann, Carl. *Der Kampf um die neue Kunst*. Berlin: Walther, 1897.

Nietzsche, Friedrich. *The Birth of Tragedy: or, Hellenism and Pessimism* (1872, 1876). Translated by W. Kaufmann. New York: Random House (Vintage Books), 1967.

————. *Untimely Meditations* (1873–76). Translated by R. J. Hollingdale. Cambridge: Cambridge University Press, 1983.

————. *Daybreak: Thoughts on the Prejudices of Morality* (1881). Translated by R. J. Hollingdale. Cambridge: Cambridge University Press, 1982.

————. *The Gay Science* (1882, 1887). Translated by W. Kaufmann. New York: Random House (Vintage Books), 1974.

————. *Beyond Good and Evil* (1886). Translated by W. Kaufmann. New York: Random House (Vintage Books), 1966.

————. *On the Genealogy of Morals* (1887). Translated by W. Kaufmann. New York: Random House (Vintage Books), 1967.

————. *The Portable Nietzsche.* Edited by W. Kaufmann. New York: Viking, 1954.

————. *Werke: Kritische Gesamtausgabe.* Edited by G. Colli and M. Montinari. Berlin: de Gruyter, 1967–78.

————. *Werke in drei Bänden.* Edited by K. Schlechta. Frankfurt: Ullstein, 1979–84.

Oldenberg, Karl. *Deutschland als Industriestaat.* Göttingen: Vandenhoeck, 1897.

Oncken, Hermann. *Rudolf von Bennigsen: Ein deutscher liberaler Politiker nach seinen Briefen und hintergelassenen Papieren.* 2 vols. Stuttgart: Deutsche Verlags-Anstalt, 1910.

Parsons, Talcott. *The Structure of Social Action.* Glencoe, Ill.: Free Press, 1949.

Rickert, Heinrich. "Lebenswerte und Kulturwerte." *Logos* 2 (1912): 131–66.

————. "Urteil und Urteilen." *Logos* 3 (1912): 230–45.

————. *Die Philosophie des Lebens: Darstellung und Kritik der philosophischen Modeströmungen unserer Zeit.* Tübingen: J. C. B. Mohr (Paul Siebeck), 1920.

Riesebrodt, Martin. "Einleitung" and "Editorischer Bericht." In *Die Lage der Landarbeiter im ostelbischen Deutschland. Max Weber Gesamtausgabe,* vol. I/3, 1–33. Tübingen: J. C. B. Mohr (Paul Siebeck), 1984.

————. "From Patriarchalism to Capitalism: The Theoretical Context of Max Weber's Agrarian Studies." *Economy and Society* 15 (1986): 476–502.

Rilke, Rainer Maria. "Thomas Mann's *Buddenbrooks.*" In *Thomas Mann,* edited by Henry Hatfield, 7–9. Englewood Cliffs, N.J.: Prentice-Hall, 1964.

Rolfes, Max. "Landwirtschaft, 1850–1914." In *Handbuch der deutschen Wirtschafts- und Sozialgeschichte,* vol. 2, edited by H. Aubin and W. Zorn, 495–526. Stuttgart: Klett, 1976.

Rorty, Richard. "Habermas and Lyotard on Postmodernity." In *Habermas and Modernity,* ed. Richard J. Bernstein, 161–75. Cambridge: MIT Press, 1985.

Roth, Guenther. "Introduction." In *Economy and Society,* by Max Weber, edited by G. Roth and C. Wittich. New York: Bedminster, 1968, 1: xxvii–civ.

————. "Marianne Weber and Her Circle: Introduction to the Transaction Edition." In *Max Weber: A Biography,* by Marianne Weber, translated by H. Zohn. New Brunswick, N.J.: Transaction Books, in press.

Roth, Guenther, and Schluchter, Wolfgang. *Max Weber's Vision of History: Ethics and Methods.* Berkeley: University of California Press, 1979.

Rücker, Silvie. "Totalität als ethisches und ästhetisches Problem." *Text und Kritik* 39/40 (1973): 52–64.

Salomon, Albert. "Max Weber." *Die Gesellschaft* 3 (1926): 131–53.

————. Review of *Max Weber: Eine Gedenkrede,* by Karl Jaspers, and *Max Weber: Ein Lebensbild,* by Marianne Weber. *Die Gesellschaft* 3 (1926): 186–90.

Scaff, Lawrence. "Max Weber's Politics and Political Education." *American Political Science Review* 67 (March 1973): 128–41.

————. "Max Weber and Robert Michels." *American Journal of Sociology* 86 (1981): 1269–86.

Schluchter, Wolfgang. *Rationalismus der Weltbeherrschung: Studien zu Max Weber.* Frankfurt: Suhrkamp, 1980.

————. *The Rise of Western Rationalism: Max Weber's Developmental History.* Translated by G. Roth. Berkeley: University of California Press, 1981.

Schmoller, Gustav. "Volkswirtschaft, Volkswirtschaftslehre und -methode." In *Handwörterbuch der Staatswissenschaften,* vol. 6, edited by J. Conrad et al., 527–63. Jena: Fischer, 1894.

Schorske, Carl E. *Fin-de-siècle Vienna: Politics and Culture.* New York: Random House (Vintage Books), 1981.

Schulze-Gävernitz, Gerhart von. "Die gegenwärtige Mittel zur Hebung der Arbeiterklasse in Deutschland." *Ethische Kultur* 3 (1895): 137–39, 149–52.

Schumpeter, Joseph A. *History of Economic Analysis.* New York: Oxford University Press, 1954.

Shaw, William. *Marx's Theory of History.* Stanford: Stanford University Press, 1978.

Simmel, Georg. "Zur Psychologie des Geldes." *Schmollers Jahrbuch* 13 (1889): 1251–64.

————. *Über soziale Differenzierung: Sociologische und psychologische Untersuchungen.* Leipzig: Duncker & Humblot, 1890.

————. "Das Problem der Sociologie." *Schmollers Jahrbuch* 18 (1894): 271–77.

————. "Elisabeth Försters Nietzsche-Biographie." *Berliner Tageblatt* 26 August 1895, 481.

————. "Friedrich Nietzsche: Eine moralphilosophische Silhouette." *Zeitschrift für Philosophie und philosophische Kritik* 107 (1896): 202–15.

————. Review of *Der Nietzsche-Kultus,* by Ferdinand Tönnies. *Deutsche Litteraturzeitung* 42 (1897): 1645–51.

————. *The Philosophy of Money* (1900). Translated by T. Bottomore and D. Frisby. London: Routledge & Kegan Paul, 1978.

————. "Zum Verständnis Nietzsches." *Das Freie Wort* 2 (1902): 6–11.

————. "Rodins Plastik und die Geistesrichtung der Gegenwart" (1902). In *Ästhetik und Soziologie um die Jahrhundertwende: Georg Simmel,* edited by H. Böhringer and K. Gründer, 231–37. Frankfurt: Klostermann, 1976.

————. *Kant: Sechzehn Vorlesungen.* Leipzig: Duncker & Humblot, 1904.

————. *Die Probleme der Geschichtsphilosophie: Eine erkenntnistheoretische Studie.* 2d, rev. ed. Leipzig: Duncker & Humblot, 1905.

————. *Schopenhauer und Nietzsche: Ein Vortragszyklus.* Leipzig: Duncker & Humblot, 1907.

————. *Soziologie.* Berlin: Duncker & Humblot, 1908.

————. *Philosophische Kultur* (1911). Berlin: Wagenbach, 1983.

————. "Soziologie der Geselligkeit." In *Verhandlungen des Ersten Deutschen Soziologentages,* 1–16. Tübingen: J. C. B. Mohr (Paul Siebeck), 1911.

————. *Grundfragen der Soziologie (Individuum und Gesellschaft).* Berlin: Göschen, 1917.

————. "Der Konflikt der modernen Kultur" (1918). In *Das individuelle Gesetz: Philosophische Exkurse,* edited by M. Landmann, 148–73. Frankfurt: Suhrkamp, 1968.

————. *The Sociology of Georg Simmel.* Translated and edited by K. Wolff. New York: Free Press, 1950.

————. "The Conflict in Modern Culture." In *The Conflict in Modern Culture and Other Essays*, translated by K. Peter Etzkorn, 11–26. New York: Teachers College Press, 1968.

———. "On the Concept and Tragedy of Culture." In *The Conflict in Modern Culture and Other Essays*, translated by K. Peter Etzkorn, 27–46. New York: Teachers College Press, 1968.

———. *On Individuality and Social Forms, Selected Writings*. Edited by D. Levine. Chicago: University of Chicago Press, 1971.

———. *The Problems of the Philosophy of History*. Translated by Guy Oakes. New York: Free Press, 1977.

———. *Georg Simmel: On Women, Sexuality, and Love*. Edited by Guy Oakes. New Haven: Yale University Press, 1984.

———. *Das Individuum und die Freiheit [Brücke und Tür]*. Berlin: Wagenbach, 1984.

———. *Schriften zur Philosophie und Soziologie der Geschlechter*. Edited by H.-J. Dahme and K. C. Köhnke. Frankfurt: Suhrkamp, 1985.

———. *Schopenhauer and Nietzsche*. Translated by H. Loiskandl, D. Weinstein, and M. Weinstein. Amherst: University of Massachusetts Press, 1986.

Skocpol, Theda. *States and Social Revolutions*. New York: Cambridge University Press, 1979.

Sombart, Werner. "Zur Kritik des ökonomischen Systems von Karl Marx." *Archiv für soziale Gesetzgebung und Statistik* 7 (1894), 555–94.

———. *Der moderne Kapitalismus*. 2 vols. Leipzig: Duncker & Humblot, 1902.

———. *Wirthschaft und Mode: Ein Beitrag zur Theorie der modernen Bedarfsgestaltung*. Wiesbaden: Bergmann, 1902.

———. *Gewerbewesen*. Leipzig: Göschen, 1904.

———. *Warum interessiert sich heute jedermann für Fragen der Volkswirtschaft und Sozialpolitik?* Leipzig: Dietrich, 1904.

———. *Das Proletariat: Bilder und Studien*. Frankfurt: Rütten & Loening, 1906.

———. ["Kulturprobleme der Gegenwart."] *Vossische Zeitung* 25 January 1907, Supplement 5.

———. ["Kultur und Persönlichkeit."] *Vossische Zeitung*, 6 December 1907, Supplement 2.

———. *Kunstgewerbe und Kultur*. Berlin: Marquardt, 1908.

———. "Karl Marx und die soziale Wissenschaft." *Archiv für Sozialwissenschaft und Sozialpolitik* 26 (1908): 429–50.

———. *Socialism and Social Movement*. London: Dent, 1909.

———. *Das Lebenswerk von Karl Marx*. Jena: Fischer, 1909.

———. "Technik und Kultur." In *Verhandlungen des ersten deutschen Soziologentages*, 63–83. Tübingen: J. C. B. Mohr (Paul Siebeck), 1911.

———. *Die Juden und das Wirtschaftsleben*. Leipzig: Duncker & Humblot, 1911.

———. *Liebe, Luxus und Kapitalismus: Über die Entstehung der modernen Welt aus dem Geist der Verschwendung* (1913). Berlin: Wagenbach, 1983.

———. *Der Bourgeois: Zur Geistesgeschichte des modernen Wirtschaftsmenschen*. Leipzig: Duncker & Humblot, 1913.

Stauth, Georg, and Turner, Bryan S. "Nietzsche in Weber oder die Geburt des modernen Genius im professionellen Menschen." *Zeitschrift für Soziologie* 15 (1986): 81–94.

Strauss, Leo. *Natural Right and History*. Chicago: University of Chicago Press, 1953.

Tawney, R. H. *The Agrarian Problem in the Sixteenth Century*. New York: Franklin, 1912.

Tenbruck, Friedrich H. "Formal Sociology." In *Georg Simmel, 1858–1918*, edited by K. H. Wolff, 61–99. Columbus: Ohio State University Press, 1959.

———. "Wie gut kennen wir Max Weber? Über Maßstäbe der Weber-Forschung im Spiegel der Maßstäbe der Weber-Ausgaben." *Zeitschrift für die gesamte Staatswissenschaft* 131 (1975): 719–41.

———. "The Problem of Thematic Unity in the Work of Max Weber." *British Journal of Sociology* 31 (1980): 316–51.

———. "Das Werk Max Webers: Methodologie und Sozialwissenschaften." *Kölner Zeitschrift für Soziologie und Sozialpsychologie* 38 (1986): 13–31.

Tocqueville, Alexis de. *The Old Régime and the French Revolution* (1856). Translated by S. Gilbert. Garden City, N.Y.: Doubleday (Anchor Books), 1955.

Tolstoy, Leo. *Complete Works*. New York: AMS Press, 1968.

Tönnies, Ferdinand. *Community and Society (Gemeinschaft und Gesellschaft)* (1887). Translated by C. Loomis. New York: Harper & Row, 1963.

———. *Ethische Kultur und ihr Geleite*. Kiel: Feincke, 1893.

———. *Der Nietzsche-Kultus: Eine Kritik*. Leipzig: Reisland, 1897.

———. *Die Sitte*. Frankfurt: Rütten & Loening, 1909.

———. *Custom: An Essay on Social Codes*. Translated by A. Borenstein. New York: Free Press, 1961.

Tribe, Keith. "Prussian Agriculture—German Politics: Max Weber 1892–7." *Economy and Society* 12 (1983): 181–226.

Troeltsch, Ernst. "Max Weber" (1920). In *Max Weber zum Gedächtnis*, edited by R. König and J. Winckelmann, 43–46. Cologne: Westdeutscher Verlag, 1964.

Turner, Bryan S. *For Weber: Essays on the Sociology of Fate*. London: Routledge & Kegan Paul, 1981.

———. "Simmel, Rationalisation and the Sociology of Money." *Sociological Review* 34 (1986): 93–114.

Turner, Stephen P., and Factor, Regis A. *Max Weber and the Dispute over Reason and Value: A Study in Philosophy, Ethics, and Politics*. London: Routledge & Kegan Paul, 1984.

Veblen, Thorstein. *The Theory of Business Enterprise*. New York: Scribner's, 1904.

Vromen, Suzanne. "Georg Simmel and the Cultural Dilemma of Women." *History of European Ideas* 8 (1987): 563–79.

Weber, Alfred. "Der soziologische Kulturbegriff." In *Verhandlungen des zweiten deutschen Soziologentages*, 1–20. Tübingen: J. C. B. Mohr (Paul Siebeck), 1913.

———. "Neuorientierung in der Sozialpolitik." *Archiv für Sozialwissenschaft und Sozialpolitik* 36 (1913): 1–13.

————. "Prinzipielles zur Kultursoziologie." *Archiv für Sozialwissenschaft und Socialpolitik* 47 (1920): 1–49.

Weber, Marianne. "Die Beteiligung der Frau an der Wissenschaft" (1904). In *Frauenfragen und Frauengedanken: Gesammelte Aufsätze*, Tübingen: J. C. B. Mohr (Paul Siebeck), 1919.

————. "Die Frau und die Objektive Kultur" (1913). In *Frauenfragen und Frauengedanken: Gesammelte Aufsätze*, 95–133. Tübingen: J. C. B. Mohr (Paul Siebeck), 1919.

————. *Max Weber: Ein Lebensbild*. Tübingen: J. C. B. Mohr (Paul Siebeck), 1926.

————. *Max Weber: A Biography*. Translated by H. Zohn. New York: Wiley, 1975; New Brunswick, N.J.: Transaction Books, 1988.

Wellmer, Albrecht, "Reason, Utopia, and the *Dialectic of Enlightenment*." In *Habermas and Modernity*, edited by Richard J. Bernstein, 35–66. Cambridge: MIT Press, 1985.

Williams, Raymond. *Keywords: A Vocabulary of Culture and Society*. London: Croom Helm, 1976.

Winckelmann, Johannes. *Max Webers hintergelassenes Hauptwerk*. Tübingen: J. C. B. Mohr (Paul Siebeck), 1986.

————, ed. *Die protestantische Ethik II: Kritiken und Antikritiken*. Munich: Siebenstern, 1968.

Winkel, Harald. *Die deutsche Nationalökonomie im 19. Jahrhundert*. Darmstadt: Wissenschaftliche Buchgesellschaft, 1977.

Wittgenstein, Ludwig. *Tractatus Logico-philosophicus*. London: Routledge & Kegan Paul, 1961 (1921).

Wolf, Erik. "Max Webers ethischer Kritizismus und das Problem der Metaphysik." *Logos* 19 (1930): 359–75.

Wolfe, Tom. *The Painted Word*. New York: Bantam, 1975.

Index

Compositor: G & S Typesetters
Text: 10/13 Sabon
Display: Sabon
Printer: Braun-Brumfield, Inc.
Binder: Braun-Brumfield, Inc.